Theoretical Foundations of Comparative Politics

Theoretical Foundations of Comparative Politics

Subrata Mukherjee
Sushila Ramaswamy

Orient BlackSwan

THEORETICAL FOUNDATIONS OF COMPARATIVE POLITICS

ORIENT BLACKSWAN PRIVATE LIMITED

Registered Office
3-6-752 Himayatnagar, Hyderabad 500 029, Telangana, India
e-mail: centraloffice@orientblackswan.com

Other Offices
Bengaluru, Chennai, Guwahati,
Hyderabad, Kolkata, Mumbai,
New Delhi, Noida, Patna

First published by Orient Blackswan Pvt. Ltd. 2017
Reprinted 2018, 2021, 2024

ISBN 978-93-86296-30-6

038131

Typeset in
Adobe Garamond Pro 10/12
by Shine Graphics, Delhi 110 094

Printed in India at
B.B. Press, Noida 201 301

Published by
Orient Blackswan Private Limited
3-6-752 Himayatnagar,
Hyderabad 500 029, Telangana, India
e-mail: info@orientblackswan.com

Dedicated to

The pioneers of New Institutionalism, James G. March and Johan P. Olsen, for having brought back the state and institutions to the centre-stage of Comparative Politics.

Contents

Tables and Images

Tables

Images

PREFACE AND ACKNOWLEDGEMENTS

Comparative Politics is one of the core areas of study and research in Political Science. The other two core areas are political theory and international relations. In its evolution and contemporary status, its subject matter is closer to international relations than to political theory because unlike in the latter, where the major focus continues to be on the classical tradition which began with Plato and ended with Hegel, the dominant concerns in the other two revolve round contemporary issues within different theoretical formulations.

Contemporary debates in comparative politics originated in the United States of America in the mid-nineteenth century, with primary emphasis on pragmatism and scientism. Even in recent times, the US has initiated and dominated the debates from the Behavioural Revolution of the 1950s to the New Institutionalism of the 1980s, unquestionably the dominant theme of contemporary comparative politics. However, unlike the early years of the Behavioural Revolution, the present debates have transcended the academic circles of the US to become global. The basic assumption of our understanding following Montesquieu's precept is that there are no accidents but only cause and effect in the process of politics, the analysis of which provides the foundation for studying comparative politics.

This worldwide attention and interest in comparative politics is a consequence of a shrinking world, made possible by technological innovations, from tape recorders to super conductors and collective efforts beyond the nation-states in space research, climate change and global warming. But this does not mean an end to debates in comparative politics, with regard to both methodology and conceptions of a desirable political order. Rather, it can be argued that the debates within the discipline today are as diverse as they used to be 200 years ago. The present work accepts this wide divergence and even plurality within the arena of comparative politics and analyses these in a detailed and objective manner.

Professor Frank Thakurdas introduced us to the need for and joy of continuous and sustained research work in the core concerns of political science, with the advice that there is no finality in what we research. We have tried to follow his advice throughout our academic endeavours. We wish to gratefully acknowledge the continued support, encouragement and appreciation that we have received from our students, friends and colleagues. Special thanks are due to Professors Milton Fisk, Barbara Goodwin, David McLellan, Alan Ritter, Jon Quah, and Timothy A. Tilton. Mr Rama Rao Suresh took a special interest in this work and read many chapters. Many of his comments and suggestions, particularly with regard to the chapters dealing with economic ideas and concepts, have been helpful. We would like to express our gratitude to the editorial and production team of Orient BlackSwan, the Publishers, for their painstaking efforts in bringing out this book. However, we alone are responsible for any shortcomings.

1

NATURE AND SCOPE OF COMPARATIVE POLITICS

Within political science Comparative Politics is a subfield that compares the struggle for power across the countries.

O'Neil 2009: 3

Comparative Politics is a discipline that deals with the very essence of politics where sovereignty resides in the state: Questions of power between groups, the institutional organization of political systems and authoritative decisions that affect the whole of a community.

Caramani 2011: 3

Even with the same source material to examine, individuals have disagreed about its meaning or the subjective value of what it depicts. Where values, ideals or strategic objectives are in fundamental contradiction, exposure and connectivity may on occasion fuel confrontation, as much as assuage them.

Kissinger 2014: 355

Comparative Politics is one of the three core components of political science, the other two being political theory and international relations. However, it is only in recent times that comparative government and politics, or comparative politics, has emerged as a distinguishable sub-field within political science. Since then, it has undergone tremendous transformation in terms of its nature and ambit of study. The modern study of Comparative Politics emerged in the late nineteenth century, and since then has evolved largely due to the research in US universities. The role and influence of US academia reached its high point in the 1970s, and declined thereafter. By the late twentieth century, it became truly international; however, the role of US scholars remains crucial. Blondel (1999) stressed the need to distinguish 'comparative politics' from 'comparative government', with the

> former being markedly broader and relating to politics in the most general fashion and in particular outside the state. Such studies are scarcely undertaken as things are; what passes and is typically referred to as 'comparative politics' is in reality 'comparative government'; it is concerned exclusively with politics within the state or in relation to the state (ibid.: 152).

Reiterating Holt and Turner, Blondel pointed to the ambiguous nature of the subject matter of comparative politics, stating that only few studies in comparative politics have used the comparative method. There is no unanimity concerning the methodology to be pursued; yet comparative politics constitutes a substantive branch of political science. Blondel noted that prior to 1914, comparative politics took two forms. First, until the middle of the eighteenth century, the main approach was normative and philosophical, wherein blueprints for how to organise society were proposed. From the middle of the eighteenth century, there emerged a legalistic and constitutional approach that dominated till the beginning of World War I. According to Blondel, Charles-Louis Secondat Montesquieu (1689–1755) was the link between the two phases as he took into account factors like climate, geography and location to explain the different consequences of constitutional rule in different countries. With an overall emphasis on cause and effect, there was no scope of an accidental happening in politics, according to Montesquieu.

I

ARISTOTLE'S CONTRIBUTION

Image 1.1: Aristotle (384–322 BC)

Source: https://commons.wikimedia.org/wiki/Aristotel%C4%93s#/media/File:Aristotle_Altemps_Inv8575.jpg.

Politically, institutionally and socially, comparative politics began with Aristotle (384–322 BC). Through a massive study of 158 constitutions and emphasising the stabilising factor of the middle class, he provided a framework of study that has withstood the challenges of the last 2,500 years. Based on the study of these 158 constitutions, Aristotle devised the classification of constitutions based on two indices—goals of the regime and the number of people who wielded political power. Ancient Greece had a bewildering variety of constitutional systems which Aristotle mentioned in *Politics*.[1] The Greek city states (800–500 BC), despite their wide variety, continued mainly because of their homogeneity and self-sufficiency.

Aristotle's Typology and its Bases

Accepting the following precepts, (*i*) what is feasible, is desirable; (*ii*) any state to be better than anarchy; (*iii*) collective opinions and judgements as more satisfying than individual ones; (*iv*) faith in moderation, his principle of the Golden Mean; (*v*) that many,[2] rather than a few, should rule; and (*vi*) elite accommodation, Aristotle's main focus was on the best practicable state or constitution. He arrived at this by extending Plato's (428/427–347 BC) arguments in *Laws* (350 BC) in favour of the mixed constitution as the best and most stable, and a panacea against the cycle of development and degeneration. Aristotle adopted the scheme, perfected and elaborated it, and since then it 'has served as a basic taxonomy through the ages and into the 19th century.... It is the first explanatory theory in the history of political science, in which institutions, attitudes and ideas are related to process and performance. It is the ancestor of separation of powers theory' (Almond 1996: 54). Of the six regimes, only four, according to Aristotle, are important—oligarchy, democracy, polity and tyranny. He considered a mixed constitution the best as it reconciled virtue with stability, the many with the few, quantity with quality. He pointed out that while social structures of cities differ according to their economies, occupations, professions and statutes, these variations can be reduced in terms of the rich and poor sections of citizens. If the rich dominate, it becomes an oligarchy, and if the poor control affairs, it becomes a democracy. In a society ruled by the middle class, extreme forces are kept at bay and such a regime has an inbuilt stability. His faith in the middle class state as a 'save' state, a term borrowed from Euripides (480–406 BC), fulfilled two important ideals: consensus and equality. The larger the middle class, the greater the possibility of tranquillity and stability, as it would steer clear of the insolence of the rich and the unruly behaviour of the poor.

Aristotle's Legacy

Aristotle's faith in the middle class[3] was reiterated by Adam Smith (1723–90) and the English liberals—Jeremy Bentham (1748–1832), James Mill (1773–1836) and John Stuart Mill (1806–73). The theme of mixed constitution found resonance in the writings of Polybius (203–120 BC), Marcus Tullius Cicero (106–143 BC), St. Thomas Aquinas (1225–74) and Niccolò Machiavelli (1469–1527). The notion of mixed constitution was central to Renaissance political theory and was integrated into the emerging notion of republicanism. John Calvin (1506–64) advocated a mixture of aristocracy and democracy to minimise the misuse of political power. Of course, what added to Aristotle's insight was not only the then prevailing order, but also the existence of a number of schools of thought that were essentially non-political in nature—Cynics, Epicureans, Sceptics and Stoics. These schools criticised Aristotle for ignoring the diversity that existed in the world, and for projecting the moral values of the Athenian middle class as universal. Aristotle continued to eulogise the self-governing and self-sufficient city state or *polis* as the ideal type at a time when his pupil, Alexander (356–323 BC), extended the frontiers of his empire and forged links between Greeks and non-Greeks over a period of 16 years. Aristotle excluded large segments of society because of the narrow social base of Greek politics, which left out women, slaves and foreigners from the citizen body. His rejection of democracy was also a reflection of his acceptance of the existing social order, a prejudice that continued till the end of the nineteenth century.

POLYBIUS: PRECURSOR TO MODERN THEORIES OF POWER SHARING

Polybius, a Greek historian taken prisoner by the Romans, was the first analyst to concentrate on measuring the success of power sharing and differentiation. His *Universal History* (146 BC) analysed the virtues of the Roman system—the mixed constitution that combined monarchical, aristocratic and democratic systems—compared to the Greeks and explained its success. He viewed the Roman Republic as the manifestation and realisation of Aristotle's theory. He believed a mixed constitution with checks and balances would provide stability, a conclusion reached after analysing the causes of constitutional change that goes through the progress and fall of government systems in a cyclical manner.

> Every variety of constitution, which is simple and formed on one principle, is precarious, as it is soon perverted into the corrupt form, which is proper to it and naturally follows on it.... Each constitution has a vice engendered in it and inseparable from it. In kingship it is despotism, in aristocracy oligarchy, and in democracy the savage rule of violence; and it is impossible, as I said above, that each of these should not in course of time change into this vicious form (Polybius, cited in Curtis 1961a: 119).

Within the Roman system, each of the several groups possessed power, which was limited by that of the others. The consuls, the executive monarchical element, depended on the Senate and the people for support. The Senate, the most powerful and comprising of aristocratic elements, needed the masses for support. The Tribunes, representing the democratic element, executed the decisions of the people. Each group checked the other but united in the face of a common enemy, both internal and external. All cooperated in the passage of a legislation.

> ...The three kinds of government that I spoke of above all shared in the control of the Roman state. And such fairness and propriety in all respects was shown in the use of these three elements for drawing up the constitution and in its subsequent administration that it was impossible even for a native to pronounce with certainty whether the whole system was aristocratic, democratic or monarchical. This was indeed only natural. For if one fixed one's eyes on the power of the consuls, the constitution seemed completely monarchical and royal; if on that of the senate it seemed again to be aristocratic; and when one looked at the power of the masses, it seemed clearly to be a democracy (Polybius, cited in Curtis 1961a: 119–20).

Polybius' theory did not accurately depict the true nature of Roman politics for it ignored the essential aristocratic nature of the Roman system (Curtis 1961a: 115). However, his theory of mixed constitution and of the checks and balances within it inspired and influenced Cicero and the Founding Fathers of the US constitution.

CONTRIBUTIONS OF ROME

The Romans did not innovate, but popularised ideas as they were perfectly content to inherit the rich Greek treasures. Unlike the Greeks, whose constitutions were the work of single founding figures, the Roman political system was a result of collective efforts of the community, evolving over a period of time. This is comparable to modern Americans, who have innovated within the framework provided by John Locke (1632–1704). Roman civilisation was the first human effort to provide enduring institutions like the Senate, an elaborate and uniform system of laws,[4] and the first institutions of civil society by assuring the right to private property and providing for universities as centres of independent learning. This impact was so enormous that even after the decline of the Roman empire, the institutions it had created continued to yield enormous importance; this is felt even today as the bulk of the European legal system combines Roman with the 1804 Napoleonic code. The abandonment of the mixed constitution, according to Edward Gibbon (1737–94), was the reason for the decline of Rome and acceptance of Asiatic values of luxury[5] (Mukherjee and Ramaswamy 1995: 434).

EUROPEAN ENLIGHTENMENT AND EUROCENTRICISM

After the Romans, it was the period of European Enlightenment in the eighteenth century that provided an impetus to build a framework to comprehend the entire world history. This was made possible by the arrival of standardised secondary sources, with which broad frameworks could be conceived of the entire world. It also inaugurated the age of Eurocentricism, which meticulously developed the notion of forward Europe and a backward non-European world. From Montesquieu to J. S. Mill, this pronounced Eurocentricism was manifest, culminating in George Wilhelm Friedrich Hegel (1770–1831), Karl Heinrich Marx (1818–83) and Max Weber (1864–1920). The underlying assumption among many post-Renaissance European thinkers vis-à-vis the non-European world was that there was a marked and qualitative distinction between advanced European cultures and other backward civilisations. Montesquieu pioneered this perception. Using climatic conditions as the yardstick, he noted that tropical climates were unsuited for democracies and individual freedom. Gibbon also believed that climate plays an important role in building different kinds of personalities. A cold climate produces hardworking people, while a warm climate produces soft people. Adam Smith clubbed China, Egypt and India together for the special attention that irrigation received in these societies. James Mill observed the difference between European feudalism and governmental arrangements in Asiatic societies. J. S. Mill used the term 'Eastern Society' in 1848. Others, like Herbert Spencer[6] (1820–1903), Vilfredo Pareto (1848–23; see Chapter 13) and Émile Durkheim (1855–1927; see Chapter 5) analysed Asiatic societies from a comparative perspective.

SIGNIFICANCE OF HEGEL AND MARX

Hegel was the most influential among these thinkers. His philosophy of history not only concurred with this prevailing European perception of the East, but also influenced, to a very large extent, left Hegelianism with respect to perceiving colonisation as a modernising force. For Hegel and his preferred Eurocentricism, India and China had no history as they were 'stationary and fixed'. This was true of all Asiatic societies. Hegel's belief that the East lacked history influenced Marx, who also perceived the oriental societies of India and China as lacking in history, incapable of change from within and essentially stagnant. Marx considered the imperialist West destructive and degenerative, yet also constructive and regenerative. It was a dialectical understanding; it was regenerative as it created the modern techniques of production, brought political unity and social change, and it was degenerative as it destroyed indigenous institutions and practices (Avineri 1969: 56).

Marx, like Hegel, described the Oriental societies of India and China as lacking in history, incapable of changing from within and essentially stagnant. Since they had blocked historical progress, the industrialised West, after becoming socialist, would turn into the agent of liberation. According to Marx, the chief characteristic of Asiatic societies was the absence of private property, particularly private ownership of land. In contrast to the European state, which was an instrument of class domination and exploitation, the state in Asiatic societies controlled all classes. It did not belong to the superstructure, but was decisive in the entire economic arena, building and managing water supply, the life breath of agriculture in arid areas. It performed economic and social functions for the whole of society. Social privileges emanated from the service of the state and not from the institution of private property, as was the case in Europe. Asiatic societies had an overdeveloped state (see Chapter 6) and an underdeveloped civil society. Military conquests and dynastic tussles ushered in periodic changes without affecting the economic organisation, for the state continued to be the real landlord. The unchanging nature of Asiatic societies was also buttressed by self-sufficient, autarchic villages, which sustained themselves through a delicate balance of agriculture and handicrafts. Satyajit Ray's famous film *Shatranj ke Khiladi* (1977), based on Munshi Premchand's (1880–1936) 1924 novel, depicted this view extremely well.

In *Grundrisse* (1857–58), Marx and Friedrich Engels (1820–95) developed these preliminary sketches of Asiatic societies to highlight the key differences between the urban histories of the West and the East. In the West, the existence of politically independent cities was conducive to the production of exchange values, which determined the development of the bourgeois class and industrial capitalism, whereas in the East, the city was artificially created by the state and remained a 'princely camp' subordinated to the countryside. The city was imposed on the economic structure of society. Social unity represented by the state lay in the autarchic self-sufficient villages, where land was communally owned. Stability was ensured by the simplicity of production. The state appropriated the surplus in the form of taxes. Factors like free markets, private property, guilds and bourgeois law, which had led to the rise of the capitalist class in the West, were absent in Asiatic societies due to a centralised state that dominated and controlled civil society. For Marx, imperialism would act as a catalyst of change since these societies lacked the mechanism for change. Imperialism had to be analysed dialectically; the non-European world is non-dialectical.

WEBER'S CONTRIBUTION

Weber was one of Marx's critics. He demolished Marx's theory of economic determinism through a new formulation that highlighted the cultural underpinnings in the development of capitalism, attributing its rise to the Protestant ethic in general and to Calvinism in particular. Calvinism rejected the earlier formulation of Martin Luther (1483–1546), which had stressed on simple life in an agrarian society, as inadequate to understanding the rise of Western European capitalism. Calvinism was the starting point of his thesis, which advocated increasing production in a commercial society, but restricted consumption by what is referred to as Puritan Ethics. The emphasis was on frugality, thrift and simplicity. This inaugurated a new dimension in which comparative politics could be comprehended within the larger framework of culture. However, there were many critics, the most important of whom was Richard Tawney (1880–1962; see Chapter 5). Alexis de Tocqueville (1805–59), who preceded Weber, saw the Protestant ethic as encouraging individualism and freedom, but with proper respect for political authority. The major difference between Marx and Weber lay in the fact that Marx considered capitalism irrational, while for Weber it was rational and natural. Weber is also important for his formulation of three types of authority: traditional, charismatic and rational-legal. His personal preference was for the rational-legal, the basis of modern capitalism and the modern state. His emphasis on an independent, competent, hierarchical bureaucracy is also an important component of modern comparative politics.

FRENCH ENLIGHTENMENT AND GREAT BRITAIN

Image 1.2: Charles-Louis Secondat Montesquieu (1689–1755)

Source: https://commons.wikimedia.org/wiki/File:Montesquieu_1.png.

Another dominant theme of the French Enlightenment was the adulation of England as the more advanced system worthy of emulation. Montesquieu's appreciation of the English constitution and commercial way of life set the tone. England was the only nation in history dedicated to liberty, which did not mean political participation or power so much as security of each individual's life and family, and peaceful or non-exploitative pursuit of property and commercial interests. In England, the old monarchical system was integrated into a broader and more effective system of checks and balances, thereby maximising individual freedom. François-Marie Arouet, better known by his pseudonym Voltaire (1694–1778), a contemporary of Montesquieu,[7] admired the English for enjoying literary freedom, freedom of person and of property as secured by law, and freedom from prejudice, thus unleashing enormous creative input. Unlike France, the English economy and commerce were free from restraints. He also appreciated the level of tolerance in England, which was the outcome of freedom, abundance, affluence and happiness. England, for him, was a just and prosperous society. He liked the Englishmen for their practicality, respect for facts, realism and their simple manners, habits and dress. Above all, he liked the English middle class, which he compared with their beer: froth at the top, dregs at the bottom, but excellent in the middle. Interestingly, Rammohun Roy (1772–1833) welcomed British rule in India on the grounds that Britain was ahead of India in three basic things: scientific temper, rule of law and tolerance.

TRIUMPH OF LIBERAL INDIVIDUALISM

With the inauguration of the US constitution in 1787, the study of constitutionalism, constitutionally sanctioned bill of rights, centrality of minority rights, separation of powers and federalism became important components of the study of comparative politics. In sharp contrast to US constitutionalism, the French Revolution gave rise to another important debate about the nature and ambit of revolutions (see Chapter 17) and the nature of the state, best exemplified in the debate between Edmund Burke (1729–97) and Thomas Paine (1737–1809) (see Chapter 6). Both revolutions brought individual rights to the centre of modern society, ending the medieval notions of guild and community.

IMPACT OF THE INDUSTRIAL REVOLUTION

With the spread of the industrial revolution in England towards the end of the eighteenth century, the debate moved towards understanding the role of technology and scientific knowledge in society and their use in a changing society. The first important theorist of this new age was Claude Henri de Rauvroy, Comte de Saint

Simon (1760–1825), with the debate about the positive and negative aspects of this new civilisation dominating much of the nineteenth century. Saint Simon could foresee the emergence of the new social forces that political revolution and scientific advancements would unleash. He did not look at the ugly side of early industrial capitalism. He clearly foresaw four developments that are visible even today: first, the role of corporate bodies in making and imposing their decisions on society; second, hierarchy, based on science and the exercise of knowledge; third, the conception of partnership among the different European states; and fourth, the inadequacy of the nation-state to cope with the internationalism unleashed by industrial and technical forces. He also emphasised on solving social problems with the help of positive and natural science. Interestingly, Saint Simon's famous disciple and one-time secretary, Auguste Comte (1798–1857), was the founder of positivism. Industrial society brought with it important offshoots like the debate on the abolition of slavery,[8] extension of franchise[9] and the general scepticism about democracy that continued till the end of the nineteenth century. The debate around the superiority of liberal versus socialist democracy continued till the collapse of communism in 1991. Challenging both liberal democracy and communism, a third alternative, fascism, emerged and remained till its defeat in World War II (see Chapter 4 and 11). A distinct elitist school proclaiming the impossibility of meaningful democracy also emerged in the late nineteenth century, exemplified in the works of Vilfredo Federico Damaso Pareto (1848–1923), Gaetano Mosca (1858–1941) and Robert Michels (1876–1936) (see Chapter 13).

DISTINCTIVENESS OF THE AMERICAN CONTRIBUTION

The popular American saying, 'what is functional is beautiful', exemplifies the quest for practical knowledge with a scientific basis. Political Science as a discipline is an American invention and this explains the absence of Americans in the classical tradition of normative political theory. This tradition of pragmatism began with James Madison's (1751–1836) classic defence of factions in *Federalist Papers* (see Chapter 6). Since then, with the assertion of American exceptionalism, there developed a distinct American science of politics, as observed by Crick (1959). Tocqueville's *Democracy in America* (1832) is an early understanding of American democracy by a French observer, whose essential purpose was to emulate the American system and replace a feudal and non-democratic regime in France. He analysed the federal constitution, the question of people's sovereignty and the role of the constitution, warning against the tyranny of the majority, a theme that J. S. Mill subsequently developed. He grasped the new and universal trend, namely the desire for equality and its intricate relationship with individual liberty and democracy. He stressed the importance of local self-government, decentralised administration, widespread ownership of property, and voluntary associations for the maintenance of political liberties, stability of government and protection against the tyranny of the majority. He did not consider it necessary for Europe to imitate American political institutions, but stressed that the study of America would yield useful instructions.

Tocqueville's striking originality lay in his recognition of the extraordinary importance of religion in strengthening democracy in America. He considered religion a 'political institution' vital to the preservation of freedom in a democratic society, particularly from the despotic tendencies unleashed by an equality of conditions. The Church in France considered democracy antithetical to religion, and consequently an enemy, while in America the two were closely linked (thereby explaining the success of American democracy). America, the nascent Puritan commonwealth, rejected Europe's aristocratic heritage and accepted the principles of democracy. The Puritans brought to the New World a Christianity that was democratic, constitutional and republican. They introduced such principles as people's participation, the right of the people to rule, free voting in matters of taxation, fixing the responsibility of political representatives, guarding personal liberty and trial by jury. They instilled a love of freedom anchored in religious conviction and taught Americans that freedom is a gift from God, which needs to be taken seriously and used wisely. Christianity associated itself with the principles of liberal democracy that it helped to create, and hence could hope for an autonomous space that would be both enduring and timeless.

COMPARATIVE GOVERNMENT TO COMPARATIVE POLITICS: SHIFT FROM INSTITUTIONS TO PROCESSES

With the exception of works like Herman Finer's (1898–1969) landmark text *Theory and Practice of Modern Government* (1932) and that of Carl J. Friedrich (1901–84), comparative politics during the first three decades of the twentieth century was by and large dominated by books that adopted in-depth country-wide analyses. Finer restricted his study to liberal democracies; his book analysed a set of institutions of all the countries together in a comparative perspective. He influenced K. C. Wheare[10] (1907–79) and his own brother, Samuel Finer[11] (1915–93).

Liberal democracy faced a challenge from Communism and subsequently from fascism and Nazism, which threw up different kinds of constitutional systems and political arrangements at variance with liberal ideals and principles (see Chapter 6). The newly emerging nations of the developing world also made the older, restricted methodology irrelevant. The existing state of theory was found wanting, as evident from David Easton's (1917–2014) 1953 critique (see Chapter 2), followed by Roy Macridis' (1918–91) criticisms of traditionalism in comparative politics. The latter pointed out that the traditional approach was parochial, monographic, descriptive, focused on Western Europe, excessively formalistic, historical and legalistic, and insensitive to theory building and theory testing. Its primary emphasis was on written documents like constitutions (Macridis 1955). He stated that the works of Walter Bagehot[12] (1826–77) and Albert Venn Dicey[13] (1835–1922), the two pioneers of comparative politics, remained important for their foresights on parliamentary government and the seminal importance of the rule of law. Lord James Bryce[14] (1838–1922), Ivor Jennings[15] (1903–67), Shotwell, Ogg, Zink, and the like provided country-by-country studies with very little comparison. Traditionalism contributed little to empirical theory. Slowly but surely comparative government, the study of selected institutions in Western democracies, moved towards the study of processes involving the entire world.

THE BEHAVIOURAL REVOLUTION

Till World War II, institutionalism was the major paradigm in most well-established democracies of the West. However, this was challenged by the behavioural revolution of the 1950s and 1960s. In a rudimentary sense, the behavioural approach began in the USA in the 1920s. Political behaviour came into circulation during World War I (1914–18). Frank Kent, an American journalist, used it for the first time in the title of a book—*Political Behaviour: The Heretofore Unwritten Laws, Customs, and Principles of Politics as Practised in the United States* (1928). The book discusses the difference between appearance and reality, which, according to Dahl (1961: 763), is still relevant. However, the first major breakthrough in a scientific sense came when Herbert Tingsten, a Swedish scholar, published *Political Behaviour: Studies in Election Statistics* (1937). Interestingly, Tingsten's study was restricted to European elections, but became a buzzword in the USA; it is identified with the American school, its high point being the 1950s and 1960s.

Behaviouralism, as articulated by Easton, organised research in political science along the same lines as natural sciences. It emphasised theory-building exercises and in the process, rejected political theory as a merely chronological and intellectual history of ideas with no practical relevance in comprehending contemporary political reality. It focuses on a simple question: Why do people behave the way they do? It insists that (*a*) observable behaviour, both at the level of an individual and a group, is the basic unit for analysis; and (*b*) that it is possible to empirically test any explanation of that behaviour. With the conviction that experience alone forms the basis of knowledge, it analysed the reasons for mass political participation in democratic countries and elite behaviour in the contexts of leadership and decision-making processes. Behaviouralism was considerably influenced by functionalist anthropologists Bronislaw Malinowski (1884–1942) and A. R. Radcliff-Brown (1881–1955), and sociologists Max Weber and Talcott Parsons (1902–79).

Historically, the quick spread of behaviouralism in the USA can be linked to the American sense of pragmatism, belief in scientific methodology, preference for finding solutions and lack of major contradictions in the system, reinforced by a long, uninterrupted constitutional government and a belief in American exceptionalism and its capacity to lead the world. However, apart from this favourable climate for behavioural research, there were six other catalysts, according to Dahl (1961: 763–65), in the rise of behaviouralism. The first major initiator was Charles E. Merriam (1874–1953), who in his historic Presidential speech at the American Political Science Association in 1925 stated: 'Some day we may take another angle of approach than the formal, as other sciences do, and begin to look at political behaviour as one of the essential objects of enquiry' (cited in ibid.: 763).

Merriam contended that a study of human behaviour enabled an intelligent understanding of political institutions and the political process. The borrowing of data and theories from psychology, economics and other social sciences, modern techniques of experimentation, statistical analysis and mathematical modelling would enable the discipline to become more scientific and relevant.

Precursors of Behaviouralism

Many consider Behaviouralism to have begun with Graham Wallas (1858–1932) and Arthur F. Bentley (1870–1957). Wallas contributed to the development of political science and the psychology of politics. 'The single most enduring contribution of Wallas made to the study of politics lay in his simple but eloquent plea that a discussion of human nature be made the foundation of all political enquiry' (Kamp 1981: xiii).

Wallas rejected Bentham's view of human nature as that of rational self-interest and contended that as people normally do not always behave in a rational way, it would be dangerous for politicians to assume that people would behave intelligently. In *Human Nature in Politics* (1908), he argued that irrational forces such as custom, prejudice and accidents do affect political decisions more often than rational ones, and hence advised politicians to study psychology. Political candidates, according to Wallas, were similar to salespersons selling products like toothpastes, breakfast cereals and ladies' hosiery. Marketing is an act of creating captive human beings, which leads to a false sense of both security and insecurity, as well as of need and satisfaction. He was also of the opinion that trained persons ought to be part of the government, as that would help in choosing the latest scientific discoveries in the fields of both natural and social sciences. With modern societies becoming more complex, he recommended a shift in thinking from individualism to collectivism, believing that collectivism, along with the study of the individual mind, would lead to the establishment of a 'good society'. Wallas' work provides a counter-balance to rational utilitarianism. His advocacy of the use of psychology in political science helped in the development of the empirical study of human behaviour, an important component of the discipline in the mid-twentieth century.

Walter Lippman (1899–1974) agreed with Wallas and argued that the fundamental concern of a social, political and economic system is a portrayal of human nature that shapes all human activity. This clear understanding of human nature would lead to the enduring success of the capitalist system. The basic truth is that human beings are driven by self-interest and are not angels; however, they have the capacity to be virtuous in reasonable situations. It is this understanding that accounts for the success of Adam Smith and the Founding Fathers of the US Constitution.

Bentley sought a proper methodology for studying the political process and to comprehend the process of social change. To find an appropriate answer, he was critical of social scientists who concentrated on the state and related institutions. His attempt was interdisciplinary, with emphasis on history, economics, sociology and political science. Bentley's inclination towards the behavioural sciences manifested itself early, in his essay 'The Units of Investigation in the Social Sciences' (1895). He made his intention clear in *The Process of Government* (1908), declaring that his attempt was to 'fashion a tool' (1908: vii). Bentley viewed all politics and all government as the result of the activities of groups. Bentley, according to Norman Jacobson (1963), provided the link between early American constitutional theory and later American political science. He built on the proposition central to *Federalist Papers* that social groups are given, and of the need to theorise about politics around it. He was not concerned with groups per se so much as with social activity, which he constantly referred to as 'men actually doing something in the world'. This activity, according to Bentley, simply exists.

One positive aspect is that Bentley, while critical of the methodology employed by other social scientists, provided solutions along with his criticisms. He rejected the proposition that feelings, faculties and ideas have independent causes; rather, their source was 'overt behaviour', which was to be discovered by concentrating on the activities of individuals. Doing, talking and organising to reach one's goal, conflict, organised and unorganised behaviour, all become a part of comprehending the process of politics. This was to be achieved in two ways: observation of all activity, and balancing quantity against quality. He rejected unmeasurable elements and sought a mechanism that could enable a move towards dependable knowledge. This could be achieved by arranging the political data of groups, interests and pressures. However, as critics point out, he never elaborated on these terms. This, however, was deliberate, as Bentley perceived that providing definitions would be premature and create hurdles in investigation. He never provided a detailed framework for comprehending group behaviour either. His attempt was modest and he never claimed to have undertaken any comprehensive verification. His work can be described as pre-theory, a precursor to the behavioural revolution of the 1950s and 1960s, and as providing a rudimentary scheme for empirical research.

The Chicago School

The 1930s and 1940s were crucial as, under Merriam's leadership, the Department of Political Science at the University of Chicago became the centre of this approach. Important behaviouralists like Harold D. Lasswell (1902–78) as teacher and David Truman (1913–2003) and Gabriel A. Almond (1911–2002) as students strengthened this new line of thinking. There were other important behaviouralists like George Catlin (1896–1979) at Cornell University, but it was the Chicago School that became the catalyst (just as later, in Economics, it became the centre for Monetarism under Milton Friedman [1912–2006]).

The second important factor was the arrival of a large number of European scholars, who brought with them the tradition of political sociology influenced by Weber. Third, World War II saw a large exodus of academicians to the war administration, which led to a profound change in their perception of politics as it is actually played. Fourth, the funding from the Social Science Research Council also facilitated research in this area. Fifth, the rapid rise of survey methodology strengthened the behavioural approach in US universities. Sixth and last was the enormous funding support that came from the Carnegie, Rockefeller and Ford Foundations. As Dahl said, due to the combined effect of all these factors in the 1950s, 'the behavioural approach grew from the deviant and unpopular views of a minor sect into a major influence. Many of the radicals of the 1930s (professionally speaking) had, within two decades, become established leaders of American political science' (1961: 766).[16]

The 1950s and 1960s

Mair (1998) labelled the 1950s and 1960s the golden period in the development of comparative politics, with elaborate schemes to comprehend the divergence of world politics. This was made possible by Almond and his colleagues at the American Social Science Research Council, which founded the committee on Comparative Politics in 1954. The most striking aspect of the new approach developed by the Committee was the attention it gave to 'large-scale comparisons', unlike the traditional approach, where the focus was on the developed world—on western Europe and the United States. Almond and his colleagues developed a theory and a methodology that allowed for the comparison of different political systems—democratic, non-democratic,[17] developed and developing, Western and non-Western. In the process, the formal and legal approach to political institutions was abandoned; instead, the focus was on realism and on subjects like political parties, interest groups and public opinion, and the newly emerging countries of Asia and Africa (Almond 1970: 14). The state was replaced by 'political system', enabling scholars to take note of the 'extra-legal', 'para-legal' and 'social' institutions so crucial to the understanding of non-Western politics (Almond 1990: 192). As Finer suggested, this was required in order 'to encompass pre-state/non-state societies, as well as roles and offices which might not be seen to be overtly connected with the state' (1970: 5). The introduction of statistical research was another key and novel method. *The Civic Culture,* by Almond and Verba (1963), belongs to this tradition (see Chapter 5).

The focus was not only on the legal powers of the agencies, but on their actual practice: what they did, how they related to one another, and the roles they performed in making and executing public policy (Almond and Coleman 1960; Macridis 1955). This was how structural functionalism emerged, comparing certain functions perceived as necessary in all societies. As the world was now divided into three broad categories—advanced capitalism, developed socialism and the emergence of new actors in the form of post-colonial societies—the new studies concentrated on these. New idioms of political understanding, like 'system' replacing the 'state', emerged, although, as there was no Kuhnian consensus, the earlier view of comparative politics as highly contested remained. Mair's (1998) assertion that the 1950s and 1960s represented 'the golden period' is grossly exaggerated as the larger universal frameworks projected could not match the actual reality.

This period also saw a proliferation of literature based mainly on Anglo-American experiences of development and modernisation (see Chapter 16). Walter Rostow (1916–2003) developed a theory of stages of development with the idea of 'take-off'. Lucian Pye (1921–2008) elaborated a scheme of modernisation and Samuel P. Huntington (1927–2008), in his classic *Political Order in Changing Societies* (1968), was critical of modernisation theory, pointing out that rapid social and economic changes lead inevitably to economic growth, social mobility and political participation. This disturbs stability, creating an uncertain and revolutionary situation. He was sceptical of a smooth process of modernisation, as lack of institutionalisation leads to increasing demands and wider participation leads to chronic instability and decay. The choice, for him, was not between liberal democracy and communism, both of which reflected a large degree of order, but between order and disorder. A critique of modernisation theory was spearheaded by dependency theorists (see Chapter 16), mainly from Latin America.

Rejection of Behaviouralism

Dahl's observation (1961: 766) was a somewhat gross exaggeration of the behaviouralists' sway in the USA in the 1950s. In Chicago University itself, Leo Strauss (1899–1973) continued with his research on and teaching of the classical tradition. The year 1960 was when Sheldon Wolin's[18] (1922–2015) masterpiece *Politics and Vision: Continuity and Innovation in Western Political Thought* (1960) was published. Wolin accused behavioural political scientists of abdicating their true 'vocation' in their concern for method. Behaviouralism, like positivism, has been criticised for its mindless empiricism. Both Carl Hempel and Popper rejected the 'narrow inductivist view' of scientific enquiry, whereby a proper enquiry is possible only if relevant facts are supported by clear minimum theoretical expectations. They dismissed enquiries based on 'all the facts up to now' as irrelevant, as mere fact-gathering could never accomplish much, 'for a collection of *all* the facts would have to await the end of the world, so as to speak; and even *all the facts up to now* cannot be collected since there are infinite number and variety of them' (Hempel 1966: 11). Unlike the positivists, behaviouralists continued to remain committed to the inductive method in research. Their emphasis on data and consequent downgrading of theory led to two undesirable tendencies within the behavioural persuasion, first, a tendency to stress what could be easily measured, rather than what might be theoretically important; and second, a tendency to concentrate on phenomena that is readily observable, rather than study the covert and profound structural factors that contribute to change and stability within the political system.

The heydays of the behavioural revolution were short-lived, as the high priest of behaviouralism, Easton, admitted in his Presidential Address to the American Political Science Association in 1969. Merriam's optimism in the 1920s ended in a question mark in 1969. Greater stress was placed on public responsibilities within the discipline, and less emphasis on the scientific method and empirical theory. There was an acceptance that theoretical analysis had to remain the starting point of any serious empirical research. Theory played an important role in post-behaviouralism, with the acceptance of the possibility of different theories yielding different observations and a plurality and diversity of approaches. Easton (1997: 16–17) pointed out that dissatisfaction with behaviouralism led to revisions in method and content, favouring a revival of interpretative understanding and historical analysis. The emergence of new concerns such as feminism, environmentalism, ethnicity, racial identity and equality, as well as the Vietnam War led to greater focus on the subject matter and consensus about methodologies. Easton announced the beginning of neo-behaviouralism in order to bring about a new unity in the theoretical focus of the discipline.

The major reason for the sharp decline of behaviouralism was the absence of a Kuhnian consensus, wherein an old paradigm is replaced with a new one accepted by most practitioners (Kuhn 1962). It is easy to describe 'what behaviouralism is not but it is difficult to say what it is' (Dahl 1961: 763). Interestingly, fascism has been described in a similar manner: 'What happened was ... complicated—and somewhat obscure' (Waldo 1975: 58). Almost all those trying to define behaviouralism have confessed that 'every man puts his own emphasis and thereby becomes his own behavioralist' (Easton 1962: 9). Terence Ball (1993: 220–21) pointed out that behaviouralism succeeded in the short run because of successful self-promotion, but failed in the long run because the promises it made could not be met. The basic problem with behaviouralism was its attempt to replace the state with system, as behaviouralists believed the state was a contested concept and that contradictory explanations were unavoidable. The notion of state lies at the heart of political enquiry and theorising. To ignore the state is counter-productive. For instance, Rajni Kothari (1928–2015) applied structural functionalism to his classic study of Indian politics (1970), but abandoned it in subsequent works.

Behaviouralists could hardly exercise any influence across the border in Canada, where classical political theory remained alive in the works of Crawford B. Macpherson (1911–87) and Christian Bay[19] (1921–90). This was the case in Western Europe, too. In Britain, Sir Friedrich Hayek (1899–1992), Michael Oakeshott (1901–90), Sir Karl R. Popper (1904–94) and Sir Isaiah Berlin (1909–97) rejected behaviouralism. In France, different strands of existentialism and post-modernism—Jean Paul Sartre (1905–80), Raymond Aron (1905–83), Albert Camus (1913–60), Michael Foucault (1926–84)—as well as liberalism, and in Germany, the critical theory tradition of Theodore W. Adorno (1903–69) and Jurgen Habermas (1929–) continued. The biggest criticism of behaviouralism emerged in the USA itself with its rejection by subsequent generations of political scientists, who recovered the gist of institutionalism and articulated a New Institutionalism.

Rediscovery of the State

The 1970s inaugurated the period of new institutionalism, which continues even today as the dominant mode, with Theda Skocpol stating that 'we are all institutionalists now'. Since the 1980s, the primacy of the state has been restored. The state is perceived as a relevant actor in its own right, with autonomous interests and is part of 'real' politics (Skocpol 1985; Mitchell 1991). Institutions are seen as having a major determining effect on individual behaviour (March and Olsen 1984). Five trends have been discernible from the 1980s, suggesting a new research agenda—greater attention to the economic aspects of politics, increased interest in the international context in domestic politics and institutions, an altered and sharpened focus on interest groups, revival of interest in state structures and their performance, and nationalism and ethnic cleavages (Rogowski 1993: 431).

COMPARATIVE METHOD: ADVANTAGES

Comparison is attempted to secure a near accurate picture of the political world and its institutions. The political world has many models and methods with which to grapple with existing complex issues, and a comparison of these provides a balanced view of the pros and cons of the subject at hand. Comparison is always about the comparable; establishing similarities and dissimilarities and arriving at plausible explanations of the observed variables. In doing so, comparison gives us a powerful set of explanations and theories that nuance our understanding. When comparing countries, it is imperative to recognise the differences that exist with reference to language, size, culture, system of government, etc. Comparison also helps us to understand the uniqueness of each country. Comparative research is an essential requirement for studying the intricacies of politics. Comparative research enables us to make intelligent judgements.

As mentioned earlier, there is no unanimity in the field of comparative politics. Different scholars have different preferences. Several kinds of studies exist:

(*i*) Studies of one country or a particular institution (political parties, militaries, parliaments, interest groups), political process (decision-making) or public policy (labour or welfare policy) in that country. When the focus is on a single country or institution, it is important to place the study in a larger comparative framework, which means stating why the subject is important and where it stands in a larger context among a comity of nations.

(*ii*) Studies of two or more countries which are genuinely comparative in nature.

(*iii*) Regional or area studies where countries of a specific region—Latin America, Africa, East Asia, Southeast Asia, the Asia-Pacific region, South Asia, Europe—are studied in a comparative framework. Such studies are useful because they involve groups of countries that may have several things in common, namely a similar history, cultures, language, religion, colonial background, and so on.

(*iv*) Studies across regions are more challenging but are undertaken to establish comparisons and dissimilarities. As such, comparative politics is concerned with significant regularities, similarities and dissimilarities in the working of political institutions and in political behaviour, as different political systems could display similar characteristics.

Transparency International is a yardstick to measure corruption levels among countries. It was established in 1993. **Human Rights Watch** Rankings assesses human rights issues in roughly 90 countries. It was founded in 1978. **Freedom House**, established in 1941, conducts research on democracy, freedom and human rights. It ranks countries as free, partly free and not free. The **Asian Barometer Survey** assesses public opinion and citizens' perceptions on matters of governance, democracy, and the like across Asian countries.[20]

New Yardsticks of Comparison

Attempts are also made to rank and assess countries on different yardsticks beyond the political. The **Human Development Index (HDI)** was devised and launched by Pakistani economist Mahbub ul Haq (1934–98) in 1990 with an explicit purpose: 'to shift the focus of development economics from national income accounting to people-centered policies'. The HDI was created to emphasise that people and their capabilities should be the ultimate criteria for assessing the development of a country, not economic growth alone. The HDI is a composite statistic of life expectancy, education and income per capita indicators, which are used to rank countries into four tiers of human development. In 2010, the Human Development Report introduced an **Inequality-adjusted Human Development Index (IHDI)** to state the actual level of human development. In the same year, the **Gender Inequality Index (GII)** was introduced to measure gender disparity with the help of three dimensions: reproductive health, empowerment and labour market participation. The new index was introduced as an experimental measure to address the shortcomings of the previous indicators, the **Gender Development Index (GDI)** and the **Gender Empowerment Measure (GEM)**, both of which were introduced in the 1995 Human Development Report. **The Economist Intelligence Unit (EIU)**, founded in 1946 by *The Economist* magazine, helps us with analysis of country, industry and risk. It focuses on the costs of living of the world's major cities.

Using the price of Big Mac as the benchmark, *The Economist* instituted in 1986 the Big Mac Index, also known as Big Mac PPP, to measure the purchasing power parity (PPP) between nations. However, the major focus of comparative politics is essentially on political indicators, while taking note of related factors.

CONCLUSION

The present mood in comparative politics is one of moderation, renouncing broad generalisations and concentrating on smaller and more manageable issues; of trying to deduce the particular from the general, thus negating the behavioural paradigm that moved from the general to the particular. As comparative politics develops with close links with developments in political theory, it goes through (just as in political theory) a period of refinement rather than innovation, concentrating on older issues like federalism and corporatism, but situating these in a context where liberal democracy's triumph is becoming increasingly uncertain and more complicated than it seemed after the collapse of communism in the early 1990s. In the 1980s, Huntington raised the question of culture in the context of democratic expansion in East Asia; although he has been proved wrong, it is becoming an important point of reference in issues like democratic expansion, the Chinese economic miracle, the Arab Spring, and terrorism. While Huntington's theory of a clash of civilisations (1996) has few takers today, Friedman's (2005) thesis that the world is flat has also proved a gross exaggeration and simplification.

One marked difference between the twentieth and twenty-first centuries is that in the twentieth century, strife and rebellion in the search for an alternative paradigm created certain ambiguities and uncertainties. But the twenty-first century is moving towards a more settled system of nation-states in Asia, Africa and Latin America, along the pattern in Europe and the West as established by the Westphalian Treaty of 1648 (see Chapter 6).[21] In this context, Comparative Politics will continue to deal with nation-states, the primary actor, in its diverse forms, impacted by different social, cultural, economic and technological evolutions, all of which will result in more contradictions than consensus in the search for alternative paradigms. A major challenge among and within nation-states is the rising inequalities. Globalisation and liberalisation accentuate these inequalities even more. The phrase 'think globally but act locally' in a world where distances are shrinking, but which is still dominated by nation-states, sets the agenda of comparative politics today. In this sense, any work describing the past, present and future possibilities would at best be conjecture rather than near certainty.

NOTES

1. Aristotle's *Politics* consists of many books. Barker (1979) believed that three distinct sets of lecture notes combined together to form *Politics*. Ross (1924: 236) saw it as a compilation of five separate treatises. Jaegar (1923: 300) saw it as a unified, well-written treatise composed over a period of 15 years. The central theme of *Politics* was the polis, an institution that was unique to fifth century BC Greece. It examined in detail the nature of the state and its origins, the different constitutions of actual states, and concepts of citizenship, law, constitution and revolution.
2. Aristotle, unlike Plato and more like Pericles (493–429 BC), did not fear the masses, having faith in their ability to collectively articulate their judgement vis-à-vis policies and the ability of their rulers.
3. Recently, former Indian Reserve Bank Governor Raghuraman Rajan had said that Indian democracy would become a lot more stable and better when it attained a per capita income of US$ 6,000.
4. Rome's lawyers devised a number of textbooks, case books and codes of law in theory and for practical use by officials. The Romans established a system of jurisprudence, or general rules by which actions could be classified clearly with definitions. Gaius, Paulus and Ulpain's treatises are systematic delineations of constitutional and political institutions. A uniform system of law became necessary to unify the divergent peoples through a common

notion of citizenship within the empire, and to settle commercial cases with foreign traders. A distinction was established between public law (in essence, constitutional law) and private law (which concerned individuals and the institution of private property).

5. Gibbon was of the view that the success of a political order is heavily dependent on civic virtue, the basis of true freedom. The decline of civic virtue, besides the unwillingness of the Roman army to serve at distant places, led to degeneration and loss of control on the part of the centre, and the shifting of capital from Rome to Constantinople was among the other factors leading to the decline of the Roman Empire.
6. Spencer divided societies into military and industrial. The former is one with a hierarchy, where cooperation is enforced through forces. In industrial societies, cooperation is voluntary and spontaneous. As societies evolve, they would become more complex and differentiated, marked by an increasing division of labour. Advanced societies are industrial in nature. Durkheim shared the same view.
7. Like Montesquieu and Voltaire, de Tocqueville admired English political institutions and the English aristocracy. Unlike in France, the English aristocracy constantly renewed itself and was in a position to wield its authority through the proper exercise of political experience and wisdom. The momentous changes sweeping through his time led to him describing it as the end of an era and the beginning of a new one. Both Montesquieu and de Tocqueville dissected the merits and demerits of different forms of governments, not in an abstract, timeless sense, but in its historical, political and social contexts.
8. Slavery was abolished throughout the British Empire in 1833. Following American independence in 1776 and the industrial revolution, eighteenth-century Britain no longer needed slaves to produce goods. Cotton, rather than sugar, became the main produce of the British economy, and English towns such as Manchester became industrial centres of world importance. Slave revolts in Barbados in 1816, Demerara in 1822 and Jamaica in 1831–32 also stressed the point that enslavement would not be tolerated. The British realised the high costs of maintaining slavery in the West Indies. Moreover, the once powerful West Indies Lobby lost its political strength with the reform of parliament in 1832. Abolition campaigns by non-conformist churches as well as Evangelicals in the Church of England also played a significant role in ending slavery.
9. Till 1832, only 4 per cent of the British population had the right to vote. By 1884, all males, including the working class, had the right to vote. Women's suffrage took longer. In 1919, women above 30 years of age were granted the right to vote, which was subsequently reduced to 21 in 1928.
10. K. C. Wheare is considered an expert on the constitutions of the British Commonwealth. He is the author of *Federal Government* (1946) and *Modern Constitutions* (1951).
11. Samuel E. Finer's notable works are *The History of Government from the Earliest Times* in three volumes, published posthumously in 1997, wherein all significant government systems are comparatively analysed; *The Man on Horseback: The Role of Military in Politics* (1962); and *Comparative Government: An Introduction to the Study of Politics* (1970).
12. Bagehot's *The English Constitution* (1867) observes and describes the actual working of England's institutions as Bagehot himself had witnessed it, arising from his contact with the ministers and heads of government departments. His essential thrust was that the strength of the English constitution lay in the sovereign cooperation between the dignified, 'the ones that excite and preserve the reverence' of the people, and efficient parts, the others by 'which it works and rules', of the Constitution, and not because of separation of powers as previously theorised.
13. Dicey, an English jurist and theorist of constitutional law, authored *An Introduction to the Study of the Law of the Constitution* (1885), wherein he argued for the impartiality of the courts and insisted that all, including those in the highest position of power, should be subject to the law. He insisted that 'no person is above the law and it is the law that rules all'. Sovereignty of parliament and the supremacy of common law were the two pillars of the British constitution, and a society organised on these principles made it possible to preserve political freedom and ensure the harmonious functioning of a democracy. The parliament makes the law. 'The principle of Parliamentary

sovereignty means neither more nor less than this, namely, that Parliament thus defined has, under the English constitution, the right to make or unmake any law whatever; and, further, that no person or body is recognized by the law of England as having a right to override or set aside the legislation of Parliament' (Dicey 1885). These laws are interpreted by the courts, the judges thus ensuring the need for a system of checks and balances for a just and harmonious society.

14. Bryce, a British observer, analysed the same from a British perspective in *American Commonwealth* (1888). He rejected Tocqueville's account as impractical and abstract, and as an alternative, provided a concrete, detailed account of the real undercurrents of American politics. His thrust was empiricism and not broad generalisations. It must stand the test of objectivity. He tried to draw a map of both American politics and society, and rejecting the idea of history being prescriptive, concentrated on its form of government, accepting American exceptionalism. He also conceded that the prediction of physics is not applicable in politics. He emphasised the special relations between Great Britain and the USA, which was similar to Dicey's assertion of a common political culture between the two. Bryce's *Modern Democracies* (1921) examined two continental democracies (France and Switzerland), two Atlantic democracies (USA and Canada), two Australasian democracies (Australia and New Zealand). He focused on Anglo-Saxon individualist democracies, ignoring corporatist and collectivist ones, that of Belgium and the Netherlands and the Scandinavian countries. In the Preface, he pointed out that the greatest obstacle to comparative government lay in the lack of factual knowledge about other systems of government.
15. Sir William Ivor Jennings (1903–65) was an authority on constitution law. He is famous for his analysis of the British Constitution. He described the Indian Constitution as a lawyers' paradise.
16. Dahl even went to the extent of asserting, 'there is every reason to think that unities can be forged anew. After all, as the names of Socrates, Aristotle, Machiavelli, Hobbes and Tocqueville remind us, from time to time in the past the study of politics has been altered, permanently, by a fresh infusion of the spirit of empirical inquiry—by, that is to say, the scientific look' (1961: 772). This optimism was negated by the limited application of behaviouralism in the contexts of both time and place.
17. In the 1950s, there also developed a new theory of convergence between advanced capitalism and developed socialism. See Karr, Bell and Marcuse.
18. C. Wright Mills' *The Sociological Imagination* (1959) echoed Wolin's sentiments.
19. According to Bay (1965), political behaviour was unable to clearly explain its actual value bases. It is far from neutral, and in reality is conservative and anti-political (see McCoy and Playford 1967).
20. The Asian countries are 13 from East and Southeast Asia—Japan, Mongolia, South Korea, Taiwan, Hong Kong, China, the Philippines, Thailand, Vietnam, Cambodia, Singapore, Indonesia, and Malaysia—and five South Asian countries (India, Pakistan, Bangladesh, Sri Lanka, and Nepal).
21. The Brexit referendum endorses the continuing relevance and importance of the nation-state.

2

APPROACHES

Political System, Structural Functionalism and Political Sociology

Functionalism seeks to uncover the requisites which are necessary for the maintenance, modernization and stability of social and political systems.

Axford, et al. 1997: 26

Behaviouralism and functionalism were the major foes of the old institutional school represented by Carl J. Friedrich and Herman Finer.

Beyme 2006: 749

The critics of the institutional approach do not do justice to his (Finer's) sophisticated analysis.

Rhodes, et al. 2006: 95

What constitutes the area of study for comparative politics is a highly contested matter. The subject matter and boundaries of the discipline are loosely defined, with a 'messy centre'. The basic purpose of comparative politics is to analyse political similarities and differences between nations, both historically and on the basis of contemporary experience. This analysis is situational and also has a value premise of finding out which one, on a comparative scale, is better than the rest. On the basis of a detailed cross-country analysis, the methods of comparative politics use a set of data and frameworks that can provide a universal yardstick of judgement. The understanding is more descriptive and less explanatory; the descriptive mechanism of comparative politics focuses on institutions, states, societies, cultures and political economy. The study of comparative politics involves both an understanding and development of a theoretical framework and its application to individual countries or a set of nations. The latter involves different levels of analysis, for example the developed and underdeveloped countries or the process of democratic consolidation in the contemporary world.

THE INSTITUTIONAL APPROACH

One of the earliest approaches to the study of comparative politics concentrated on the governing institutions of a country. This approach derived its strength from the fact that the very subject matter of comparative politics revolves around the study and analysis of formal political structures. The constitutional structure of the legislative wing became the focal point of enquiry in this approach. The institutional approach was heavily inclined towards the constitutional framework and placed less emphasis on political parties, the bureaucracy and local government. It was based on the understanding and analysis of organisations, which were supposed to identify the actual role of the members. These roles were defined by constitutional provisions, practices and conventions and had the following essential characteristics: (*a*) expectations; (*b*) well-accepted and somewhat mechanical operating guidelines; (*c*) a shared culture of belief and behavioural pattern; and (*d*) rigid rules of governing conduct which makes governance predictable. The net result of such an overwhelming presence of rules of behaviour makes it clear that the assigned and designated roles become more important than the individual characteristics of players. It means that the office of President or Prime Minister is more important than particular office bearers; and the same is the case with the legislature and the judiciary. The assumption is that institutions have an autonomy and independent behaviour pattern of their own, and that subordinates individual preferences to the basic minimum of what is expected from the office or position. There is a clearly demarcated behaviour pattern, characterised by uniformity, continuity and predictability. The institutions, however, are neither static nor stale, but grow and develop with both universal and particular characteristics. The influence of history, culture, situations, circumstances, and the initial founding values and purposes become an integral component of this study. The slow consolidation of institutions leads to their overwhelming presence, curbing the individual role within the parameter of official rules. The collective character of an organisation or a state becomes open and routine, developing trust in the totality of a state's governing apparatus. This means the subordination of individual preferences and power to a larger collective with a larger framework of accountability. The rights and duties of individuals are clearly defined and respected.

The institutional approach restricts the role of individuals, however powerful. This assumes that no individual is indispensable and that limiting individual power and tenure is essential for the proper functioning of modern organisations, including political ones. It is exemplified by the saying that a good manager is one whom nobody misses when s/he leaves the organisation. Institutionalisation is the opposite pole of personalisation, and the effectiveness and longevity of a modern social, economic and political apparatus is mainly dependent on the level of institutionalisation and predictability of the leaders' behaviour.

Institutionalised politics is more orderly than personalised ones, and the higher the level of sophistication and development of a political society, the higher is the level of institutionalisation. No single actor can individually twist and turn events, and this leads to the building of trust both within and outside. Individual and group interests are protected and accommodated within the arena of institutional politics, where the rules of the game are known to all players and are more or less observed universally. In such an order, political actions assume their own legitimacy and no action is reduced to a zero sum game. Bryce, Dicey and Friedrich were pioneers of the institutional approach (see Chapter 1: 13 and 14n).

LIMITATIONS OF THE INSTITUTIONAL APPROACH

The institutional approach restricted itself to comparing the comparable with an emphasis on the validity and sanctity of the formal institution. Who governs is not its primary concern; rather, who governs as a president or a prime minister is more important. The actors are identifiable within a transparent political apparatus of mostly well-established Western democracies. However, in the post-World War II phase of the 1950s and 1960s, there was widespread dissatisfaction with the emphasis on the analysis of constitutions and governmental institutions. This crystallised mainly through the emergence of a world divided into three segments: the Western capitalist democracies (called the First World); the developed Soviet-led socialist countries of East Europe (the Second World); and a very large number of newly emerging nations, where formal institutions were less in existence, as the Third World.

As a consequence of such monumental changes, the framework of comparative politics moved away from the institutional approach, which was essentially limited in its focus to well-established Western democracies only. Two interconnected developments led to the quest for a new paradigm to study the wide variety of governments that emerged in the post-colonial world. These emerging non-Western nations vary widely, from one-person dictatorships to liberal democracies, where the typology practised in the analysis of well-established democracies do not lead to any fruitful research framework. The Western doctrines of separation of powers, accountability, difference between state and civil society, respect for the public-private divide, or respect for elementary human rights exist more in their violation than in their observance. For instance, even in a relatively peaceful transition to power, as in the case of Ghana, Kwame Nkrumah declared himself president for life and was ultimately ousted from power through a military coup. He spent the rest of his life in exile. The communist world is also far from the institutionally based Western democracies, as its leadership is highly personalised and the Communist Party dwarfed all the other institutions, including civil society. As Antonio Gramsci (1891–1937) had prophesied with regard to the Soviet Union, 'where the state was everything and civil society, nothing' (cited in McLellan 1979: 189).

Apart from the impact of such widespread changes in the world, the post-World War II period also witnessed new developments like attitude surveys and opinion polls, which were applied to political studies by younger researchers. The study of constitutions and governmental institutions were regarded as inadequate as they missed out the real currents of political and societal change, which were often better understood by informal mechanisms rather than through the study of formal institutions. As a consequence, the comparative method increasingly concentrated on (*a*) generalised principles; (*b*) the political attitude and behaviour of individuals; and (*c*) the structure and functions that operate universally, whatever be the political superstructure.

EASTON'S *POLITICAL SYSTEM* (1953)

In this shift from the study of formal institutions to a larger societal paradigm, Easton's model of the political system proved a turning point in the early years of what is referred to as the behavioural revolution. He defined a system[1] as 'any set of variables regardless of the degree, of inter-relationship among them' (Easton 1953: 147). A political system is distinct from other systems because it concerns itself with 'the interactions through which values are authoritatively allocated for a society' (ibid.).

Easton stressed the long lineage of the history of political enquiry, which Aristotle called the master science. He was equally conscious of the fact that the promise does not match the subsequent developments, and conceded that while the discipline of Political Science is 2,500 years old, the results even today are disappointing. He found a major lacuna in the inability of contemporary political scientists to adapt to a scientific method with three important attributes: (*i*) valid thinking, (*ii*) observation, and (*iii*) description. He identified the shortcomings in the discipline as its 'failure to clarify the true relationship between facts and political theory and the vital role of theory in this partnership' (Easton 1953: 4).

According to Easton, just as in other areas of knowledge, political scientists must make an effort to base their enquiries on scientific knowledge based on facts. Such knowledge must have a general frame of enquiry for ordering facts and clarifying the links and relations which would lead to a broader and better formulation for explanation and understanding. A general theory would make political science much more meaningful by making it profound and extensive. Reliable knowledge would emerge from such a comprehensive theory.

Easton tried to reinforce his argument by invoking the scientific works of Nicolaus Copernicus (1473–1543), Johannes Kepler (1571–1630), Galileo Galilei (1564–1642) and Isaac Newton (1643–1727), and their cumulative impact on the development of a specific trend of scientific enquiry in Europe. Thomas Hobbes (1588–1679) was the first product of the scientific revolution. However, his conclusions did not match the expectation of the basic verification of the facts of a generalised theory. Hobbes is important for his spirit and not for his result. The philosophers of the Enlightenment, like Jean Jacques Rousseau (1712–78), Claude Adrien Helvetius (1715–71), Marquis de Condorcet (1743–93), Denis Diderot (1713–84) and Montesquieu, were more speculative than empirical. But they were also pioneers in emphasising 'the necessity of scientific reason'.

In the nineteenth century, the overall temper was scientific, and Easton called it 'the age of scientific method'. The examples of Comte, Marx and Spencer proved the sway of the scientific method on the century, with a great deal of optimism with regard to their projections (Easton 1953: 10–12).

However, in sharp contrast to the slow but definite consolidation of an optimistic projection, the twentieth century has been a period of pessimism, with an onslaught on the usefulness of the scientific method in the social sciences. A very large section of intellectuals believed in the thesis that 'the world is not rationally ordered'. The rise of logical positivism is one example of this retreat. Oakeshott is an important example of this movement against rational scientific enquiry through 'a belief in the virtues of the intuitive art of the statesman as against the conscious deliberations of the social scientist' (Easton 1953: 18). The criticism of the scientific method is a reflection of the mood of the age. The severe limitations of scientific reason accrue from a loss of faith in reason itself. This is followed by the argument that reliable theoretical knowledge is not attainable. The laws of social interaction cannot be discovered (ibid.: 19–24).

Easton decried this general pessimism and was hopeful that generalised frameworks of social enquiry could be discovered in even disciplines like political science. He rejected the argument that political principles can never be universally valid as they are products of a particular time and place and lack the universal characteristics of science. However, while rejecting the notions of cultural and historical specificity, Easton believed it was possible to build social science theories with broad generalisations. The American tradition of looking into facts began after the Civil War. Bryce (see Chapter 1: 15n) dealt admirably with this new awakening of dealing with facts. He tried to bridge the gulf between fact and theory. Bentley, et al. reinforced this scientific enquiry amongst political scientists in the USA (see Chapter 1: Section II. See also Easton 1953: 38–47).

CRITICISM OF THE CONCEPT OF STATE

Easton rejected the use of the term 'state', both historically and in its contemporary use. It is not an analytical tool and came into frequent use only since the sixteenth and seventeenth centuries, developing fully in the nineteenth century. In between, it served two important functions: (*a*) the universalistic claims of the Medieval Church, and (*b*) rivalries and competitions of local feudal lords. To combat these two challenges, 'the state concept became a crucial myth in the struggle for national unity and sovereignty. It is both vague and imprecise because of the many conflicting claims and interpretations which cannot provide the basic tools of a scientific analysis' (Easton 1953: 106–15).

The concept of state has no utility for empirical work and 'its importance lies largely in the field of practical politics as an instrument to achieve national cohesion rather than in the area of thoughtful analysis' (Easton 1953: 112). The use of the concept of state has three serious limitations: (*a*) it does not allow any distinctiveness of political science analysis from the other social sciences; (*b*) it does not help in working out a satisfactory definition; and (*c*) it concentrates on particular episodes rather than emphasising the general characteristics. The basic limitation of the concept of state is that it concentrates on the specific and the particular rather than on the general framework, which would allow the study of a wide variety of institutions. It does not allow the study of formations where the state does not exist. The state is just one form of political institution and not the only one, as social anthropology has established. The universality of the political is restricted by the state, and the fact remains that the state originates only in some specific historical setting.

LIMITATIONS OF THE POWER APPROACH

Power as the key concept has been popularised by Morgenthau, Odegard, Holms and Key. However, in spite of its popularity, it is inadequate for identifying the boundaries of research in political science as power, instead of being the only variable, is one of the important variables. There is a larger world beyond the narrow view of power, and Easton demonstrated this by examining the works of Catlin and Lasswell. In his transformative criticism of Catlin, he acknowledged the latter's contribution by highlighting the utmost urgency to conceptualise the concept, but left the other areas unattended. Lasswell's approach was broader than Catlin's, but his essential conception also revolved around power, with concentration only on a small segment of the entire process. It did not provide a general framework for studying the entire process of political life (Easton 1953: 115–24).

Easton termed Catlin's and Lasswell's perceptions as elitist as their essential concern was with the examination of the power of certain groups, rather than with the powers of the majority of the people. Their failure lay in their neglect of a distinction 'between power in general and power in a political context'. Rejecting the claims of state and power as providing satisfactory frameworks of political analysis, Easton concentrated on finding a more general framework of political enquiry which would provide for a reasonably acceptable mechanism of macro analysis of political objects. It had two essential concerns: (*i*) to identity the variables that influence an authoritative policy formulation, and (*ii*) their application in actual practice (Easton 1953: 115–25).

AUTHORITATIVE ALLOCATION OF VALUES

In this effort to broaden the meaning of political participation, Easton included all political activities that affect the entire policymaking process. The cumulative effect of all these factors forms the political system. A political system, with its unique characteristics, would be different from other systems, for example, the economic system. These concepts become crucial in comprehending this differentiation and identification, policy, authority and society. Policy refers to the allocation of values. It has two parts: formulation and execution of a policy. Policy is much wider than a formal or legal decision-making process. Political science is not concerned with all value allocations, but only 'with authoritative allocations or policies' (Easton 1953: 129). The distinctiveness of political research lies in identifying the values that influence and affect authoritative allocation.

The concept of authority is linked to obedience. The societal basis of authority lies in the notional concept of universal application, although a particular policy normally affects a small segment of the entire society. The data for political research is broadly differentiated between the situational and the psychological. Within situational data are three different categories: (*i*) the physical environment; (*ii*) the non-human organic environment; and (*iii*) the social environment as a consequence of social interaction. The basic distinction between situational and psychological data leads to the adoption of the idea of political behaviour, which allows for a departure from the traditional approach (which ignores this distinction). However, a moral framework is also essential to a constructive approach, both for rational enquiry and in formulating a systematic theory. In order to elaborate on this moral framework of research, Easton made a critical assessment of the value premises of traditional political theory based on historical research (Easton 1953: 132).

Easton defined political system as the system of interactions in any society through which binding or authoritative allocations are made. He spoke of inputs from the various environments into the political system, which are converted into outputs, that is, authoritative decisions. Feedback mechanisms put outputs back into the system of inputs, thus completing a complex, cyclical process. Many demands will be made or articulated, but some are lost in the conversion process and do not reach the output stage. If there are too many demands, or particular types of demand, stress arises and the channels are then overloaded. There are various regulatory mechanisms to control demands and to minimise overloading—first, there are structural mechanisms that function as 'gatekeepers', that is, pressure groups and political parties; second, the cultural mechanisms, the various norms which consider the appropriateness of the demands; third are the communication channels; and fourth, demands may be controlled in the conversion process itself by legislators, executives and administrative bodies.

For Easton, the social process represented an uninterrupted flow of different activities by which a limited number of valuable objects are transferred to and from interacting individuals, whose principal interest is in adopting and enjoying such objects. These objects may extend from physical goods to abstract ones like power and the right to deference. The allocation process is not a haphazard one. It is to a large extent institutionalised if social life is to have any pattern and continuity. It must produce or validate the assignment to certain individuals of certain objects, devalued as well as valued. In three ways—custom, exchange and command—this allocation process is structured, which makes it relatively predictable and stable.

Easton defined the whole ambit of politics with reference to command as the basis of allocation, for political allocation necessarily involves the submission of one party to another's will. Customary allocations reflect consensus among the participants, while parties to an exchange are equal and they agree rather than submit. Since the objects in question are valued and scarce, political allocations cannot rest solely on someone's will and need binding. Submission to a command does not depend on a person's spontaneous goodwill or indifference, but could be enforced against her/his will. The command-giver should be able to support her/his statements with sanctions, which entail punishment for non-compliance rather than reward for compliance. Politics then deals with the allocation and handling of a resource, which in turn can be used to make further allocations of other valued objects. Understood in this way, politics seems a mundane business, even as one intuitively considers it important and pivotal to social business involving major players and occupying centre-stage in society. Easton tried to reconcile these views by stating that it is not proper to consider any command-based allocation as political; rather, only that which takes place within relatively broad and durable social contexts with broadly defined constituencies should be considered political. A parent's commands, the rulings of a club's chairperson or even the decisions of a corporation's executive are not in the proper sense political. Memberships in local groupings are often voluntary, and even if it is not, it can be surrendered without much loss to oneself. However, such groupings form a part of a much wider group with membership that cannot be easily relinquished, and this comprehensive grouping that is also territorially bounded is termed 'society'. Easton applied the term 'political' only to those command-based allocations whose consequences are directly or indirectly valid for society as a whole.

Political business involves particular visible, diverse and demanding relations of superiority-inferiority, and ultimately can sanction the uniquely compelling one of physical coercion. For Easton, politics necessarily took place within bounded interaction contexts that can co-exist together. It dealt with a functional problem—that of allocating values among interacting units, which can in principle be dealt with by two other institutional methods, custom and exchange. This leads us to the question of whether politics is a necessary feature and ingredient of social life. The answer is unequivocally in the affirmative, except in the very simplest contexts of interaction. It is clear that custom and exchange, singularly and collectively, can do all the allocation that has to be done. There are bound to be contingencies which can be met only by command-based allocations. Custom-based allocation cannot, by its very nature, allow for the mobilisation of resources, the evasion of routines, the inquiry into new lines of action that becomes necessary from time to time if society is to endure, to safeguard its values, to defend and maintain its boundaries with nature and with other societies. A wholly custom-controlled society can endure and meet new eventualities only if its customs empower some members to mobilise others in response to such contingencies, to devise new routines, to choose among alternative patterns of action and have their choices accepted. This implies the necessity of command. With regard to exchange, Durkheim had shown long ago the need for enforceable, policed rules for even the most sophisticated and flexible exchange system. Effective contracts depend on the existence of the institution to guide and implement them; these contracts are not merely theoretically contractual, but are binding by a command. Easton contended that some allocations will take place through command, for that suggests the necessity of politics. The three modes of allocation do not exist in water-tight compartments and can be interchanged and combined.

Wasby noted that the 'authoritative allocation of values does not distinguish politics adequately from other means of social control. Values are authoritatively allocated within the family, church, and business corporations, as well as government, political parties and interest groups' (1970: 10). It is therefore imperative to distinguish between informal means of social control and those that are coercively enforced. A police officer using force to enforce a value is visible, while there can be situations where the use of force is not visible and where it is not easy to tell who is allocating values. Furthermore, consider a case where companies, through their separate decisions, have been able to establish a similar price while the government, because of paucity of evidence or lack of investigative officers, ignores the action taken by the companies separately. Is this tantamount to authoritatively allocating values, even if these are economic and not directly political (ibid.: 11)? The approach is criticised for its failure to cater to concepts such as political power or for its inability to handle mass political behaviour, for example, aspects like voting. However, Easton, through his emphasis on different boundaries and the input–output mechanism, could have dealt with a situation where an economic issue becomes a political one. He constructed a theoretical model that can be modified and changed (as he had done himself).

FAULTS OF HISTORICISM

Traditional political theory believes that all human ideas are historically formulated and as a consequence, both moral and causal ideas are relative in nature. As Easton put it, 'there can be no universal truths, except perhaps the one truth, that all ideas are a product of a historical period and cannot transcend it' (1953: 235). This makes the search for universal truths impossible, as the conception of truth is related to the period of its formulation. The sociology of knowledge is an extreme form of this historicism. Easton said, 'political theory today is interested primarily in the history of ideas' (ibid.: 236). This has led to concentration on a few areas: (*i*) values are related to the period in which they appeared; (*ii*) historical exposition of the emergence of such ideas; (*iii*) on the basis of the first two objectives, the meaning and consistency of these ideas are found out. As such, the premise is empirical and logical, and not value-based. This has not resolved the conflict between facts and values. Attention is focused on mastering the values of others, and not on clarifying their own values and premises. This has led to the assimilation of political theory within the empirical and causal aspects of social sciences without any link with the moral aspect. Instead, the purpose of historical knowledge is to inspire the construction of one's own 'political synthesis or image of good political life' (ibid.: 237). Within this broad parameter of historicism, some distinctions can be seen between the followers of this approach, namely William A. Dunning (1857–1922), Charles H. McIlwain (1871–1968) and George H. Sabine (1880–1961) (ibid.: 234).

Dunning's three volumes on political thought were published at the beginning of the twentieth century, and subsequent work in this area owes much to what he had laid down as the basic requirements of theory building. He was trained as a historian and his entire outlook was coloured by this. Historical changes and their impact on political theorising is the main ambit of his research. History for him was the interaction between contemporary societal practice, institutions and political thought. He attempted a historical narrative with emphasis on its influence in the formulation of political thought. In doing so, he investigated the prevailing cultural and political moorings and linked them to the formulation of political ideas. Given his firm commitment to historicism, he refused to deal with moral questions even in the context of history. Political theory for him was a portrayal of actual notions and theories. Easton was critical of Dunning's exclusion of moral questions from his query. Dunning's basic postulate was to portray as accurately as possible the linkage between ideas and the social setting, and he was careful to build his analysis logically (Easton 1953: 237–41).

However, Easton conceded Dunning's value premise of supporting representative democracy; yet 'moral views found only a grudging place in his thinking'. He agreed that Dunning also dealt with logic, moral interpretations and even empirical verification, but his major thrust was on analysing political ideas in the context of political moorings. The contemporary trend towards historicism in American political theory began with him. He continues to inspire contemporary research in political theory.

McIlwain's Historicism

The second type of historicism is reflected in McIlwain's work. Political ideas for him were a reflection on political events. He treated political theory as a rationalisation of a historical event, and not as a guide to action. Political activity is rarely influenced by theory. Ideas do not influence action; at best, they have a limited effect. Their influence is restricted to the field of ideas. Political theory often assumes a branch of sociology of knowledge, with primary focus on the role of the circumstances that build knowledge. The task of the political theorist is to discover how larger societal factors shape political theory; and the major task of political theory is to discover the factors that determine the formulation of an ideology.

As such, political theory is merely the study of a particular aspect of history. Political practice, institutions and observation form the components of political theory. McIlwain was concerned with the good political life because of its importance in our lives. His own preference was for a constitutional democracy, a discussion of which he found rewarding. One of his major motives was discovering the origin of contemporary moral convictions. However, in spite of such concerns, McIlwain considered values relative and subjective. Easton rejected this notion of moral relativism in McIlwain's work. Moral theories and the realm of ideas remain open-ended and he ignored the important question: If the assertion of moral views does not guide action, what is the need to attempt it? (Easton 1953: 241–48).

Sabine's Historicism

For Sabine, the value of the historical method in studying political theory was self-evident. However, Sabine's views were different from those of Dunning and McIlwain as he synthesised both their views. He agreed with Dunning that the history of political thought was worth studying because as part of the political process, it influences social action. On the other hand, he agreed with McIlwain that the moral judgement that exists in each theorist is also an essential aspect of study. For Sabine, political theory could be examined in two basic ways: (*i*) social philosophy, and (*ii*) ideology. The task of the theorist is to discover the extent to which such theories have shaped the historical process. The contents of this study are both factual and moral. Evidence can be gathered of facts, but moral utterances cannot be characterised as either true or false; they are reflections of human preferences. Values are not 'reducible to facts, they are expression of emotions' (Easton 1953: 250).

Sabine did not ignore the moral element in political theory, and placed it in the realm of psychology. Easton noted that Sabine called himself 'a social relativist' (Easton 1953: 251) and agreed that his approach facilitated an understanding of the historical evolution of concepts like democracy and liberalism. However, he found Sabine's position unacceptable because 'when we approach values, there is little to guide the student of history with regard to what he is to learn from the research that passes beyond a mere report of theorist's moral speculation' (ibid.: 252). Sabine's analysis does not help a theorist to build his own moral values. A historical perspective is essential for comprehending a good political life, but is not enough by itself. As such, historicism 'is manifestly unsuited for training political scientists in the skills and knowledge of genuine moral clarification' (ibid.: 254). A moral basis is necessary for constructing a systematic political theory and is the surest way to bridge the gulf between fact and value. A moral clarification needs the approach of a constructivist, and not of a historicist. Easton, after rejecting historicism mainly because of its indifference to or neutrality on the question of morals, tried to provide a new framework for a systematic political theory based on an explicit commitment to a moral framework.

IDEA OF POLITICAL EQUILIBRIUM

In his quest for uniformities as a measure of a collective consciousness of the discipline, Easton provided a theory of political equilibrium. It is a key concept in a broader theory and has two aspects: (*i*) to comprehend the political process in a political system, and (*ii*) balancing and restraining the different power groups within a constitutional political system. In the second category, balancing of power is an important ingredient, in which general equilibrium coexists with constitutional equilibrium. General equilibrium means (*a*) interdependence of units, and (*b*) reaching a point of stability. This idea of equilibrium was first seen in Bentley's work (see Chapter 1: Section II), with its emphasis on the balance of groups with the idea of the equilibrium principle based on coherence. It means (*a*) that equilibrium implies a marked tendency towards cooperation, and (*b*) political change is to be understood in the context of attempts at equilibrium. Revolutionary changes and revolutions have been rejected because of their 'uninspired philosophies of history'. This mechanism provides a reasonable alternative with which to study political change. General equilibrium implies an emphasis on empirical work, accepting the idea that political activity is a component of a larger empirical mechanism that emphasised change over a period of time (Easton 1953: 267).

WHAT SHOULD POLITICAL THEORY DO TODAY?

Traditional and historical analysts operated on a broad canvas, attempting to depict the entire political life. Political theory was not treated as a 'moral enterprise'. Political theory consists of four major elements: factual, moral, applied and theoretical. The focal point for political theory today is comprehending political life based on a systematic theory. The task is to unite causal and moral theory to provide a research framework for all political scientists. The purpose is to attain 'reliable knowledge about political life' (Easton 1953: 310).

The purpose of political science research is to provide a mechanism that would not be restricted to just one political system, culture or civilisation. The current research paradigms of contemporary comparative politics are unsatisfactory and need drastic revision. The focus today is on institutional descriptions of particular political systems. Beyond this, comparison between different systems is merely descriptive. But if we use political system as a general framework, it can move research from the descriptive to the theoretical. Related to this present emphasis is another lacuna: it is only static situations that are concentrated on. The new method will achieve two purposes: (*i*) study the alterations in political systems over a period of time, and (*ii*) facilitate an understanding of the process of political change (Easton 1953: 314).

THE NEW REVOLUTION IN POLITICAL SCIENCE

In 1969, in a drastic revision of his earlier thesis, Easton advanced a new revolution in political science after the initiation of the behavioural revolution in the 1950s necessitated by social and political crises not perceived earlier. The impact of these changes has been felt in political science as well, and Easton termed the new challenges 'the post behavioural revolution'.

The focal point of this new urge revolved around the question of relevance and action. As was the case in the earlier behavioural revolution, this too was rooted in dissatisfaction with political research, especially of those who wished to mould political science research on the model of the natural sciences. The earlier challenge to behaviouralism had come from the classicists and traditionalists, whereas this challenge was futuristic, with emphasis on seeking new directions for the discipline. Easton considered this a 'genuine revolution' and not merely a reaction or counter-reformation (1969: 324). It was a movement and an intellectual path-finding, with similarities to the behavioural movement in its infancy. The present movement had no particular methodological framework and had adherents from conservatism to the left. In its various manifestations, the one unifying theme was its deep dissatisfaction with contemporary political research. This was a reflection of the 'collective heritage of the discipline'. It was a call for change, and Easton reminded readers that his political system was a call for change in the early 1950s. As Hiroshima changed the perception of natural scientists with regard to a broader role to prevent atomic wars, social scientists are also to have a greater obligation to the commitment to truth and links with the people. He also acknowledged a link between the outcome of scientific research and social relevance. Political system is a general theoretical framework for performing research on social issues. The scientific method is an important tool of research, and the search for basic frameworks is to be a continuous process. Few question the futility of this effort. What is required today is a commitment to a more rigorous 'application of whatever knowledge we may have to transparently critical problems' (ibid.: 325).

In 1969, Easton was more accommodative of other approaches and views than he had been in 1953, when he proposed his political system as an alternative to contemporary political science in the US and Great Britain. In 1969, there was an acceptance of a larger plurality and an assertion that all divergent views within the discipline enrich the discipline cumulatively. His own commitment to scientific research is reaffirmed; this time, however, he expressed this not to bridge the gulf of fact and value, but to pursue his own commitment more vigorously (Easton 1969: 328).

EASTON'S INNOVATIONS IN SYSTEMS THEORY

The systems approach in political science is not new. However, earlier approaches emphasised the probabilities and did not speak in terms of a general law in the Newtonian sense. Drawing on biology, the natural sciences, cybernetics, operational research and sociology, Easton tried to provide a general framework for political science research that was similar to the scientific paradigms followed in science.

Easton attempted to build scientific knowledge upon a theoretical basis of facts. The ordering of the facts would encompass the entire political process as no solution to a particular problem is possible without a well-formulated general scheme. To arrive at this point of reliable knowledge, it is imperative to analyse both empirical and psychological data, like the personalities and motivations of participants. Situational data shaped by environmental influences would also form a part of the latter.

For Easton, political life reflected the forces of disequilibrium—change and conflict—as well a countertendency towards equilibrium, of accommodation and interdependence. A general framework of the system replaced the notion of state, as the term is confusing, with a variety of meanings attached to it. Power, for Easton, was one of many significant concepts and related to authoritative politics in society. Like Dahl, he looked at power as the ability to influence the actions of others while determining policies. Policy is the outcome of a web of decisions and allocation of values. The key concepts in Easton's system are power, decision-making, authority, policy, units, boundaries, inputs, outputs, differentiation with the system, and integration.

Easton provided a highly organicist view of the political process as a living object. It adapts, survives, reproduces and changes. It is a total rejection of the view that politics is to be analysed by concentrating on different levels of analysis. Formulated in the heydays of the behavioural revolution of the 1950s, Easton's political system was highly influential. One very important offshoot of Easton's theory is the application of structural functionalism to the study of comparative politics.

THE FRAMEWORK OF STRUCTURAL FUNCTIONALISM

Structural Functionalism originated in sociology; its early proponents were Radcliffe-Brown, Bronowski and Durkheim, although its beginnings can be traced back to the ancient Greeks and to Aristotle's writings (Susser 1992). However, it owes its systematisation and popularisation to the achievement of Parsons. Structural Functionalism emphasised the structural aspect of any social system. It concentrated on the process that maintained a social structure, ordered internal stability, and on the reasons for its survival. Its key focus was on cohesion and stability.

In the 1960s, Almond and Powell (1966) considered structural functionalism an application within Easton's framework of a political system. The emphasis here was to comprehend both institutions, that is, structures and functions, in a historical and situational context. It was an alternative to the fragmentary theories of both state and society, and to dependency theory (see Chapter 16). The essential requirement for understanding a political system is an analysis of the structures and responses, or inputs and outputs. Almond and Powell developed key concepts to understand different political systems: (*i*) political socialisation (see Chapter 5), and (*ii*) recruitment and communication. Political socialisation implies larger belief structures like the civic virtue[2] as an indicator of a citizen's belief structure, and also its non-existence. The recruitment system reflects the process of incorporation of citizens' interest, engagement and participation. Communication is the mechanism through which a political system implements its values and information. The focus is not on institutions, organisations and groups, but on the role, structure and interaction within units. The structure refers to patterns of interactions indicated by political culture, which reflect the patterns of orientation and a guide to political action. These patterns will enable cross-country surveys beyond the boundaries of particular political systems.

FRAMEWORK FOR STUDYING THE POLITICS OF DEVELOPING COUNTRIES

In 1960, Almond and Coleman employed structural functionalism to understand the politics of newly emerging countries where change was widespread, and institutions weak or non-existent. System replaced the state and emphasis shifted from the legal institutional approach of traditional political science to newer functional categories. Function substituted power, role substituted office and structure, institution. This substitution was claimed to be a solution to the problem of studying different categories of political systems, both advanced and backward. The claim was that it would overcome the limitations of the institutional approach by identifying the universal characteristics. This claim was based on the logic that while all political systems provide different political structures, all of them perform the same function. Political structures are multifunctional and in a cultural sense, all political systems are mixed. It incorporates all of Easton's categories—input, output, feedback, functional categories, interest articulation, interest aggregation and political communication in the category of inputs, and rule making, rule application and rule adjudication in the output categories.

Almond and Powell argued that state building is related to the extractive and regulative capabilities of the political system. They viewed nation-building exercises as essentially a structural problem as it involves the differentiation of new rules, structures and sub-systems. For instance, penetrative and centralised bureaucracies might exist, but in the absence of a homogenous pattern of loyalty, there is neither loyalty nor commitment to the central political institutions. Examples are the Austro-Hungarian empire, Italy, the former Soviet Union and the new states of Africa, as these display incompleteness due to societal factionalism.

CONCLUSION

Easton's model viewed the political system as a device that would transfer societal demands to policy formulation. The most significant aspect for Easton were the inputs and not the institutions. The institutions were a small 'black box' As a part of the behavioural revolution, Easton's model emerged as a critic of the institutional approach. Instead of focusing on institutions, it focused on human beings. The role is emphasised because of the freedom of the players within their broad assigned roles, and also because the players have the ability and the inclination to change the institutions itself. The study of legislative behaviour replaces the focus on formal procedures with emphasis on the social backgrounds of legislative representatives, the individual record of voting, and their own definitions of their roles within the institution. In the judicial section, attention shifted from the courts to the judges. With the widespread use of statistical techniques, social backgrounds, political leanings and their links to legal judgements became the main area of study.

Easton's view was mechanistic and its emphasis on equilibrium with a balance between inputs and outputs proved to be static, something he indirectly admitted to in his later writings of 1969. Much of the problem with Easton's model lies in the fact that it ignored specific contexts. It attempted to build a grand theory that would be coherent and permanent, but without focusing on specific details. In this, he followed Comte and Engels rather than Marx and Weber, who moved to generalise theory on the basis of the particular to the general and not vice versa. As a consequence (as happens with all grand theories), its particular contextualisation remains problematic. His criticism of traditional political theory and historicism operated at a superficial level by emphasising a code of morality that is final and static. Instead of limiting the task and ambit of political theory, as reflected in the writings of Oakeshott (1956) and Berlin (1962, 1980), he attributed an undefined and large canvas for a homogenous political theory. This is impossible to achieve as political theory is an arena for ideas in conflict. As Berlin said (1962), Easton, with his overriding concern for equilibrium and stability, had little or nothing to say about system breakdown and conflict.

Like Marxism, Easton's theory too did not provide for safeguards, and in defining the political, left no scope for inputs from other systems to drastically change or alter the political system itself. Because of this rigidity, the political system ignored the problems of variation and differentiation. While Easton's underlying assumption was the universal validity of the American system, he did not examine the factors of American exceptionalism, making the model inoperative in many other areas of the world. However, Easton's political system and its follow-up in the application of structural functionalism to comparative politics brought out the limitations of the formal institutional approach. Its criticism of the institutional approach and the state is the most important component in the study of political science. The revival of the state as the most important focal point emerged in the 1980s in the writings of Skocpol (1979) and Evans (1985). The reason for this change in perception lay in the incapacity of the behavioural approach to understand political change. However, in broadening the ambit of comparative politics and in pointing out that political activity is complex and cannot be comprehended by merely looking to the formal institutional apparatus of the state, Easton and his associates have played an important, albeit transient, role in the evolution of modern political analysis.

Political Sociology

Traditional political science comprised mainly three aspects: (*i*) the descriptive, formal institutional organs of the central and local governments; (*ii*) practical, contemporary problems of organisation, procedure and implications of constitutional provisions; and (*iii*) philosophical, normative concerns in political philosophy (Bottomore 1979). With its emphasis on formal characteristics, there were no broad generalisations and no overall generalisation of regimes on a world scale, the motto being 'compare the comparable'.

The situation changed with sociology claiming a much broader field and insisting that a comprehensive understanding of the political process demanded the attention of both the formal and the informal as key to broad generalisations and explanations, and to building a more accurate and scientific framework of analysis. Political behaviour is to be studied in a much larger context. Initially, Marxist influence was predominant as the political superstructure was inherently based on an economic system. However, by the end of the nineteenth century, there was a shift towards the critics of Marxism with the important foresights of Pareto, Mosca, Michels and Weber. With a variety of studies of political parties, elites, voting behaviour, political ideologies and culture, a distinct area of political sociology emerged.

Political Sociology and Behaviouralism

Political Science originated in the United States. The very name suggests a hankering for a more scientific study of the subject, distinct from the subject's more philosophical growth in England and continental Europe. Within this broad paradigm, the influence of political sociology is predominant in the field of political behaviour.

A trend developed to refine and elaborate upon the concepts that originated with early sociologists—political parties, pressure groups, elite behaviour and concentration on the actual processes of government and administration. The most important feature of these studies was that all of them used a comparative scale; they not only compared the comparable, but also evaluated systems with wide differences. International conferences on comparative political sociology became common. However, after practically dominating political science research and training in the 1950s and 1960s, the influence of political sociology declined. The fate of Marxist sociology was not very different either. One important reason for the rapid decline of this trend was the fact that the behaviouralists grossly underestimated the need to comprehend the formal structure of government. The replacement of the state, which lies at the very core of political science, by the political system remained problematic and elusive.

NOTES

1. Systems Theory emerged in biology in the nineteenth century, but its complete articulation took place in the 1920s. The general systems theory developed in the writings of Ludwig von Bertalanffy (1901–72; 1950, 1951, 1969) and was established as a field of study. Easton and Karl Deutsch's (1912–92) systems approach to study politics grew out of sociological and communication theory. Anatol Rapoport (1911–2007; 1965, 1966, 1970) defined a system as a set of interrelated entities connected by behaviour and history. He stated that a system must specifically satisfy the following criteria: (*i*) one can specify a set of identifiable elements; (*ii*) among at least some of the elements, one can specify identifiable relations; (*iii*) certain relations imply others; and (*iv*) a certain complex of relations at a given time implies a certain complex (or one of several possible complexes) at a later time (Rapoport 1966: 129–30).
2. The notion of civic virtue or virtù figures prominently in the writings of the Italian Renaissance political theorist, Machiavelli. In a ruler, civic virtù is a martial quality needed to defend the state against external aggression and internal disunity. In an ordinary individual, it means public spiritedness and patriotism, necessary for ensuring freedom and deterring tyranny. Civic virtue is usually fostered by governments that are republican and in societies that have cities. It became popular during the Enlightenment. It became a matter of public interest and discussion during the American Revolutionary War. Benjamin Franklin (1709–90), an articulate exponent of the notion, underlined that republics can be sustained only through the cultivation of specific political beliefs, interests and habits among its citizens, reverting in its absence to authoritarian rule, such as a monarchy. Wood (1969) called it a universal eighteenth-century assumption of republics as intrinsically beautiful, but depended on people's willingness to submit their own interests to that of the government voluntarily, and to obey laws for the sake of conscience and not out of fear of the ruler's wrath.

3

APPROACHES
New Institutionalism

We live through institutions.

Bellah, et al. 1991: 740

The indifference which political scientists displayed traditionally with respect to what constitutes political institutions is remarkable: indeed, at any rate up to the emergence of the behavioural movement, the empirical study of politics seemed to be viewed as co-existence with the study of political institutions.

Blondel 2006: 718

By the mid twentieth century, intellectual and cultural currents were taking an increasingly dim view of institutions.

Heclo 2006: 731

Compared with other areas of the social sciences, political science emerged late as an independent discipline. In its formative period, the study of political institutions was the pivot around which the entire discipline revolved. The distinguishing characteristic of political science is an in-depth study of formal governmental apparatus and legal norms. However, for a time institutions, as March and Olsen remark, 'receded from the position they held in the earlier theories of political scientists' (1984: 734). Its revival came with a larger analytical framework, which provided a broad rather than a specific outline. Two important characteristics of an institution are a longstanding observation of rules and conventions, followed by orderly, organised practices in which individual players play a subordinate role and the enduring institution is insulated from (*a*) individual expectations, and (*b*) the changing external environment. The emphasis is on appropriate behaviour played out through rational actions for a long time; for instance, the British practice of 'once a speaker, always a speaker'. Over a period of time, institutional structures develop codes of behaviour, and common motivations while stressing predictable behaviour leads to a justification of a legitimate behavioural pattern. March and Olsen term such a development 'prescriptive rules of appropriateness' (Rhodes, et al. 2006: 3). Institutions 'are also reinforced by third parties in enforcing rules and sanctioning non-compliance' (ibid.).

The basic premise of new institutionalism is that 'institutions matter . . . scholars can achieve greater analytic leverage by beginning with institutions rather than individuals' (Peters 2005: 155). It implies the importance of collective action. For the new institutionalists, although institution is the core area of political analysis, a wide divergence exists amongst them with regard to its contents. They use it in the sense of a general approach. Its major components are time-tested and enduring structures, well-formulated codes under which to develop a standardised operational practice. An institution evolves and develops its own strength and plays an autonomous role in the political sphere. The basic purpose of institutionalism is a normative concern with improving the political system. Institutionalism develops by interacting, learning and deviating from rational choice theory and political culture theories. The first approach sees political life as interactions between calculating self-interested persons, while the second emphasises shared values, a common cultural setting and experience, and a common vision. Institutionalism provides a transformative criticism of both approaches, while incorporating the frameworks and insights of both.

Order and predictability are the two important foundations of new institutionalism. What is emphasised is the appropriate function of all participants. The primacy of institutions enables an order to build its 'character, history and visions' (March and Olsen 2006: 4). They provide unity in diversity and order institutional change within the larger framework of 'historical inefficiency' (ibid.: 5). March and Olsen, who pioneered the study of New Institutionalism in 1984, accept the fact that 'a full blown theory of political institutions' is not available, and that the theory has encountered criticism and a constant process of elaboration is continuously developing (ibid.). There is no unified body of thought. At least three different analytical approaches have emerged over the past 15 years, each of which calls itself new institutionalism. These are Historical Institutionalism, Sociological Institutionalism and Rational Choice Institutionalism.

POLITICAL INSTITUTIONS: SEARCH FOR A THEORETICAL FOUNDATION

March and Olsen reflect on the historical antecedents of the past 50 years, culminating in the famous phrase articulated by Skocpol and Pierson: 'we are all institutionalists now' (2002: 706). In the post-World War II phase, the behavioural revolution attempted a 'paradigm shift' with a frontal attack on traditional political science's primary occupation with formal and legal institutions. Its obsolete and limited vision is reflected in the fact that this approach ignores the vitally important ingredient of political life, that is, the non-political attributes of governmental institutions (Macridis 1963: 43). With the purpose of discovering in politics—as Lasswell (1936) puts it, 'who gets what, when, and how'—there is a desire to comprehend political behaviour scientifically as well as the real working of the political process.

The major emphasis is on diversity and on political and societal interaction. This assertion rejects the claim of the state and the visible symbols of political institutions, that is, the legislature, the executive, bureaucracy, judiciary and the electoral system. March and Olsen argue in favour of a reassessment of political institutions, that is, to measure their 'independent and endurable implications' (March and Olsen 2006: 6). To achieve this, they reject (*i*) contextualism (politics purely as society's reflection) and reductionism (macro aggregation) of individual players; (*ii*) instrumentalism and the reduction of politics to only policymaking and the allocation of resources; (*iii*) the perception that political action is solely determined by calculating, self-interested behaviour; and (*iv*) the 'standard equilibrium models' as history, is 'inefficient' and thereby recommend functionalism (ibid.). Rejecting all these methodologies, they propose that 'political order is created by a collection of institutions that fit more or less into a coherent system' (ibid.). These patterns are not static as they change over time and are structured not on the basis of one set of principles, but on different principles. Politics is played not in a vacuum, but in a social construction which is public knowledge, and has two crucial characteristics—anticipation and acceptance. This framework is essential as 'by virtue of these rules and practices, political institutions define basic rights and duties, shape or regulate our advantages, burdens and life chances are allocated in society and create authority to settle issue and resolve conflicts' (ibid.: 7).

The values of an institution are manifold: (*a*) it injects order into social relations; (*b*) it minimises flexibility in individual behaviour; and (*c*) it avoids one-sided and selfish pursuit of self-interest. This basic Weberian principle compels individuals to follow general principles and rules and develops 'a logic of appropriateness'[1] (March and Olsen 2006: 7). Legitimacy becomes a common denominator. Institutions do not need to be static, nor is their emergence inevitable. While inside operators and beneficiaries defend institutions, their validation must be done by outsiders. One very important characteristic of an institution is that change is to be orderly and within the larger rules and routines, and never arbitrary.

March and Olsen are careful to not project an ideal type of institution. Such institutions are historically inefficient and the effort is to optimise rather than reach an optimal point. They also admit that institutions are slow to adapt to changes in the environment (March and Olsen 2006: 7). Authority and power are the two important determinants for new institutionalists. Within an overall framework of appropriate behaviour, the emphasis is on normality and orderly change. Rules and roles are intermingled. Appropriate procedure normally leads to appropriate behaviour. New Institutionalism, unlike the old one, is not implicitly identified with organisational structures. Instead, its focus is on rules and norms. It also focuses on both informal and formal institutions. New Institutionalism is also more theoretical and is interested in the processes of institutional change.

MULTICULTURALISM AND INSTITUTION BUILDING

As coherence is an important consideration, New Institutionalists also take up the problem of achieving political order in multicultural societies. To overcome strong national identities and the absence of a common centre with regard to a large number of concerns, for example education, the idea of shared institutions has been advocated in order to develop a pan-European identity. However, the problems concerning the building of common political institutions and protecting cultural diversity remain.

Institutions and the Process of Change

Institutions change because of both internal and external factors. The quest for new institutionalists is to evolve a 'standard process of change' (March and Olsen 2006: 11). Involving the doctrine of 'historical inefficiency' and the denial of any optimism, March and Olsen remark, 'adaption is less automatic, less continuous and less precise than assumed by standard equilibrium models and it does not necessarily improve efficiency and survival' (ibid.). In democracies where political institutions are of pivotal importance, the source of change is political debate and competition. However, institutions occasionally encourage obstruction to enable 'reflection, criticism and opposition' (ibid.). Even a competitive party system can be 'frozen' (Lipset and Rokkan 1967).

The link between institutional persistence and external factors is not accepted by institutionalists. Of greater importance is the distance that exists between institutional practice and an institutional ideal. They emphasise change as a natural process. Streeck and Thelen (2005: 12) focus on 'critical junctures', but also point out their limitations. They argue that transformative results can emerge out of incremental, or what Popper calls piecemeal, social engineering.[2] An example is Western European democracies, where a large public sector and welfare state emerged after World War II. But in the late 1970s, the same democracies moved in a neoliberal direction, totally transforming the relationship of the individual to the state—from a citizen as a social self to that of a customer with concern only for the self.

Balance between Exploitation and Exploration

Exploitation is concerned with the lessons of history, whereas exploration is more futuristic. While balance between the two is an important consideration, optimal balance remains indeterminate and difficult to realise. Conflict is also a persistent problem, termed as 'institutional irritants'. The basic principles of an institution are never accepted by a whole society. Batora (2005: 14) discusses the inherent tensions in areas like diplomacy between the interests and perceptions of a nation and the accepted norms of diplomatic conduct.

Political Institutions Beyond the Political System

A plurality of structures in political institutions is a fact in liberal democracies. No single set of principles can be prescribed. An integrated and coherent institutional basis and the doctrine of political system ignores this elementary fact, as 'politics is eternally concerned with the achievement of unity from diversity' (March and Olsen 2006: 14). The details of competing institutions form the subject matter of political institutionalists. Reality itself remains a contested concept. Rationality and values are themselves to be explained and changed with the pressure of time and place.

Limits of Enlightenment Rationality

The Enlightenment belief in uninterrupted and continuous progress may not match the human capacity. Gandhi's dictum of one step at a time is advised, to check arbitrary action with the consciousness of 'modest knowledge' (March and Olsen 2006: 15) and to be extremely careful to initiate substantive changes.

Questions Relating to New Institutionalism

New institutionalism is the dominant trend in contemporary political science. It has consolidated its hold during the past three decades. However, a lot of questions still remain unanswered by the practitioners of this new and novel approach. The very idea of its newness has been questioned, as has its capacity to sustain theoretical and empirical claims. However, defenders claim that modern political institutions like the legislature, the judicial process and diplomacy can only be meaningfully studied by concentrating on their institutional characteristics (March and Olsen 2006: 16). Rhodes believes that 'there is a future for the institutional approach' (ibid.). A claim has even been made that this methodology may well represent the 'next revolution in political science' (Goodin and Klingemann 1996: 16). Its strength lies in the fact that it aims to supplement, rather than reject other approaches. But they also concede that the nature of their work is modest and rudimentary, and that there are miles to go 'before the different conceptions of political institutions, action and change [can] be reconciled meaningfully' (March and Olsen 2006: 16).

Political institutionalists also envisage a change in the subject matter of political science itself, which has been traditionally dominated by sovereign territorial nations and the European Westphalian state system (see Chapter 6). Order within the state system and disorder and anarchy in relations between states, they argue, are moving towards a drastic revision. Their major example for this change is the European Union, and this leads them to argue that 'there is a need for new ways of describing how authority, rights, obligations, interaction, attention, experience, memory and resources are organized beyond hierarchies and markets' (Brunsson and Olsen 1998: 16). They also contend that the task is to go beyond rational plans and environmental constraints. Instead of responding to all the concerns, institutionalists limit their enterprise to asking a number of fruitful questions:

> Which institutional characteristics favour change and which make institutions resistant to change? What factors are likely to disrupt established patterns and processes of institutional maintenance and regeneration? What are the interrelations between change in some (parts of) institutions and continuity in others, and between incremental adaptation and periods of radical change? Under what conditions does incremental change give a consistent and discernible direction to change and how are the outcomes of critical junctures translated into lasting legacies? Which (parts of) political institutions are understood and controlled well enough to be designed and also to achieve anticipated and desired effects? (Rhodes, et al. 2006: 17).

DOMINANT SCHOOLS IN POLITICAL INSTITUTIONALISM

Rational Choice Institutionalism

Rules and incentives lie at the core of rational choice institutionalism. Institutions are to be analysed as legal institutions, with a vision of political engineering to promote the common good. The pioneers of US political science believed that neither corruption nor partisanship has a place in modern politics, and that politics is to be seen and analysed as an administrative process. Rules, designs and structures are key concerns for them. US exceptionalism, with its strong legal tradition and written documents—coupled with the fact that the US had never seen a struggle between the aristocracy and commerce; nor had it seen a well-organised working class mobilisation—has greatly influenced this school. Seeking immediate advantage, the arena of politics remains a contested one. Rules change, and so do advantages and disadvantages. There is nothing like a neutrality of rules; rather, they evolve in the tussle between the holders of power and their challengers.

However, along with this endemic conflict situation, agreement as a key concept was also developed by some members of the school. Derived from economics, this model is based on Pareto's optimality, in which one party is made better off, but none is made worse off. Institutional arrangements evolve out of log rolls, reciprocities and consideration of mutual advantages. With the emergence of reciprocal relationships, certain institutions develop on the basis of a fragmented power structure, and opportunities for a number of veto options lead to coherent change and provide a precise and proper direction. The emergence of a central and enduring leadership is unlikely in this scheme.

Some of the big names of this approach are Olsen, North, Levi and Rothstein. Rational choice institutionalism accepts that individuals have a fixed set of preferences and they behave in a manner that maximises the attainment of these preferences. They see politics as a series of collective action problems (Hall and Taylor 1996). It arises from the study of American Congressional behaviour. Rational choice institutionalists are unable to provide an adequate predictive theory of action as it is not easy to know how preferences come about, and why they vary from individual to individual. Rational choice institutionalism also ignores the social structure.

Historical Institutionalism

This approach defines institutions as the formal or informal procedures, routines, norms and conventions embedded in the organisational structure of the polity or political economy. Continuity and preservation are the key concerns for this school. The transaction costs of changing the course are prohibitive. Institutions are compared with dried cement; in the initial period it can be dismantled, but it becomes very difficult later on. The old hats will always like to preserve institutions, whereas new entrants may try to extricate from the post. A consequence of this is the likelihood of institutions failing. With uncertainty surrounding future political control, ineffective institutions may emerge. Institutions emerge at both procedural and programmatic levels. In a democratic structure, durable and popular programmes are more difficult to alter than they are in an authoritarian one. Such programmes strike a balance between financial and political costs. The cost of change always remains a key factor. Another important factor is the number of actors and the prevalence of heterogeneity or homogeneity; if the decision-making process is cumbersome, it tends to preserve the existing institutions. However, all these factors are tentative; none is absolute.

In the 1960s and 1970s, historical institutionalism developed in response to the group theories of politics and structural functionalism. While it borrows from both these approaches, it goes beyond them. From group theory, it accepts the argument that politics is about the conflict between rival groups for scarce resources, and from structural functionalists, it borrows the assumption that the state is made up of interacting parts. Building on the older tradition of institutionalism in political science, which accorded importance to formal institutions, historical institutionalism develops a more expansive conception of which institutions matter, and how (Eckstein and Apter 1963). Historical institutionalists are also influenced by the way structural functionalists view polity—as an overall system of interacting parts (Almond and Bingham Powell Jr 1966). However, unlike structural functionalists, who view the social, psychological and cultural traits of individuals as the driving forces of the system's operations, historical institutionalists see the institutional organisation of the polity or the political economy as the principal factor structuring collective behaviour and generating distinctive outcomes. They emphasise the 'structuralism' implicit in the institutions of the polity rather than the 'functionalism' of earlier approaches, which viewed political outcomes as a response to the needs of the system (Hall and Taylor 1996: 937).

In response to structural functionalism and group conflict theories (both pluralist and neo-Marxist variants), historical institutionalists in the 1970s took a closer look at the state, which was no longer seen as a neutral agent among competing interests but as a complex of institutions capable of structuring the character and outcomes of group conflict.

> Historical institutionalists tend to conceptualize the relationship between institutions and individual behaviour in relatively broad terms. Second, they emphasize the asymmetries of power association with the operation and development of institutions. Third, they tend to have a view of institutional development that emphasizes both dependence and unintended consequences. Fourth, they are especially concerned to integrate institutional analysis with the contribution that other kinds of factors such as ideas can make to political outcomes (Hall and Taylor 1996: 938).

Regarding the question of how institutions affect the behaviour of individuals, historical individualists use two approaches—the calculus and cultural approaches. The calculus approach emphasises the fact that individuals seek to maximise their goals through their preference, and act strategically in pursuit of those goals (ibid.). Institutions affect human behaviour mainly by providing information, rules and norms to actors, thereby decreasing the level of uncertainty about the behaviour of other actors. The cultural approach argues that human behaviour is bound by an individual's worldview, which views the individual not as utility maximisers but as 'satisficers', whose actions are dependent on context rather than on strategic calculation (ibid.). Institutions also provide the ethical or rational model for interpretation, which in turn affects the identities, self-images and preferences of individuals. Historical institutionalists stress the relationship between institutions and ideas. While institutions are important, other factors such as socioeconomic development and the diffusion of ideas are equally important. Its strength lies in comprehending the effect of political struggle on institutional outcomes, and vice versa. Historical institutionalists underline the role of institutions in political life, but do not insist that institutions are the only casual factor in politics. Its weakness lies in its ignoring of individual decision-making in its analysis.

Sociological Institutionalism

This is also referred to as 'cultural' or 'normative' institutionalism and draws heavily on the works of Durkheim and Weber as its concern is with the forms of social control that collective institutions exert on individual action. It also draws on the sociological study of organisations, particularly the work of Philip Selznick (1948). March and Olsen, considered the founders of new institutionalism, are sociological institutionalists as they define institutions as a 'relatively enduring collection of rules and organized practices' (2006: 5).

Norms and culture are the key factors for this school. This approach has emerged from organisational theory. The bases of institutions are exogenous, as the history and norms of a political order are integrated within it. No single political actor(s) can create them. Institutions have an independence and autonomy of their own, which over a period of time influence the player's preferences, perceptions and identities. With rules and routines, appropriate and predictable behaviour emerges. Duty and obligations overtake rational self-interest, with the players adjusting themselves to the prevailing rules and routines. When preference is non-antagonistic and homogenous, self-interest as a motivation drives the players towards observation, as the cost of deviance is enormous. Sociological institutionalism underlines the importance of values and norms in constituting institutions and in socialising individuals into conformity through what March and Olsen call the 'logic of appropriateness' (2006: 7). Civil society is one institutional setting that is heavily researched; this includes Putnam's highly influential empirical analysis of social capital.[3] Unlike Rational Choice Institutionalism, sociological institutionalism stresses that individuals will be circumscribed by institutions and their norms and rules.

Institutions themselves set the process of change, not through conscious design but through significant social, cultural or political change. They change in an indeterminate manner. In the early twentieth century, scholars like Edward Said developed the geological view, comparing institutions to 'coral reefs' and 'show accretions' (Rhodes, et al. 2006: xvi). Sociological institutionalists define institutions more broadly than any other approach. Institutions are not just rules, procedures, organisational standards and governance structures, but are also conventions and customs (Koelble 1995). Sociological institutionalism, however, does not explain how institutions originate.

A wide diversity of institutional approaches include the above-mentioned approaches, as well as a number of others, like international institutionalism, constructed institutionalism and network institutionalism. In spite of these wide differences, institutionalists try to build a 'collective experience' rather than score over one or the other approach. They look to all the differences as a journey forward to institutionalism. Jourbert's (1842) advice is worth heeding:

> One of the surest ways of killing a tree is to lay bare its roots. It is the same with institutions. We must not be too ready to disinter the origins of those we wish to preserve. We disinter institutions, not to kill them, but rather to learn from them as repositories of our collective experience (cited in Rhodes, et al. 2006: xvii).

Blondel's View of New Institutionalism

'If institutions are regarded as central in a social science discipline it is in Political Science' (Blondel 2006: 716). Till World War II, there was an agreement on this. However, two decades after the war, the behavioural revolution became dominant and institutions assumed importance with the emergence of new institutionalism. The pioneers in the 1980s were March and Olsen and since then, there has been a resurgence in mainly rational choice theory. Blondel reminds us that even during the relative decline in the study of institutions during the behavioural revolution phase, with the dominance of structural functionalism, the word structure was used instead of institutions for its supposed neutrality; however, it covered 'at least in large part the same reality' (ibid.).

In spite of the long tradition and widespread use of the term 'institutions', it continues to be debated, unlike in economics or sociology. Blondel refers to Huntington's attempts to provide a broad definition of institutionalisation in his *Political Order in Changing Societies* (1968): 'the process by which organizations and procedure acquire value and stability' (Blondel 2006: 12, 717). It is defined by four characteristics: adaptability, complexity, autonomy and coherence. The emphasis is on procedures and not on activities. Institutions develop, but they also decay. The efficiency of institutions cannot be taken for granted, and they depend both on internal and external factors. Where institutions do not exist, they are to be created and designed.

Traditionally, universities in the USA emphasised political institutions and empirical politics, and not political philosophy. But there was no urgency to mention institutions, and they found no mention in the classic works of Finer and Sartori (Blondel 2006: 718). However, the discussion arose when the ambit of political science went beyond the study of institutions with the incorporation of the study of groups. Representing this new outlook, Truman stated that institutions do not carry a 'meaning sufficiently precise to enable one to state with confidence that one group is an institution whereas another is not' (ibid.).

Almond and Coleman (1960) distinguished between interest articulation function and three others—non-associational groups, anomic groups and associational groups (Blondel 2006: 718). Blondel refers to a similar statement made by Almond and Powell in 1966; the behavioural attempt to replace institutions with structure is bound to lead to important questions 'by the sheer fact that a second notion was introduced without abandoning the first' (ibid.: 719). The wheel turned full circle with the publication of 'The New Institutionalism' by March and Olsen in the *American Political Science Review* in 1984. However, even they refused to provide a definition of institutions by clearly demarcating them from other elements that also play a role in the political process.

Blondel admits that a common definition acceptable to all the social sciences may not be possible. In Political Science, he quotes Easton to assert that a

> search for a definition has to be around the concept of bodies able to take authoritative decisions, these bodies being in a position to develop practices—that is to say, procedures and rules—which those who recognize these bodies have to accept as being, so to speak, the 'arms and legs' of these organizations (2006: 723).

Quoting Huntington (1968) and Polsy (1962), Blondel accepts the fact that 'institutionalization takes time' (ibid.: 724). He also agrees that political scientists accept institutionalisation as being of seminal importance, and yet its basis for development 'has not been systematically explored' (ibid.: 725). Quoting Huntington, he asserts that there is no co-relationship between longevity and the level of institutionalisation. The process is not linear as reversals also take place, and there have been examples of the collapse and decline of well-established regimes (ibid.: 726). Huntington observes that where 'a function is no longer needed, the organization faces a major crisis: it either finds a new function or reconciles itself to a lingering death' (ibid.). Blondel accepts the problem of defining institutions in a political context. The extent of support to either stabilise or destabilise them is also difficult to arrive at. He concludes: 'the difficulties are such that one is tempted to conclude that what makes an arrangement, an institution, in politics as elsewhere, is merely whether that arrangement is a "stable, valued and recurring pattern of behaviour"' (ibid.: 728).

The crux of the problem, according to Blondel, is the essential distinction that is to be made between institutions and institutionalisation. De-institutionalisation and pseudo institutions are also derivate accounts of institutionalisation. It leads to a situation where 'the concept of institutionalization' is more commonly used than the 'concept of institution' (2006: 728). Blondel accepts that 'a coherent concept of institutionalization' still eludes us (ibid.). It is not a puzzle whose solution is sought, 'but a serious gap in our understanding of social life, as studies of institutions and institutionalization are likely to provide major clues about key variations in approach among the social sciences' (ibid.: 729).

Hugh Heclo concentrates on the debate around institutions in the context of the 1950s and 1960s. He begins his account with an event in the mid-1960s. There was an assembly of known scholars of the 'behavioural revolution' in Yale University's seminar room—Dahl, Deutsch, Lane, Lindblow, Danelski, Barber, and the much older but towering figure of Lasswell. The readings concerned Truman, Key and Schattsheider, all of whom were influenced by the writings of Arthur Bentley. The general thesis was that 'government was the process of adjustment among groups: with that insight, institutions faded into the background and process came to the fore' (Heclo 2006: 731). The general mood was that the formal institutional and legal framework did not reflect reality. The search had to go beyond the institutions.

Reasons for Change

Heclo stated that against the background of the ongoing liberation struggles, institutions received another setback. Habermas' phrase, 'colonization of the lifeworld by system' (Heclo 2006: 732), offers enough reasons to rebel against the system or the establishment, where the institutions lay. The dismissal of institutions also meant an awareness of the oppressive power that lies behind it. As Heclo sums up: 'institutions were both the icing on the cake of behavioural reality and the iron cages of social control' (ibid.).

What does Institutional Thinking Mean?

Institutions made a grand comeback in political science (as well as in economics and sociology) in the 1980s. But the answer to the question of what institutional thinking means is cloaked in ambiguity. As Sabine (1973) observed, political theory developed as part of politics; similarly, institutional thinking takes shape in the contest of some known and specific institutions. To arrive at a reasonable conclusion, Heclo answered this in the context of a four-fold plan:

(*a*) *What institutional thinking is not*: Institutional thinking is not critical thinking; nor does it reflect a 'hermeneutics of suspicion' (Stewart 1989: 764). Institutionalist thinking rejects the proposition that good quality thinking refers to critical thinking. Critical thinking devalues institutions and this is precisely what is avoided by institutional thinking. Heclo (2006: 735) claimed that 'thinking institutionally is still thinking'; however, institutional thinking does not mean conformity, but thinking positively; 'it means exercising a particular form of attentiveness to the world' (ibid.).

(*b*) *Institutional thinking as faithful reception*: Novelty, newness, originality, invention or creation are not the essential ingredients of institutional thinking. The essence of institutional thinking is to value and cherish what has been followed till now. The arrangements are neither transitory nor a quick fix, but are authoritative in the context of function and durability. But this does not prohibit adaptability or innovation as 'institutional thinking eagerly seeks to understand what has been received in light of new circumstances that are always intruding' (ibid.).

(*c*) *Institutional thinking as infusion of values*: Heclo is categorical in stating that 'institutional thinking is about value diffusion as well as infusion' (ibid.: 736). Institutions inculcate a larger value system beyond personal preference. Independent standards of evaluation evolve and individual players are judged by such values. Appropriateness is appreciated and expediency is decried. It teaches a 'central fact': 'there is something estimable that is larger than yourself and your immediate interests' (ibid.: 736).

(*d*) *Institutional thinking as lengthened time horizons*: Institutional thinking stretches 'the time horizon backward and forward' (ibid.: 737). Both past and future determine present action. It follows the Burkean principle of a partnership between the past, the present and the future that is still unborn. It accepts change and its inevitability, but situates it within an appreciation of the past, with consideration for what would likely happen when one is no more. 'The present is never only the present'; rather, 'it is one moment in a going concern' (ibid.).

Institutional thinking is based on the logic of long-term rather than short-term calculations. Heclo also answers the question of whether institutional thinking is unimportant or archaic by stating that while addictive behaviour is not desirable, 'steady habits' possess 'immense survival value for society at large' (2006: 738). Social order is strengthened by it as 'the multitude of nameless people "just doing my job" amounts to a sheet anchor sustaining civilized life together, something we are never likely to notice until disaster strikes' (ibid.). Both in ordinary times and in times of crises, institutional thinking survives, although it is subdued and restricted in the latter. The most important point is that it provides 'a voice independent of the claims of personal power'. It also protects one from 'wilful ignorance called presentism'; both 'memory and anticipation speak together in the present tense' (ibid.: 739). It secures predictability of human conduct and without institutions, it is hell. However, the solace is the need to think beyond institutions, distinguish bad and good institutions like a mafia; but this does not mean that institutional thinking is discouraged or absent. An Aristotelian balance is what is required.

Klaus von Beyme studied institutions historically since 1789. He linked the emergence of new institutions to three waves of democratisation: the first is the constitution, which spread all over the world except in Great Britain. This new constitutionalism does not break completely with the past; rather, it adapts it to, first, the representative government, and second, to universal franchise. Even dictatorships have come under the spell of constitutionalism, incorporating 'a bill of rights which the regime rarely respected' (Beyme 2006: 749). Continuity with the past is reflected in a number of ways. Old assemblies become modern parliaments. Advisors to the king develop into the modern cabinet, with an office of the prime minister. What is important is 'not so much in the internal change of institutions, but in their mutual relationship within the system' (Beyme 2006: 744). One major innovation is the dependence of the cabinet on parliamentary majority.

Second, two major institutions, the bureaucracy and political parties, which originated with the Romans, have been resurrected in a big way in modern times. Weber linked bureaucracy to the modernisation process itself. Political parties, which are extra-constitutional and which George Washington decried at the time when liberal democracy began, have developed as the best possible coordinator of all state institutions.

Unlike the first two developments, the evolution of the constitutional courts is a modern phenomenon. Beginning with the unprecedented judgement of the US Supreme Court in *Marbury vs. Madison* in 1803, the Supreme Court (along with the Senate) has fulfilled the constitution makers' desire for a need for checks and balances.[4] Although this doctrine of judicial review is the negation of the doctrines of both republican tradition and popular sovereignty, this idea has received slow but steady support, and has become part of the constitutional code even in Europe, which has countries with a long republican tradition (for example, France). The idea of the Ombudsman precedes the democratic age. However, the idea of a planning commission or an authority evolved in the twentieth century as part of the command economy, but disappeared with the acceptance of a market-oriented neoliberal order by most democracies.

Beyme contends that 'institutional theories always developed in cycles, after revolution', that is, in 1789, 1830, 1848, 1871, 1918 and 1945 (2006: 745). A sudden change took place in regimes in 1989 when many communist nations embraced liberal democracy. The French semi-presidential and German constitutional court proved the most popular with the post-communist states moving towards Western liberal democracy. The old ways are preferred to any new experimentation.

THEORIES OF INSTITUTIONS: THE CLASSICAL TRADITION

Theories of institutionalism are unable to dissect the actual functioning of the institutions they analyse. An example is 'Montesquieu's doctrine which ignored the institution of parties and adhered to a schematic view of the British system' (cited in Beyme 2006: 746). There is always a differentiation between theory and method. A theory can prove to be incorrect, whereas methods survive even if some theories employing the method are falsified. For instance, a separation of powers may not be applicable to modern democracies. But pluralism and federalism 'can be put into empirical operation with institutionalist, behaviouralist or rational choice methods' (ibid.: 747). The old institutional approach derived its inspiration from the Aristotelian view of politics, where the political process is open and the citizens equal. Classical institutionalists like Montesquieu and de Tocqueville are not 'ontological analysts' and describe 'institutions in comprehensive social settings of a system' (ibid.).

RECENT TRENDS

After 1945, institutional theory oscillated between 'waves of neglect and rediscovery of institutions' (Beyme 2006: 748). Making a science of political science meant not 'accepting institutional analysis as the centre of research' (ibid.). The old institutionalists became the target of the behaviouralists, but even the latter could not avoid the use of the term 'institutions'. It is to the credit of Easton's system theory that a broad general theory of institutions emerged after Weber. New scientific terms, such as 'rule setting', 'rule applying', and 'rule adjudicating' and 'rule enforcing' institutions, were invented. However, there is an inherent flexibility in 'structural functionalism' as it emphasises particular solutions and localised political institutions that emerge to solve the problems of a given society.

Old institutionalists like Friedrich and Herman Finer were severely criticised by the behaviouralists. But paradoxically, they were supported by neo-Marxists and radical post-behaviouralists who brought back the notion of state in political science discourse. There is an inherent hostility on the part of behaviouralists towards such revivals. For instance Easton, who invented the term 'political system' to replace the state, feared a 'romantic backlash' from theorists like Miliband and Poulantzas (Beyme 2006: 749). However, the fear was exaggerated as the concentration of the dissenters remained on economic relationships, and 'they failed to develop a differentiated theory of institutions' (ibid.). Rational choice theorists also attempted to rediscover institutions; however, a basic fallacy in their paradigm lay in their focus on utility-maximising rational individuals, making them unable to effectively comprehend the larger political behaviour of groups and parliaments. Interestingly, in the US the state never plays the role of a major institution. However, 'the citizens were more proud of their institutions than in other countries' (ibid.).

However, by and large theorists disagree with the view that national characteristics can be reflective of institutions as a permanent feature. For instance, Huntington discovered a gap between ideals and institutions. The new social movements also question such assertions. The problem with institutional theorising is that 'institutions develop less quickly than theories in institutions' (Beyme 2006: 752). It is quite difficult to change obsolete past practices, such as the US Senate, the electoral college or the executive second chamber of Germany. Beyme raises an important question regarding the permanent cleavage in political science between 'hard' proponents like behaviouralists and rational choice theorists who want to formulate universal laws and 'soft' historical analysts (ibid.: 753). The purpose of new institutionalism is to work out a synthesis and strengthen the discipline. Beyme notes the many novelties of new institutionalism: (*a*) unlike old institutionalism, it is theory-oriented; (*b*) it incorporates the earlier achievements of behaviouralists and rational choice theorists; and (*c*) it is much more comparative than earlier institutional theories (ibid.). Beyme concludes that 'neo institutionalism cannot substitute for the behavioural and the rational choice revolts but can only correct their theoretical and methodological exaggerations' (ibid.).

CONCLUSION

Today, there is a general agreement that there cannot be a Kuhnian consensus in the contested field of political science. In the heydays of Behaviouralism, Strauss continued with his normative work along with Easton's political system approach at the Chicago University. Unlike pluralism in a liberal democratic approach, pluralism in the study of political science is a settled fact. Easton himself admits this in his presidential address at the American Political Science Association in 1969.

Accepting this broad limitation of the discipline, the new institutionalists are not propagating a paradigm shift in the study of political science and comparative politics. They view all earlier efforts of different perspectives to enrich political science with respect, and incorporate the valuable points that have been made. Their attempt is to build on the old foundations to make political science timely and relevant. This modesty and acknowledgement has made new institutionalism the dominant school in contemporary times, with a near total acceptance that we are all new institutionalists now.

NOTES

1. Appropriateness, according to March and Olsen, refers to a specific culture. There is no assumption about normative superiority. A logic of appropriateness may produce truth-telling, fairness, honesty, trust and generosity, but also blood 'feuds, vendattas and ethnic conflicts in different cultures' (March and Olsen 2006: 7).
2. Piecemeal social engineering is gradual and evolutionary, in contrast to both holistic utopian revolutionary change and conservatism. Popper associates piecemeal change with an open society, one that is committed to freedom,

democracy and pluralism. He rejects social revolution as a political method because, first, to abolish all institutions and traditions—what he often terms 'canvas cleaning'—leaves the utopian engineers confused and at a loss as to how to act. The second reason is the fallibility of both scientific knowledge and social science knowledge. It is therefore rational to resort to piecemeal change that can be executed all the time by private individuals and groups, as well as the government. There is a constant process of learning from the inevitable errors and expectations are to be adjusted accordingly. In the absence of any finality, it is wise to adopt a wait and watch policy and go by the trial and error method that allows us to rectify mistakes as and when they occur, for it is not possible to anticipate all contingencies. Reforms through this method are modest but democratic as it tries to accommodate differing points of view and public discussions, and makes open its conclusions and consequences. Change for Popper is gradual and modest as there is nothing called an absolute truth; he doubted anyone who proclaimed the existence of one. Truth is at best relative, depending on the perception of the one who perceives it. Holistic revolutionary change proceeds on the assumption that it is possible to anticipate all eventualities, and that the person creating the master plan can never go wrong. It is unscientific and irrational (Mukherjee and Ramaswamy 2011: 14–15).

3. Social capital is a term that Robert Putnam, borrowing from James Coleman (1990), develops. Social capital refers to 'features of a social organisation such as trust, norms and networks, that can improve the efficiency of society by facilitating coordinated actions' (Putnam 1993: 167). The idea of social capital has been in vogue in the social sciences for decades, but it has recently changed its meaning and become important once again particularly due to the efforts of the World Bank, which defines social capital as 'the internal social and cultural coherence of society; the norms and values that govern interactions among people and the institutions in which they are embedded. Social capital is the glue that holds societies together without which there can be no economic growth of human well-being. Without social capital, society at large will collapse, and today's world presents some very sad examples of this.' At first, it was mostly applied to the sociology of education. It referred to the numerous connections and experiences of the more fortunate in society, which were helpful for success. It has considerable affinity with the older conception of civil society and civic culture.

The current usage is different, as it refers to a set of intangible social or collective attributes that make for stable and effective political systems. It is that set of expectations and social habits that make it possible for governments to reply on public support at times of stress, or to call forth great public effort or a period of stoicism. Conventions of mutual help and neighbourliness and a strong commitment to public charity on the part of the educated elite are seen as integral to the notion of social capital. Its advocates contend that the government or the state ought to increase social capital, but are unclear as to how this is to be done. Many see this as an invasion into the private space and as an artificial creation, and therefore difficult to sustain. Furthermore, social capital refers to sub-cultures rather than to states. Social capital is not anathema to *laissez faire* capitalism (Cunningham 2000: 135) as Smith, its high priest, clarifies that self-interest alone cannot be the motivating factor for the success of capitalism. There are other motivations, like responsibility, trustworthiness and social values, as is evident from his extensive discussion of values such as sympathy, generosity and public-spiritedness. Smith is also categorical about the key functions of a government, which are education, healthcare and labour laws, and this means that the creation of the very basis of social capital did not escape the notice of the pioneer *laissez faire* theorists. Social capital complements economic analysis and it is the non-market counterpart to market imperfections.

Until recently, economists assessed growth, whether of individual economies or sectors of the economy, by measuring productivity on the premise that the free flow of capital and technology would lead to per capita growth rates. However, empirical evidence points to differences in growth rates, which is attributed to non-market imperfections that include technology, saving, education, finance, economies of scale, externalities, intergenerational transfers, level of inequality and type of political regime. Social capital is the defining characteristic of a society that is both liberal and democratic. Putnam points out, for instance, that in the US, social capital is declining, as evident from the decrease in voter participation, declining membership in groups and declining levels of trust, to the extent that neighbours no longer know each other. A high level of social capital is good for democracy, while less spells trouble.

4. In the *Marbury v. Madison* case the Supreme Court applies the principle of judicial review wherein the federal courts have the power to declare void acts of Congress considered to be ultra vires of the Constitution. In doing so, Chief Justice John Marshall paves the way for the Supreme Court to become a separate branch of government on par with the Congress and the President.

4

APPROACHES
Political Economy

By making it impossible to believe any longer in an automatic reconciliation of conflicting interests into a harmonious whole, the General Theory of Employment, Interest and Money (1936) of John Maynard Keynes brought out into the open the problem of choice and judgement that the neoclassicals had managed to smother. The ideology to end ideologies broke down. Economics once more became political economy.

Robinson, cited in Gamble 1983: 64

Political Economy is not a fixed subject or discipline but a recurrent mode of conceptualizing social life.

Vig 1985: 6

Political economy is the methodology of economics applied to the analysis of political behaviour and institutions.

Weingast and Wittman 2006: 5

Economic interaction amongst people began with the invention of agriculture, and especially after agriculture started to produce a surplus. Since then, markets have become an integral part of human existence. The barter system prevailed before the invention of money; however, money, which makes enduring storage possible, stabilised the rise of cities and the merchant class market. Demand automatically led to greater supply, and this also meant a role for the state in order to deal with the market through regulations. In the beginning, political economy was all-comprehensive and was based on a larger number of disciplines. This was reflected in Smith's *The Wealth of Nations* (1776), with which the modern period of economic thinking began. The framework within which the state deals with economic questions and the interdependence of politics and economics is called Political Economy.

In his *History of Economic Analysis* (1954), Schumpeter defined political economy as an exposition of a comprehensive set of economic policies on the strength of certain unifying normative principles, such as the principles of economic liberalism and socialism (Gamble 1983: 64). This differentiation of political economy as an arena of normative philosophy and economics as a value free science can be traced to the origins of political economy itself. As Vig (1985: 6) observes, 'to some extent it still holds, since political economy raises fundamental value questions about the proper role of the state and private markets and often gives rise to critical evaluations of existing arrangements'. The Marxian critique of capitalism continues to provide the basic structure of critical political economy, whereas theories of microeconomic choice and market equilibrium favour the framework of liberal bourgeois society; and as Myrdal (1969) says, no study of the social sciences can be value-free. The ideological moorings of seventeenth and eighteenth-century liberalism and socialism provide the two broad divisions of the political economy approach, as well as the general philosophical framework to formulate the arguments (Weingast and Wittman 2006: 5).

THE DIFFERENCE BETWEEN THE OLD AND THE NEW

However, there are reasons for the contemporary interest in and revival of political economy: (*i*) there has been a great deal of effort to study democratic countries, which are more adaptable than non-democratic regimes;

(*ii*) data and close observations are easily accessible in democracies; (*iii*) political and economic comparisons are more plausible for application in 'developed institutions of the advanced industrial democracies', rather than the less stable and less institutionalised politics in the developing world (Weingast and Wittman 2006: 5); (*iv*) An added reason for confining the enquiry to advanced capitalism is that large comparisons are possible today, unlike in the past (ibid.).

This has led to a situation where normative theories and presumptions can be empirically tested because, first, of the easy accessibility of sophisticated tools and methodologies for quantitative research; second, social scientists are increasingly being trained in statistics and mathematics; and third, the increasing use of econometric methods to political questions (Weingast and Wittman 2006: 7). With all these recent developments, 'it is no longer possible to write political economy off as a field for amateur economists and moralists, through mutual interest and the cross fertilization of disciplines it is now pressing forward at the boundaries of social science research' (ibid.).

POLITICAL ECONOMY AND INTERNATIONAL ECONOMICS AND POLITICS

The international economic structure is of crucial concern to political economy. International trade, finance and the role of important players like the IMF and the World Bank are critical as by their money power they exert considerable influence and control over many nations. Their neutrality remains suspect as they are supposed to benefit the host and key contributors, at the cost of recipients who have to follow diktats such as structural adjustments for domestic issues like inflation and unemployment. Such an indirect but crucial remote control creates dependency and a lack of autonomy for the recipient nations (Frank 1980; Wallerstein 1974–89).

Contribution of Political Science to Political Economy

Traditionally, the field of political economy was dominated by economists and sociologists. But the situation is changing with the increasing role of the state in economic areas, even in countries committed to a free market economy. It has also to do with reasonableness. John Rawls (1921–2002) had stated that human beings do not want to be equal at a subsistence and starvation level and that a prosperous society is to have both incentives and specialisation, which can only happen when the government is efficient. In such a state, the Weberian values of efficiency, rationality and impersonality are indispensable. Zuckert (1985: 35–36) comments that 'democracy defined as equality of condition—income, occupation, influence and information is thus not merely inefficient but fundamentally unfeasible'. In order to match democracy with efficiency—which John Maynard Keynes (1883–1946) always emphasised—serious attention is to be paid to institutions, interest groups, elections, bureaucracies and political parties. Pluralism and corporatism, two crucial areas of concern for political scientists, are also of great interest to political economy. In terms of its evolution, the political economy approach is both older and younger than Political Science.

ORIGINS OF POLITICAL ECONOMY

Bronowski and Mazlish (1960) acknowledge the impact of scientific enquiry and its movement from the Mediterranean, brought about by Galileo's torture, humiliation and imprisonment to Northern Europe, especially England, in comprehending the rise of Northern Europe and, commensurately, the decline of Southern Europe. This is also of crucial significance in understanding the rise of political economy. The background to this was provided by 'writers on science, from Bacon to Locke, (who) slowly brought about an intellectual climate in which scientific laws, the laws of nature, were equated with the law of God, immutable, rational precepts and also with an equally immutable moral law' (Hill 1972: 89). As both culture and science are conditioned by economic development and abundance, the climate for scientific enquiry led by Newton was facilitated by the flowering of the glass and paper industry in Britain. This new scientific attitude was all-pervasive, with attention focused on preserving accurate records, the balance of trade, public revenue and expenditure, mortality rates of plagues and life insurance.

In this evolution, Sir William Petty (1623–87), who contributed immensely to the development of political arithmetic, is acknowledged as the father of political economy. He developed the art of reasoning with the help of figures relating to governmental expenditure and administration. His advocating of free rein to different forms of individual self-interest served as the precursor to the later development of *laissez faire* economic theory. He considered the maintenance of a high degree of employment to be the duty of the state, and advocated the requirement of labour for production as the main determinant of exchange value. As Tawney observes, 'the contemporary progress of economic thought fortified no less the mood which glorified the economic virtues' (1926: 157). He also adds that the development of economics in England was different from that in Germany and France. In Germany, it flowed from public administration and in France, from philosophers and important celebrities. But in England, continues Tawney, 'with the exception of Petty and Locke, its most eminent practitioners were business men, and the questions which excited them were those neither of production nor of social organization, but of commerce and finance—the balance of trade, tariffs, interest, currency and credit' (ibid.: 160).

POLITICAL ECONOMY AND THE SCOTTISH ENLIGHTENMENT

In the eighteenth century, in a more definite form, political economy emerged as a precursor to modern economics, political science and sociology. It was first consolidated in eighteenth-century England as a branch of moral philosophy as part of the Scottish Enlightenment (1740–90). Scotland was traditionally allied to France, and England was its enemy. However, against the background of three rebellions, a union between England and Scotland took place in 1707. The major worry of Scottish thinkers was the future of the poor, backward, stagnant Scottish economy when integrated into a common market with England, a world-class dynamic economy. Scotland was sandwiched between a prosperous England and an impoverished Ireland. In the context of the French Enlightenment, Scotland, which had a long association with France, shared the spirit of France's age of reason and because of this emphasis on the rationalist spirit, a new kind of sceptical and utilitarian philosophy developed under the influence of David Hume (1711–76). But unlike the French Enlightenment, which had a broad canvas, the chief concern of Scottish Enlightenment was economic growth and rapid development, international trade and the emergence of an urban, commercial, bourgeois society in post-1707 Scotland.

The central task of the moral philosophy of Scottish Enlightenment was to analyse the societal consequences of human greed and acquisitiveness. Bernard de Mandeville (1670–1733) propounds the thesis that private vices lead to substantial public benefit, that virtuous simplistic behaviour on the part of an individual does not lead to any social benefit, and that private virtue need not be idealised as it does not lead to any public good. Hume linked the question of private morality with a utilitarian calculus. Pleasure is virtuous and pain is vice. He showed little concern at the rise of corruption and its effect on morality under capitalism. He was confident that a moral code for individuals would rise subsequently. Francis Hutcheson (1694–1746) interpreted virtue in the moral sense of providing the greatest good to the greatest number, and considered pain unnatural. Smith reconciled these different strands by bringing in the concepts of moral sympathy and the invisible hand of God to control human passions. He also brought in the concept of stages of economic growth within a larger historical pattern. This scheme of the stages of human history was followed both by Hegel and by Marx. Smith, along with Adam Ferguson (1723–1815), propounded the theory of the division of labour as the key factor in the expansion of commerce. Montesquieu linked commerce to civilised behaviour, with a mutual stake in perpetuating prosperity. Smith in his masterpiece, *The Wealth of Nations*, gave industry and

Image 4.1: Karl Marx (1818–83)

Source: https://commons.wikimedia.org/wiki/File:Karl_Marx.jpg.

manufacturing a special position of honour. Ferguson, in his *Essay on the History of Civil Society* (1792), noted the increasing specialisation of professions that debase the lower ranks of commercial society, which seem to threaten the upper ranks with imminent moral corruption. To check this trend, he advocated a recreation of the ancient classical ideal of virtue, to be calculated by the militia and the citizens. Machiavelli also championed civic virtue, but his essential concern was not with economics or social change. But Hume's and Smith's perceptions are different as they are shaped by the emergence of commercial society, which makes new demands on institutions: (*a*) limiting the burden of government to defence, administration of justice and execution of public woks; and (*b*) broadening the political participation of citizens.

The broad framework of these Enlightenment thinkers centres on economic life. They were not interested in developing a theory of the modern state (as attempted later by Hegel), but were concerned with dissecting the institutional settings crucially related to economic life. Within this broad framework that gave primacy to economics, the related yet vital questions of political life—for instance, the public/private divide and the question of political liberty—came to the fore. Hume and his associates created this new discipline of political economy. It examined questions relating to economic life and growth, seen as key concerns of social science. Smith subsequently reinforced the fact that an ordinary wage labourer in Britain or Holland was much better-off than an American Indian King.

This tradition of analysing economic arrangements as they affect life dominates the writings of Smith, J. S. Mill and Marx. However, the late nineteenth and early twentieth centuries saw the rise of distinct scientific disciplines like economics, sociology and political science. With increasing specialisations and detailed, specific enquiries, the social sciences were compartmentalised, and different independent perceptions evolved (Routh 1975).

THE MARGINALISATION OF POLITICAL ECONOMY

Apart from this separation of individual social science disciplines, there was another important reason why mainstream Western social scientists ignored the questions of political economy. Political scientists ignore economic development and economic policies, considering them the problems of the post-colonial societies of Asia and Africa after World War II. In the West, steady economic growth and affluence within the framework of a neo-Keynesian consensus is taken for granted. The advanced capitalist democracy is supposedly stable; theories espousing the end of ideology and convergence posited that both advanced capitalism and developed socialism were areas where fundamental problems of economics had been solved. This led to the rise of the behavioural movement, and attempts to explain the sociological and psychological roots of partisan voting and similar political activities.

With emphasis on the pluralist nature of advanced capitalism and the interplay of interest group politics, economic questions have been relegated to secondary importance. Simultaneously, the attribution of Western capitalism as post-industrial and post-material has distanced social science research from key political economy questions. With large areas of consensus amongst political parties and decision-makers, economic policy options within the political process have been reduced to a minimum, exemplified by Lipset's famous assertion that politics has become boring. The issues that dominate are whether metal workers ought to get a nickel more an hour, or whether the price of nickel ought to be raised. These may be important, but are hardly the grounds to stimulate ideological debate. Since the fundamental political problems of the industrial revolution have been solved, it has spelled the 'end of domestic politics for those intellectuals who must have utopias or ideologies to motivate them into political action. . . . The ideological issues dividing the left and right has been reduced to a little more or less of governmental ownership and economic planning' (Lipset 1964: 290; 1973: 406).

REVIVAL OF POLITICAL ECONOMY

However, this apparent tranquillity of the social sciences with the indifference to political economy questions began to break in the late 1960s with the onset of the Vietnam War, and the subsequent student unrest in many developed capitalist countries. The 1970s and 1980s saw an unexpected revival of political economy. In the 1970s, advanced capitalist countries faced a great deal of stagnation, inflation, unemployment and economic difficulties because of the decision of the Organization of the Petroleum Exporting Countries (OPEC) to raise the price of oil fourfold. This adversely affected all non-petroleum exporting countries, especially the developing ones, but the impact was felt more in the West as one of the major reasons for the spectacular post-World War II recovery of Western Europe was the supply of cheap oil from the Middle East (West Asia). As a consequence of these factors, economic issues regained central focus within the social sciences. There was also a realisation that economic problems could not be understood in isolation from other social realities; no one discipline is capable of finding satisfactory answers and as such, the interdisciplinary nature of political economy was advocated.

THE NATURE OF POLITICAL ECONOMY

However, the subject of political economy is varied and can be termed an umbrella ideology. It is a normative area of study where the laws of physics do not operate. It deals with many important aspects, such as the market, property, the intricate problem of supply and demand, and the selection of priorities and consequent allocation of resources. The questions of a minimum wage and labour welfare to tackle the problem of organised versus unorganised labour, the formal and informal markets, and the world economic system all come under the purview of political economy. The priorities and limits of social expenditure, that is, whether to spend more on education or on medical aid for the poor and the aged, taxation, money supply, inflation, corruption, structure of the state, regulation, competition and the comparative advantage of trade and commerce, natural resources and human resources are all components of political economy.

As it covers such a wide variety of subjects, political economy is neither a rigid nor a fixed subject of study. It is a continuous process of comprehending the many linkages that compose economic life. Its relative importance shrinks and broadens at different times and in different places. For instance, US society is often described as apolitical, with minor contradictions and a near total approval of capitalism with a Calvinistic spirit. But even in the US, following the depression, there has been a great deal of debate about political economy, which ultimately led to the passage of the New Deal legislations, and a compromise with many essential presumptions of traditional American capitalist values. Political economy, to a very large extent, is an expression of economic belief systems, like the contemporary supporters and critics of globalisation.

In spite of this primacy of value preferences in political economy, some key variables are present in all the different formulations, for example the question and nature of human equality, growth, impact of scientific inventions and discoveries, change in the world system (the rise and fall of fascism and communism), the emergence of post-colonial societies, and the emergence of the newly industrialising countries of East and Southeast Asia and China, which is why the twenty-first century is said to belong to the Asia-Pacific region.

Another key aspect of political economy is the critical dissection of prevailing ideologies and thought processes. Within the larger interlinking of economy and polity, some key characteristics manifest themselves in the following manner:

(a) Political economy as a discipline is both normative and empirical. It combines the speculative perceptions of an ideal economic arrangement with an emphasis on hard empirical facts. This combination began with Smith and continued with contemporary commentators like Friedman. Both the defenders and critics of a political-economic arrangement follow the same pattern. In political economy, facts do not always speak for themselves but are interpreted to carry a particular meaning. For instance, when Marx says that 100 years of capitalism had done more wonders than all the preceding civilisations put together, he is trying to interpret the impact of capitalism in civilisational terms and speculate on the liberating role played by capitalism in the normative sense. However, when he details the intricacies of contemporary economic facts, including surplus value, he is interpreting the facts in a particular manner to build his thesis.

(b) Political economy is policy-oriented, but cannot be termed a branch of policy analysis. Political economy has a practical aspect—recommending policy preferences within the larger ideological preference—which makes it both a macro and micro-based discipline. The classic example of such initiatives can be traced back to the Fabian Society pamphlets, which dealt with particular problems of Great Britain's economic, social, cultural and political issues within a larger framework of Labour Party programmes. Similarly, the Adam Smith Institute is the think-tank for the British Conservative Party. In India, during the initial years of planning, the contrasting framework of policy formulation followed the Fabian collectivistic model with state-directed import substitution, which Chakravarti Rajagopalachari (1878–1972) within liberal economics opposed, terming it the permit-licence-quota-raj. In contrast, the ambit of policy sciences is much more restricted and specific.

(c) Political economy incorporates both structural and behavioural levels of analysis. The basic questions pertaining to social, political, cultural and economic structures constitute the essential framework of political economy. Questions concerning a weak or a strong state, order and disorder, a soft or effective state are important considerations for political economy. But the question of leadership, levels of consensus in society, levels of social discipline and motivation are also emphasised by political economy.

(d) Emphasis is placed on both international and national political economies. Political economy incorporates both as an integral part of study, as one is not comprehensible without the other. Increasingly, political economy is paying more attention to international players like multinational corporations and international financing agencies like the International Monetary Fund (IMF) and the World Bank. Wallerstein speaks of a world capitalistic system within which is a rise and fall of national economies. The emphasis on an integrated study received further impetus after the collapse of the Soviet economic management, which followed a highly secluded economic structure. In contrast, the economies that were integrated with the West, namely the Newly Industrialised Countries (NICs) of South Korea, Taiwan, Hong Kong and Singapore, did very well and now China, with its integration, has achieved spectacular results. However, the question of desirable levels of integration or isolation continues to be hotly debated in political economy.

(e) Political economy has a critical dimension. With marked value preferences, political economy reflects heavily on the critical dimension of enquiry. It does not lead to a Kuhnian consensus and like political theorising, it continues with many alternative paradigms, more in the nature of a zero sum game. The basic reason for this is that much of contemporary political economy is derived from the value orientations of the age of ideologies of the eighteenth and nineteenth centuries, within the larger categories of liberalism and socialism. The same tradition continues today with the incorporation of new issues like sustainable development and environmentalism, making the issues more complicated and sophisticated.

The larger frameworks of political economy can be classified under the following categories: Liberalism; Mercantilism; Communism; Social Democracy; and Developmental state. Two other frameworks for analysing political economy, namely Anarchism and Fascism, have been relegated to history and are rarely referred to in contemporary debates of political economy.

Liberalism

Laski (1936) described Liberalism more as a mood than a doctrine. It took shape in England in the late seventeenth century. Early liberalism, from the late seventeenth to the early eighteenth centuries, was essentially libertarian in outlook. It was based on the idea of plenty and a rough parity of individuals, both in the enjoyment of freedom and ownership of property. Liberalism defends both private property and the market as these encourage competition and innovation, and only the critical areas of defence and education are to be the responsibility of the state. Early Liberalism defended a limited state with little regulation of market and property, and supported capitalism, a system of production based on private ownership and market. The state should provide for social goods only in critical areas such as education.

The essential framework of liberal political economy was provided by Smith in *Wealth of Nations*, in which he portrayed a realistic picture of economic operation in the context of the increasing internationalisation of commerce and industry, and the role of the government in managing the complex interplay of trade, commerce, governmental regulation, economic well-being and growth. For economic development, there is no need for the presence of an all-powerful leviathan; on the contrary, what is needed is a limited government with least interference in an individual's political and economic freedom. He considered an average individual responsible enough to rationally control his own behaviour and interests, and look after his own well-being. He advocated the twin principles of market and the institution of private property, the sanctity of which was first established in Europe through Roman law. He dealt at length with the questions of harnessing individual initiative and entrepreneurship to the furthest possible extent. To achieve the optimum capacity of each individual, he advocated a limited government with the possibility of maximising individual autonomy. He rejected a paternalistic, top-down policymaking process; legislation would be limited to defence, maintenance of law and order, protection of labour and the provision of public goods, leaving the rest to the individual.

Smith placed tremendous faith in the capacity of the individual, and therefore regarded elaborate regulatory mechanisms as stifling individual initiative and enterprise. He supported competitive capitalism and provided numerous examples of innovation that ordinary entrepreneurs make in their daily work. Private ownership and free markets are the essential pre-requisites for the successful operation of an economic order. He remarked, 'little else is requisite to carry a state to the highest degree of opulence from the lowest barbarism, but peace, easy taxes and a tolerable administration of justice all the rest being brought about by natural course of things' (Smith 1980: lxxx). His philosophy of free trade and free market was ultimately to be regulated by the Invisible Hand. However, although he advocated a limited government, he also wanted an effective government that would guarantee laws to protect labour and provide for health and education.

Smith laid down the essential framework of a liberal economic order that remains relevant till date. Along with Locke and Montesquieu, he exerted a seminal influence in all subsequent economic formulations. The US Constitution is the first modern constitution to sanctify Smith's recommendation (following Locke and Montesquieu) of a limited government, with state power restricted by means of checks and balances. Montesquieu pointed to the importance of commerce and the need for social balancing to achieve the desired equilibrium between politics and economics. This tradition of liberal economics continued till Marshall, and the US, Canada, UK, Australia and New Zealand are the best examples of countries that followed the prescription of limited government.

However, within this broad liberal economic framework are many innovations to tackle crises. One such example is the Keynesian revolution after the Depression of 1930. The depression dealt a shattering blow to the capitalist order, placing a question mark over the entire framework of the free market. Keynes recommended state intervention, which led to the New Deal legislations in the US and to the inauguration of the welfare state with the help of the Beveridge report of 1944 in Britain to tide over the crisis the Depression had brought about. Keynesianism accepts that the political problem of humankind has to combine three things: economic efficiency, social justice and individual liberty.[1] By the middle of the 1920s, Keynes realised that Leninism was out to historically destroy capitalism; that fascism had sacrificed democracy to save capitalism; and the option left to him was to save democracy by adapting capitalism through the control of expenditure and demand, rather than ownership and supply by the state. Focusing on aggregate demand defuses class struggle since vigorous demand leads to high profits and full employment with rising wages. The key issue was employment. Since the market by itself fails to provide for a full utilisation of resources, the state ought to step in to manage the economy. If the economy grows too fast, the total amount of people's spending could be reduced through higher taxes, cutting down public spending and making it harder to borrow money, thereby slowing down the boom. In the case of recession, with goods unsold, factories closing down and people losing their jobs, the remedies would be to cut taxes, increase government spending and make the process of acquiring credit easier, as this would increase the demand for goods. This means there would be a need for more factories and more workers to fulfil demands. Through these measures, it would be possible to break out of the cycles of boom and slump and replace them with steady economic growth and permanent full employment. For Keynes, these measures civilise and humanise the market, ensuring welfare and equality of opportunity, as the state would remove the disadvantages imposed by social circumstances After World War II, advanced capitalism was largely governed by Keynesian consensus till it was challenged by the rise of the New Right, spearheaded by Hayek in Britain and Friedman in the US.

In the meantime, Rawls' *A Theory of Justice* (1971) provided a new blueprint for a liberal political and economic order. Accepting the continuous growth model of traditional liberalism, it emphasised the need to elevate the worst-off while accepting inequality as a given. Like traditional liberalism, he accepted the primacy of liberty, but also emphasised equity, efficiency and stability as necessary for a well-ordered society.

The 1970s also saw the rise of neo-liberalism after the coup that overthrew the social democratic president of Chile, Allende. This plank, drawn mainly from the Chicago school led by Friedman, advocated limited governmental regulation, low taxation and limiting social expenditure. Free market and not democracy was advocated. Friedman later defended his assertion by arguing that subsequent events and the restoration of democracy in Chile proved that a free market ultimately ensures freedom. In today's world, Singapore is an anomalous example as it is one of the freest economies, but imposes severe restrictions on individual political and civil rights. If Friedman is correct, then Singapore will become more liberal. So will China, with its fast growing economy and expanding middle class.

Communism

The core idea of communism is collective equality and not individual freedom. It was first established in Russia in 1917, and then extended to Eastern Europe, China, Cuba, Vietnam, and a few other countries after World War II, with stress on full employment, universal state-sponsored education, elimination of a privileged economic class (which is inevitable in capitalism) and people's democracy, with only non-antagonistic contradictions surviving. The communist philosophy rejected in *toto* the twin institutions of free market and private property as providing human liberation and a true basis of an egalitarian democratic order. Private property leads to the domination of a few over the vast property-less multitude, and an increase in this divide would lead to a revolution resulting in the abolition of property, which in reality means state control over property. Similarly, the market would be eliminated as all kinds of private transactions would be banned. This is a total negation of Smith's formulation of the invisible hand of the market and an acceptance of a highly centralised decision-making process, expected to rationalise economic decision-making that would in turn benefit the entire society and do away with the problems of a market economy.

Convinced about a highly centralised decision-making process as the defining characteristic of communism, Lenin distinguished Marxism from Anarchism on the grounds that while the former believes in centralisation, the latter emphasises decentralisation. However, this highly centralised decision-making process could not compete with the decentralised market with regard to efficiency or innovation, reminding us of Popper's succinct observation, 'who plans the planners'. The monolithic state and a command economy led to inefficiency, highly lopsided and wasteful decisions, shortage, rationing of essential food items, stagnation, ecological destruction, low productivity, non-competitiveness, and a declining Gross National Product (GNP) from 4.9 per cent in 1966–70 to 2.2 per cent in 1981–85. There was stagnation in coal and steel production. Agricultural production, too, was below the plan level. Officially, statistics are not available since 1980 with regard to grain production, but it was estimated to be a mere 1.8 per cent in 1981–85. Rationing in important food items was introduced in some Soviet cities in the late 1970s and early 1980s. The death rate, which was 6.9 per 1,000 in 1964, rose to 10.3 in 1980. The life expectancy of men and women declined from 67 to 62 years and from 76 to 73 years, respectively. Soviet Union was the only industrialised country to experience such a decline. There was a steep rise in the infant mortality rate. 'By the early 1980s it was obvious that the Soviet Union was failing to make the transition from a fairly primitive stage of economic development based on exports of primary products into a modern Western-based economic system' (Elliott 1991).

The isolationist economic policies pursued by communist states with the aim of self-sufficiency and independence led to a GNP of less than 25 per cent; their export was merely 14 per cent of the world's share. This resulted in these states being left out of prevailing trends towards internationalisation of the production process. The three important components of modern business organisation—increased efficiency, product quality and consumer choice—did not become a part of socialist culture, and remained the exclusive preserve of capitalism. The inconvertibility of their currencies aggravated their lack of competitiveness. Galbraith pointed to this lack of competitiveness and adaptability in meeting new requirements and challenges: 'Capitalism in its original or pristine form could not have survived. But under pressure it did adapt. Socialism in its original form and for its first tasks did succeed. But it failed to adapt' (cited in Hague, et al. 1992: 417).

This, coupled with the success stories of the East Asian Tigers (see Chapter 16), made the communist model unattractive. The spectacular success of the Asian NICs proved that economic liberalism allowed late modernisers to catch up with the others within a short span of less than two generations. Their hardships and privations seem more bearable when compared with the large-scale social terror unleashed by the former communist regimes (Fukuyama 1992: 41–42). Khrushchev's promise that the USSR would overtake the West remained an empty one. In a comparative perspective, the communist regimes, as opposed to liberal democracy, lacked resilience, adaptability and the capacity to respond to and absorb societal and technological changes, thus becoming in the process a dinosaur. Moreover, with the emergence of a commercial world, military alliances and adventures look both illegitimate and unprofitable. The former Soviet Union attained rough armaments parity with the United States, but lagged behind in terms of economic power. Japan occupied the second position. The former Soviet Union lagged behind in technology, a fact taken note of by Andrei Sakharov (1921–89), who commented that all important innovations and discoveries had originated in the West since World War II. 'Socialism was incapable of moving fully into, let alone generating, the new hi-tech economy, and was therefore destined to fall even further behind ... it failed to achieve the mass production of consumer goods' (Hobsbawm 1990: 21).

The worldwide failure of Marxist–Leninist Communism was also due to a fallacious and erroneous conception of the market. The mistakes can be categorised as anthropological and economic (Roos 1990: 6). The anthropological mistake was to presume, as Marx did, that the 'law of history' dictated a fundamental antagonism between capital and labour. 'The dream of socialism with a human face will always be a dream: it is based on a mistaken view of man' (ibid.: 16). Democratic institutions and culture, extensive social security measures, trade union activities and labour welfare laws have improved the position and working conditions of the proletariat. The economic mistake was compounded by continuing to view capitalism as it had existed in its early phase of development, ignoring the structural changes that took place subsequently. Moreover, the idea of a free market solely governed by the principle of profit, which the Marxists attacked, was a myth. Even Smith, the guru of *laissez faire* and the market, granted to the state three duties: (*a*) defence, (*b*) administration of justice and the protection of every member of society, and (*c*) maintenance of public works and public institutions, which meant universal public education, public health and labour laws. Thus, within the ambit of the last two functions he 'offered an intellectual framework for a generous and compassionate government consistent with a competitive market economy' (Meyerson 1989: 67).

Ernesto 'Che' Guevara (1928–67), an advocate of planning, could comprehend the problems of stagnation within the Soviet economy as early as 1964. He advocated a combination of economic planning with market, or what he called the 'law of value'. This suggested the need to accept complexity if economic regulations were to be effective, and also indicated a willingness to check results against what was happening elsewhere (Blackburn 1991: 216).

> The starting point is to calculate the socially necessary labour required to produce a given article, but what has been overlooked is the fact that socially necessary labour is an economic and historical concept. Therefore, it changes not only on the local (or national) level but in world terms as well. Continued technological advances, a result of competition in the capitalist world, reduces the expenditure of necessary labour and therefore lowers the value of the product. A closed society can ignore such changes for a certain time, but it would always have to come back to these international relations in order to compare product values. If a given society ignores such changes for a long time without developing new and accurate formulas to replace the old ones, it will create internal interrelationships that will shape its own value structure in a way that may be internally consistent but would be in contradiction with the tendencies of more highly developed technology (for example in steel and plastics). This would result in relative reverses of some importance, and, in any case, would produce distortions in the law of value on an international scale and making it impossible to compare economies (Che, cited in Blackburn 1991: 215–16).

Nove contended that the bureaucracy's dominant role within communist societies could be reduced by relying on markets and commodity production, for that would encourage participation and self-management (Nove 1983: 227–28). The Yugoslavian leader Ante Markovic (1924–2011) admitted that contemporary socialism could not solve the problems of either efficiency or political democracy. Economic failure undermined the legitimacy of an already unpopular political system in the former Soviet Union.

Social Democracy

This is an off-shoot of Marxism, and questions some of its basic presuppositions. In England, it was consolidated under the banner of Fabian socialism in 1884 and in Germany, it was spearheaded by the Social Democratic Party (SPD). Ferdinand Lassalle (1825–64) was the first theorist to think in terms of reforming the state and using it for the welfare of the people. The framework of social democracy as a better and more acceptable formulation than Marxism was provided by Eduard Bernstein (1850–1932). Rejecting Marxism as rigid, deterministic and ideological, he points out that many Marxist predictions like increased pauperisation of the poor, the disappearance of the middle class, and the widening gulf between rich and poor had not taken place. In the altered situation, the working class would be better-off if they worked within the institutions of parliamentary democracy.

In the background of the realisation of universal franchise in the late nineteenth century, social democracy combined both liberal and communist values and accepted both private property and market economy. It broke ranks with Marxism with its rejection of violent revolutionary transformation and its insistence on realising democracy and socialism simultaneously. To maintain social equilibrium, the state intervenes to create positive social rights. Individual initiative is balanced within a framework of collective equality. Although public ownership is inevitable in any kind of economic management, state ownership in social democracy is more extensive when compared to liberal democracies. However, it rejects a free market economy as it leads to intolerable inequalities and polarisation of society. To meet this challenge, it emphasises the need to moderate capitalism and guarantee basic rights to every citizen. There is an overriding emphasis on social solidarity as evident from the manifesto of the Party of European Socialists, which states: 'for socialists and social democrats, a modern economy can only be developed in close cooperation with social partners. We know that economies are stronger when societies are just. The poverty of some diminishes the lives of all who live in a divided society.' The state plays a crucial role in ameliorating economic injustice, which means quite a bit of state control in economic affairs. It also means that in many areas of social welfare, like healthcare, education and mass transit, the state has an obligation to its citizens. The monetary situation is strictly controlled by the state, with overriding powers given to the central bank. Although competition is encouraged, the economy is regulated to ensure that domestic jobs and businesses are not affected. State ownership exists in many sectors of the economy, for example large industries, steel, automobile production and banking, and there is governmental regulation of the professional fees charged by doctors and lawyers. The general slogan of social democracy is 'yes' to market economy and a 'no' to market society.

A common element in social democratic systems is the use of 'neocorporatism', a system of policymaking involving the state, labour and businesses. It rejects the combative relationship between labour and business and instead emphasises consensus by creating a limited number of associations that represent a large segment of business and labour. For example, the German Federation of Trade Unions comprises 11 different trade unions and more than eight million workers. The confederation of German Employers' Associations includes nearly every large and medium-sized employer in the country. These associations are recognised by the state as legitimate representatives of their members, and together these associations and the state decide on important economic policy matters such as wages, compensation, taxation and unemployment.

Mercantilism

Mercantilism was the economic system of the major trading countries for three centuries, from the sixteenth to the eighteenth. It believed that national wealth and power are best achieved by increasing exports and accumulating precious metals, especially gold and silver. The focus of mercantilism was on the needs of the state; it was less concerned with individual freedom or collective equality, unlike liberalism, social democracy and communism. National power is paramount. Mercantilist states concentrated on their position within the international system and believed that economic weakness undermined national sovereignty. They considered wealth crucial to political power and believed that wealth should be directed towards national ends. Friedrich List's (1789–1846) *National System of Political Economy* (1841) is considered a classic in mercantilism.[2]

Mercantilism supersedes the medieval feudal order and was first manifested in the Italian city states at the time of Renaissance, like Bologna, Florence, Genoa, Milan and Venice. These were successful centres of trade and generated unprecedented fortune. A good example is the Medici family who were part of the patrician class and not the nobility, and acquired enormous wealth through banking and commerce in the thirteenth century, and subsequently political influence in the fourteenth. However, because of a lack of unity within the Italian nations and intense rivalry between city states, this localised mercantilism was short-lived. A passionate clamouring for Italian unification is reflected in Machiavelli's writings.

Under mercantilism, the political and social elite came from the merchant class. Western Europe—Holland, France and England—also practised mercantilist policies successfully, till the *laissez faire* economic system proved more stable than mercantilist policies. Mercantilism is based on a zero sum theory which leads to both religious and commercial wars, resulting in huge expenditures because of the growing costs of the army and the civil government. The clamour for gold is based on its universal demand as a medium of exchange for any other commodity. It imposes foreign trade, giving it precedence over domestic trade, as well as severe state control over the economy. Corporations and trading companies were established and severe regulations imposed on production with the aim of producing high quality goods at low costs in order to be competitive in the foreign market. The trading nations formalised treaties to secure exclusive trading privileges for their commerce, which subsequently resulted in colonial expansion with exploitation benefiting the mother countries. The most successful mercantilist nation is England; through navigation and wars, it destroyed the commerce of Holland, its chief rival. England also benefited from its skilled industrial population and existence of a large shipping industry. However, mercantilism had other economic problems as well, which restricted its benefit even to the mother country, such as the over-supply of money which resulted in high inflation. Mercantilism declined with the onset of industrialisation and *laissez faire*-ism.

Developmental State

This is a term used by Johnson while referring to the governmental system that Japan pioneered from the mid-1920s, and which was later emulated by other NICs. The term has been used with greater frequency since the 1980s. The emphasis is on rapid industrialisation, with the state assuming responsibility for deciding national growth priorities accompanied by policies pertaining to taxation and subsidies, helped by a powerful economic bureaucracy insulated from democratic/parliamentary and other political interests. An elite core of technically trained members supports the bureaucracy. The state aims to bring about consensus and cooperation between the public sector, private entrepreneurs and other domestic interests. Like social democracy, it advocates total or partial state ownership of specific industries; however, it focuses less on welfare as compared to social democracy. As pointed out by Hobsbawm, the 'industrializing countries today develop in the context of strong labour movements and social world powers, which make the idea of industrializing without any provisions for social security or trade unionism politically almost unthinkable' (1990: 21).

A developmental state is driven by the urgent need to promote economic growth and industrialise in order to 'catch up' either economically or militarily, or both, in order to ward off competition or threat in a global or regional context. While critics have questioned the capacity of the state to set proper priorities and achieve the target, they have failed to provide an alternative. With capitalism being inherently weak and without state intervention, the basic infrastructure for capitalist expansion and productivity becomes impossible to conceive. Successful developmental states are Japan, South Korea and Taiwan.

CONCLUSION

Political economy is a hotly contested subject. The wide and divergent views prove that unanimity is practically impossible. However, in the practical application of the various models the twentieth century witnessed, there was a keen contest and rivalry between three different forms of economic management: liberal capitalism, fascism and communism. Fascism, which arose after World War I and was characterised by brutal political, economic and social experiments, ended with World War II. As Nolte observed, fascism was conditioned by the specificities of the economic conditions created by the Great Depression. The communist movement, with its theoretical framework provided by Marx and Engels, took into account nineteenth-century capitalism in Western Europe. It consolidated itself first in the former Soviet Union after overthrowing the repressive Czarist regime, and then expanded in East and Central Europe—with the exception of Yugoslavia—at the end of World War II with Soviet help. Subsequently, it spread to China, North Korea and Vietnam. However, the collapse of communism and the disintegration of the Soviet Union brought communism to an inglorious end in 1991, 70 years after its establishment in 1917. The unpredicted but inevitable collapse of the Marxist regimes is as significant as the fall of the Roman Empire. The collapse came about as a result of its internal contradictions. Fukuyama (1992) proclaimed the triumph of liberal democracy over its rivals as the end of history, meaning the end of the ideological debate that began with the contrasting views of Hegel and Marx.

Understanding the process of economic change is the major aim of political economy. This process depends on the intention and perception of the players. North pointed out that the process of economic change 'is for the most part a deliberate process shaped by the perceptions of the actors about the consequences of these actions' (2005: 12). In the contemporary post-communist world, there is a larger consensus evolving around the process of economic change. According to North, there are four basic requirements for pursuing a sound economic order: (*i*) a shared belief structure 'about the legitimate ends of government and the rights of citizens; (*ii*) constitutional limitations on governmental powers at decision-making; (*iii*) a clear definition of property and personal rights; and (*iv*) credible commitment of the state to protect these rights against severe curtailment and abuse by public officials' (ibid.: 15).

Within this larger conceptual framework, the alternative models of political economy conditioned by geography, resources and size would likely move towards increased refinement, with schemes for practical solutions, greater elite agreement and consensus. Within the parameters of political economy, grand alternative proposals are unlikely in the contemporary world dominated by technology and quick change. Against the background of the collapse of the highly centralised authoritarian regimes, both of the left and the right, political economy is likely to move towards solving actual problems as the Fabians did—they called it 'Gas and water socialism'—or what Popper termed piecemeal social engineering, in opposition to highly centralised planning.

NOTES

1. The first, efficiency, was a bitter lesson learnt from World War I and the Great Depression. This led to the second lesson, namely social justice, where social liberals learnt that humane concerns as underlined by Leonard Hobhouse (1864–1929) and John Dewey (1859–1952) could not be relinquished. The third, individual liberty, is the most enduring and is the legacy of J. S. Mill. It states that liberty is as important as social security.
2. According to List, the prosperity of a nation depends not upon the wealth it has amassed but upon its ability to develop 'productive forces' that would create wealth in the future. Productive forces are not those that create material products, but scientific discoveries, advances in technology, improvements in transportation, provision of educational facilities, the maintenance of law and order, an efficient public administration and sustaining self-government. List contrasts the economic behaviour of an individual with that of a nation, noting that while an individual's concern lies with his personal interests, the nation is responsible for the needs of the whole. Therefore, according to List, a nation must first develop its own agricultural and manufacturing processes sufficiently before it can fully participate in international free trade. He recognised the existence and power of nationalism, and that a unified and harmonious world could not be achieved till individual nations reached sufficient levels of development to avoid being overwhelmed by the already developed nations. List made Smith the starting point of his analysis; however, the slump in Germany following the collapse of Napoleon's continental system led him to revise his views on fiscal policy. He opposed the cosmopolitan principle in the contemporary economical system and the absolute doctrine of free trade in harmony with that principle, and instead developed the infant industry argument as enunciated by Hamilton. He gave prominence to the national idea and insisted on the special requirements of each nation according to its circumstances, and especially the degree of its development.

5

APPROACHES

Political Culture and Political Socialisation

For our purposes we may regard the political culture as a shorthand expression to denote the set of values within which a political system operates. It is something between the state of public opinion and an individual's personality characteristics.

Kavanagh 1983: 49

The concept of political culture offers itself as an ideal token of and catalyst for behaviouralism since it fulfils the two central aims of the approach: it can be defined so as to be measured quantitatively, and it marks the ultimate expansion of the territory of political science.

Welch 1993: 4

The term 'political culture' first appeared in modern empirical political science in the late 1950s and the 1960s and is chiefly associated with American political scientist, Gabriel Almond.

Bove 2002: 2

The importance of attitudes, values and beliefs and their role in promoting the stability and survival of a regime have been acknowledged by thinkers throughout the ages. Aristotle focused not only on institutions, but also on social structures and their attendant value systems, thereby emphasising civility, consensus and partnership in politics as middle-class values.[1] Rousseau wrote about the importance of morality and custom as the basis of political stability. Burke wrote about custom and tradition, Marx about ideology and Johann Gottfried Herder (1744–1803) about national spirit. Tocqueville categorically stated that democracy does not rest only on constitutional arrangements or laws, but also on the mores of society, which embrace habits and opinions made possible by religion, as religion inculcates moral habits and respect for all human beings. This is necessary in a free society in the absence of political control. Durkheim and Weber, followed by Parsons, emphasised the crucial role of culture in the evolution of a modern, complex industrial society, and since then, many scholars have been attracted to the study of culture to explain the nature and features of democracy. Williams (1958), one of the foremost theorists of culture, admits that the concept is both complicated and elusive. Patrick (1976) details 30 different meanings of culture. Culture deals with habits, behaviour and outlook within a comparative framework between two groups, cultures and nationalities. The behavioural revolution brought to the fore the importance of political culture as it displaced the traditional institutional approach. In the particular context of politics, political culture deals with norms, rules, habits, conditions and beliefs, and their cumulative effect on the political process. Some even argue that these values and attributes lie at the very heart of the political system as they shape political behaviour and participation in the political process. In 1983, Kavanagh described political culture as a set of values within which the political system operates.

GRAND THEORIES OF CULTURE

Durkheim divided societies into two basic categories, traditional and modern, arguing that the two have very different kinds of social cohesion. In a traditional society, interaction is limited to the confines of an agrarian community composed of a group of families and clans in a rural setting. There is a lot of similarity and commonality in these settlements, with a great degree of cohesion emerging on the basis of a common lifestyle and habits, which Durkheim described as 'mechanical' solidarity based on conformity. This rigid pattern of traditional norms and beliefs exists within self-contained, small communities concerned with farming, social control, child-rearing and defence. Division of labour is restricted within the capabilities of the small number of people in the group. It is a 'segmented society'. When Rousseau idealised the direct participatory society, he had such a community in mind. With near conformity of all, the phrase 'forced to be free' appears rational and appropriate. The recent post-colonial one-party Solidarist philosophy in Africa[2] was free in Rousseau's sense of the term, and Macpherson considers it one of the models of democracy. It would fit the description that Durkheim provided (Giddens 1978: 26).

Modern society, according to Durkheim, is entirely different. It is characterised by a high density of population, with acute competition among people for the control and enjoyment of scarce resources. It leads to an increasing social division of labour and quests for new resource generation. Division of labour, in turn, creates increasing interdependence, social differentiation and the establishment of specialised institutions. This society, although complex, is integrated, and Durkheim termed it 'organic solidarity' (cited in Giddens 1978: 21–33). It leads to the emergence of a new pattern of morality with new, flexible norms. Social rules emerge to guide complex and diverse activities. In this altered situation, the individual enjoys a greater freedom of action within a set of general moral guidelines than is possible in the traditional social order. But the potential danger of modern society lies in the possibility of an individual's desire and ambition going beyond the general moral code. Large-scale dissatisfaction leads to a collective code of morals in society. Durkheim attributed the progress of modern society to the evolution of flexible rules of social conduct, which enhances the scope for individual creativity and expression. But he also warned that flexibility can become the source of individual frustration and unhappiness (ibid.: 21–33).

Weber limited his enquiry to answering a vexed question about the rise of capitalism in Western Europe, which he attributed to the distinctive evolution of a cultural process that enabled the establishment of a rational state, allowing modern business organisations to flourish through the accumulation and most efficient use of capital and cost reduction, thereby providing a proper climate for investment. All of this brought about a psychological transformation that inculcated the competitive spirit of capitalism as a rational tool to meet consumer demands. Together, these factors led to a transformation from a leisurely, pre-capitalist culture to contemporary hardworking modern capitalism.

Weber demarcated the ancient from the modern through what he called the 'spirit of capitalism'. Making money has been a factor in all societies at all times. The key difference is that in modern capitalism, increased profit is not wasted. With hard work, capital is acquired, which is then carefully re-invested. This was the pattern in West Europe but not elsewhere, and this fundamental departure made West European evolution neither easy nor natural, but a consequence of the emergence of Protestant ethics. A particular religious practice—Calvinism—contributed to the economic evolution of West Europe. Success is acclaimed, provided it is based on diligence, discipline, moderation and work ethics. Historical evidence of the rise of this kind of rationality can be found in the modern social birth of the individual. This rational individual is not tied to old customs and traditional values or to the rigid conformism of the past, but is an agent free to experiment.[3]

Durkheim and Weber are considered the grand theorists of the development of modern culture, emphasising functional differentiation, rationalisation, business motivation, individual ambition, and a spirit of adventure and glory. This is the process underlying the rise of Western Europe, which imbibed the spirit of the Renaissance leading to the period of the Enlightenment, which inaugurated the modern age.

IMPACT OF THE GRAND THEORIES OF CULTURE

Image 5.1: Max Weber (1864–1920)

Source: https://commons.wikimedia.org/wiki/File:Max_Weber_1894.jpg.

In the 1950s and 1960s, there was, in the grand tradition of Durkheim and Weber, considerable concern and debate about the basic features of development. As a consequence of this concern, attempts were made to build holistic models to measure the stages of development in a society. Against the background of the breakdown of colonial empires, the socioeconomic and cultural conditions necessary for development received special attention from well-known social scientists. Parsons, like Durkheim before him, identified the basic differences between a traditional and a modern society.

Parsons delineated three crucial features of traditional society: (*i*) a pronounced dominance of traditionalism where people by and large were oriented towards the past. In such a situation, people lack the cultural ability to adjust to new circumstances and situations; (*ii*) in traditional society, positions were ascribed and not achieved. Social positions changed only with change in the family status, and status is neither earned nor achieved, but is conferred by kin groups; (*iii*) the approach to the world is emotional, superstitious and fatalistic.

In contrast, a modern society has different value systems. (*i*) People may have traditions, but also have the ability to transcend them without becoming the slaves of tradition. Since people do not suffer from traditionalism, they continue to make cultural progress. (*ii*) Kinship and family ties become loose, leading to geographical and social mobility. Position in the economy, politics and society is not dependent wholly on family or kin pedigree. (*iii*) The attitude is not of fatalism but one of innovativeness, forward-looking with the courage to face obstacles. This is reflected in an entrepreneurial spirit, business challenges and a rational, scientific and pragmatic approach to the world. In the tradition of classical sociology, for Parsons, the choice of actions and behavioural orientations are different in these two types of societies. In traditional society, a sense of achievement is virtually absent. There is a predominance of the role of ideas and psychological factors in modern society.

In 1960, Rostow placed all societies within a broad economic scale of five categories: (*i*) traditional society, (*ii*) pre-conditions for a take-off, (*iii*) the take-off stage, (*iv*) drive to maturity, and (*v*) the age of mass consumption. The general framework of Rostow's analysis emerged from the study of the British industrial revolution and its subsequent stages. For him, the take-off was the great watershed in the evolution of modern society, with the removal of obstacles to economic growth through an adequate rate of capital investment, which sustains growth continuously.

NOTION OF CIVIC CULTURE

The emphasis on political culture arose out of dissatisfaction with the study, which limited itself to the constitutional and institutional feature of a few select Western societies. With the rise of post-colonial states, structural-functional theorists like Almond and Verba concentrated on the study of political culture. In 1983, Kavanagh described political culture as a set of values within which the political system operates. Almond and Verba emphasised the pattern of orientations to political objects among the members of a nation. This is reflected in parliament, political parties and history, and not merely in the belief structure but also in behaviour. The idea itself is not new, but its extensive use in comprehending behaviour in democracies in the context of a variety of regimes, value systems and stability stems from the impact of the Behavioural revolution and movement in the 1950s and 1960s.

> This work was stimulated in part by a desire to explain the collapse of representative government in interwar Italy, Germany and elsewhere, and the failure of democracy in many newly independent developing states after 1945. Although interest in political culture faded in the 1970s and 1980s, the debate revitalized in the 1990s as a result of efforts in eastern Europe to construct democracy out of the ashes of communism, and growing anxiety in mature democracies such as USA, about the apparent decline of social capital and civic engagement (Heywood 1997: 186).

The high-water mark of this new dispensation was reflected in the notion of civic culture formulated in 1963 by Almond and Verba, which emerged after a comparative study of five nations—US, UK, Italy, Germany (West) and Mexico.

Almond coined the term 'political culture'[4] in 1956. Almond (1956) acknowledged that his conception of political culture was inspired from Weber and Parsons' traditions of social theory. The key concepts are attitudes and orientations, pattern, and political objects. Almond and Verba (1963: 15) defined political culture as the 'pattern of orientations to political objects among the members of the nation'. They pointed out that every political system is entrenched in specific form of political action, which indicates whether the system is consensual or polarised. Political objects refer to a large number of questions regarding public policy, including power, well-being, respect and enlightenment, and their distribution. It also includes institutions such as parliaments and political parties. One key area of concern is whether political attitudes and orientations are distributed among the entire population, or among a particular section of citizens. It also describes political sub-cultures, which means that certain attitudes and attributes develop a distinct political culture. One key function of political culture is to discover the level of agreement or disagreement on political issues on the part of a group or country, and to measure it. The best possible methods are public opinion polls, attitude surveys and cross-national comparisons. For Almond and Verba, the key question concerns the attitude of people regarding the distribution of political power between the rulers and the ruled. It is not only what one believes, but also how one behaves politically. The application of this paradigm leads to the formulation of the notion of civic culture.

In Almond and Verba's comparative analysis of the political values of the five countries, Italy and Mexico rank below the others. Of the two, Mexico is behind Italy. There are striking differences between the political cultures of Italy and Mexico. Mexicans have less pride in their government than the Americans and the British, but are more proud than the Germans and Italians. Mexicans do not recognise the role of the government in their lives; however, the overwhelming majority takes an interest in politics. The citizen competence is also high. Mexico also exhibits a politics of aspiration, which means that people have expectations for the future from their government, but nothing for the present. The legitimacy of the systems rests on hopes and aspirations, described as 'the promise of the Revolution'.

In contrast, Italians have an alienated political culture. They distrust one another and are generally preoccupied with self-protection, are doubtful of governmental help in times of need, and believe that the government is managed by the few in the interests of the few. In West Germany, people are politically detached but competent. People are well aware of politics and voter turnout during elections is high. The primary preoccupation is with economics and not with politics. They believe they are not competent enough to influence political events, and the majority think they should not even try. As subjects, the people are competent, consuming the goods and services provided by the government. A very large percentage has trust in the government, the administrators and the police, and expects fair treatment.

Great Britain and the USA fall under the category of civic culture, that is, their citizens value popular participation in political affairs and believe that political power is evenly distributed. They are sufficiently content with the political system, but are not motivated enough to participate in politics very actively. Great Britain is more passive than the USA and is a case of 'deferential civic culture', while the USA exemplifies a 'participant civic culture'. But these differences are not fundamental. Both are strongly committed to democracy. In both societies respect for and trust in the government is high, and there is a wide acceptance of one's duty to participate in the political process, along with the belief that such participation could make a difference. A balanced and limited participation is one in which there is no constant intervention or possibility of overload. The normal channels function efficiently and there is no threat of destabilisation. Civic culture provides a solid underpinning for stable democracy, which means the future of democracy is more certain in Great Britain and the USA than in West Germany and Italy. Mexico was not a democracy at the time of the survey.

Almond and Verba attempted to arrive at some definite conclusions by comparing data based on a public opinion survey with approximately 1,000 respondents in each country. Three sets of questions were posed to the respondents: (*i*) cognitive questions, which tested the factual knowledge and belief structures of respondents towards their respective political systems; (*ii*) affective questions that tested feelings about political objects; and (*iii*) evaluative questions, which tested political opinions and judgements within the framework of a wider political value system. They make both influential and provocative statements about political culture and formulate three ideal types of individual, as well as collective or national political cultures: parochial, subject and participant. Parochial culture leads to a general ignorance about political subjects and a consequent lack of involvement in political activity. In the subject category, citizens have widespread knowledge about the political process, but are disinclined to participate in political activity because of a feeling of powerlessness. Participant political culture combines knowledge of politics with willingness to participate in the political process. There is a confidence in the average citizen that s/he is capable of influencing and/or changing policies through political activity, and that her/his reasoned and active involvement will make a distinct difference. Almond and Verba are interested in both individual properties and the political system as a whole, and are confident that it is possible to measure aggregate individual orientations. They are also confident of linking a micro study with a macro one, which would enable them to arrive at certain definite, testable conclusions.

The three categories with an apex ideal would provide a framework of analysis within the disordered reality of actual political processes with the aim of aiding and motivating future investigations, and systematising and providing order to our thought process. Almond and Verba accept that the majority of political culture manifestations in different set-ups is mixed; yet they assert that on the basis of painstaking investigation, it is possible to provide a framework to understand the cultural underpinning for a stable democratic polity. For instance, a parochial political culture is a reflection of a traditional society and not a mature democracy, which is based on a very different value system. Similarly, subject political culture is unsuitable for any democratic consolidation because, while citizens possess the requisite political knowledge, they can in no sense be effective. But participant political culture also has its disadvantages as it may lead to an overload. Too many citizens trying to effect change through mass participation might become a serious source of instability, as this could undermine the very basis of the normative ideal of democratic stability.

The best possible system of political structure is a mixed one of both subject and participatory culture. This is the model of civic culture, where a high level of knowledge about political processes exists, empowering one to become a political activist while also realising the legitimacy and necessity of political elites to take decisions on their behalf. This balance is achieved through elite sensitivity to the preferences of the population. Echoing the sentiments of Aristotle and Cicero, the emphasis is on accommodation, restraint and the capacity of the political process to absorb new demands and filter them into policy.

In 1980, Almond and Verba updated their study of civic culture, taking into account the political fallout from Vietnam and student activism in the 1960s, the economic recession of the 1970s, and the growth of non-conventional forms of political participation in the 1980s. They acknowledged the impact these events have had on Western political cultures. In both Britain and the USA, trust in the government declined. Civic culture shifted towards a more pragmatic and instrumental perception of politics; however, this did not signify a change in political culture. The discontent was more towards governing parties than the entire political process.

Recent surveys point out that the pattern identified by Almond and Verba is still valid. In a study of European countries, Inglehart (1977, 1990) noted that the French, the Italians and the Greeks ranked low on measures of political satisfaction, trust in others, life satisfaction and happiness. These countries are characterised by large anti-system parties. Inglehart observed that more stable democracies have a reservoir of support which can sustain them through bad times.

CRITICISMS OF CIVIC CULTURE

The civic culture theory that provides a basis for democratic stability has met with a number of criticisms. It has been accused of an Anglo-Saxon bias because of its assertion that Germany, Italy and Mexico lack the necessary cultural basis for democracy. Lijphart (1968, 1989) demonstrates that democratic stability can be achieved in even non-consensual societies with elite accommodation and a properly conceived political structure. Through examples from both Western and non-Western democracies, he asserts that deft management can overcome divisiveness and reduce antagonistic contradictions to non-antagonistic ones. He contends that the political elite can create consensual behaviour by evolving appropriate institutional support, which can ensure both effective government and democratic stability even in plural and divided societies based on religion, ideology, language, region, culture and race. A proper mechanism of power sharing (see Chapter 10) rather than culture is the key to achieving democratic stability. The civic culture formulation is also criticised on the grounds that culture is not static but dynamic, and that there is a process of evolution within democratic politics of accommodation. It is generally agreed that if the democratic practice of reasonableness, accommodation and compromise is played for a long time, a consensual basis is created, which Almond and Verba ignore. Another important criticism is that the theory rests on a very small survey restricted by a short time period, which is inadequate as a basis for a long-term conceptualisation. Marxists criticise the theory for ignoring the key determinants of politics, namely the economic basis and the domination of classes. This criticism follows two traditional lines: (*a*) false consciousness, and (*b*) it is in line with modern structuralism initiated by Gramsci and Althusser (see Chapter 6), which states that ideas are more an expression of material circumstances than culture. Furthermore, Almond and Verba view civic culture as a consequence rather than a cause of stable democracy, and leave unanswered the question of what makes a stable democracy (Hague, et al. 1992: 138). Very little importance is given to sub-political cultures; there are always groups in societies whose political attitudes are at sharp variance with the national cultures.

Kavanagh (1972) departs from Almond and Verba in his emphasis of sub-culture. His theory stresses the importance of: (*a*) elite versus mass culture; (*b*) cultural divisions within elites; (*c*) generational sub-culture; (*d*) social structure; and (*e*) attitudinal differences. He also mentions Lijphart's (1968, 1979, 1984) theory of cultural consensus between divergent groups and the division between groups into coalescent and adversarial, considering it the basic key for understanding democratic politics. He also emphasises the generational dynamism of political culture. Articulating the necessity of accepting generational change, he points out the distinctive value premises of a particular generation, which leads to a change in agenda and its adaptation in a democratic framework by political institutions and political parties. Here, Kavanagh's emphasis echoes the sentiments of Jefferson—that to absorb new ideas and the spirit of the fast-changing modern times, the constitutional validity of a particular type should be restricted to 20 years. Kavanagh cites the example of 1970s Europe, when it was changing from materialism to post-materialism, from a pursuit of economic and physical security to a quest for identity, self-expression and identification with a larger cause without any consideration for personal advancement. Participation and articulation became more important than basic needs. Such a shift in perception led to a sea change in politics; from a concern with military security and economic welfare, emphasis shifted to ecology, community and popular participation. During such significant generational change, the older generation is materialist and the young, post-materialist. In the background of the two World Wars and the Depression, the older generation was more cautious and less critical; but the young, growing up in the relative prosperity and security of West Europe under a Keynesian consensus, became bolder with a larger societal concern.

Lipset (1973, 1979) concentrates on the cleavages that become apparent during the national and industrial revolutions. In a situation of turmoil and quick change, the centralised elite gains control over a territory and endeavours to standardise norms and education, and create a common legal framework. Such acts lead to a series of conflicts when peripheral communities resist the centralising tendencies of the state elite. The process of industrialisation comes into conflict with pre-industrial forms of production. Yet another arena of conflict appears between the landowning rural elite and the new urban bourgeoisie, and between the urban bourgeoisie and the working class. All the different categories vigorously pursue their distinct interests, identities and value systems. Failure to resolve these conflicts during the period of democratisation finds institutional expression with the emergence of new political parties. Lipset points out that the boundary between political identity, attitudes, dispositions and belief on the one hand, and the political process on the other cannot be easily drawn.

A. D. Smith (1971, 1991) hypothesised that every individual in the modern world has multiple identities. An individual's identity can be broken down into gender, social class, ethnicity, religion, territorial location and family. All these identities co-exist, preventing the attribution of an individual to a single political identity. Smith points out that universal, mass political identities like gender are bound to be less cohesive as geographic separation, class, ethnicity and religion lead to fragmentation rather than to building a cohesive identity.

Hobsbawm (1968) asserts that tradition can be invented by the repetitive assertion of values and norms and cites the example of Scottish nationalism to explain his point. Giddens (1991) emphasises the emergence of identity politics in modern times. The forces of globalisation have created a great deal of uncertainty, which has made people more self-reflective. This ensures the construction of plausible narratives that seek to discover what we are and what we should be.

SUBJECT-PARTICIPATORY CULTURE AND THE COMMUNIST VARIANT OF POLITICAL CULTURE

The erstwhile communist countries functioned within the framework of a dominant political culture, which was subject-participatory. The latter referred to the prevailing beliefs and opinions that define and limit political life in the communist state within a model set of values. Soviet leadership tried to integrate three long-term goals within the framework of subject participatory political culture: (*i*) continued party leadership for industrialisation; (*ii*) rise in the standard of living after a careful scrutiny of available alternatives; and (*iii*) to convince the rationality of communist politics to people with a centralised political leadership which facilitates long-term planned growth through coordinated decision-making, effective implementation and execution. The rationale behind the dominance of a small group of decision-makers states that centralised politics is better than a pluralist one.

Analysing the nature of political culture in the former Soviet Union, Tucker (1987) pointed to a deep-rooted crisis of belief that existed within Soviet society. There was no belief in the myth of communism. The majority felt that no useful purpose would be served in even attempting to realise communism. He estimated that not more than 1 or 2 per cent of Communist Party members believed in the policies and programmes of the Party. There was universal indifference to official pronouncements and the officially controlled press. Alcoholism was widespread, coupled with a strong desire to emigrate. It came as no surprise when—within months after the publication of Tucker's work—communism collapsed in Europe and the Soviet Union disintegrated.

Solzhenitsyn (1973) pointed out that the Gulag, the concentration camp system, originated during Lenin's time, with the terror and cruelty increasing during Stalin's time. Many people who suffered under Stalin's regime were angry for they knew that Stalin's victims were innocent. This anger was compounded by the fact that the regime did not accept responsibility for the heinous crimes perpetrated against its own citizens. There was a complete lack of political democracy, a suspension of liberties and an abrogation of civil society.

From the moment the Bolsheviks seized power in 1917, the Soviet state systematically attacked all potential competing sources of authority in Russian society, including the opposition political parties, the press, trade unions, private enterprises, and the Church. While some institutions continued to exist and retain their names till the end of the 1930s, they were all ghostly shadows of their former selves, organised and completely controlled by the regimes. What was left was a society whose members were reduced to 'atoms', unconnected to any 'mediating institutions' short of an all-powerful government. The human relations that make up a society's fabric—the family, religion, historical memory, language—became targets, as society was systematically and methodically atomised, and the individual's close relationships supplanted by others chosen for her/him and approved by the state. The ultimate goal of totalitarianism was not simply to deprive the new Soviet man of his freedom, but to make him actively fear freedom in favour of security, and to affirm the goodness of his chains even in the absence of coercion (Fukuyama 1992: 24).

The presence of a self-serving, corrupt and privileged elite, which Djilas characterised as the 'new class' or the *nomenklatura,* did more to alienate the masses from a system that prided itself on being equal and just. Morally, the communist systems did not respect the self-worth and self-esteem of the ordinary citizen. Havel condemned communist societies for undermining and humiliating the ordinary person's moral character and dignity, and their belief in their own capacity to act as moral agents. It is to Rabindranath Tagore's (1861–1941) credit that he could, as early as 1930, see Bolshevism as transitory and as a medical treatment for a sick society. He commented, 'Indeed the day on which the doctor's regime comes to an end must be hailed as a red letter day for the patient' (Tagore 1960: 111). The collapse of Communism in the former Soviet Union and its Eastern Europe satellites has led to the realisation that the choice today is not between shades of capitalism and that of socialism, but between constitutionalism, rule of law, independence of judiciary and democracy on the one hand, and authoritarianism on the other. The experience of the past four decades demonstrates that democracy is as much a necessity for economics as it is for politics. This is true of both developed and developing countries. The reasons for this shift lie mainly in the track record of revolutionary regimes, with regard to both economic growth and the protection of basic human rights. In both spheres, their performance was dismal. The excesses committed during the cultural revolution in China, the pathetic economic situation of Cuba, the horrors in Kampuchea and the famine in Ethiopia have made it clear that such regimes were unable to deal with the basic problems and requirements of their people.

Among the many questions that preoccupied Gramsci was: Why has there not been a successful communist revolutionary overthrow of a regime in an advanced Western capitalist country (Rosamond, cited in Axford, et al. 1997: 65)? According to Gramsci, the answer lies in the ability of advanced capitalist regimes to rule by consent through intellectual and moral leadership rather than through coercion, and military and political repression. Hegemony is a key and unifying concept in *Prison Notebooks,* and in his entire theoretical edifice. The basic idea is that people are not ruled by force alone, but by ideas. Hegemonic crises arise when ruling is done through force, rather than being a part of the ideological apparatus of civil society. Differentiating between political society and civil society, Gramsci points out that civil society consists of private institutions like schools, churches, clubs, journals and parties, which are instrumental in crystallising social and political consciousness, while political society consists of public institutions like the government, courts, police and the army, which form the instruments of direct domination. It is in civil society that intellectuals play an important role by creating hegemony. If hegemony is successfully created, the ruling class can rule by controlling the apparatus of civil society. If it fails, then rule occurs through coercion.

Among the advanced countries, Northern Ireland occupies an anomalous position. It is characterised as sub-cultural hostility. Both in terms of religious and social divisions, the cleavage between Protestants and Catholics are rooted deep in history. Edmund Burke attempted to deal with it and towards the end of the nineteenth century, Gladstone's liberal party disintegrated on the Irish question. In a deeply divided society, there is no consensual basis for power sharing amongst the elite. Instead of promoting a framework of coherence and a common platform, it adds to inter-communal hostility and distrust. Lijphart (1968, 1989) conceded that his consociational model is not operative in Ireland because of the lack of accommodative politics. He also found that an absence of inter-elite accommodation can be a serious impediment to peace. However, the process of European integration and the idea of a larger federal Europe have enhanced the possibility of Northern Ireland joining the mainstream of Western European consensual politics.

A **consensual democratic culture** exists among the five states of Denmark, Finland, Iceland, Norway and Sweden, located in the northwestern corner of Europe. They are smaller democracies with a strong regional identity, and are collectively called the Nordic or Scandinavian countries. In contrast to the present scenario of minimal conflict, the region had earlier been sharply polarised between the two metropolitan powers of Denmark and Sweden. But a continued historic interrelationship, cultural affinities and diffusion have resulted in the emergence of a strong, unifying regional consciousness, paving the way for a consensual region with each maintaining its national identity, but within an enduring framework of regional cooperation that extends to the micro level. However, in the context of crucial security and defence, this region, till recently, was in sharp contrast to the Benelux countries of Belgium, The Netherlands and Luxembourg; the countries were grouped together first in 1948 as a customs union, which was then replaced by the Benelux Economic Union in 1960. Norway, located on the Atlantic Ocean, had a powerful mercantile marine, while Finland, more inland, had to be careful about Soviet security considerations during the Cold War. Demark had close economic ties with Britain, Germany and Switzerland, and followed a policy of distance from alliances during peace and neutrality in times of war.

In the evolution of constitutional democracies, too, each state followed its own particular pattern. Denmark, Norway and Sweden are constitutional monarchies, while Iceland and Finland are distinctive republics. However, a larger unity has been achieved amongst the neighbouring states through a free flow of ideas, political exchanges and inter-governmental elite accommodation, leading to the evolution of a federal spirit that acknowledges that they have more in common amongst themselves than with nations outside the circle. It is generally accepted that for a successful liberal democratic order, there has to be agreement on some fundamental issues. Some liberal democracies, though, are more consensual than others, and this is reflected in three broad dimensions: (*i*) the general framework of rules and regulations for resolving political conflict; (*ii*) the nature of the conflict that develops within the framework; and (*iii*) the mechanism by which a resolution of these conflicts is attempted. De-politicisation signifies greater consensual politics, while increased dissension indicates a movement towards destabilisation.

However, despite the marked preference for unity, there has been no attempt to create a regional parliament or a federal state of Scandinavia. This is not essential because each Nordic country takes the others into account while making decisions. This example vindicates de Tocqueville's understanding that people's attitudes are more important than formal institutions in making democracy a success. One very important unifying force in the region, in the background of one of the highest standards of living in the world, has been the search for moral authority and not instruments of domination or control. This is reflected in their high level of commitment to Third World development programmes during the Cold War, initiatives for détente, support for United Nations activities, and individual country initiatives, for example the Norwegian scheme to break the deadlock between the Sri Lankan government and the rebel Liberation Tigers of Tamil Ealam (LTTE). There is overriding concern with enhancing global security, stabilising the international system and ending terrorism. A key to regional consensus is that within the context of different security demands, perceptions and commitments, individual national action is always in harmony with collective regional interests called the 'Nordic balance'. The recognition of the different security demands of these smaller nations led to the development of 'high politics' during the Cold War years. The foreign and defence policy of each nation was excluded from the agenda of the Nordic Council founded in 1952; yet, within the Nordic balance, a successful consensual foreign and defence policy evolved.

Lucian W. Pye and Sidney Verba (1965) described an ideal type of modern life, dominated by mass media, institutions, press, radio, television, popular arts and mobility. He incorporated the Weberian scheme of rational bureaucracy with Almond's civic culture transcending the nation-state. Communication breaks down barriers between nations and makes development possible on a world scale. Pye talked about three broad stages: the traditional, transitional and modern stage of communication. Pye regarded Asian political development as a product of cultural attitudes towards power and authority. He contrasted Confucian East Asia with the Southeast Asian cultures and South Asian traditions, and explored national differences within these larger civilisations. In Asia, societies are group-oriented and respectful of authority, and its leaders are concerned with dignity and collective pride.

Asian Values Debate

In the context of the East Asian countries, a common inheritance based on Confucianism is often asserted. In this distinctive theory of Eastern-ness (in contrast to theories of Westernisation), it is often stated that the phenomenal economic success of the region can be attributed to Confucianism. The points emphasised are the crucial role of the family as provider of social security, which negates the need for an expensive paternalistic welfare state. The Confucian culture helps to build a cohesive moral standard, which effectively binds the individual to the community network. The expanded security provided by this cultural heritage leads to excellence and economic development. Confucianism is perceived as the most profound challenge to the ideological hegemony of the West. It has been argued that Confucianism, with its high premium on obedience and hierarchy, helps to promote authoritarian rule. The ruling elite acts in public interest, but is not controlled by the people.

The former prime minister of Malaysia, Mahathir Mohammed, summarised these distinctive Asian values: 'when citizens understand that their right to choose also involves limits and responsibilities, democracy does not deteriorate into an excess of freedom.... These are the danger of democracy gone wrong, and in our view it is precisely the sad direction in which the West is heading.' However, several commentators have criticised this authoritarian interpretation of Asian values. East Asia, like any other region in the world, is diverse, and it is futile to place the entire region within a rigid framework of one set of values. Differences and not unity characterise this region. Disputing this authoritarian interpretation of cultural heritage is Kim Dae Jung, former South Korean President: 'culture is not necessarily our destiny, democracy is'. The increasing consolidation of democracy in South Korea and Taiwan vindicates this later assertion that East Asia is as important a component of the universal march towards democracy as any other. Amartya Sen (2003) rejected the entire idea of Asian values and Confucianism. Growth takes place when there is a 'friendlier economic climate rather than a harsher political system'. He also found a wide variety in Confucian teachings, which challenges two sacred edifices of Asian values, loyalty to family and obedience to the state. Sen demonstrated that the contradictory loyalties can be in severe conflict with one another. He also pointed out the inevitability of wide diversities within culture. The terms 'Asian values', 'Western civilisation' or African Culture' are 'unfounded readings of history and civilization, are intellectually shallow, they also add to the divisiveness of the world in which we live'. Sen was categorical that authoritarian readings of Asian values would not survive a close scrutiny. They add little to our comprehension and add 'to the confusion about the normative basis of freedom and democracy'.

Another serious failing of the Asian values theory is that if it really builds such a solid social harmony which is the need of Singapore's soft authoritarianism, then it also promotes a fear psychosis where none can talk freely in Singapore. Press is muzzled and is dull and boring, in comparison to South Korea's vibrant press. Opposition Party politicians have been hounded through a series of legal actions.

POST-MATERIALISM

From the early 1950s to the early 1970s, the unprecedented prosperity in the Western world, which British Prime Minister Harold Macmillan summed up in the memorable phrase 'you have never had it so good', coupled with a period of international peace led to a 'silent revolution' in the political cultures of the Western world (Inglehart 1977, 1990). A new generation of 'post-materialists' emerged—the young and well-educated, brought up in prosperity, took to concerns that were post-materialistic, like ecology, nuclear disarmament, human rights and gender justice. They became advocates of a new politics, rather than continue with the old one. Post-materialism first made inroads into the wealthiest democracies, such as Denmark, The Netherlands and West Germany. With the exception of Norway, the affluent Scandinavian countries have been receptive to post-materialist ideas (Knutsen 1990). The United States also witnessed its first wave of post-materialism. In relatively poorer democracies with lower levels of education—Greece, Ireland, Spain and Portugal—post-materialism is less common (Inglehart 1990). It ought to be noted that in the richest countries, post-materialism is confined to a small minority; however, that small group is significant, and active and influential in opinion-making. The recession of the 1970s and early 1980s following a steep hike in oil prices saw a decrease in the spread of post-materialism. The youth in the Nordic countries became more materialistic than the previous generation. Some writers dismissed post-materialism as nothing more than a fragile flower of sunshine politics (Hague, et al. 1992: 141). This criticism seemed short-lived; as the world economy recovered by the end of the 1980s, so did post-materialism. However, Hague, et al. (ibid.) are of the view that an increase in educational standards—and not income, as projected by Inglehart—is the single best predictor of post-materialism. Post-materialism is also the least popular among the oldest and least educated; with greater education, the spread of post-materialism will be wider, provided the young do not lose their post-material commitment (ibid.: 142).

Huntington (1996) put forward his thesis of the clash of civilisations, which underlined the enormous cultural differences in the world, both in terms of geography and religion, and perceived that such differences would be the major basis of global conflict in the post-communist era. The modern revolution in information and communication technology and the increasing mobility of people have also highlighted hitherto invisible difference between different cultures. However, the opposite is also true: such innovations and interactions also reveal similarities between people everywhere, irrespective of differences in ethnicity, region, religion or language, thereby demonstrating that the human race has enough common bonds and unity within diversity. The 'political' is a dynamic and not a static concept. Like culture itself, it changes over time. Many factors, including technology, mould this change, as also the relative success or failure of a particular ideology or system. In the post-communist world, with the twin forces of economic globalisation and technological innovation, there are enough indications that an exchange of views, values and habits, as well as the Internet, will lead to a fusion of culture with increasing collective concerns such as the environment, individualism, human rights and tolerance. It has long been established that human civilisation is a cooperative enterprise in which no single group can be excluded or elevated. Sakharov has stressed the need for one single universal criterion for judging right from wrong; similarly, political culture in this democratic age highlights the common shared heritage of humankind, rather than the differences.

The idea of 'national culture' is questioned by many; some believe there is no national culture. While culture is important, it is equally important to understand that many political cultures coexist within any given political system. The term 'sub-culture' is used for societal groups with a particular identity (see Chapter 18). Kavanagh (1972) identifies four distinct bases on which sub-cultures develop: (*i*) elite versus mass culture; (*ii*) cultural divisions within elites; (*iii*) generational sub-cultures; and (*iv*) social structure.

POLITICAL SOCIALISATION

Aristotle commented that man is by nature a political animal. But we still have to understand the process by which one formulates political ideas, becomes a liberal or a socialist, a Marxist, a conservative, or an anarchist. The process that determines the crystallisation of political ideas, party loyalties, voting behaviour, etc., is the subject of political socialisation. It is believed that childhood plays an important role in formulating the belief structures of most people throughout their lives.

Important categories of political socialisation are broadly divided into personal or general factors. Personal factors include family, social and economic categories, education and local environment. Among general factors are the general political environment in which one grows, the role of mass media, domestic politics—manifested as adversarial or consensual—the role of the state, and important world events.

Family influence plays an important role and is the core support base of political parties. This is consolidated in childhood itself. We are familiar with life-long communists or life-long Congress or BJP supporters in political life. Although children view politics more as amusement, the fact remains that elders in the family wield considerable influence on children throughout their lives. The post-independence generation in India provided firm support in the formative years, nurtured by the magic of Gandhi and Nehru. Even after their deaths, their memories lingered for a long time, with many who were in their mid-20s at the time of India's independence continuing to vote for them throughout their lives. Political discussions in the presence of children also leave a lasting imprint. For decades, communists in Bengal could not understand why the Bihari jute mill workers voted for the Congress. They ultimately realised that it was not local politics that determines voting; rather, such voting is influenced by the politics in the home towns and villages of the migrants.

Political socialisation is also largely determined by the socio-economic condition of a person. In the US and Great Britain, the rich tend to vote for the Republicans and the Conservatives, respectively, while the less well-off form the support base of the Democratic party in the US and the Labour party in Britain. In Western European democracies, there is a gender divide, with men supporting the Social Democratic Parties and women overwhelmingly supporting the Christian Democrats. In India, although different combinations vote differently in states, a general national pattern is discernible: the upper castes vote for the BJP while the lower castes and minorities veer towards the Congress. In Tamil Nadu, it is interesting to note that the men overwhelmingly vote for the DMK while the women for the AIADMK.

Influence of Schooling

The values taught—freedom, equality and liberty, liberal democracy—inculcate their own opinions. Participation in class elections and student bodies also helps in formulating opinion. At the college level, political beliefs are sharpened through interactions within a larger informed community. Religious groups also help in consolidating political views. As early as the 1930s, Merriam acknowledged the power of films and radio to educate and influence political opinion formation. In recent years, this influence has been enhanced manifold by the Internet revolution, especially given that in today's democracies, there is no personal access to either government or politicians and all major decisions are taken secretly. There has also been a dramatic decline in family ties, teachers and friends (by more than 60 per cent), with television and social media now occupying that space. This leads to a process of individualised political socialisation in the form of exchanges on Facebook and the like. The links that the media has established between leaders, institutions and citizens are now direct and instant. Almond and Bingham Powell (1966) detail the functions of the process of political socialisation: (*a*) shaping and transmitting a nation's political culture; (*b*) maintaining a society's political culture from one generation to another; (*c*) this process has the capacity to transform the population—or a part of it—towards viewing and experiencing politics in different dimensions; (*d*) rapid changes or extraordinary events have the capacity to generate political culture even where none existed (through cultural diffusion).

Political Socialisation and Indoctrination

Normally, it is assumed that political socialisation will lead to the assertion of what is perceived as the correct dominant political culture in a given society. The best negative examples of this view are George Orwell's *Nineteen Eighty-Four* (1949) and *Animal Farm* (1945). The process is detrimental to reason, individual thinking and free speech; it cultivates statist propaganda and disinformation, resulting in conformity and subservience. Peer pressure diminishes self-esteem and individualism. I. F. Stone ran the *IF Stone Weekly* with the conviction that the government is supposed to lie, and the task is to find out the lies: 'Every government is run by liars and nothing they say should be believed'. Vaclav Havel, former President of erstwhile Czechoslovakia, in *Power of the Powerless* (1978), tried to illustrate how people were 'living a lie' through the example of a greengrocer who placed the slogan 'workers of the world, unite' in his shop window; this is a good example of political socialisation and indoctrination. Havel asked:

> [W]hy does he [the greengrocer] do it? What is he trying to communicate to the world? Is he genuinely enthusiastic about the idea of unity among the workers of the world? Is his enthusiasm so great that he feels an irresistible impulse to acquaint the public with his ideals? Of course not. He is signaling his readiness to conform. But if the greengrocer had been instructed to display the slogan 'I am afraid and therefore unquestioningly obedient', he would not be nearly as indifferent to its semantics, even though the statement would reflect the truth (Havel 1985: 6–7).

CONCLUSION

Culture contributes to the study of comparative politics in five different ways: first, it frames the context in which politics occurs. Second, it links individual and collective identities. Third, it defines group boundaries and organises actions within and between them. Fourth, it provides a framework for interpreting the actions and motives of others, and fifth, it provides resources for political organisation and mobilisation (Ross 2009: 139–41). Theorists of culture underline the importance of values, beliefs and attitudes in political life as they affect political behaviour and stability. 'Even in its current state,' observed Pye and Verba (1965: 197), 'the theory of political culture represents a significant advance in the direction of integrating psychology and sociology with political science to produce richer and fuller understanding of politics.'

NOTES

1. Polity or middle-class state, which balances oligarchic and democratic tendencies, is what Aristotle considered the best practicable state.
2. The Solidarist philosophy that Julius Nyerere, the first President of Tanzania, and most other most well-known leaders of Africa propound is a model of democracy in the Rousseauean sense, applicable to societies that are relatively homogenous and lacking the experience and institutions of a conventional parliamentary system. The primary reason for this was the increasing trend of consolidation of power by the majority party after gaining independence. This is exemplified by Tanzania. Nyerere was not a Marxist, nor did he believe in a one-party state of the Leninist type. He is a Roman Catholic and a believer in social democracy. However, he was conscious of the situation of the newly independent countries where a multi-party system could not work. The Solidarist one-party state, according to Nyerere, is democratic, with open membership and no restrictions on personal freedom. He understood the importance of a legitimate opposition in a political system, but pointed out that this could not work in newly emerging nations like Tanzania. He asserted that the notion of democracy does not exactly require organised opposition; what it demands is not the actual existence, but a theoretical acceptance of the idea. The central fact that he emphasised was the internal backwardness of the newly emerging nations. Since classes are not well-developed, class politics has to be ruled out. Added to this is an important fact: the common aspiration among the entire population for development. In the absence of a differentiated industrial society like

Europe and America, the introduction of a pluralist system is not possible in Africa. There is no organised group that could exercise its hegemony over others. The challenge of development needs firm, strong and centralised control from above, a fact that Western societies never had to contend with.

In the African context, the task is to democratise society from the top. Independence enhanced the role of the state. Mobilisation of resources and the exercise of authority increased the authority of the state. National consolidation took place through the active participation of the state. The crux of the matter was that the backwardness of traditional societies did not allow for the immediate adaptation of a Western-type parliamentary democracy. However, this does not mean an absence of democracy. The absence of viable class divisions ensures equality; and since traditional African society is democratic, with free discussion, government is established with the approval and participation of the people. Unlike the erstwhile Soviet system, which had a low level of discussion compatible with its totalitarian political structure, Africa had an indigenous democratic experience.

This democratic experience is linked with the African version of socialism—*ujamaa*—which has the following features: (*a*) in traditional society, mutual respect exists with a recognition of the place and rights of each member of the family; (*b*) a belief in communal life exists with a theory that all goods are held in common; inequalities exist, but are not marked or offensive to social cohesion; and (*c*) every single person has an obligation to work. However, there were two inadequacies in the pre-colonial situation: (*a*) inequality between man and woman; and (*b*) a low standard of living. There was optimism that with the use of technology and an increase in economic activity within the framework of three basic principles—traditional life, mutual respect and communal ownership, and a commitment to work—these could be eliminated within a short period. Such a philosophy fitted perfectly well with a Solidarist one-party democracy. In reality, the *ujamaa* movement suffered from many economic difficulties like low productivity and limited output, and the dual strategy of public sector and cooperatives along with private enterprise created tension in the implementation of democratic and socialist principles. In view of this, Nyerere's call for a multi-party democracy in the early 1990s acknowledged the fact that the specific conditions faced by newly independent countries in the post-independence phase were over, and that the one party state reflected this extraordinary circumstance. This acknowledgement indicated the entry of the Third World into the modern age of multi-party democracy.

3. Weber's thesis was critiqued by R. H. Tawney. The latter agreed that capitalism and Protestantism are connected. In *Religion and the Rise of Capitalism* (1926), Tawney stated that Protestantism adopted the risk taking, profit-making ethic of capitalism and not the other way round; he substantiated this by pointing out that Venice, Florence, South Germany and Flanders, the greatest commercial and financial centres of that time, had a great deal of capitalist spirit. In Holland and England in the sixteenth and seventeenth centuries, capitalism developed not because these were Protestant countries, but because of the large number of discoveries that made the development of capitalism possible. According to Tawney, the strongest connection between capitalism and Protestantism is rationality. Protestantism revolted against traditionalism and advocated rationality as an approach to life and business. Rationality became inherent in capitalism because of Protestantism. Catholicism subscribed to traditionalism. Tawney considered Weber's thesis too simplistic to explain historical events. History is not linear, as Weber assumes. Tawney pointed out that while capitalism was the result of the Protestant ethic that stressed hard work, thrift, etc., Protestantism itself was also influenced by capitalism.
4. A variant of political culture can be found in Lipset's formative events theory, which states that key events at the time of a nation's founding shape its political culture. Hartz developed the Fragments theory, which stated that colonised countries such as Canada are 'fragments' of European society. Colonisation shapes the political culture of the colonies. Inglehart advanced the post-materialism theory, which explained the long-lasting effects of economic and social conditions of childhood on a person.

6

DEBATES ON THE STATE

The true State is the ethical whole and the realization of freedom. It is the absolute purpose of reason that freedom should be realized. . . . The State is the march of God through the World, its ground is the power of reason realizing itself as will. We must . . . worship the State as the manifestation of the Divine on Earth.

Hegel 1929: 443–44, 447

The state is not 'abolished'. It withers away.

Engels 1977: 303

The State is a soulless machine. It can never be weaned away from violence to which it owns its very existence.

Gandhi 1935: 413

A theory of the state is crucial to political analysis and political theorising as it is the pivot around which politics is organised. As with most concepts in political science, there is no agreement on the meaning of the state. It remains a contested concept. This is despite the fact that it lies at the centre of any meaningful discourse. It is because of these contested notions that, in the heydays of the behavioural revolution, Easton substituted the word 'system' for 'state'. State is used in the following senses: a historical or philosophical idea, and an eternal form of political community, which is a specifically modern phenomenon (Forsyth 1987: 503). A state is defined as a political entity that comprises people, territory, a government and sovereignty. The state is an abstraction, while a government is a concrete reality. A state remains unchanged while governments may change structurally and can be removed, altered or amended. A government is the policymaking body that makes, declares and enforces a law. Government differs from administration, although both are used interchangeably in casual language. A government is the political executive while administration is the permanent executive that represents continuity and expertise in policymaking. An administration is a set of persons and bodies that works under the direction of the government to discharge ordinary public services. Governments change, but administration continues.

THE STATE IN THE MODERN AGE

A modern state is highly differentiated, specialised and complex, upholding the difference between the private and the public spheres. As a modern phenomenon, the state developed with sovereignty as its distinguishing trait. The concept of sovereignty reinforces the public-private divide, and also that between one body politic and another. Concurrently with the idea of sovereignty—and partly in opposition to it—grew another idea, which emerged with the American and French Revolutions of 1776 and 1789, respectively, and distinguished the state as a modern phenomenon—the idea that it is the people as a single entity who rightly decides and constitutes the form of rule within the body politic, and that the proper end of the state is primarily the protection of the lives and liberty of individuals.

> The state as a modern phenomenon may, thus, be defined as the institutional representation of the people's will, enabling it to act effectively in both the normal and extreme situation to secure the defence and welfare of the whole and the rights of the parts—together with this very activity itself (Forsyth 1987: 506).

The political apparatuses of modern states are distinct from both rulers and ruled, with supreme jurisdiction over a demarcated territorial area, backed by a claim to a monopoly over coercive power and enjoying a minimum level of support or loyalty from their citizens (Giddens 1985: 17–31, 116–21; Skinner 1978: 349–58).

The modern state is territorial with an impersonal power structure, that is, it is an institutional mechanism under which one operates, and which legitimises and provides total control over the means of violence. The modern state system with its core principles—that of state sovereignty, the legal equality of states, and non-intervention of one state in the affairs of another—emerged in Europe with the Treaty of Westphalia in 1648.[1] Evolving alongside were ideas of constitutionalism and the rule of law; a separation of temporal from ecclesiastical authority; and a separation of the state and church, captured in the statement 'the things that are Caesar's and the things that are not Caesar's'. Acceptance of the limits to political power and the authority of the state is also the acceptance of a private sphere. Between the state and the family lies civil society.[2]

A state is distinguished from society, community, association and nation. A society, like the state, consists of people within a given territory, engaged in cooperative activity; however, a society concerns itself with social order while the state is occupied with legal order. Society is a whole made up of a range of voluntary associations, each with specific tasks and purposes, from the family right up to an international forum. Like society, the idea of community stands for fellowship, personal intimacy and wholeness, and is characterised by common ends or feelings. The state is a bureaucratic government body of institutions and officials with the special purpose of maintaining a compulsory scheme of legal action, acting through laws enforced through direct and positive sanctions. The state, like society, is national in scope, but it differs from society in two respects: (*a*) it consists of all people who inhabit a particular territory and it has the power to use legal coercion, enforce obedience through sanction of punishment, and decree rules of behaviour; and (*b*) other associations, because of their voluntary nature, can enforce social discipline, expect obedience to its conventions and rules, and may, only as a last resort, expel a deviant member. The state is an association in the sense of being a union of human beings who would act as partners to realise a common purpose. However, it is an association with a difference, for it can exercise an all-embracing compulsory jurisdiction within a given territory and is in a position to act competently to decide conflicting claims, whether of individuals or associations. Michael Walzer (1935–) characterizes the state as a primary association. People who live in a country may differ in religion, race, language and ethnic composition; but when people identify with others who live within the state, they constitute a nation. Nationalism supplies the reasons for people to set aside internal divisions within a state, a process that has been going on since the sixteenth century. A state can exist as a juridical entity while a nation needs emotional props. A nation-state means political institutions that combine the concepts of nation (an anthropological idea) with state (a legal notion). All modern states are nation-states. In a technical sense, a state can be defined with reference to four components—population, territory, government and sovereignty. However, there are different theories and ideological standpoints with regard to the origins, nature and functions of the state.

LIBERAL-DEMOCRATIC STATE

The liberal-democratic state comprises two distinct yet interrelated ideas. One refers to the limits of state power (the liberal component) and the other, the democratic component, deals with people's rule, participation and representative institutions. With the extension of adult franchise and consolidation of representative institutions and the rule of law, the liberal constitutional state evolved into a liberal constitutional democratic state by the middle of the twentieth century. A liberal state evolved into a liberal democratic state with the widening of suffrage, which brought in the working class and women into the political fray, and through improved techniques of participation. A liberal state is also a representative democracy, with a system of elected rulers to represent the interests and views of citizens within a framework of the rule of law. Elections through two or a multiparty system constitutes the life breath of representative governments.[3]

A liberal state, by definition, is a limited state, for it confers upon persons the rights and claims of justice which governments must acknowledge and respect, and which can be invoked against the government. The liberal component signifies the limits to state power by rejecting political absolutism backed by the Divine Right of Kings theory,[4] which was the dominant idea in the sixteenth and early seventeenth centuries, also the period when liberal ideas crystallised and began to evolve. A limited state refers to the way power is exercised, as there are constitutional restraints on the way state power is exercised rather than on the form of government. State power can assume the form of constitutional monarchy as in Britain, or a republic as in the US. The former is essentially a unitary system with a largely unwritten constitution, while the latter is a federal system with a written constitution; both, however, are classic liberal states. Most large liberal states follow the American practice of acknowledging a written constitution, federalism, and separation of powers and bicameralism as constraints. The English (1640–88) and French (1789) Revolutions marked the transition from absolutism to the modern state, with the features of fixed territory, control over the means of violence, impersonal power structure and legitimacy. These revolutions helped to stress the importance of consent (of the people) as the primary source of legitimacy for governments and regimes.

The basic outlines of a liberal state emerged in Locke's writings. The ideas that form the core of the liberal state, namely political authority as trust between the governors and the governed, based on consent[5] of the governed, government existing for the people and not vice versa, instituting the government for a stipulated period of time, the principle of majority rule, sovereignty with the people but in abeyance as long as there is a government, supremacy of the legislature, separation of executive and legislative powers, a limited government, and the natural right of the individual to alter and remove a government, are Locke's. These principles became the bases for a constitutional order that emerged with the decline of absolutism.

Image 6.1: Niccolo Machiavelli (1469–1527)

Source: https://commons.wikimedia.org/wiki/Niccol%C3%B2_Machiavelli#/media/File:Santi_di_Tito_-_Niccolo_Machiavelli%27s_portrait_headcrop.jpg.

Montesquieu enunciated ways and means of protecting civil society against the sovereign's arbitrary powers, proceeding on the Lockeian premise that a government based on law, as laid down by the legislator, is the best bulwark against tyranny. He also proposed the principle of separation of powers, with the legislature, executive and judiciary in separate hands, each checking and balancing the other, as the best mechanism for protecting freedom. The US constitution embodies this principle. Montesquieu stressed factors like climate, which shape societies, and regarded politics, law, legislation and form of government as the main determinants of any society. He favoured a republic as it guarantees virtue, namely unreflective patriotism that prompts citizens to subordinate their selfish pursuits to the good of the community. Like Machiavelli, Montesquieu believed that such virtue entailed freedom, security and equality, made possible through conformism, vigilance and austerity, which suppress the strongest of the natural impulses.

The Lockeian principles found concrete expression in the two Revolutions—American and French—towards the close of the eighteenth century; with it came a re-examination of liberal theory. Thomas Paine (1737–1809), the most articulate liberal theorist of the eighteenth century, defended the French Revolution in response to Burke's critique by affirming Locke's rational and egalitarian principles with a new emphasis: that liberal theory no longer represented people's collective rights against the king, but individual rights that guarantee and safeguard one's independence against the state or government. The Bill of Rights of the United States Constitution (1789) exemplifies this shift. Paine staunchly supported representative democracy, rule of law and manhood suffrage without property qualifications.

From the 1760s to the 1790s, there were demands made in England by rational dissenters—for example, Mary Wollstonecraft (1759–97), a close associate of Dr Richard Price (1723–91) and Reverend Joseph Priestly (1733–1804)—for democratisation of the parliament, annual elections, equal electoral districts, secret ballots, and abolition of property qualifications for MPs, payment to MPs and manhood suffrage. These demands were strengthened and influenced by revolutionary events in France in 1789. Wollstonecraft questioned the male bias in notions of rationality and citizenship, and demanded equal opportunity for women. She desired the extension of the liberal values of economic independence, individual achievement and personal autonomy to women in general, and to middle-class women in particular. She established a close link between liberalism and feminism by accepting the liberal challenge to aristocratic and patriarchal rule. Wollstonecraft is the pioneer on equal rights and status for women; she pointed out the incompleteness of the natural rights doctrine, which understood the individual as male, leaving out the female completely.

Image 6.2: Title page of Thomas Paine's *Rights of Man* (1791)

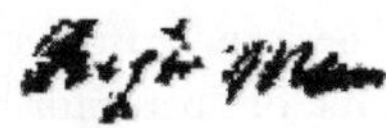

RIGHTS OF MAN:

BEING AN

ANSWER TO MR. BURKE's ATTACK

ON THE

FRENCH REVOLUTION.

BY

THOMAS PAINE,

SECRETARY FOR FOREIGN AFFAIRS TO CONGRESS IN THE AMERICAN WAR, AND

AUTHOR OF THE WORK INTITLED "COMMON SENSE."

LONDON:

PRINTED FOR J. S. JORDAN, No. 166, FLEET-STREET.

MDCCXCI.

Source: https://commons.wikimedia.org/wiki/File:PaineRightsOfMan.png.

The Federalist Papers and the US Constitution

After gaining independence from British rule, the United States became the first liberal state. In the years leading up to the 1776 Revolution, the Americans described their resistance to British rule as the need to protect individual liberty from the state. According to them, certain fundamental rules and principles ought to form the basis of government, the violation of which would not be tolerated by well-informed citizens. The various acts of the British government—taxing the Americans without their consent, restricting trial by jury, curbing popular control of the government, and stationing a large number of soldiers in the colonies—prepared the grounds for the Revolution. By 1775, it became apparent that confrontation was the only remaining alternative to loss of liberty, as immortalised in Patrick Henry's words, 'give me liberty, or give me death'. The initial American resistance and ultimately the Revolution reflected three basic perceptions of their leaders: (*i*) the value of liberty for human beings; (*ii*) the threat that British actions posed to American liberty, leading to the establishment of an absolute and arbitrary government; and (*iii*) the need to attack despotism in its embryonic stage; when well-entrenched, it would be difficult to defeat. The Americans fought for peace, stability and liberty. In their main concern with limiting state power, the founding fathers, as evident from the *Federalist Papers*,[6] created a republic based on representative institutions. Alexander Hamilton's (1755–1804) fear of mob rule, a democratic phantom since Plato's time, was reflected in the provisions for indirect elections to the Senate and the Presidency, and in allowing state legislatures to stipulate restrictions on franchise. He contended that in popular governments, the greatest danger to liberty comes from those who love power and that demagogy could sway the ordinary, inexpert, parochial and short-sighted people. Free government, he reasoned, needs those who love fame to check those who crave dominion. For this reason, he admired the British constitution—'the best in the world'—with its aristocratic features.

Madison brought in three important arguments: (*i*) from Hobbes, the maxim that self-interest is the basis of politics; (*ii*) from Locke, the importance of protecting individual freedom through the institution of public power that is legally limited and accountable ultimately to the people, as well as the principle of toleration regarding religious freedom as a fundamental natural right, and a legitimate government as instituted by a compact not for heavenly salvation, but for earthly utility; and (*iii*) from Montesquieu, the principle of separation of power as crucial to the formation of a legitimate state. Madison accepted factions as inevitable and the fact that politics has to effectively deal with dissent, argument, conflicts of interest and clashes of judgement, as these are inescapable because their roots lie in human nature. Madison regarded every country as divided into classes based on property; however, he did not consider the elimination of private property a way of resolving class conflict. The mechanism to regulate diverse and intruding interests in such a manner that they become part of the necessary and ordinary operation of government is the creation of a powerful American state that would act as a bulwark against tyranny, and as a means to control the violence unleashed by factions. This Republican state would periodically face the judgement of citizens and the ballot box would overcome political difficulties caused by minority interest groups.

For Madison, the republican form of government is the least imperfect constitution as it establishes majority rule through a scheme of representation. His support for majority rule is the most brilliant argument on the subject. The typical defects of popular government, in which majorities ultimately prevail, are majority folly (short-sightedness and instability) and majority tyranny (injustice to minorities). Madison argued that the cure for these defects is not, contrary to traditional republican thinking, to keep republican societies small and simple—for that helps to keep the public good in view and integrate minorities—but to enlarge and to diversify them. The problem of folly could be addressed through a system of representation by electing proper representatives, and by having larger electoral districts so as to get more worthy candidates; also, since electoral competition is difficult when more interests and voters are involved, worthy candidates would have greater success. Thus, the greater the number of representatives, the more possible it is 'to guard against the cabal of a few'. The problem of majority tyranny can be addressed if there is a greater variety of parties and interests, as that would make it impossible for the majority to intrude into the rights of the minority. Social diversity creates political fragmentation which prohibits a disproportionate accumulation of power, a view that has exerted considerable influence on the pluralist tradition after World War II. Madison advocated the representation of different groups and interests and favoured cooperation, deliberation and bargaining as methods of decision-making, as opposed to majority rule and voting in the English Parliament.

This is the difference between American and British versions of the democratic idea, although Locke is the common factor in both. To offset the possibility of representatives becoming remote and impersonal in a large state, Madison proposed a federal constitution with separation of power between the three branches of government to ensure just rule, and a bicameral legislature where the upper house lends steadiness and useful delay to allow for a cool and measured response from the community to prevail over the passions of the lower house, the popular chamber. The federal representative state would protect individual interests and their rights and sustain the security of persons and their property, and make politics compatible with the complex modern state through its trade, commerce and international relations. Madison championed popular governments as long as the majority did not run roughshod on the minority's privileges with the help of the state. Thomas Jefferson (1743–1826) restated Locke's conception of natural rights as those that protect the individual from governmental intrusion by securing life, liberty and property; and the best government is one in which citizens have the most freedom, even if that means reducing the government to being ineffective. He also sanctioned the right of every generation to choose for itself a government which it believed would give it happiness.

The English Utilitarians

In the late eighteenth century, following Hume's rejection of social contract theory along with the notions of natural law and natural rights, a new conception of the state based on the principle of utility that is legal, with rights enacted and enforced by a duly constituted authority, emerged with Bentham as its chief exponent. A state will be judged by its usefulness to the individual and Bentham insisted on the need for a watchful and interested government that readily and willingly acts for individuals' happiness. Reiterating Montesquieu, he instructed a legislator to take into cognisance factors like people's customs, prejudices, religion and traditions while codifying laws.

For Bentham, as with James Mill, universal suffrage makes governments accountable and less whimsical; in 1817, it was considered an impregnable principle. A good government makes possible what he calls democratic ascendancy. He granted to the people the power to select and dismiss their rulers, made possible by the American and French Revolutions that demonstrated that 'people were capable of acting politically for themselves', and this 'was converted to the general principles of political democracy' (Arblaster 1997: 42–43).

Bentham drafted a complete scheme of parliamentary democracy in his magnum opus *Constitutional Code* (1822–30), pleading for secret ballot; annual elections to maximise aptitude and minimise expenses and ensure high quality officials and representatives; equal electoral districts; annual parliaments; a scheme for elementary, secondary and technical public education; election of the prime minister by the parliament; abolition of the monarchy, the British House of Lords and unicameralism; checks on legislative authority and a rejection of plural voting; central inspection, a public prosecutor, recruitment of the young in government, and competitive civil service examinations; the threat of dismissal, which ensures accountability and responsibility; and a code of penal sanctions and representative government for empowering people and finding experts to rule. Unlike Burke, Hamilton and Madison, for whom representation was a means of limiting popular participation and control and preserving the actual powers of governments in the custody of an enlightened elite, Paine, Bentham and James Mill viewed representation as preventing elected representatives from acquiring too much independent power or becoming a self-perpetuating oligarchy. It was also the means of adapting the democratic principle to large and populous societies. Measures such as annual or biennial elections, two terms for representatives and prohibition of single chamber would ensure the core of popular power as far as possible (Arblaster 1997: 60).

In the nineteenth century, the need to check majority tyranny became important with J. S. Mill making a cogent case for liberty, individuality and plurality. The liberal state had to become more responsive to the interests of the working class and women, two major concerns of the time. The demand for the right to vote intensified, and in response the Reform Act of 1832 was enacted, enabling the liberal state to evolve into a liberal democratic state. By then, theoretically, the debate on whether democracy should be representational or direct was also settled within the liberal tradition. Moreover, by the end of the nineteenth century, liberal doctrine as revised by Green underlined that the function of the state was not merely to maintain law and order, but also to remove the obstacles in the way of individuals' moral development. Compulsory education and universal suffrage were important demands in the late 1890s.

Green's revisionist liberalism found systematic exposition in the writings of Leonard H. Hobhouse (1864–1929), who supplanted the older conception of natural liberty with the ideals of distributive justice and social harmony to shape progressive opinion in England, which was not outright socialist. He accepted the need for government intervention not on paternalistic grounds, but to ensure some level of well-being for all—an essential precondition for a liberal society. The idea of liberty shall not prevent the general will from acting where it must for the common good. He stressed on the contribution of welfare measures to the realisation of the liberal value of equality of opportunity. The welfare measures of Lloyd George's reforming budget of 1909 were explained not as an intrusion into the working of the market and individual freedom, but as a justified extension of public control on humane grounds. It was clear that the old liberal order was waning, and during the inter-war years, Keynes, Sir William H. Beveridge (1879–1963), and other revisionist liberals tried to steer the middle way between the old capitalist order and new socialist ideals. The post-World War II Keynesian consensus in England and Roosevelt's New Deal in the United States led to the revival of economies and ushered in an era of prosperity and full employment by the mid-1950s. Equally important is the fact that it marshalled the support of socialists both in Europe and in Britain, furthering the wedge between Western Marxism and Soviet Communism. Public opinion was not overtly socialist, but favoured an activist state and a mixed economy rather than a free market.

However, there were those who swam against the current, claiming allegiance to classical liberalism; its most noteworthy exponent was Hayek, who rejected central planning and collectivism as leading to totalitarianism, and pleaded a return to a free market and spontaneous social order. In his view, these spontaneous or un-designed social patterns and orders existed to serve human purposes. The 'footpath example' demonstrated that useful social institutions could arise and function without any overall organisation, without the exercise of power or authority, without coercion, and thus without compromising individual liberty. The other important exponent of a liberal outlook was Popper, who rejected the wholesale transformation of society that Marx advocated and justified a piecemeal reform of social institutions as the path of reason. Talmon developed a powerful critique of totalitarianism, and Berlin offered an eloquent defence of the importance of negative liberty. The most extraordinary revival of liberalism was seen in the writings of Rawls. Robert Nozick (1938–2002; it would be appropriate to regard him as libertarian), criticising Rawls, provided a powerful defence of the minimal state.

Laissez Faire, but not a Minimal State

It is often argued that the early liberal emphasis on a minimal or night-watchman state stemmed from the belief that an extension of state activity and/or power erodes individual freedom. In the early part of liberal doctrine, the functions of the state were limited to guaranteeing life and property. This was because Europe in the seventeenth and early eighteenth centuries was ravaged by intense religious and civil conflicts, and everything else had to wait till peace was restored. This explains why, in spite of England having a relatively well-developed parliamentary tradition, Locke, Montesquieu, and his eighteenth-century successors did not share Hobbes' conclusion of an irrevocable sovereign, while agreeing that the state has to be an instrument for civilising people. Even as late as 1790, Bentham continued to consider the state a machine in a strictly utilitarian sense, with the sole aim of maximising the happiness of the largest number of people (Creveld 1999: 189). In spite of the commitment of early liberals to *laissez faire*, free trade and the motto that the 'best state is one that governs the least', they, like Smith, supported a large number of government programmes: universal public education, public health measures against contagious diseases, and safety regulations for labour that protected them against the fraudulent practices of employers. Smith stressed the need for government action in six key areas: moderate taxes as an incentive to growth; finance of public works, which should come from those whom it benefits; public responsibilities for private organisations; programmes benefiting a locality to be the responsibility of local authorities (for that ensures accountability and efficiency); and accountability of the market to the government.

Bentham, a supporter of *laissez faire*, insisted that the government maximise happiness, which meant security, abundance, subsistence and equality. Of these four, security and subsistence were most important. He thus proposed free education, guaranteed employment, minimum wages, sickness benefit and old-age insurance (Mack 1955: 85). He also proposed a system of agricultural communes and industry houses to take care of the indigent, as distinguished from the working poor. The indigent would be encouraged to become part of the normal labour market as soon as possible. Care should be taken to ensure that the lot of the indigent was not more beneficial than that of the poor, for that would mean rewarding shirkers, thus acting as a positive disincentive to the industrious poor, a point that Rawls subsequently developed. Bentham recommended an interventionist state in a backward country, but preferred private enterprise in advanced ones. He justified intervention on the grounds that if its advantages outweighed the costs, then it was good rather than bad. In the nineteenth century, the expanding economy, both internally (due to maturity of capitalism) and externally (from overseas trade and colonial empires), demanded an extension of state activity. Equally important are the criticisms levelled against capitalism and the liberal state by socialists, conservatives and other radicals, which liberals like J. S. Mill confronted. He realised the need to change capitalism by incorporating an ethic of social welfare, and supported local workers and retail cooperatives, workers' participation in management, schemes of profit sharing between workers and managers, and other workers' savings. A larger community should not 'dispense with the inducements of private interests in social affairs'. He supported trade unions and the right to strike, but rejected compulsory membership of unions. While aware of the exploitation under capitalism, he was more perturbed by the uniformity that socialism/communism enforced. Capitalism, according to J. S. Mill, would decrease misery and injustice in the long run, and socialism would succeed only if it remained true to its liberal heritage. He disliked the inherent statism of the socialist doctrine, fearing a submersion of individuality, a point that Bernstein developed in great detail.

CONSERVATIVE STATE

The conservatives, like the idealists, adhered to an organic and hierarchical conception of society, rejecting the ideas of contract and consent. They dismissed the mechanistic interpretation that views state as an entity that can be replaced or destroyed at any time and rejected the atomistic view of society, although they saw society as an aggregate of individuals pursuing their self-interest. Individuals are considered in the context of groups, and conservatives stressed the importance of family and neighbourhood communities for the security and meaning they provide. They regard society as fulfilling human needs, with each part—family, church, work and government—playing a particular role in sustaining and maintaining the health of the social fabric. Each part understands its role and perceives society as a whole that is continuously evolving and changing. They understand authority as a hierarchy, with each level playing a major role in society. Burke categorically identified the state with everything truly and properly public—public peace, public safety, public order and public property—precluding the private. Here, Burke echoed the sentiments of early liberals like Smith, whom he greatly admired. Louis Gabriel de Bonald (1754–1840), reiterating Aquinas, asserted that authority and power were derived directly from God.

Conservatives emphasised the social importance of religion as not only a spiritual phenomenon, but also a cementing force that provides a set of shared moral values that hold society together. They regarded the nation with great respect, for it is a product of affinity among people who share the same language, history, culture and traditions; they are sceptical of multicultural, multi-racial and socially plural societies. The conservatives did not favour a weak central government. Tocqueville's distinction between government and administration in *Democracy in America* is implicitly present in almost all shades of conservative thought. He advocated a strong and unified government while administration, in the interests of liberty and order, should be as decentralised, localised and generally inconspicuous as possible. Joseph de Maistre (1753–1821) considered the public executioner the very cornerstone of proper governmental power over people. While the executioner both prevents and punishes crime, that does not mean he is omni-competent, responsible for daily existence, and worst of all, a 'pretended moral teacher, guide to virtue and mother of spirit'. Burke warned that the price of erosion of all natural authorities in society was the increasing military domination of government. This stress on state, family, authority, religion, order and tradition found resonance in Neo-conservatism, which arose in the mid-1960s in the US and obliterated the distinction that existed in conservative thought in the US and in Europe. Neo-conservatives stress on intermediary institutions like ethnic groups, churches, labour unions, universities, family and community as integral parts of a decent society; the absence of these, in their view, led to alienation and to a spiritual vacuum, resulting in totalitarianism and a secular, rootless mass society (Nisbet 1962, 1975).

MARXIST/COMMUNIST STATE

Unlike Hegel, who worked out the details of a modern state through his distinction between the realm of the state and the realm of civil society, Marx's account was sketchy. This was despite his professed aim to provide an alternative to the Hegelian paradigm, as outlined in his *Critique of Hegel's Philosophy of Right* (1844). His views on the state were largely determined by his perceptions and analyses of the French state, the Revolution of 1848 and the *coup d'etat* of Napoleon III, and his ideas resulted from an elaborate misunderstanding of the 1789 French Revolution, the role of classes and the very nature of the revolution. Keeping the French experience in mind, Marx advocated a violent revolutionary seizure of power and the establishment of a dictatorship of the proletariat. Interestingly, he accepted the possibility of a peaceful and parliamentary transfer in 1872 in England, America and Holland, where the state was not as highly centralised and bureaucratic as it was in France. However, by and large he remained committed to the idea of a violent revolution.

According to Marx, the state belonged to the superstructure. So in the course of history, each mode of production gave rise to its own specific political organisation to further the interests of the economically dominant class. The *Communist Manifesto* declared, 'the executive of the modern State is but a committee for managing the common affairs of the whole bourgeoisie' (1975: 44). The state expressed human alienation and was an instrument to further class exploitation and class oppression. In the *Eighteenth Brumaire of Louis Bonaparte* (1852), Marx denounced the bureaucratic and all-powerful state and advised its destruction. Bonapartism was a regime in a capitalist society in which the executive branch of the state, under the rule of one individual, attained dictatorial power over all other parts of the state and society. Examples of such regimes during Marx's lifetime included that of Louis Bonaparte, the nephew of Napoleon I, who came to be known as Napoleon III after his *coup d'etat* of 2 December 1851. Engels drew a similar parallel with Bismarck's rule in Germany. Bonapartism arose when the ruling class in the capitalist society was no longer able to maintain its rule through constitutional and parliamentary means, and the working class, too, was unable to wrest control. It gave rise to a temporary equilibrium between the rival warring classes. The independence of a Bonapartist state and its role as 'ostensible mediator' between rival classes did not mean that it was in suspended animation. In reality, it ensured the safety and stability of bourgeois society and guaranteed its rapid development. The relative autonomy of the state was based on cancelling out the forces in a state of temporary equilibrium. Marx provided the outline of relative autonomy which Gramsci subsequently developed into a systematic theory.

Dictatorship of the Proletariat

This controversial and ambiguous concept emerged in the writings of Marx and Engels as a result of a debate with the German Social Democrats, the Anarchists and more significantly, from the practical experiences of the Paris Commune of 1871. Their observations on the subject have to be pieced together from remarks made solely *enpassant* and from different sources. The two major texts, however, are *Civil War in France* (1871) and *Critique of the Gotha Programme* (1875). This concept holds the key to understanding Marx's theory on the nature of communist society and the role of the proletarian state. It is a concept that divides Marxists and Leninists from the Anarchists on the one hand, and from Social Democrats on the other. Neither the phrase 'Dictatorship of the proletariat' nor the idea of eliminating state power is mentioned in the *Manifesto.* Instead, Marx and Engels spoke of the 'political rule of the proletariat', advising workers to capture the state, destroy the privileges of the old class and prepare the basis for the eventual disappearance of the state. Bearing in mind the experiences of the French Revolution of 1789, Marx advised the proletariat to seize the state and make it democratic and majoritarian. Irrespective of form, the state machinery was powerful, something the proletariat had to contend with. The initial 'capture' thesis of the state, however, subsequently yielded to the 'smash' thesis. In a book review written around 1848–49, Marx observed that destruction of the state had only one implication for communists, namely the cessation of the organised power of one class aimed at the suppression of another class (Draper 1977: 288). In the *Manifesto,* Marx described the nature of communist society as classless and 'an association, in which the free development of each is the condition for the free development of all' (1975: 76). Socialisation of the means of production would be through the following 10 measures:

1. Abolition of property in land and the application of all rents of land to public purpose;
2. A heavy progressive or graduated income tax;
3. Abolition of all rights of inheritance;
4. Confiscation of the property of all emigrants and rebels;
5. Centralisation of credit in the hands of the state;
6. Centralisation of the means of transport in the hands of the state;
7. Extension of the factories and instruments of production owned by the state;
8. Equal liability of all to labour;
9. A combination of agriculture and industries; gradual abolition of the distinction between town and country; and
10. Free education for all children in public schools (1975: 74).

Marx modified his views on the state between 1848–52 as a result of events in France, and more significantly after 1871. In March 1850, the phrase 'dictatorship of the proletariat' was used to signify the complete and total power needed to destroy the remnants of the old order and for the creation of a new one. It did not mean the permanent rule of one person or group. This phrase was incorporated into the first of six statutes of the Universal Society. The 1871 Paris Commune revived the debate on the notion (Hunt 1975: 305–06). Marx regarded the Commune as the 'glorious harbinger of a new society' and in his amendment of the *Manifesto* in 1872, he acknowledged that 'the working class cannot simply lay hold of the ready-made state machinery and wield it for its own purpose' (Marx 1975: 8). The notion was criticised by many of his contemporaries and fellow travellers within the socialist movement. Michael Bakunin (1815–76), in *Statism and Anarchy* (1873), contended that the Marxist political order could turn out to be a rigid oligarchy of technocrats and officials, eventually resulting in bureaucratisation and a government by the intelligentsia. The task of the proletarian revolution was not to transform, but to abolish the state as it symbolised power and authority. Speaking at the First International (formerly, the International Working Men's Association) in 1869, Bakunin stated:

> I detest Communism because it is the negation of liberty and I cannot conceive anything human without liberty. I am not a communist because communism concentrates all the powers of society and absorbs them into the hands of the state while I want to see the state abolished. I want the complete liberation of the authoritarian principle of state tutelage which has always subjected, oppressed, exploited and depraved men while claiming to moralize and

> civilize them. I want society and collective or social property to be organized from the bottom up through free associations and not from the top down by authority of any kind . . . in that sense I am a collectivist and not at all a communist (Bakunin, cited in Woodcock 1944: 41).

On the other hand, the German Social Democrats, following the views of Lassalle, articulated the possibilities of using the existing state to realise socialism and enhance human freedom. They favoured reforms as opposed to revolution, and believed that the spread of suffrage would give workers a decisive role in parliament and in the institutions of the state. These demands were incorporated in the Gotha programme adopted by the German Social Democratic Party (SPD) in 1875. In response to both the Anarchists and the German Social Democrats, Marx wrote the *Critique of the Gotha Programme* emphasising the transitional nature of the dictatorship of the proletariat, outlining the attainment of full communism following a revolutionary transformation of society through a two-tier process. '. . . between the capitalist society and communist society lies the period of the revolutionary transformation of the one into another. There corresponds to this also a political transition period in which the state can be nothing but the revolutionary dictatorship of the proletariat' (Marx 1977, Vol. III: 19).

Marx contrasted the higher form of communism with primitive or crude communism, the first stage in historical materialism. In primitive communism, all are compelled to work, individual talents are levelled down, women are communally owned, all essentially indicating a negation of the human personality. Marx did not specify the mechanisms of change from stage I to stage II in the post-revolutionary phase of human history, casting serious doubts on how this development would take place, and whether the development would be as intended (Avineri 1976: 329). Since the process is not explained, the ultimate aim—'free development of each will lead to the free development of all'—might not be realised (Wilson 1941: 335–36). In *Anti Dühring*, Engels introduced the notion of 'withering away' of the state, in which the 'government of persons' would be replaced by an 'administration of things'. Both he and Marx accepted central planning and direction without force or coercion as a feature of the proletarian state, but failed to resolve the possible conflict between centralised planning and individual freedom in communist society.

Thus, Marx and Engels reacted sharply to Bakunin's criticism about the statist implications of their conception and Lassalle's conception of 'free state'. By 1875, it became clear that the German Social Democrats had begun to think of using the existing state apparatus and were settling down for reformist socialism. Marx continued to advocate the revolutionary overthrow of the existing bureaucratic-military state and replacing it with the dictatorship of the proletariat, which was considered more truly democratic and majoritarian. Bakunin insisted on the immediate elimination of all forms of political authority, replacing it with spontaneous and voluntary organisations. Hoping to counter both critics, Marx accepted the anarchist demand for the abolition of the state, but emphasised the majoritarian content of the transitional state as purely a temporary measure.

In exploring the possibilities of a world proletarian revolution, Marx and Engels showed an interest in the non-European world and set out the idea of the Asiatic Mode of Production. Unlike the European state, which is an instrument of class domination and exploitation, the state in Asiatic societies controlled all classes. It did not belong to the superstructure but was decisive in the entire economic arena, building and managing water supply as the life breath of agriculture in arid areas. It performed economic and social functions for the entire society. Social privileges emanated from service to the state and not from the institution of private property (as in Europe). Asiatic societies had an overdeveloped state and an underdeveloped civil society. Military conquests and dynastic tussles ushered in periodic changes without affecting the economic organisation because the state continued to be the real landlord. The self-sufficient autarchic villages sustained by common property, agriculture and handicrafts buttressed social unity in Asiatic societies. In Europe, cities rose independently, helping the production of exchange values, which in turn determined the development of a bourgeois class and industrial capitalism. In the East, the city was created artificially by the state and superimposed on the economic structure, remaining therefore a 'princely camp' subordinate to the countryside. The state appropriated surplus in the form of taxes; this centralised state prevented the rise of free markets, private property and guilds, and bourgeois law.

For Marx and Engels, communist society eliminated all forms of alienation for the individual, from nature, society and from humanity. It would be a true democracy with the majority ruling for the first time. The transitional state—dictatorship of the proletariat—lay between the destruction of capitalism and attainment of communism. Interestingly, one well-known utopia is among the least delineated. Marx's own epistemological premises cautioned him about the future. To describe an object that exists in the consciousness of a thinking subject is philosophical idealism. Moreover, Marx did not compete with socialists he had branded as 'utopian' by constructing detailed blueprints since communist society was determined by the specific conditions under which it was established (Avineri 1976: 221). Marx projected an image of future society from the internal tensions of the existing capitalist society, implying that from the outset, communist society would perfect and universalise all the elements of bourgeois society that could be universalised.

For Marx and Engels, socialism represented the zenith of capitalism with the possibility of a proletarian revolution only in advanced industrialised societies. However, they explored the possibilities of revolution in semi-developed and backward areas with a view to fomenting revolution in developed areas. In this context, in 1882, they stated that if a revolution broke out in Tsarist Russia, it could complement the efforts of the proletariat in the advanced West. Russia's backwardness and Marx's lack of a coherent theory of post-revolutionary society attenuated the Blanquism in Leninism and Stalinism.

If Stalinism was an offshoot of Leninism, Marxism inspired Leninism. An examination of the development of 'dictatorship of the proletariat' reveals a tension between the concept's organisational necessities and Marx's vision of full communism as truly and fully free. Marx's handling of the theory of the state remains inadequate; 'Marx sketched but never developed a systematic theory of the state and hence the idea of a political economy remained overdetermined and undescribed politically' (Wolin 1987: 469). His aversion to utopian blueprinting led him to ignore the details necessary for managing a society based on equity, just reward and freedom. The concept of 'class struggle', central in Marxist thought, has become largely irrelevant in America and Western Europe (Berlin 1939: xi). Berlin's last observation about the obsolescence of class struggle in advanced industrialised countries can now be extended to the developing world. There is no more talk of a revolutionary transformation of society, or that 'East is Red'. Moreover, the possibility of using democracy as a means of realising socialism never took centre-stage in his analysis of future society. This is where Social Democrats scored over Marx. They (in particular, Bernstein) emphasised the need to combine democracy (representative parliamentary institutions with universal suffrage) with socialism, which resulted in a permanent breach between German Marxism and Russian Communism (Plamentaz 1969).

The Leninist State

Vladimir Ilyich Ulyanov Lenin (1870–1924) regarded dictatorship of the proletariat as the core of Marxist thought. In his 1916 tract *State and Revolution* (1977), Lenin reviewed Marx and Engels' ideas on the state by examining the views of other contemporary Marxist scholars on the subject. *State and Revolution* is regarded as Lenin's most substantive contribution to political theory (Colletti 1969). Using the model of the Paris Commune, he argued that proletarian revolution destroyed the bourgeois state and established a dictatorship of the proletariat, for that is the most appropriate political form during the transitional phase. Lenin argued that since the bourgeois class controlled the bourgeois state with all its democratic instruments, the primary function of which is direct coercion, it has to be destroyed totally. He clarified that Engels' notion of the withering away of the state referred to the proletarian state withering away while the bourgeois state was abolished. This differed from the anarchist notion of abolition of the state. Lenin defined the proletarian state as a special organisation of force, an instrument of violence to suppress the bourgeoisie. He emphasised that socialist revolution would lead to political rule of the proletariat, and to its dictatorship. The proletarian state wielded coercive force, but of a different kind; the majority exercised coercion over the minority, a reversal of the bourgeois state. Its *raison d'etre* was to crush the resistance of the exploiters and build a socialist democracy for all, which he believed only the proletariat could accomplish. Reiterating Marx, he outlined a two-stage development for the attainment of communist society. The first or lower stage—the socialist phase—retained vestiges of the old bourgeois order in which exploitation continued (since the state, as a coercive force, continued); however, it was a 'bourgeois state without the bourgeoisie'. The second phase would dawn when the imperative need for state machinery disappeared completely after society adopted the rule of 'from each according to his ability to each according to his needs', and when the 'Government is replaced by the administration of things'. The antithesis between mental and physical labour would also disappear. The proletarian state, like the Paris Commune, would be one where workers directly participate and manage state affairs without a bureaucracy and a standing army.

In *Left Wing Communism* (1920), he described the tactics that dictatorship of the proletariat was to employ. Lenin christened the first and second phases as 'socialism' and 'communism', respectively, and since then the two phrases have been used in common parlance. He faithfully reproduced the observations of Marx and Engels on the dictatorship of the proletariat and communist society, in the process adding a 'permanent ideology to Marxism, namely, that the attainment of the Communist society would be two phased' (Sabine 1973: 762). For Lenin, dictatorship of the proletariat is a political concept, 'a rule won and maintained by violence by the proletariat against the bourgeois rule unrestricted by any laws' (Lenin 1977: 117). It would be viable only through the Vanguard of the Proletariat, the Workers' Party, for he had little faith in the industrial proletariat as a mass.

Miliband (1977: 179–80) correctly commented that the Leninist model is illusory; for the revolution to properly succeed in Russia, a 'state proper' strong enough to organise the transition from capitalism to communism is needed. Unlike Marx, who conceived of a majoritarian revolution, Lenin spoke of a minority revolution carried out by the Vanguard Party on behalf of the proletarian mass. Given the minority nature of the revolution, it would be difficult to conceive a majoritarian government. Moreover, the proletarian state would continue to function as the state. The revolution would end the bourgeois state but not the state as such; in contrast to the bourgeois state, which protected the interests of the bourgeois minority, the proletarian state would promote and further the interests of the proletarian majority, in the spirit of true democracy. *State and Revolution*, however, neglected the problem of political articulation and political organisation. The tricky part is Lenin's emphasis on the need for and role of the Vanguard Party (Miliband 1977: 182), for he remained sceptical of the role of the Soviets and workers' councils, which represented people's spontaneity till the eve of the revolution. *State and Revolution* does not examine the relationship between the Soviets and the Vanguard Party. It was when Karl Johann Kautsky (1854–1938) accused the Bolshevik regime of violating democracy that Lenin described the role of the Soviets as evolving from local bodies to national organisations, organising the workers directly. However, a short time after the revolution, the Soviet regime became the dictatorship of the Bolshevik Party as the Party came to enjoy an irretrievable and irrevocable position, largely because of the failure to distinguish 'between the dictatorship of the proletariat and the dictatorship of the party', and Lenin's declaration 'that dictatorship of the proletariat is impossible except through the Communist Party' (Carr 1979: 230).

Critics of Leninism

The Leninist experiment was severely criticised both within and outside Russia. Most critics pointed unanimously to the absence of democracy and the lack of sufficient institutional checks against an abuse of power. From a social democratic standpoint, Bernstein dubbed the Revolution as a counter-revolution and regarded Bolshevism as a 'brutalized' version of Marxism, for it relied on terror and violence and abhorred civilised behaviour. He believed that socialism ought to eschew all forms of dictatorship and violence. Julius Martov (1873–1923) and the Mensheviks were sceptical of Bolshevik methods and tactics and argued that Russia was not yet ready for a socialist revolution, given its backwardness. Martov rejected the Leninist conception of a minority revolution led by a disciplined, well-organised Workers' Party with covert or overt mass support on the grounds that it would institutionalise dictatorship or 'Commissarocracy'. Regarding the Leninist model as a flagrant departure from the majoritarian perceptions of Marx and Engels, he accused Lenin of imposing the will of a 'conscious revolutionary minority' on an unconscious majority, thereby reducing the latter to a passive object of social experimentation. The Social Democrats, on the other hand, remained committed to realising both socialism and democracy. Martov's position coincided with that of Kautsky. Lenin's reply to Martov in *Will the Bolsheviks Retain State Power* was weak, as he wrote that if 130,000 landowners could govern Russia in the past, why could 240,000 members of the Bolsheviks party not do so now? To this, Martov and others replied: 'Yes, you may be able to stay in power with your 240,000 members, but only insofar as you approach and then exceed the repressive measures of the 130,000 landowners.' In response, Lenin retreated partially and launched the New Economy Policy (NEP), acknowledging the need for more time to build socialism and liberalise the economy without introducing political democracy and civil liberties. Later, lack of political liberalisation only strengthened the autocracy under Josif Vissarionovich Stalin (1879–1953), who introduced forced collectivism, industrialisation and nationalisation, and also simultaneously increased mass terror, mass murders and purges, thus confirming Martov's worst fears.

The suspension of the Constituent Assembly and the suppression of universal suffrage provoked both Kautsky and Rosa Luxemburg (1871–1919) to virulently denounce the Revolution and Leninism and castigate Lenin for disregarding democratic norms and procedures. They believed that the minority revolution would lead to militarisation and bureaucratisation. Kautsky pointed out that dictatorship of the proletariat meant power of the workers through a majority in parliament; and according to Luxemburg, abandoning spontaneity would encourage centralisation and personal dictatorship. Lenin, in *Proletarian Revolution and Renegade Kautsky* (1918), stated that the contrast between the Bolshevik and non-Bolshevik socialist movements was a contrast between two diametrically opposite methods, dictatorial and democratic. For Lenin, dictatorship of the proletariat had to be understood with reference to the relationship of the proletarian state to the bourgeois states, of the proletarian democracy to the bourgeois democracy—a fact that Kautsky overlooked. Lenin clarified that dictatorship does not mean the absence of democracy; and for a Marxist, the class connotation of a regime is crucially important. Leon Trotsky (1879–1940) justified the use of violence and terror to combat reactionary forces to enable workers to transform society. Subsequently, he too conceded that backwardness and socialism were incompatible, and that the measures he advocated as temporary means could become permanent and the ends of the regime. He blamed poverty for the bureaucratisation of the former Soviet Union as the bureaucracy had become a 'caste', depriving the proletariat of its political rights and introducing brutal despotism.

Prince Peter Kropotkin (1842–1921), Bakunin's successor, anticipated the establishment of the Marxist state in Russia and the fact that in Marxism, there exists both an embryonic form of Leninism and its malignant form, Stalinism. Like Luxemburg, Bakunin is confident that party dictatorship would eventually deaden the spontaneous creativity of the masses, destroy the Soviets and the popular revolution, and impressed upon Lenin the need for initiative by local forces. He contended that Bolsheviks had replicated a centralised state that closely resembled the one with full dictatorial power proposed by Babeuf. Such a state, in his opinion, paralysed the reconstruction work of the people, undermining their success.

The important gaps left by Marx in his theory of the state led to controversies and debates in the first two decades of the twentieth century. As far as the basic principles are concerned, there was considerable disagreement between Bernstein, Kautsky, Lenin and Luxemburg. Significant differences existed amongst Russian Marxists, too, as the opposing views of those led by Lenin and those of the Western Marxists reflected two different situations. In Germany, which had the single largest following of Marx and the influential SPD, the lot of the working class had actually improved, a fact completely at variance to Marx's predictions. The collapse of capitalism was not imminent. The British Labour Party established in 1904 was reformistic in its attitude towards capitalism, as was France.

Dictatorship of the proletariat would have ceased to be controversial had Lenin not resurrected it during his campaign against Bukharin, who advocated the need to smash rather than capture the existing state apparatus during the revolutionary seizure of power. In 1917, on the eve of the October Revolution, he remained confident of the spontaneous role assigned to workers and the rise of the Soviets, which explained his libertarian outlook in *State and Revolution* as opposed to the authoritarian tone of *What is to be done?* (1903). In view of an imminent proletarian revolution, it became imperative to define the post-revolutionary state and the nature and form of socialist democracy, and set the rules for dealing with problems of real politics. Marx was hardly helpful on this issue.

As Milovan Djilas (1911–95) pointed out, Marxism lacks a theory of political liberty. Having visualised his classless communist society as non-conflictive and harmonious, Marx never comprehended the dynamics of a democratic modern society. The fact is that individuals function rarely as isolated creatures but often through group(s), which serve to articulate and represent the plural and diverse interests in society. Marx's mistake was to assume that a classless society necessarily meant a homogenous and Unitarian one.

This fallacy, coupled with the Leninist emphasis on a Vanguard Party, led to the emergence of a monolithic party system in the erstwhile USSR, which straddled and terrorised all aspects of civil society. The Communist Party's monopoly, conferred upon it by Article 6 of the Soviet Constitution, was never really examined when political reforms were contemplated and initiated. It was finally revoked in 1989–90 in the wake of de-Leninisation, leading to the mushrooming of diverse political groups. In the absence of a philosophy for the post-revolutionary phase, coupled with Russia's backwardness and the lack of a democratic culture both within Tsarist Russia and the Leninist model, the minority-based Bolshevik Revolution reconstructed the state with total power under the guidance of the Vanguard party. This was inevitable since the revolution had to succeed; and given its essential minority character, it was impossible to conceive of a majoritarian government.

DEBATE ON THE ADVANCED CAPITALIST STATE

Gramsci rightly pointed out that an advanced state rules by perfecting the ideological apparatus, rather than through repressive measures like force and terror. The state consists of two elements—the coercive apparatus comprising of police, army and judiciary, which upholds the authority of the ruling class through force, and various institutions of civil society like media, church, schools, clubs, parties and trade unions, the instruments of hegemony and the means by which the ruling class secures the spontaneous compliance of society with its rule. Hegemony allows a ruling group to hold on to power long after it ceases to be the dominant class. For Gramsci, the tenacity and strength of societal forces within advanced capitalism make it possible for the capitalist class to assert its hegemony. In the process, it renders a genuine communist revolution a virtual impossibility, unless carried out in the Leninist manner.

The democratic pluralist view provides the most popular defence of advanced capitalism as a viable and relatively just system. It states that within advanced capitalism lies equality of opportunity for most, if not all people, and this crucial factor renders the concepts of ruling class, power elite and class politics largely irrelevant. In these systems, 'all the active and legitimate groups in the population can make themselves heard at some crucial stage in the process of decision' (Dahl 1956: 137–38). Since 'the fundamental political problems of the industrial and political citizenship have been solved, conservatives have accepted the welfare state; and the democratic left has recognized that an increase in overall state power carries with it more dangers to freedom than solution to economic problems' (Lipset 1973: 443). This theory of classlessness within advanced capitalism has obvious limitations. Although it is generally conceded that the welfare state has lessened inequalities to a considerable degree by improving the living standards of the poor, it is also acknowledged that far from the classes withering away, they continue with their inbuilt cleavages. In other words, the Marxist analysis of these societies retains its validity to a considerable degree.

In recent times, one of the most penetrating class analysis of the welfare state has come from Ralph Miliband (1924–94), who in *The State in Capitalist Society* (1969) provided a detailed critique of the pluralist view by asserting the superiority of Marxist analysis. He began by examining the concepts of ruling class or the power elite, which the pluralists ignore. Advanced capitalist countries are highly industrialised, and a large portion of their activity is under private ownership and control. Miliband pointed to state intervention, in varying degrees, in economic life. Their economic base is identical, resulting in notable similarities within their social structures and class distribution. A relatively small number of people own a very large and disproportionate share of wealth, deriving their incomes from ownership. This class is the ruling class in the Marxist sense. Despite 'all the instances of growing or achieved "classlessness" ... the proletarian condition remains a hard and basic fact in these societies, in the work process, in the levels of income, in opportunities or the lack of them, in the whole social definition of existence' (ibid.: 16).

These affluent societies also carry within them large sections of people who live in misery. Managerial capitalism is not a selfless neutral institution but maintains definite class interests. They appear social in character, but exist largely for private purposes. The social origins of this managerial class are similar to those of people with large incomes and ownership of property. Elite recruitment is mostly hereditary. Education is very important for success, although elite institutions can usually be accessed only by the upper and middle classes. Working-class students do not get better jobs. The differences among the dominant classes are confined to a given ideological framework. The property owners control the state system; for instance, a very small percentage of American army officers come from working-class backgrounds. The same is the case in Sweden and Japan. The main purpose of government is to further the interests of capitalism for it 'genuinely believed in the virtues of capitalism, and, have accepted it as far superior to any possible alternative economic and social system' (Miliband 1969: 70). Contrary to general belief, the higher civil service is also not neutral. The military maintains close relationships with large business houses. The government appoints judges, who in turn appoint conservative judges. All these factors combine to create an imperfect competition. This process is legitimised in different ways. For instance, bourgeois political parties can spend more money than working-class ones. Miliband also stated that the most significant political fact of advanced capitalism 'is the continued existence in them of private and ever more concentrated economic power. As a result of that power, the owners and controllers in whose hands it lies, enjoy a massive preponderance in society, in the political system, and in the determination of the state's policies and actions' (ibid.: 265). The basic fact in these societies is that unequal economic power produces unequal political power.

The capitalist context of generalised inequality in which the state operates determines its policies and actions. The prevalent view is that the state in these societies can be, and indeed mostly is, an agent of a 'democratic' social order with no inherent bias towards any class or group; and that its occasional lapse from 'impartiality' must be ascribed to some accidental factor external to its 'real' nature. But this too is a fundamental misconception; the state in these class societies is primarily and inevitably the guardian and protector of dominant economic interests. Its 'real' purpose and mission is to ensure their continued predominance, not to prevent it (Miliband 1969: 265–66).

Miliband's instrumentalist view argues that capitalists use the state as a means of domination in society. Structuralists like Louis Althusser (1919–1990) stressed the ideological and structural mechanisms that help the ruling class to maintain itself in power using both force and consent. Elaborating on Althusser's (1969) basic formulations, Nicos Poulantaz (1936–79) related it to the major function of capitalism, namely the reproduction of capitalist society in its totality. The state, along with maintaining the political interests of the ruling class, also ensures cohesion and equilibrium in society in a manner that blurs class divisions (Poulantaz 1973). As a result, social relations appear competitive and individual-based, and any notion of class and class struggle disappears. The competitive party system conceals contradictions, factions and disunity. It does not allow the hegemony of any particular class, including the bourgeoisie. Since the state is not the instrument—as

Miliband assumes—of a dominant class, it is a relatively autonomous and stabilising factor. The structuralist view, like the instrumentalist one, does not deal with the mechanism of change or with essential reasons for the continuation of the capitalist state.

SOCIAL DEMOCRATIC STATE

Unlike Marxism and Anarchism,[7] Social Democracy emphasises the transformation of the capitalist state, which is then to be used for the benefit and welfare of workers. Marxism arose as a systematic critique of this early phase of unregulated capitalism, although Marx did take note of important reforms, like the 10-hour day. However, Marx, despite writing during the Victorian era which was essentially optimistic and moving towards greater democracy, remained committed to the Jacobin idea of total and apocalyptic change. The Reform Acts of 1832, 1867 and 1884 on the extension of franchise that eventually covered the working class and the British government's decision to not expand its empire territorially after the 1857 Indian Mutiny did not alter this rigid perception; he continued to uphold the two-stage violent revolutionary transformation of society, one to destroy capitalism and the other to create socialism. However, the slow expansion of democracy in England and its initiation in many countries of continental Europe led to a large number of socialists rethinking the appropriateness of Marx's projection, and to the search for an alternative proposition. This line of thought received an impetus with the growth and expansion of the SPD, the largest and most influential socialist party, accompanied by the English Fabian Society. German, Austrian and Scandinavian social democratic parties, particularly in Sweden,[8] embraced them. Social Democracy accepted the capitalist free market as the most efficient system, yet admitted that capitalists cannot be trusted. Only the wise stewardship of public agencies could ensure public interest and common good. Social Democracy advocated a strong regulation of corporations, strong progressive tax, strong stewardship of ecosystems and social infrastructure, prevention of tax shelters and of campaign finance corruption.

Ferdinand Lassalle (1825–64), following Jean J. C. Louis Blanc (1811–82), viewed the state as representing the will of the people as a whole; this was why he supported the demand for suffrage, for that enables people, including workers, to advance their cause. He described the state as the highest form of human organisation, with the purpose of enabling individuals to maximise and realise their freedom, and not merely (as liberals argue) to protect individual freedom and property interests. For Lassalle, socialism meant political democracy, universal suffrage, freedom of press and of association, and referendum and trial by jury. He advocated the establishment of autonomous organisations independent of the bourgeoisie; representation of the working class in German legislative bodies through universal, direct and equal suffrage; establishment of state-aided producers' cooperatives to act as a counter to capitalism, to realise freedom and equity. However, he remained ambivalent on whether the state would assume the form of parliamentary democracy or a democratic order based on spontaneous popular will, guided by the revolutionary act of the leader, an idea borrowed from Johann Gottlieb Fichte (1762–1814). Unlike Marx, who defended proletarian internationalism, Lassalle's support for German nationalism rested on the hope of organising the German working class on a national scale with universal franchise. The Gotha Programme of 1875 incorporated most of his ideas—universal, direct and equal suffrage, state-aided producers' cooperatives under the democratic control of workers, and a democratic republic to be realised through reforms. Lassalle rejected the concept of a night-watchman state and sought to reform the existing state to become reflective and responsive towards workers' interests. Eduard Bernstein (1850–1932) accepted these arguments and emphasised that socialism must not unduly worship the state. Instead, following the arguments of Eugene von Dühring (1833–1921), he stated that the liberal element in socialism must never be sacrificed. He categorically stated the need to realise socialism and democracy together and to use the existing state to improve the social and economic conditions of the working class.

The Erfurt programme of 1891 that Bernstein helped to frame demanded universal suffrage, equal rights for women, proportional representation, freedom of expression and of association, free and secular schools, local self-government, free legal assistance and medical care, election of magistrates, an eight-hour day, and prohibition of employment for women and children. Most notable was his assertion that revolutionary violence is not the means to achieve these ends. As late as 1959 the SPD, through its 'Bad Godesberg' programme, finally renounced revolutionary goals at the level of theory. This programme identified five criteria that formed the core of social democracy: political liberalism, mixed economy, welfare state, Keynesian economics and a belief in equality. Besides the German SPD, Austrian and Scandinavian social democratic parties have also incorporated these ideas. This became the broad consensus between social democracy and liberalism in the post-World War II era. It remained dominant till the 1980s, when the New Right arose to challenge and revoke the consensus.

Social democracy in Britain developed due to the efforts of the Fabian society (established in 1884), comprising a small group of London-based intellectuals who aimed to create the nucleus of a future planned socialist society. In the 1880s, England experienced economic problems like stagnation and political difficulties like the disintegration of the Liberal Party primarily due to Gladstone's inability to solve the Irish question. The Conservative Party underwent substantial changes, with its dominant membership tilting in favour of defenders of British nationalism and the empire replacing the traditional majority of landed gentry and the Church. In this altered climate, there was a natural attraction towards radicalism, with sections of the middle class moving towards socialism, thus reflecting a loss of faith in the classical economic theories of liberalism and capitalism. While Green's philosophy reflected this shift and his theory of positive freedom and common good transformed the nature of English liberalism, there emerged socialist groups like Henry M. Hyndman's (1842–1921) Social Democratic Federation, William Morris' (1834–96) Socialist League and the Fabian Society, which developed out of the Fellowship of the New Life started by Percival Chubb (1860–1960) and Thomas Davidson (1840–1900).

Since its inception, the Fabian society emphasised 'permeation' of existing institutions and the 'inevitability of gradualism' and that explains its choice of name—after Roman General Fabius Cunctator, known for exhausting his enemies through protracted and patient action while avoiding, as far as possible, frontal attacks. Fabians dissociated themselves from both Anarchists and Marxists, categorically proclaiming their commitment to democratic procedures with the fundamental assertion that socialism had to evolve out of democratic welfare legislations to be administered by the civil service in order to become popular among the middle classes. They concentrated on practical but detailed and well-thought out reforms, which are often characterised as the 'gas and water socialism'. Greenleaf (1973) described Fabian society as an Institute for Social Engineering, as their tracts dealt with specific contemporary problems like factory conditions, sanitary reform, public wealth, land nationalisation and taxation. Each point was carefully analysed with facts and accompanied by detailed prescriptions for change. Some suggestions are of great historical significance, like the case for an eight-hour bill, municipalisation of gas supply, municipal slaughterhouses, and the London Education Act of 1903. Two fundamental assumptions distinguished Fabians from other socialist groups and laid the foundations for their enormous influence in Great Britain and elsewhere: (*a*) By accepting the constitutional method in a country with a long tradition of parliamentary democracy, they made socialist ideas respectable and acceptable in places where Marxism was unknown. Unlike Germany, there was no socialist movement in Britain, considering that when Kropotkin visited England in 1881, he had no audience. (*b*) Fabian emphasis on practical problems and solutions enabled it to be more realistic than continental socialists, turning it into the romantic and idealistic English left. For Fabians, socialism implied a moral transformation to be brought about by a change of opinion through democratic means. Like Marxists, they consider socialism inevitable, but believe in constitutional methods like the extension of franchise to achieve it and make it attractive to the middle class. The ideas and theorists of New Liberalism—like Hobhouse and Wallas—influenced Fabianism and helped the development of a non-Marxist form of socialism. Fabians, like the New Liberals, supported the extension of the regulatory and administrative functions of the state. Fabians desired to extend the ambit of political democracy to include the social sphere, as socialism had to grow out of capitalism and liberalism. Despite their poor opinion of the average voter, they supported the extension of franchise; they were, however, not enthusiastic about women's suffrage. Socialism combined political democracy, a welfare state, educational opportunity and greater social justice, all of which had to develop within the framework of a mixed economy.

The exposition of Fabian collectivism by the Webbs led to a lively debate between Sydney (1859–1947) and Beatrice Potter Webb (1858–1943), and George Douglas Howard Cole (1889–1959). Cole's ideal was the creation of an active social democracy far removed from Fabian collectivism. Cole, like the pluralists (see Chapter 13) and unlike the collectivists, desired a decentralised social and political structure. He differed from pluralists in his commitment to industrial democracy in the workplace or self-government both for and within the group. He espoused the idea of manual workers administering industry, and this came to be referred to as Guild socialism,[9] that is, non-Communist, non-statist, pluralist and a libertarian version of socialism, thus anticipating late twentieth-century advocates of participatory democracy by championing work experience and environment as the most decisive factors in moulding man.

In the 1930s, the New Deal in the US and Keynesianism, along with the Beveridge Report in Britain, provided fresh evidence proving the falsity of Marx's analysis of capitalism. In the wake of the Great Depression of 1929, which discredited laissez faire capitalism, and following the devastation caused by World War II, state intervention and regulation of the economy became the guiding principles. Equally important is that it marshalled the support of socialists in both Europe and Britain, furthering the wedge between Western Marxism and Soviet Communism. Keynes prepared the ideological base through a state-aided post-war reconstruction with which social democracy began to identify: the relative decline of the manual working class[10] (which made political parties more heterogeneous); the unprecedented growth rate that guaranteed full employment, economic prosperity and social security to all; structural changes within capitalism that led to the extinction of the overbearing owner-boss and the emergence of a new species of salaried managers (vividly described by Burnham; see Chapter 13); the end of family capitalism and spread of public ownership, creating a new balance between the public and private sectors and transcending the bourgeois character of capitalism; the emergence of a service economy rather than a goods producing one; and democratic control of the economy. Crosland's *The Future of Socialism* (1956) captured this synthesis between liberalism and social democracy by pointing out that twentieth-century capitalism was qualitatively different as it was less individualistic and more egalitarian and democratic. Liberals like Galbraith and Schumpeter agreed with his thesis of convergence. The British Labour Party nationalised key industrial sectors and instituted major welfare state provisions, including a national health service.

WEBER'S ANALYSIS

Weber disagreed with the Marxist premise that the state is part of the superstructure, which itself is determined and conditioned by the economic base. He stated that even if it were possible to transform class relations, the modern state and its bureaucracy could not be replaced by institutions of direct democracy. This is because only the bureaucracy can resolve the massive task of coordination and regulation. He considered the problems posed by a liberal pursuit of a balance between might and right, power and law as inescapable elements of modernity. He developed one of the most significant definitions of the modern state, emphasising two distinctive elements of its history—territoriality and violence. The modern state, unlike its predecessors (which were marked by constantly warring factions), had the capacity to monopolise the legitimate use of violence within a given territory; it is the nation-state in embattled relations with other nation-states, rather than with armed segments of its own population. Of course, 'force is certainly not the normal or only means of the state—nobody says that—but force is a means specific to the State.... The state is a relation of men dominating men, a relation supported by means of legitimate (i.e. considered to be legitimate) violence' (Weber 1958: 178). The state maintains compliance or order within a given territory; in individual capitalist societies, this crucially involves the defence of property and enhancement of domestic economic interests overseas, although not all problems of order can be reduced to these. The state's network of agencies and institutions finds ultimate sanction in its claim to a monopoly over coercion; only when there is an erosion of this monopoly does a political order become vulnerable to crises. Weber's definition brings into focus the third element—legitimacy. The state enjoys a monopoly over physical coercion that is legitimised by a belief in the justifiability and/or legality of this monopoly. Today, authority is no longer obeyed as it had been earlier—through habit, tradition or the charisma of individual leaders. Rather, there is a general compliance by 'virtue of legality, by virtue of the belief in the validity of legal statute and functional competence based on rationally created rules' (ibid.: 79). The legitimacy of the modern state rests primarily on legal authority, that is, commitment to a code of legal regulations. Weber's foremost concern lay with the administrative set-up or bureaucracy, consisting of appointed officials representing a rational legal authority. He supported the power of private capital, the competitive party system and a strong political leadership as countervailing forces against bureaucracy.

FASCIST STATE

In the fascist doctrine, the nation is supreme. The state is the organic structure of the nation, supreme and all-inclusive. This concept was summed up best by Giovanni Gentile (1875–1944) who, like Croce, identified with an Italian school of Hegelian philosophy. Fascists used the Hegelian argument; however, that did not mean they were well-versed in Hegel's philosophy. Like Hegel, they criticised individualism and parliamentarism. However, for Hegel the state implied a constitutional government with a fair amount of civil liberty and orderly legal procedure. The motto of the fascist state is: 'Everything for the state; nothing against the state; nothing outside the state' (see Chapter 11). The state is an ethical idea representing lofty ideals, as opposed to the materialism of the Marxists and the selfish, anti-social, individualist ethic of political liberalism. The fascists espoused the absolute sovereignty, moral and legal, of the national state; while the state's interests will at times coincide and at others conflict with the interests of citizens, the former will always enjoy precedence. The preservation and expansion of the state through war is justified. The fascists defended a nation that was organically and hierarchically constituted, dismissing claims of equality and rights as essentially feeble creeds. Their slogan, 'Responsibility, Discipline, Hierarchy', substituted the democratic slogan of 'Liberty, Equality, Fraternity' with a view to encouraging the individual to garner all his resources and employ them towards efficacious participation in national life. They stressed the need for law, order and efficiency rather than liberty, which they considered possible only under a strong and progressive state. The individual fulfills his true personality and freedom not by safeguarding his private interests, but by merging with the larger unions—his family, church and the state. Gentile declared that the 'maximum of liberty coincides with the maximum of state power'. The individual derives his rights from the state and his will counts in political decisions only when it coincides with that of the state. For fascists, political authority is aristocratic and also autocratic, representing the essential groups and not individuals within the state. Sovereignty resides with the state and not with the people; only elites are competent to speak, thereby repudiating democracy.

German Nazism has no theory of the state. In *Mein Kampf*, Hitler proposed that the state was a means to an end, namely the well-being of the *Volk* (the folk, the organic people). *Volk* represented a culture that was learned and could not be inherited or equated with the nation, for it was biological. Nazism spoke of the masses, the elite and the leader. The elites lead the masses, and are in turn led by the leader. Hitler and Mussolini were contemptuous of the masses and advocated the selection of the elite. The elites were selected through a natural process that represented the folk and its inner will. The leader was the head of the elite, responsible for all and served with unquestioning obedience. He symbolised what Weber called charismatic authority. The idea of the leader and folk is supported by a general theory of race, specifically the myth of the Aryan race, invented to uphold political chauvinism. It depends for effect on racial prejudice, particularly anti-Semitism.

TOTALITARIAN STATE

The term 'totalitarianism' was first used by Gentile in 1916 to describe a seamless identification predicated on a Hegelian universalism that absorbed the elements of society within the totality of the state. It became a political term and theoretical concept after World War I, applied to the three radical dictatorial regimes of the inter-war period—Italian Fascism, German National Socialism and Soviet Stalinism. It differed from earlier absolutist states in its capacity to control the mass of its subjects politically, socially, economically and technologically. Hence, in this sense it is a twentieth-century phenomenon. Arendt (1951) identified four conditions that form the foundations of a totalitarian state. First, during and after the two world wars, there was a breakdown in class and community because of rapid industrialisation and the spread of an individualistic liberal doctrine. Second, even though the non-politicised masses suddenly became enfranchised, political apathy about democratic procedure(s) rendered them vulnerable to manipulation by demagogic leaders. Third, the chaos and havoc caused by these two conditions created a 'negative solidarity'. After the confusion caused by the wars, directionless individuals searched desperately for an identity through which to link themselves with society. In order to fight isolation, individuals began to participate in mass activities like political rallies, taking membership in political parties or other elements of the political machinery. Fourth, a large population is an essential prerequisite because such states habitually generate internal cohesion and stir up misplaced nationalist fervour by creating scapegoats on a massive scale. For instance, there was genocide and persecution of Jews by the Nazis and the kulaks (peasants) by the Russians.

For Talmon (1960), the conditions for totalitarian thinking were: (*i*) a dominant ideology that offered an explicit vision of the ideal society, subordinating everything; (*ii*) a pessimistic conception of human nature as wicked, weak, selfish, anti-social, irresponsible and in need of guidance; (*iii*) a belief that human beings were incapable of knowing what was good for them because of their imperfections; the leader, on the other hand, with his vision of an ideal society, acts precisely to realise that aim; (*iv*) as a result of this conception of human nature, personal freedom is subordinated to greater material security; (*v*) all of society is politicised, obliterating the distinction between the public and the private; and (*vi*) individuals are treated as ciphers with identical wants and needs—enforced homogeneity—and subordinated to the greater whole—the state, the locus of supreme political value.

Friedrich and Brzezinski (1965: 21–22) list a 'six-point syndrome' that best characterises a totalitarian state, namely (*i*) an elaborate holistic ideology, (*ii*) a single mass party with a leader, (*iii*) system of terror, (*iv*) total control of mass media, (*v*) monopoly over weapons, and (*vi*) control over the economy. Ideology forms the most powerful means of perpetuating totalitarianism since it is a tool of persuasion and indoctrination. It appeals to the deep intuitive beliefs of the masses, to their traditions and culture, their fears, hatred and hopes. Despite the varying degrees of difference between the three totalitarian ideologies, they are similar in their manipulation of mass hysteria to the extreme. Havel (1985: 273–74) uses the term post-totalitarian to describe a system in which every individual is trapped within a dense network of the state's governing instruments … themselves legitimated by a flexible but comprehensive ideology, a 'secularized religion'. It is therefore necessary to see, argued Havel, that 'power relations … are best described as a labyrinth of influence, repression, fear and self-censorship which swallows up everyone within it, at the very least by rendering them silent, stultified and marked by some undesirable prejudices of the powerful…'.

All three totalitarian states possessed a bureaucratic and hierarchical party led by a single person. Each party emerged after successful revolutionary movements and once in power, became the only party to rule ruthlessly, suppressing all competition from other parties and groups. The party is crucial for it is the foundation of the ideology through which the regime's legitimacy flows, and is a tool that is subjugated to the authority of the leader. Weber classified such a leader as charismatic with supernatural or superhuman qualities, subjugating all institutions like the legislature, bureaucracy and their own party to their control. Totalitarian regimes use terror and force to maintain law and order, have a monopoly over communications, and invade individuals' private spaces. They exercise complete control over defence weapons and the economy with the view to mobilising resources. The corporate state in Italy, the attacks on labour and on the property and financial investments of Jews in Germany, and the centrally directed economy in the former Soviet Union had one common aim—to extract the maximum surplus value from the economic mix of labour and capital. Of the three totalitarian regimes, Fascism and Nazism were defeated by the Allied powers during World War II; communism collapsed in the 1990s due to its own internal contradictions.

POST-COLONIAL/OVERDEVELOPED STATE

States that have emerged in the Third World after the decolonisation process differ both in evolution and nature from their counterparts in the West. The fundamental difference has been that in Europe, the nations created the state, whereas in the Third World it is the state that has supposedly created the nation. Given the wide social, cultural and economic cleavages, this has been a stupendous task, compelling many to turn increasingly to authoritarianism to create the nation-state. Lacking proper institutions and burdened with an overdeveloped colonial state apparatus, the rulers have mostly advanced their own personal interests rather than that of society. The lack of entrepreneurship allows for the consolidation of a parasitical bourgeoisie, with the middle class as its junior partner.

A new clientalism with a mutually beneficial and reinforcing relationship between patrons and clients has emerged. In such circumstances, legitimate authority is further eroded by the co-existence of segmented groups of culturally divided people who, in the absence of a well-formulated plan for power sharing, do not consider the state their primary identity (as has happened earlier in Europe). This makes the majority of Third World states weak, mostly because they have continued with the legacy and instruments of a repressive colonial administration. However, the recent third wave of democratisation,[11] according to Huntington (1984, 1992), has created a new climate of optimism and with the overall acceptance of multi-party democracy, there are indications that with greater elite accommodation and power sharing, Third World states will move towards becoming nations.

Hamza Alavi (1921–2003), a sociologist, developed a theory of an autonomous overdeveloped state with a military-bureaucratic complex dwarfing all other aspects of society, and with a collaborative understanding between landed elites and the business class. In an influential essay on Pakistan and Bangladesh, 'The State in Post-Colonial Societies: Pakistan and Bangladesh' (1972), Alavi posited that the post-colonial state was 'overdeveloped' as it is a foreign construct and hence is powerful in comparison to leading agrarian and industrial classes, the latter being 'under-developed'. In a colony, if the indigenous bourgeoisie is weak, divided ethnically and underdeveloped, it will be unable to gain dominance at the time of independence over the relatively highly developed colonial state through which the metropolitan country had exercised its control. The peasantry is factionalised. However, the three propertied, exploiting classes—the indigenous bourgeoisie, the metropolitan neo-colonialist bourgeoisie, and the landed class—converge under metropolitan patronage. Their competing and no longer contradictory interests and demands are mediated by the bureaucratic-military oligarchy, which in the process acquires a relatively autonomous role and does not become an instrument of any of these three classes. This relatively autonomous role of the state apparatus is of special importance to the neo-colonialist bourgeoisie, enabling it to pursue its class interests in post-colonial societies.

Alavi's thesis is a critique of Miliband's institutionally focused analysis of advanced capitalism. Alavi portrays a static, institutionally linked elite and his analysis is based on its insular character. Its origins can be traced to the movement for an independent Pakistan in the 1903s and 1940s, which was guided not solely by religious motives, but rather by a salaried class of Muslim government servants ('salariat') who stood to gain the most from the creation of a new state. An independent united India would have seen a drastic (negative) revision in its share of jobs in pre-partition India. For instance, in the colonial era, although Muslims formed 23 per cent of the population, their share in the armed forces was 40 per cent. The new state of Pakistan—and subsequently Bangladesh—continued with this overdeveloped state and the overwhelming influence of its bureaucratic-military complex. However, in recent times Alavi's thesis has been questioned, with the rise of new institutional actors in Pakistan like the media, the judiciary and parliament. The reduced role of the state is also seen in areas of internal security and the exercise of sole monopoly over violence with the emergence of the Taliban and private mafias. Former Pakistani Prime Minister Yousuf Raza Gilani drew attention to the existence of a parallel state, which also questions the basic formulation of Alavi's thesis.

In relating Alavi to Africa, Saul (1974) noted the absence of strong internal classes and pointed out that the state's independence is due to a balance between internal and external forces, making the state dependent on strong external classes. Saul believed that the state bureaucracy was likely to become a new type of class, which would appropriate and control productive resources by regulating them or by acquiring private capital. Leys criticised this position and argued that the notion of a 'bureaucratic bourgeoisie' as a ruling class is vague: 'the contradictions of the situation are obscured by this lumping together of different elements in the state apparatus' (1977: 48). Saul also pointed out that Alavi neglected ideology, which is necessary for the state's function of holding the capitalist system together. Leys responded by reasserting the importance of class as the basis of analysing the state.

FAILED/COLLAPSED STATE

The notion of a failed state, although not new, became relevant in the 1990s and prominent in the wake of the 9/11 terrorist attacks. Such states are incapable of asserting authority and power within their territories and are chronically unstable, leading to mass migration and murder. They endanger the lives and livelihoods of their people and are a threat to world peace. In these states, living standards begin to deteriorate rapidly as elites grant financial rewards only to favoured families, clans or small groups. Foreign exchange shortage leads to shortages of food and fuel, curtailing government spending on essential services. Corruption thrives as the ruling class skims away the already scarce and few resources available and stashes away ill-gotten money in foreign accounts. Citizens see a dwindling in their healthcare and education benefits. The leaders and their cohorts subvert democratic norms, force legislatures and bureaucracies into subservience, strangle judicial independence, undermine civil society, and gain control over security and defence forces. One ethnic group is preferred over others; the latter feel discriminated against and/or excluded, as was the case in Somalia and Sierra Leone in the 1970s and 1980s. Governments once seen as benefiting all appear partisan as they provide fewer and fewer services. Ordinary citizens become poorer and rulers visibly wealthier—they live in grand boulevards, drive expensive limousines, go on frequent foreign excursions, put their faces on the local currency and display their large cut-offs in public. Unlike strong states, a failed state is tense, prone to conflict and strife-ridden, as criminal and political violence is high. It is embroiled in ethnic/religious/linguistic/cultural hostilities; its infrastructure is fragile and institutions weak. Starvation, declining life expectancy, rising levels of infant mortality, runaway inflation, and basic food shortages are its other characteristics. A rare and extreme version of the failed state is the collapsed state, symbolised by an absence of authority.

Rogue state is a term used in international politics to signify a state that is a threat to world peace. It is ruled by an authoritarian regime that severely restricts human rights, sponsors terrorism and supports the proliferation of weapons of mass destruction (WMD). The term was used frequently till 2000 by the US; since then, its usage has been abandoned. There is a general conception that a rogue state does not behave rationally or in its own best interests. Former US President Ronald Reagan stated in July 1985 that the US would not 'tolerate attacks from outlaw states by the strangest collection of misfits, Looney Tunes, and squalid criminals since the advent of the Third Reich'. The Clinton administration elaborated on the concept. National Security

Advisor Anthony Lake, in the 1994 issue of *Foreign Affairs*, referred to a recalcitrant and outlaw state as one that remains outside the family of democratic states and undermines basic values. He identified North Korea, Cuba, Iraq, Iran and Libya as rogue states. A state that pursues WMD, supports terrorism, severely abuses its own citizens and stridently criticises the US is considered a rogue state. Subsequently, Yugoslavia, Sudan, Syria, Belarus, Nicaragua, Venezuela, Panama, Afghanistan and Zimbabwe have been labelled rogue states as well. Post-2000, rogue states officially became 'states of concern', 'outlaw states', 'pariah states' and 'outposts of tyranny'. In 2002, following the 9/11 attacks, George W. Bush coined the phrase 'axis of evil' to disparage Iraq, Iran and North Korea. The Obama administration uses the term only for North Korea and Syria. William Blum, Noam Chomsky, and many in the left consider the US the biggest rogue state of all. A rogue state is differentiated from a pariah state such as Myanmar and Zimbabwe, which abuse the human rights of its people while not being considered a tangible threat beyond their own borders. The two terms have been used interchangeably.

CONCLUSION

Daniel Bell observed that the modern state is too small for big things and too big for small things, implying the fragmentation of politics both within and outside the state. This leads to a need not only for greater federalising tendencies within the state, but also when the state has to meet the challenges of a global civil society. The state as an all-powerful leviathan is a thing of the past, and the modern state now refers to a well-ordered state within a plurality of associations representing civil society both within and outside. Held (1989: 228–37) identified five gaps with regard to state sovereignty in the global context. In the economic realm, there are forces that actually undermine the power and scope of national states. In the context of world markets, given the role of multinationals, the increased social and workforce mobility, and the decisive role of technology and communications, the claim that the nation-state is sovereign in its economic policies is no longer correct. Internationalisation of production has eroded the state's capacity to control its own economic future. Sovereign states continue to place their national interest in the forefront while taking decisions concerning their economic policies; clearly, however, their autonomy in this regard has been circumscribed. Economically weak states are under greater pressure from both outside and inside to set their houses in order. For example, the International Monetary Fund (IMF), with its structural adjustment programmes, insists on certain conditions while providing loans to a government, namely a cut in public expenditure, subsidised welfare programmes and currency devaluation, thereby monitoring the policies or performance of the economically weak states. Global markets imply greater competitiveness and increased dependence among states, making the idea of splendid economic isolation redundant.

Till World War II, the state was the primary military actor. This was undermined by the emergence of power blocs, one led by the US and the other by the former USSR, through their respective alliances of NATO and the Warsaw Pact. (The disintegration of the former USSR and the collapse of communism has led to the dissolution of the Warsaw Pact.) Although the US is the world's only superpower, its dominance within NATO has diminished, primarily due to the rise of the European Union. Furthermore, there has been a decisive shift in the world mindset, which now sees economic domination as more important than military strength. The proliferation of international and regional organisations has also moderated the idea of state sovereignty. Since the Nuremberg trials following the end of World War II, there has been increasing emphasis on human rights as a yardstick to assess the conduct of states. International law subjects individuals, governments and non-government organisations to a new set of regulations (Vincent 1986). 'The International tribunal at Nuremberg laid down for the first time in history, that when *international rules* that protect basic humanitarian values are in conflict with *state laws,* every individual must transgress the state laws (except where there is no room for moral choice)' (Cassese 1986: 132). This is in keeping with the spirit of Grotius' suggestion; Grotius, while confronting the main problem of seventeenth-century Europe—how to cope with radical moral conflict and its derivative armed warfare—asserted the possibility of having universal moral standards to adjudicate questions of international conflict. He defended armed warfare as long as it was based on two principles—first, that self-preservation must always be legitimate, and second, any reckless injury of another, if not for reasons for self-preservation, must always be illegitimate. On this basis of self-preservation, it is possible to establish rules for reconciling conflict. Finally, domestic autonomy is limited, with the larger security concerns of the power blocs undermining traditional concerns of sovereignty, which conceive the state as the primary spokesperson of its citizens by determining domestic public policy and protecting their foreign interests.

The wide diversity reflected in the various theories and practices of the state indicate the extreme complexity of dealing with this important concept. Today, the debate lies within the framework of liberal democracy, between the individualists and communitarians. Owing to a larger consensus between the pluralists and the Marxists, a convergence in broad terms is also visible in theories of the state, with emphasis placed on both structure (Marxist-elitist preference) and agency (the pluralist emphasis). However, one major inadequacy of theories of the state, more so in the case of pluralists, has been their lack of comprehension of the international impact of globalisation, which makes these theories locally dated. In this age of globalisation, a theory of the state must reflect both its relative autonomy and subordination in a world where most decisions are emerging from a centre beyond the jurisdictions and control of the individual nation-state.

NOTES

1. A new system of political order emerged in Europe, which came to be referred to as the Westphalian system based on the concept of co-existing sovereign states. Non-interference in one another's domestic affairs was accepted.
2. Between 1750 and 1850, the term civil society emerged as the key concept in Western political thought. Till then, civil society (*koinōnia, politikē, civilis, sociētē, civile, bürgerliche, Gesellschaft, Civill Society, societā civile*) was used synonymously state (*polis, civitas, état, Staat, state, stato*). A member of civil society was also expected to be a citizen of the state, and was obliged to act in accordance with its laws without harming other citizens. This perception remained dominant till the mid-eighteenth century in Britain, France and Germany. The concern at this time was with the nature of civil society and the limits of state action. Civil society as a concept originated within liberalism, with an attempt to undermine absolutism. The concept was introduced into modern European political philosophy through Latin translations of the Aristotelian Greek term *politike koinonia*, which for Aristotle was the ethical-political community of free and equal citizens, ruling and being ruled under a legally defined system of public procedures and shared values. The Aristotelian identification of the political and the civil was maintained till the eighteenth century. The end of the eighteenth and beginning of the nineteenth century, after the Industrial and French Revolutions, brought about another distinction between state and society. Society no longer meant the fundamental union between human beings, which the state establishes. Civil society emerged as a network of interaction and exchange formed by individuals exercising their right to pursue the satisfaction of their needs in their own ways. Ferguson's work provided the most succinct analysis of civil society. He stated that civil society was not a sphere of life distinct from the state; the two were in fact identical. 'A civil society is a kind of political order which protects and "polishes" its mechanical and commercial arts, as well as its cultural achievements and sense of public spirit, by means of regular government, the rule of law and strong military defences' (1792, Vol. 1: 252).

   Paine, writing in the background of the American Revolution with its innovative principles—the natural rights of man, popular sovereignty, right to resist an unlawful government, and a republican and federal political structure—pointed to the utmost need to restrict the power of the state in favour of civil society, as the state is a necessary evil while civil society is an unqualified good. For de Tocqueville, a plurality of civil associations is necessary for consolidating the democratic revolution. Civil associations are permanent, open schools of public spirit within which citizens learn their rights and obligations, press their claims and become familiar with others. He considered civil associations arenas in which individuals can direct their attentions to more than their selfish, narrow, private and conflicting goals, and also realise that they are dependent on one another and hence must work for cooperation. Civil society embodies a 'system of needs' and a totality of private individuals.

Civil society, for Hegel, represented a conflict of interests that can be resolved only by the state representing all interests in society. He viewed civil society as crippling and in constant need of state supervision and control. Unlike Paine, Hegel did not consider civil society (*bürgerliche Gesellschaft*) a natural condition of freedom, but as a 'historically produced sphere of ethical life' that lay in between the simple patriarchal household and the universal state. It included the market economy, social classes, corporations and institutions concerned with the administration of welfare and civil law. The creation of civil society is the achievement of the modern world (1969: 339), and it was made possible because it developed a 'system of needs'. For Marx, civil society was the site of crass materialism, of modern property relations, the struggle of each against all, and egotism. For Gramsci, the two were interrelated. Civil society consists of private institutions like schools, churches, clubs, journals and parties, which are instrumental in crystallising social and political consciousness, while political society consists of public institutions like the government, courts, police and the army, the instruments of direct domination. It is in civil society that intellectuals play an important role by creating hegemony.

3. The Solidarist One Party system in Tanzania and the erstwhile communist one party system are exceptions to this belief.
4. The Divine Right of Kings was promulgated in 1610 by James I in England. This theory was supported by his son Charles I and his chief adviser, William Laud, the Archbishop of Canterbury. Laud argued that the king had been appointed by God and people who disagreed with him were bad Christians. The idea of the Divine Right of Kings evolved in Europe during the Middle Ages. The theory claimed that kings were answerable only to God, and it was therefore sinful for their subjects to resist them. The theory ceased to have influence after the Glorious Revolution of 1688 that saw the establishment of constitutional monarchy and parliamentary supremacy.
5. For Locke, consent is the basis of legitimate government. He proposed two types of consent, Express or Direct, and Tacit. Express or Direct consent is an explicit commitment given at the time when the commonwealth is instituted. The fundamental Constitution of Carolina, which Locke helped to draft, provided for a declaration of one's allegiance to the commonwealth when a person comes of age. If there is no explicit provision for express consent, a person's obligation will be gauged from tacit consent. Locke provided for tacit consent to counter Filmer's critique of the contract doctrine. Filmer stated that the idea of a one-time, irrevocable contract meant binding subsequent generations to what their ancestors had done, thereby making it no different from what royalists were advocating at the time—that God had given Adam the right to rule, which was bequeathed to Adam's heirs. Tacit consent is ongoing, and is demonstrated by the right of inheritance, when lodging for a week, or while travelling on a highway.
6. It consists of 86 articles that Hamilton (51), Madison (24) and John Jay (five) penned to support the campaign for the ratification of the US constitution in 1787–88. They were published under the pseudonym 'Publius' and are regarded as the classic interpretation and defence of the American political system.
7. Anarchism differs from Marxism in three key ideas. First, it rejects the Marxist notion of dictatorship of the proletariat as a transition between the destruction of capitalism and the realisation of the final stage of communism. Second, it distrusts state authority, and third, it rejects authoritarian socialism. These three themes have interlaced and constitute the anarchistic critique and challenge to Marxism, which Marxism (both during Marx's life and later) could not meet effectively. Anarchism differs from Liberalism as it does not favour a constitutional and law-based state; the latter is viewed as devices to protect and safeguard the interests of well-entrenched classes. Anarchism rejects the idea of government based on consent and contract, for most states have come into being through conquest, violence and force.
8. Social Democracy is seen as the secret of Sweden's success, where social services and quality of life remain unsurpassed in the world. At the base of this success is the concept that the whole nation is '*folkhemmet*'—the people's home—with 90 per cent of the population belonging to the Scandinavian racial group. Sweden offers all its citizens universal healthcare insurance, affordable college tuition, excellent public transport, strong labour

rights, long vacations, strong social security, good jobs, good housing, low poverty, low drug abuse and crime rates, and virtually no homelessness. The Swedish Social Democratic Party had rejected the Leninist path even before the oppression and suffering of the Stalin era had disenchanted men and women who had great expectations of the Russian Revolution. When the party came to power in 1932 as a result of the Great Depression, it did not try to nationalise key industries in the Swedish economy, but through the use of Keynesian policies, its leaders succeeded in reviving the economy. Through the use of legislation and fiscal policies, they began constructing a more egalitarian social order. This Swedish combination of an economy in which formal ownership of the means of production remains in private hands and a social policy that favours those do not own capital has come to be known as the 'welfare state'. Sweden, along with other Scandinavian countries, enjoys a consensual nature of political decision-making, considered the most distinctive feature of the Nordic model of government.

This does not mean that there are no conflicts; rather, cooperation and consensus mark collective deliberations and compromise. This is achieved by giving all parties a chance to articulate their points of view. These countries have proportional representation systems, which encourage parties to cooperate with one another and form coalitions, unlike the first past the post system, which allows the winner to take all. Most Swedes belong to four to five associations and only less than 10 per cent remain outside associational life. Suffrage was extended during the formative years of the Labour movement, which explains the strength of the Labour parties (Castles 1978). This is due to the philosophy of societal corporatism that considers the labour movement a social partner with the employers' association and the state in negotiating economic and social policies.

9. This is a sensible version of Syndicalism, a movement in France, Italy and Spain. Syndicalism's major exponent was Sorel. Syndicalism scorns parliamentarism and speaks of workers' control, but through the modicum of a general strike. It rejects doctrine Marxism.

10. In comparison with the total population, low-skilled workers constitute less than 10 per cent. The demand for those with greater education is increasing. The pyramidal shape of the occupational distribution of the working population has given way to a diamond-shaped one because of the rapid expansion in educational opportunities, allowing persons from poor and deprived families to avail of higher university degrees (Lipset 1979: 9).

11. Huntington narrated four stages of democratic development: first, the emergence of a democratic United States in the early eighteenth century; second, in the following century, democratic expansion in Northern and Western Europe, the British dominions and a few Latin American countries. The year 1920 was the peak of democratic development, with a subsequent reversal. Third, in the aftermath of World War II, there was a brief growth in democracy because of US support to the allies, US imposition in Japan and Germany, the decolonisation process and the emergence of newly independent countries, which adopted political forms of imperial powers. Fourth, from the early 1950s to the 1980s, there were mixed fortunes for democratic expansion; the net change in democracy was not good, making it difficult to argue that the world had become more democratic in the 1980s. Furthermore, many former colonies saw shifts from democratic to non-democratic systems, which was a significant departure. Equally significant was a movement in the opposite direction. In 1974, Spain, Portugal and Greece moved from authoritarianism to democracy.

7

CONSTITUTIONALISM

Constitutionalism is an achievement of the modern world. It is a very recent achievement, and it has by no means become stabilized. Indeed, it is a complex system of providing for orderly change, and there is no reason for assuming that the need for change will come to an end in the immediate future.

Friedrich 1968: 4

Constitutions are one of the most readily identifiable methods of regulating the relationship between the state and the individual.

Axford, et al. 1997: 276

Constitutions, written or unwritten can be given operational meaning only through the workings of other political institutions, any analysis of how constitutions shape and facilitate human interaction must necessarily be complex.

Shane 2006: 191

The modern state, based on constitutional rule, is very different from the preceding societal order of feudalism. The latter was organic in nature and had a complex, rigid social hierarchy, in which there existed a delicate balance of groups reflecting a functional social order based on mutual dependence and a code of social conduct. The three divisions of vassal, lord and king were intrinsically linked by duty and obligation. The structure was highly organic, reflecting an interdependence in which roles were prescribed by membership to an economic and social class. Duties, rights and obligations also accrued from the identity created by this membership. It was pyramidal in structure, with well-defined boundaries between the well-balanced groups in a hierarchal order. In such group identity and existence, individual rights were not considered important.

In Great Britain, this delicate but well-defined social boundary received a jolt with the accession of James I (1566–1625) to the throne. His reign proclaimed divine power to rule in 1610,[1] disturbing the power balance of the medieval guild order. Individual rights were severely curtailed and people were supposed to submit completely to an all-powerful sovereign. Dissent and alternative points of view were not tolerated and were suppressed. This proclamation of the divine rights theory was short-lived, as a strong opposition began to be mounted against the king's claim of divinity. The social contract theory provided a new weapon with which to challenge the king's authority and power, leading to the formulation of a constitutional state. In England, the Magna Carta[2] (1215), which established the rights of English barons and free citizens, the Petition of Rights[3] (1628) and the Bill of Rights (1688), which gave landowners and parliamentarians basic rights and freedom, laid the foundations for the modern constitutional state. However, before the rise and consolidation of modern constitutionalism, there was a long history of dealing with issues of government and aspects of constitutional practices.

GREEK HERITAGE AND ARISTOTLE'S CLASSIFICATION OF CONSTITUTIONS

Although modern constitutionalism, with its emphasis on limited government and accountability, began with Lockean liberalism, the idea of a constitution is old and can be traced to ancient Athens. The Athenians did not have a theory of limited government or of a separation of the public from the private, which led to an understanding of a constitutional framework encompassing the entire way of life, including culture, religion, education, social institutions, and administrative and law-making institutions. It is within this holistic framework that Aristotle, as an empiricist, classified the constitutions. He analysed the constitution of Athens as it manifested at the time of Solon (640–589 BC). At that juncture, an egalitarian communal life was being increasingly transformed into economic struggle between the rich and the poor. Solon introduced property qualification for the holding of offices, but not for franchise.

Aristotle was categorical that a rightly constituted law serves as the final authority and that personal authority is only desirable when, for some reason, it is not easy to codify laws to meet all general contingencies. His ideal is an order based on a constitution and laws as, being impersonal, these are less arbitrary and fair when compared to rule by a person. 'The rule of law is preferable to that of a single citizen even if it be the better course to have individuals ruling, they should be made law-guardians or ministers of the laws' (Aristotle 1979: 146). He contended that a free political relationship is one where the subject does not completely surrender his judgement and responsibility, for both the ruler and the ruled have a defined legal status. The 'passionless authority of law' gives to the magistrate and the subject a moral quality and dignity, respectively. A constitutional ruler, unlike a dictator, rules over his willing subjects through consent. According to Sabine (1973: 99), for Aristotle 'the relation of the constitutional ruler to his subjects is different in kind from any sort of subjection because it is consistent with both parties remaining free men, and for this reason, it requires a degree of moral equality or likeness of kind between them, despite the undoubted differences which must exist.' The authority wielded by a constitutional ruler over his subject is different from the one the master wields over his slave, since the latter lacks the reason to rule. Political authority also differs from the authority that a husband exercises over his wife and children. According to Aristotle, a serious flaw in Plato's reasoning was his failure to distinguish political authority from that of the household, as evident in Plato's comment in the *Statesman* that the state is like a family writ large. A political relationship is one of equality; this was reiterated by Locke subsequently. An ideal state would be neither constitutional nor political if the differences between its members were so great that they did not have the same virtue.

Constitutional rule, for Aristotle, has three main elements: first, it is a rule in the general or common interest of the populace, as compared to a rule by a faction or a tyrant which is in the interest of the ruler/s. Second, since it is lawful, a government is carried on in accordance with general regulations and not through arbitrary decrees. A government cannot act contrary to the constitution. Third, a constitutional government means willing subjects ruled by consent, rather than by force. Taking a cue from Plato's suggestion in *Laws* that laws are necessary for a moral and civilised life, he argued that civility of law was possible if one perceived law as wisdom accumulated over the ages and resulting from customs, both written and unwritten. Unlike Plato, he believed that the collective wisdom of the people was superior to that of the wisest ruler or legislator. A constitution, for Aristotle, was not only a basic law determining the structure of its government and the allocation of powers between different branches within a government, but was also a reflection of a way of life. A constitution has two aspects: ethical, or the aims and goals to be pursued by a community, and institutional, or the structure of political institutions and offices, and the distribution of power. A constitution provided an identity to the *polis,* which meant that a change in the constitution would bring about a change in the *polis*.

Aristotle's classification of 158 Greek city states in the fourth century BC has dominated the subject for the past 2,500 years. His classification is based on two categories—who rules and who benefits from that rule. As far as the nature of government is concerned, his classification emphasised that such rule could be exercised by one single individual, a small group, or by many. The question that Aristotle asked was whether the rule was in the narrow selfish interest of the rulers or for the benefit of the entire community. Based on the numbers wielding power and the ends for which power is wielded, Aristotle makes a six-fold categorisation.

Table 7.1: Aristotle's Six-fold Categorisation

	Good	*Perverted*
One	Monarchy	Tyranny
Few	Aristocracy	Oligarchy
Many	Polity	Democracy

Aristotle considered tyranny the worst possible constitution as it reduced citizens to slaves. Monarchy and aristocracy were impractical as they asked for the virtually impossible—that the rulers would place the good of the community over their own selfish interests. This view is in sharp contrast to Plato who placed tremendous importance on reason and philosophy, whereby philosopher kings could transcend their narrow self-interest without any legal binding. For Aristotle, polity, the rule by the many, was the most practical, although he was critical of popular rule as it would make the masses jealous and resentful of the wealth of the few, and therefore vulnerable to being swayed by demagogues. To meet this challenge, Aristotle advocated a mixed constitution as it was practical, combining aristocratic and democratic elements, with the government led by the middle class, the mean between the rich and the poor. In the post-Aristotle phase, the theme of mixed constitution figured prominently in the writings of Polybius, Cicero, St Aquinas and in Machiavelli (Mukherjee and Ramaswamy 2011: 145; see also Chapter 1).

ROME'S LEGACY

Rome's specific contribution to civilisation was a competent administration, the rule of law and secret ballot. It put into practice Aristotle's ideal of a mixed constitution, which according to Polybius was the reason for the success of the Rome system. Polybius took note of the inevitable degeneration of these systems, unless preventive remedies could be employed. His advocacy of the mixed constitution as producing stability was based on the analyses of constitutional change and of the cyclical recurrences, progress and fall of all government systems. Cicero accepted the traditional institutions of the Roman state—assemblies, senate and magistrates—and held that the whole must be guided by one person. However, he did not explain the workings of this guided democracy. He described the Roman system as a mixed constitution but did not analyse the relationship between the assemblies, senate and magistrates. He developed in detail the meaning of public responsibility and distinguished between power and authority. He also provided an elaborate account of Roman law as exemplifying constitutional authority and expounded the principle of stoicism as a basis of political life, thus transmitting Stoic doctrines of natural law to Christian thinkers.

AGE OF CONSTITUTIONALISM

Constitutions, like political parties, are a recent development and can be linked to the seventeenth-century crisis in England and subsequently to eighteenth-century European Enlightenment. According to Friedrich (1968), the roots of constitutionalism lay in liberalism, rationalism, individualism, capitalism and imperialism, and that of Christian belief lay in the dignity and worth of each person, each human being, no matter how lowly (ibid.: 6–7). The core objective of the constitution is to safeguard members of a political community, with a person's sphere of autonomy considered the primary and ultimate value. It is therefore a function of the constitution to define and maintain rights that are considered natural. This was not part of medieval constitutionalism, although it had laid the foundations. By developing the idea that man is entitled and indeed called upon to render resistance to a ruler who violates the Christian natural law, who becomes a tyrant interfering with man's religious (Christian) duties, it took the first step in the recognition of a universal right to any religious conviction. Both Aquinas and John Fortescue (1394–1480) considered it crucial that a government be subject to legal restraint, as a government is best when instituted by law. Another important input was the Conciliar movement. The ecclesiastical insistence upon the need to subject all authority to legal restraints was claimed to apply to the church. Effective participation of lower ecclesiastical orders, and even of the laity, was demanded in the councils called upon to formulate the law. From William of Ockham (1285–1347) to Nicholas of Cusa (1401–64), the idea of consent as a vital ingredient of law gained ground. Equally important in the development of constitutionalism was national unification. As England became unified at an early date, constitutionalism made substantial headway in England in the seventeenth century, which was not the case in Italy. Modern constitutionalism is a distinctive development and was possible only after national unification had provided an effective central government. The disappearance of the universal church as an ever-present counterpoise to national monarchies was probably also important (ibid.: 9).

The unwritten nature of the British constitution was mainly based on the practice of British common law tradition.[4] This consolidation of liberal constitutionalism emerged from a popular upsurge to clearly detail the relationship of the state to the individual, in which individual rights occupied centre-stage by virtue of reason and property. The other natural rights followed the recognition of this right. The ambit of the state was restrained to ensure the maximum freedom of every citizen. The American *Declaration of Independence* drafted by Jefferson in 1776 and the French *Declaration of the Rights of Man* of 1789 were the products of this continued evolution of liberal individualism and the spirit of the Enlightenment. The most important element championing the cause of limited government in the US is the fact that the rights of the individual propertied male became the driving force of constitutionalism. Constitutionalism also flowed from the acceptance of human nature as imperfect; therefore, any attempt at a grand design and total change would be flawed. This scepticism about the possibilities of both misuse and abuse of power led to the acceptance of gradualism and moderation.

In this period of constitutional consolidation, the most important theoretical framework emerged in the work of Montesquieu, who followed the blueprint provided by Locke, the father of both modern-day constitutionalism and liberalism, in the seventeenth century. For Locke, political absolutism was untenable. Absolute power was illegitimate and wicked, for people would never give up all their powers and rights to another, who would then exercise them on their behalf. He developed the arguments in favour of a limited and constitutional state wherein political authority is a trust between the governed and the governors. Locke was categorical that legitimate political authority was based on the consent of the governed.

Montesquieu, reiterating Locke, prescribed a separation of powers as the institutional requirement of a representative democracy in order to curtail the highly centralised authority and ensure a virtuous government through checks and balances. Montesquieu's importance lay in his realisation of the pivotal role that institutions play in ensuring an effective and good government, particularly in view of the human tendency to place their own particular interests over those of others (Krouse 1983: 61–62). For both Locke and Montesquieu, it was imperative that legally sanctioned political power have limits.

A broader and more effective system of checks and balances along with the old monarchical system had been able to maximise individual freedom. To prevent the abuse and misuse of power and to guarantee and preserve individual liberty, it was necessary that the three arms of government be in separate hands and check and balance one another. The important assertion in Montesquieu was not division but separation of power, for without it, individuals could not enjoy liberty. While classifying each kind of government, he stressed not only on the 'institutional distribution of the sovereign power', but also on the specific qualities that make each constitution work.

Hume, as part of the Scottish Enlightenment, considered the state as embodying a relationship that combined liberty with authority. He considered a mixed constitution good and identified the need for the following: (*i*) Proper governors were to be obeyed; (*ii*) Government was to perform its job; (*iii*) Government was to be neutral—equal, impartial in its penalties, judgements and positive legal activities; (*iv*) Predictability of government action; (*v*) Government could be changed for the good of society; (*vi*) Freedom of the press; and (*vii*) A non-hereditary second chamber.

THE FEDERALIST PAPERS AND THE US CONSTITUTION

The United States of America was the first representative democracy in the modern world. Conscious of the need to protect individuals from the abuse and misuse of power by the state, the American founding fathers stressed the need for certain fundamental rules and principles that would form the basis of a government. For the leaders of the American revolution, the value of liberty for human beings, the threat posed by British actions to American liberty—which saw the establishment of an absolute and arbitrary government—and the need to wrench out despotic tendencies before they became too well-entrenched were of supreme importance. Liberty and safety were the main concerns of the founding fathers.

Madison proposed a federal constitution with separation of powers between the three branches of government to ensure just rule. At the time of the formation of the US, it was generally accepted that there was no need for a Bill of Rights in view of the limited powers that the national government would wield. Madison thought otherwise, and stated that while in Great Britain a Bill of Rights was needed as the Crown posed a threat to the rights of the people, in the US, there was an apprehension about majority rule invading private rights.

In the background of the anti-federalist critique spearheaded by Patrick O'Henry, who attacked the constitution and wanted to replace it through a second convention, Madison sought the ratification of the constitution through amendments in the form of the Bill of Rights, to which Jefferson also agreed. In 1789, Madison announced in the first Congress his intention to propose amendments to the constitution to include a Bill of Rights, which would mainly concern personal rights (and which was ultimately incorporated as the first 10 amendments). It included freedom of speech and the press, the right of assembly, right to security against unreasonable searches, the right to bear arms, and the right to a speedy trial. These rights make it possible for individuals to protect themselves and the government cannot take away their rights. Madison's reasons for the need for a Bill of Rights is explained on the grounds that it would guarantee and safeguard the rights and liberties of every individual. Regarding Madison's crucial role in having the Bill of Rights included in the US constitution, Gordon S. Wood (1969) pointed out that Madison made it possible for the Bill of Rights to be an integral part of the Constitution.

The intellectual backdrop of the debate between the Federalists and anti-Federalists in the US saw a stress on republicanism and its integration with liberalism, as articulated by Locke and Montesquieu, who in turn drew from Aristotle and Polybius and the mixed constitution of Rome. The anti-Federalists made a populist case for direct democracy with citizens participating actively, which the Federalists considered naïve and dangerous. Society, for the federalists in general and Madison in particular, was to be large, diverse and commercial; it would necessarily have many antagonistic 'minority factions', and there would be a need to contain those interests safely within a republican structure. Madison wrote: 'Pure democracies have even been spectacles of turbulence and contention and have in general been as short in their lives as they have been violent in their deaths.'[5] There should be representation but in the House of Representatives, with the Senate filtering it along with the other two branches of the government to 'cool House legislation as a saucer cools hot tea', as Washington said to Jefferson.[6] Moreover, the rigidities of the electoral system would filter through the entire electoral process and build a governmental structure based on separation of powers and checks and balances,[7] but without the democratic content. The presence of the Electoral College for electing the president; the election process of the senate; and the combination of the roles of head of state and that of government in the person of the president are enough indicators of the suspicion with which the Founding Fathers viewed ordinary people. The Federalists won the debate.

PAINE'S *RIGHTS OF MAN*

Paine interpreted and popularised many of Locke's ideas. He convincingly argued that individuals have natural rights; it is to protect these that they join a society. This means that no government can violate or infringe upon these rights; rather, it has to protect them as its first and foremost duty. He criticised the monarchical and aristocratic systems of eighteenth-century Europe, viewing hereditary governments as fraudulent for they depend on people's ignorance and superstition. A hereditary legislator is an absurd idea according to Paine, 'as absurd as a hereditary mathematician, or a hereditary wise man and as absurd as a hereditary poet laureate' (cited in Jackson 1969: 111). A hereditary government is in principle irrational and prone to war, corruption and expense. In contrast, a representative government based on a constitution drafted in a convention, and written and approved by the people is free from such abuses. Paine, influenced by the American constitution, hoped that both England and France would replace their respective corrupt hereditary systems with a republican government of the American kind, which would protect rights and ensure good governance. Since the government would be accountable, it would do its best by having the wisest elected to it. Paine succinctly stressed the importance of a constitution by asserting: 'if politicians are allowed to use their own judgement, they will use this advantage to pursue their own self interest. Government without a constitution is power without right' (ibid.: 115). Paine's sentiments find resonance in the Preamble of the US Constitution:

> We the People of the United States, in order to form a more perfect Union, establish justice, insure domestic tranquillity, provide for common defense, promote the general welfare, and secure the blessings of liberty to ourselves and our posterity, do ordain and establish the Constitution for the United States of America.

NINETEENTH CENTURY—BENTHAM AND J. S. MILL

Constitutionalism and the consolidation of mass representative democracy were the highlights of the nineteenth century, with constitutional liberalism preceding mass representative democracy. During the French Revolution, Bentham developed his theory of constitutional government. Impressed by the strides made by American democracy, with its broad-based suffrage and security of property, he was convinced of the inherent value of democracy, and hoped that England would take a leaf out of the American experience. He regarded constitutional representative democracy as an overall political arrangement, with measures to protect individuals from arbitrary and despotic governments—widespread suffrage, an elected assembly, frequent elections, freedom of the press and association—serving as guarantees against misrule. Constitutional democracy, according to Bentham, was relevant 'to all nations and all governments possessing liberal opinions' (Bentham 1983: 1).

Constitutional liberalism, according to Zakaria (2003), has less to do with the exact procedure of selecting a government than with objectives like protection of an individual's autonomy by providing a bulwark against any form of coercion perpetrated by the state or society. This restates J. S. Mill's formulation, as pointed out by Sabine (1973), that a liberal society is an essential precondition for a liberal state. A related question concerns the factors that led to the broadening of franchise and its acceptance by the propertied because of the constitutional protection of private property. The answer lies in the fact that the constitutional guarantee of property rights facilitated the slow spread and universality of democracy, with one person one vote.

WEIMAR CONSTITUTION

After Germany was defeated in World War I, the first complete democratic election took place in 1919. A new government was formed, and as the social democrats emerged as the largest single party, their leader, Ebert, became the first president. The government was challenged from both the left and the right, but survived despite these challenges. By the end of 1919, a new constitution had been agreed by the National Assembly (Parliament).

This constitution, called the Weimar constitution, is often described as the most perfect constitution conceived in modern times. German unification and the defeat of France in 1870 had made Germany the most powerful nation in continental Europe, with a peculiar mixture of conscription and universal suffrage. This acceptance of liberal principles was incomplete as Bismarck, as the imperial chancellor, was not responsible to the Reichstag (Parliament) but only to the Emperor. 'Constitutionally the German Empire was far from being a liberal state' (Joll 1981: 4). The situation became more illiberal after Bismarck's exit in 1890, and although organised politics evolved in Germany in the 1890s, a proper constitutional state did not evolve till after World War I, when the Weimar Republic was inaugurated. The social democrats and their allies had won a majority in the Reichstag and wanted a constitutional monarchy accountable to it, but could not muster majority support. Constitution-making was completed by August 1919. The essential aspects of a liberal constitution—the basic freedoms of speech, rule of law, equality before law, freedom of religion—were included, along with rights of speech and of assembly. However, one distinguishing feature was the emergency powers of the president, which could suspend political rights in order to restore order. 'The legislators were still living under the shadow of the danger of communist coups and the ability of the President to act quickly and decisively seemed essential' (Grenville 1987: 250). Only later (but too late) would the destruction of the democratic republic be achieved through gross misuse of these powers. Like the US, the president would be elected for a period of seven years by direct popular vote. The president would appoint the chancellor; there was no separation of powers, nor did it resemble the parliamentary system of Great Britain. The chancellor had to win a majority in the Reichstag; if he failed to do so, the president could dissolve it and call for new elections. The incorporation of principles of proportional representation led to a multiplication of political parties and the inevitable coalition governments. It was supposed to be a scientifically structured democracy with the right to universal franchise granted to both men and women.

The failure of the Weimar constitution lay not in its flaws, according to Grenville (1987: 251), 'but in the shortcomings of the politicians of the Weimar period and in the reaction of the German people to the problems that faced them'. James Joll remarked that in Germany, criticism of parliamentary democracy was based on the belief that the 'Weimar constitution had been the product of defeat and of alien influences and that it was somehow part of the dictated terms imposed on Germany by her enemies' (1981: 270). The Nazis levelled this criticism frequently and alleged (without any foundation) that it was inimical to the German spirit. The differences between political culture on the one hand and France and Britain on the other were meticulously highlighted; this was the case in Italy as well. However, in its short life the Weimar constitution did try to institutionalise democracy, and by 1923 had provided an element of prosperity and stability. Hitler's National Socialism could overturn the Weimar Republic only in 1933, four years after the collapse of Wall Street.

The collapse of the Weimar constitution was due to a combination of several issues: the acceptance of a humiliating and unpopular Treaty of Versailles; lack of respect for a democratic government; the introduction of proportional representation in the hope of providing reasonable representation to all groups led to chronic instability, as no political party could win an overall majority and carry out its programme; the inexperience of political parties when it came to operating in a democratic parliamentary system; and a failure to permanently solve the serious economic problems facing the country. This became acute after the Wall Street crash of October 1929, which compelled the US to stop further loans and even to honour the pledges it had already made of the short-term loans. The collapse of the Weimar Republic was a reminder that a constitution, even when drafted excellently, may collapse because of serious national and international crises.

MEIJI RESTORATION AND THE MAKING OF THE JAPANESE CONSTITUTION

After the success of the Meiji Restoration in 1868, the Japanese leadership embarked on a mission to find out an appropriate constitution for Japan. Until then, there had been no written constitution in Japan. There was intense debate both within and outside the government about the idea of a written constitution. Conservative elements were suspicious of democracy and republicanism, while the Freedom and People's Rights Movement demanded the promulgation of a constitution and the immediate establishment of an elected national assembly. In 1881, Itō Hirobumi was appointed chair of a committee to study the various forms of constitutions and in 1882, Itō led an overseas mission to observe the working of various constitutions first-hand. The US constitution was rejected, as the US was in the throes of a civil war. The French constitution was rejected because of its instability. The ideal type was the British one, but the committee did not favour giving too much powers to the parliament. The Prussian constitution was considered suitable to the requirements of Japan. The key issue was the balance between the sovereignty of the Emperor with that of an election representative legislature, which would limit the power of the sovereign. The Emperor was an active ruler with considerable powers over foreign policy and diplomacy, while the elected Diet (parliament) took care of domestic policy. The final version of the constitution was submitted to the Emperor in April 1888. There was no public debate on the drafting of the constitution. The Meiji Constitution, as it came to be known, was promulgated on 11 February 1889 and came into force on 29 November 1890. Interestingly, the Meiji Constitution inspired the 1931 Ethiopian Constitution. Japan's post-war constitution came into effect on 3 May 1947. It stripped the Emperor of all but symbolic powers, abolished peerage, incorporated a bill of rights, granted universal suffrage, and outlawed Japan's right to make war.

PACIFIST CONSTITUTIONS

The Axis powers—Japan, Italy and Germany—in the post-World War II period embraced pacifism and explicitly renounced war. Article 9 under Japan's constitution, drafted under US occupation in 1947, declares that the Japanese people 'forever renounce war as a sovereign right of the nation'. Article 11 of the Italian Constitution declares that Italy 'rejects war as an instrument of aggression'. Article 26 of Germany's Basic Law forbids 'activities tending and undertaken with the intent to disturb peaceful relations between nations, especially to prepare for aggressive war'. Article 9 of Japan's constitution goes to the extent of pledging that Japan will never maintain 'land, sea and air forces, as well as other war potential' and that it will not recognise the 'right of belligerency'. Japan's Self-Defence Forces exist to protect the Japanese homeland. In 2015, the Japanese Diet passed laws that allowed Japan to mount military action in support of a 'close ally' who was attacked. The landslide victory by the Liberal democrats in July 2016 has given Shinzo Abe, its leader and the incumbent Prime Minister, the chance to realise his lifelong ambition of revising Article 9 of the constitution, and making Japan a military power for global leadership and responsibilities.

PLAN FOR PAN-AFRICAN UNITY

The Berlin Conference of 1884–85 divided the African continent amongst the imperial powers without any consideration of geography, ethnicity, language or religion. This led to many insoluble problems in the entire continent in the post-colonial period. Kwame Nkrumah (1909–72) proposed a pan-African unity on the basis of the US constitution in his well-known work *Africa must Unite* (1963), which he thought would help in overriding the artificial divisions imposed by the Western powers. However, though well-conceived, it was never implemented. Nkrumah proposed integration at the continental level, which would be primarily economic, with a loose cooperation of regional institutions in technical, administrative, economic and trade areas.

JUDICIAL REVIEW AND CONVENTIONS

Modern constitutionalism is primarily based on the rule of law.[8] The concept of rule of law establishes a common codified conduct that is equally applicable to all members of a society. Both private citizens and government officials come under its jurisdiction. The rule of law provides the basic foundation for constitutionalism, accountability and limited government. This is reflected in the German concept of *Rechtsstaat*, which means a state order based on law. In the US, it derives sustenance from the constitution and the doctrine of due process. In the UK, as Dicey observed, rule of law is embedded in common law, which provides an alternative model to a codified constitution. He offered a three-fold description of the English constitution. First, it means that the law excludes the exercise of arbitrary power. This means that an Englishman could be punished for breaches of law and for nothing else. Arbitrary punishments resulting from prerogative power or uncontrolled bureaucratic discretion are inconsistent with the rule of regular law. Second, rule of law means the equality of persons before the law, and the equal subjection of the ruler and the ruled to ordinary law administered by ordinary law courts. Third, rule of law in England stands for the idea that citizens' rights are not derived from the constitution, but result from the benefits and liberties conferred on individuals by the remedies provided by the ordinary law of the land.

The task of the judiciary in a modern constitutional system is to interpret or construct the law. Judicial review highlights the constitution as an important basis of government. To perform this important function, judges are to be strictly non-political persons. They are to be above politics; this is seen as safeguarding the important idea of the separation of law and politics. The systems that did not believe in judicial neutrality and impartiality, like Nazi Germany or Communist Soviet Union, could not be described as constitutional states. The show trials in Stalinist Russia in the 1930s, the Soviet constitutions of 1936 and 1977, and the 12-year rule of Hitler in Germany are examples where the judiciary, as an extension of authoritarian regimes, was used only as an agent of ideological repression and political persecution. In contrast, liberal constitutionalism is based on the legality and political neutrality of judges. Any doctrine, like a committed judiciary, is also a negation of liberal constitutionalism. The independence of the judiciary is ensured by the security of tenure of judges, and by strict restrictions on the comments of judges and on court decisions. However, there is a wide gap between theory and practice as this ideal of complete independence and neutrality may be compromised by the involvement of political organs in both recruitment and promotion. Miliband believed that in well-established liberal democracies, conservative judges were mostly appointed and promoted.

The power of judicial review is the most important aspect of the judiciary's role in modern liberal constitutional states. It can review and invalidate laws, decrees, and other directives of other branches of the government, mainly the legislative and the executive. In a codified constitution, the court has the power to declare actions and acts unconstitutional—as being incompatible with the constitution. In un-codified systems, the review is limited to executive actions as ultra views (beyond the powers) to determine whether the executive has exceeded its powers. This principle ensures a government in accordance with the laws and also goes beyond the doctrine of separation of powers by establishing the supremacy of the judiciary.

In the US, the doctrine of judicial review was established in the Marbury versus Madison case in 1803. The critical importance of Marbury lay in the assumption of several powers by the Supreme Court. One was the authority to declare acts of Congress, and by implication acts of the president, unconstitutional if they exceeded the powers granted by the Constitution. But more importantly, the Court became the arbiter of the Constitution, the final authority on what the document meant. As such, the Supreme Court became, both in fact and in theory, an equal partner in government, and it has played that role ever since.

Equally important in the evolution and adaptability of a constitution is the role of customary practices, which have over a period of time evolved to become an integral part of the decision-making process. These practices are called conventions, and although unwritten and unenforceable in the courts, are as important as written rules and are seldom violated.

CONCLUSION

The idea of liberal constitutionalism is intrinsically linked to other ideals like individual freedom, reason, equality, toleration and consent. In the absence of any of these essential pre-requisites, constitutionalism will lose all value. Within the larger parameters of a liberal society, as Bell (1990) remarked, the constitution and the Supreme Court are the bedrocks of modern civil society. They are the most recognisable and identifiable ways of regulating and maintaining the delicate balance between the state and the individual.

Duchacek (1973) described a constitution as a power map which reflects the formal distribution of authority and power within the state. The success of a constitution depends on its capacity to reflect the dominant values of society. The success and stability of a constitutional order and its successful operation depend on this important factor.

A constitutional document, like any other, must be adaptable to changing circumstances and needs; this is performed through amendments. The most successful written constitution of modern times, the US constitution, has been amended only 26 times, which includes the first 10 amendments that form the Bill of Rights. There is also a less formal process of constitution adaptation through judicial interpretation. In many cases, the latter has played a more decisive role than the amendments. This is evident from the US Supreme Court's role during the Roosevelt years of the New Deal legislation and the post-World War II period of the Civil Rights movement.

In contrast to the smooth evolution of US constitutionalism, Canada has seen constant change, which puts considerable strain on the political system. This stems from the uncertainties in the Canadian constitutional process—is it a partnership of two people (the English and the French), or is it a federation of 10 provinces? There is a lack of consensus on fundamental issues like the provincial and federal relationship, and virtually insoluble linguistic, ethnic and cultural conflicts. This contrasting picture of the US and Canada reveals that the success of a constitution is determined by two basic factors: (*i*) when the ambit of the constitution is limited and its attempt confined to the political and not extended to the social; and (*ii*) when constitutional provisions reflect dominant social interests and values. The success of the US constitution is because of its limited central government, which continues—except during the civil war of 1861–65; there is larger societal cohesion and only minor contradictions exist in their society. Simon Bolivar (1783–1830), was a lifelong devotee of ideals of freedom, reason and progress, but not a slave of the Enlightenment. He rejected not only the absolutist state, but also the colonial state. He pleaded for true independence under the liberal constitution.

However, in contemporary complex mass societies, a functioning constitutional machinery is the basic pre-requisite of a well-ordered society. For instance, Dahl's group-based democratic theory of polyarchy (see Chapter 13) accepted the utmost necessity of a constitutional order. As Medvedev (1982) observed, democracy is as much a necessity for economics as it is for politics in today's world; and a basic constitutional document is necessary for a vibrant and successful democracy. In the background of the failures of recent examples of strong unconstitutional states, both of the right and the left, a liberal constitutional framework is seen as neither cosmetic nor superfluous, but as an essential requirement of our age. Aristotle envisaged the value of constitutional rule and rule by the middle class in different circumstances, which still form the bedrock of liberal constitutionalism. This institutional approach received fresh vindication in contemporary, worldwide democratic consolidation, with its emphasis on a constitutional order. It brought into the open the basic flaws of the structural-functional and political economy approaches as they undervalued the need for constitutionalism for good and proper governance. The primacy of a constitutional order was accepted by New Institutionalism, the dominant school of contemporary comparative politics.

NOTES

1. In a speech delivered to the Lords and Commons of the Parliament at White Hall in 1610, James I stated: 'The state of monarchy is the supremest thing upon the earth. For kings are not only God's lieutenants upon earth, and sit upon God's throne, but even by God himself they are called gods.' See also Chapter 6.

2. The Magna Carta, also known as the Magna Carta Libertatum (the Great Charter of Freedoms) was introduced by some notable barons of the thirteenth century as an act of rebellion against their King, King John I (1166–1216). John I became unpopular among his subjects because of increased taxes, his excommunication by Pope Innocent III in 1209, and his unsuccessful and costly attempts to regain his empire in Northern France. His oppressive rule, according to the barons, did not adhere to the Charter of Liberties. The Charter consisted of a preamble and 63 clauses and dealt mainly with feudal concerns which had little impact outside thirteenth-century England. However, at the heart of the Charter was the idea that the law is not simply the whim of the king or government; that all are equal under the law and all can be held to account. Clause 39 of the Charter contained in an embryonic manner the guarantee of trial by jury and of habeas corpus, and inspired England's Petition of Right (1628) and the Habeas Corpus Act (1679). Among them was the right of the church to be free from government interference, the rights of all free citizens to own and inherit property and to be protected from excessive taxes. It established the right of widows who owned property to choose not to remarry, and established principles of due process and equality before the law. It also contained provisions forbidding bribery and official misconduct. Lord Denning (1899–1999), a distinguish British Judge, described the Magna Carta 'as the greatest constitutional document of all time—the foundation of the freedom of the individual against the arbitrary authority of the despot'.
3. King Charles I (1625–49), having failed to receive a grant of taxation for the war with Spain, resorted to a forced loan, effectively a tax which the parliament had not authorised. This forced loan met with substantial resistance, with some prominent gentlemen imprisoned for their refusal to comply. When five of those men tried to secure their freedom by issuing a writ of habeas corpus, the Crown argued that it had the power to commit people to prison at its own discretion without stating a specific legal reason. By 1628, Charles had no option but to turn again to Parliament. When it met, the House of Commons expressed its determination to secure a commitment from the King to observe the rule of law, since the Crown had breached clause 39 of the Magna Carta. The House of Commons presented a Petition of Rights which, as suggested by Edward Coke, had the same status as an Act of Parliament, and was therefore as strong a guarantee of the subject's rights as the Magna Carta itself. The *Petition of Right* contained four main points: (*i*) No taxes could be levied without Parliament's consent; (*ii*) No English subject could be imprisoned without cause—thus reinforcing the right of *habeas corpus*; (*iii*) No quartering of soldiers in citizens' homes; and (*iv*) No martial law may be used in times of peace.
4. The common law tradition is one that is generally un-codified and based on customs across the country. It emerged in England in the Middle Ages. It was largely based on precedent, meaning the judicial decisions that have already been made in similar cases. These precedents were maintained over a period of time by the courts through its records. Common-law systems extensively use statutes and judicial cases are regarded as important sources of law, giving judges an active role in developing rules. Common-law systems are found in countries that have been England's colonies or have been influenced by the Anglo-Saxon tradition, such as Australia, Canada, India and the United States.
5. Most mass societies of today, being representative democracies, have incorporated features of direct democracy. For instance, Switzerland is one of the oldest democratic republican constitutions, going back to 1848, with a federal structure composed of 26 cantons (since 1976) with far-reaching autonomy. The Swiss confederation consolidated from below and since the Napoleonic wars, has faced a situation similar to America. Its federal structure is integrated with its traditional devices of direct democracy, with initiatives and referendums becoming a regular part of national governance. Any amendment to the Swiss constitution requires a referendum, but also needs a simple majority of the cantons in the legislature; this effectively means that half the cantons that might represent a minority of Swiss voters can overrule the majority in a referendum, thus addressing Madison's concern about majoritarian tyranny or the 'cooling' that Washington spoke of. In Sweden, a representative parliamentary democracy, the office of ombudsman, linked to the Parliament and not the executive, was established. It was designed to be a supervisory agency independent of the executive branch of government, charged with the responsibility of protecting the rights of the people.

Recall is another measure to secure greater accountability of elected representatives by providing a method wherein the electorate may vote to terminate the appointment before the normal date on which re-election would occur in the event of certain rules being breached, or on account of misdemeanour. This measure is normally associated with direct/plebiscitory democracies. The Paris Commune of 1871 contained the principle of the workers' right to recall their elected representatives at any time, emulated subsequently by the 1905 and 1917 revolutions in Russia. Marx took note of this feature while writing about it, viewing it as intrinsic to majoritarian workers' democracy, as opposed to the formal bourgeois democracy. This device became popular in the USA in the 1890s to 1920s, which was known as the Progressive era. South Dakota adopted initiatives in 1898, followed by Utah, Oregon, Montana and Oklahoma, mixing in their own cocktails of direct democracy. Eighteen states permit recall elections to remove state officials, although some states require specific grounds for recall. The recall device was first adopted in Los Angeles municipality in 1903. Michigan and Oregon were the first states to adopt recall procedures for states officials in 1908. In 1911, California adopted the three tools of modern direct democracy—referendum, initiative and recall. Minnesota is the more recent example. The most common threshold in terms of signatures required is 25 per cent of the total number of votes in the last general election. Only two governors, Lynn Frazier in North Dakota in 1921 and Gray Davis in California in 2003, were removed through recall over a dispute about state-owned industries and mismanagement of the state budget, respectively. Usually, recall works better in local bodies than at the state level. The California system, unlike Switzerland, is designed to be 'confrontational', with no safeguards against what Madison termed as the majority tyrannising the minorities and the minority factions overtaking the system. It encourages special interests to wage war through the ballot until one lobby prevails over the other. The California state has become 'dysfunctional', 'ungovernable' and 'failed'. Enacted in 1995, British Colombia in Canada is the only parliamentary system, similar to Britain, which has the right to recall. Voters in that province can petition to have a sitting representative removed from office, even a premier leading a government. If enough registered voters sign the petition, the Speaker of the legislature announces before the House that the member has been recalled and a bye-election follows as soon as possible. In January 2003, a record 22 recall efforts had been launched. However, no one has technically been recalled.

Article 72 of the 1999 Constitution of Venezuela also enables the recall of any elected representative, including the president. The recall clause has been used in the Venezuelan recall referendum of 2004, which attempted to remove President Hugo Chavez. Of the techniques of direct democracy, it is believed that referendum does not subvert representative democracy, but makes it accountable. Initiatives damage representative democracy. Had referendum and not initiatives been the order of the day in California, it would perhaps not be in such a mess. In California, the problem is not with regard to recall. In Britain, a referendum was recently held on Britain's membership in the European Union.

6. Rule of law refers to the procedures, principles and constraints contained in the law, in which the citizen can find redress against another, however powerful and/or influential, and against the officers of the state itself, for any act which involves a breach of the law. It is not merely important to declare that the constitution is supreme. It is equally important, for the citizen, that the law is enforced. This, at the minimum, suggests an independence of the judiciary if the law is to be enforced against the state. However, it ought to be remembered that it is the state that makes and revises the law, and it is the state that controls the appointment and dismissal of judges. Rule of law is opposed to 'rule of persons', which is normally equated with an unfettered and arbitrary exercise of power. As far as arbitrariness is concerned, there are three related concerns—first is the danger that rulers will simply govern willfully and capriciously, resulting in inconsistency or incoherence of policy and leaving people confused; second, people will feel dominated by the rulers; and third, arbitrariness could result in oppression, leading to an overriding of people's legitimate expectations and needs. Aristotle, writing about the merits of constitutional rule as opposed to personal rule, said: first, it is a rule in the general or common interest of the people rather than one or few (as is the case with personal rule); second, it is lawful as government is carried on in accordance with general regulations and not by arbitrary decrees. A government cannot act contrary to the constitution. Third, constitutional government signifies rule by consent of the people rather than by force.

In the international arena, rule of law refers to the generally agreed-upon rules by nation-states, applied by international courts or adjudicators whose decisions are generally accepted and obeyed by those subject to their jurisdiction. Aristotle's *Politics* was the first to recognise that individual human judgement on each and every case of social conflict that comes before a judge was not likely to produce fairness and equity, and thus recommended that the judge limit himself to applying previously fixed rules to factual cases. Following this idea, the rule of law was seen as a major contribution to equality and liberty. It requires legislatures to look only at the abstract feature of a problem and to lay down a general rule, and judges need to look only at relevant characteristics under the immediate rule in deciding cases. A judge should decide according to the rule laid down and not according to their own sense of justice or personal preferences. This can at times lead to largely similar cases being judged very differently due to marginal circumstantial variations. In the wider sense, the rule of law is associated with the notion of limited government, procedural guarantees of the due process of law, fair legal procedures, fair trials, natural justice, judicial independence, and access to courts for the enforcement of rights conferred by the law. This means that laws have to be drafted with precision, not retrospectively in operation, at least in criminal matters, and they should not impose penalties on named individuals or delegate ill-defined or unduly broad discretionary powers.

7. The idea of bicameralism came up to check the tyranny of the majority. In the US, with the exception of Nebraska, there were bicameral legislatures in every state. Bicameralism is strongly linked to Federalism. The US is an example of strong bicameralism, with both houses exerting equal or offsetting powers, and legislations must be received and approved by both houses. There are just about 63 countries that have bicameral legislatures, compared to over 100 countries with unicameral legislatures.
8. An important safeguard is Gerrymandering, wherein the boundaries of electoral districts are drawn in a way that does not give one party an unfair advantage over its rivals. Filibustering is a legislative procedure employed during debate to delay or prevent a vote on the bill. Filibustering goes back to the days of the Roman Empire. Senator Cato was known to be its best practitioner.

8

FEDERALISM

> *...federal principle consists in the division of power in such a way that the powers to be exercised by the general government are specified and the residue is left to the regional governments. It is not enough that general and regional government should each be independent in its own sphere; that sphere must be marked out in a particular way. The residuary powers, as they are called, must lie with the regional governments. On this view a government is not federal if the powers of the regional governments are specified and the residue is left to the general government*
>
> Wheare 1963: 11

> *Federalism is a state of states.*
>
> Forsyth 1981: 15

> *Federalism is self-rule plus shared rule.*
>
> Elazar 1987: 350

Nation-states as a unit create the world political map. However, equally important is the fact that within this façade of unity, nation-states and their political structures are fragmented, with different levels of power and authority. The most significant division in this plural power structure is the division of power and function between a union or central government and different types of provincial, state and local outfits. The three major models of this distribution of power are broadly categorised as three different forms of government: the unitary system, federal system and con-federal system. The divergent pressures of centripetal and centrifugal forces are accommodated differently under these three categories.

ADVANTAGES OF CENTRALISATION AND DECENTRALISATION

All modern nations are geographically divided into a central or national government, regional outfits and local bodies. The central or national government is a prime necessity for two important reasons: (*i*) the nation-state acts on the world stage through the central government, which performs all facets of international relations like treaties, alliances, trade, defence and other agreements, representing the nation or providing the personnel for membership to international organisations. The central government looks after the key areas of foreign, diplomatic and defence policies exclusively. (*ii*) The central government mediates between provincial outfits and local bodies in order to facilitate cooperation between the different units in matters of mutual interest. This necessitates the central government assuming a supervisory role for regulating economic aspects like internal trade, transport, communication, and other related areas. The modern planning process and even the processes of globalisation and liberalisation have increased the role and powers of the central government. There are advantages and disadvantages of both centralised and decentralised governments. The debate centres around two propositions:

efficiency and effective administration, and responsiveness to the democratic aspirations of the people. Both arguments overlap, but usually, the former supports centralisation and the latter, decentralisation.

Arguments in favour of centralisation are the following:

(*a*) First and foremost is national unity; the central government speaks for the entire nation, keeping in mind the overriding national interests, and not giving into the particularistic and narrow interests of pressure groups, and/or ethnic, regional and linguistic groups. A strong centre defends national interest, which refers to the common interests of all inhabitants, whereas a weak central authority reflects the intense rivalry among sectional interests, disharmony and distrust. In certain exceptional and extreme cases, such a polity becomes a failed state.

(*b*) The second concerns a uniform pattern of legality and governance. A central authority can and does formulate laws and provide the guidance and framework applicable throughout the country. This is an essential pre-requisite for efficiency and order, as this widens the scope for mobility and commerce within a common legal, educational and infrastructural order. In the absence of such universally accepted norms, given the wide variations in legal and administrative structures, localism will predominate over efficiency and the rule of law.

(*c*) Decentralisation may be advantageous to the more prosperous regions with abundant natural resources and geographical features like a coastline, but would be disadvantageous to less prosperous regions. The intervention of the central government with its policy of transfers would create a mechanism of rough equality and parity, without which discontent and protest would become permanent destabilising factors in the political process. Aristotle's (Barker 1979: 247) dictum that everywhere, inequality is the cause of revolutions remains valid within the internal arrangement of modern mega-nations.

(*d*) The presence of a unifying central government is necessary for managing a single currency and implementing taxation and spending policies. Even in the context of planned economic growth, it is important in providing the infrastructure of roads, railways and links to airports and sea routes.

(*e*) In the absence of a central government, local or provincial governments may not be interested in protecting individual or minority rights. Due to the inherent localism of local parties, pressure groups may be more powerful in subverting the democratic process in a small area. Accountability may also suffer in the absence of a larger legal apparatus. Local considerations may allow sub-human practices like slavery or bonded labour, which are not possible in larger units.

(*f*) The central government legitimises power on the basis of a larger mandate, which allows it to formulate national policies.

(*g*) It is also argued that a strong central government is necessary for good governance and implementation of the rule of law, and to stop the secessionist designs of some peripheral groups. However, it is generally agreed that over-centralisation is counter-productive; the disintegration of the former Soviet Union reinforces this contention.

THE ARGUMENTS FOR DECENTRALISATION

Hobbes remarked that human desire is the desire for power, which ceases only in death.

(*a*) This uncontrollable urge to exercise power in its absolute form can have disastrous consequences, as Lord Acton pointed out. A strong central government in the absence of countervailing state governments may act tyrannically.

(*b*) Citizen participation is more visible in a decentralised political system. Such participation results in a widespread dispersal of political knowledge, leading to a well-informed citizenship which also helps in broadening the base of political recruitment.

(*c*) Democratic accountability is easier to establish in a small place rather than in a larger unit, where the average citizen feels insignificant and powerless.

(*d*) The central government is a distant outfit, both in terms of geography and politics. It is impersonal and remote, and in a situation of mass indifference and alienation, legitimacy is better established through smaller identities.

(*e*) Efficiency increases with compactness and when politicians and administrators have a thorough knowledge of their areas.

(*f*) The right to make decisions can be educational and develops (as J. S. Mill had pointed out) a responsible citizenship.

(*g*) Interesting experiments and political initiatives may emerge from such wide participation.

(*h*) The administrative burdens of the centre can be shared.

(*i*) Decentralisation can lead to healthy competition between different political units.

(*j*) Local services are managed more efficiently and economically through local efforts.

(*k*) In mega-democratic nations of our times, a decentralised administration helps to perpetuate the distinctive identities of various groups.

In recent years, decentralisation theories have been supported by both political theorists and politicians. But it is an accepted fact that decentralisation leads to increased inequality and retards the development of a common identity, which is an essential requirement for a successful democracy.

ORIGINS OF FEDERALISM

Huntington (1966)[1] rightly declared federalism as the only significant institutional innovation of the US. Like political parties, federalism is one of the major attributes of the modern political system. The significance of these two developments has to be understood in the context of a fundamental divergence between traditional and modern politics. At the level of both political consciousness and political development, traditional political structures accommodate only a small segment of society, for instance, as was the practice in Athenian democracy. But the modern political system derives its sustenance from mass participation. Political parties and federalism emerged to facilitate the accommodation of this mass participation in an orderly manner. They are the modern innovations, whereas other important institutions like bureaucracy, elections, or a constitution have ancient roots. It is modernity that explains the exclusion of federalism from Aristotle's classification of the constitutions. The term 'federalism' derives from the Latin word '*foedus*', meaning a league, pact, covenant; a federal system is based on the idea of a permanent contract between political units that creates a new political entity without abolishing the original constituent units. According to Dicey (1908: 141), a federation balances forces of centralisation with those of decentralisation.

Image 8.1: Albert Venn Dicey (1835–1922)

Source: https://commons.wikimedia.org/wiki/File:Albert_Venn_Dicey.jpg.

A federal state, unlike a unitary one, is a conscious creation that emerges from a deliberate constitutional settlement. The US emerged from a meeting of the 13 American states in Philadelphia in 1787. Similar conventions took place in Switzerland in 1848; Canada in 1867; and Australia in 1897/98. Four of the largest states in the world—Australia, Brazil, Canada and the US—are federal states.

The emergence of federalism in modern times is intrinsically linked to the US constitution-making process after it won independence from Britain in 1776. In the immediate aftermath of the victory, patriotic sentiments were replaced by assertions of local sovereignty, not as Americans, but as New Yorkers, Georgians, Marylanders, Vermonters, and the like, acting as members of independent nations. Frantic and rival claims for unsettled land became apparent and the states developed their own currency systems and taxes, ignoring the other states of the Union. Even relations with foreign countries were established. There were no sentiments for a nation and national debt became somebody else's headache.

The Congress was the only national body in existence as the army, the navy and the Marine Corps were immediately abolished against the background of a deep distrust of standing armies. The Congress was the only institution to devise the form of a national government. Nine days after the *Declaration of Independence* in 1776, it appointed a committee to draw up the Articles of Confederation, which would be effective after ratification by the States. In a month's time, the debating agenda was fixed, but it took almost five years for it to become a law of the national government. Under the Articles of the Confederation, the Congress was to be the only governing body in which each state would have equal voting rights. Its function was restricted to foreign affairs, and to the appointments of national naval and military commanders. The States were required to pay for the costs of defence and of the central government itself on the basis of the value of the land that each state owned. The land question remained a disputed one, and there were other complexities, such as the extradition of criminals, free exchange of state citizenship, and the proper quota of troops from each state on the basis of its white population.

With regard to the Articles of Confederation, there is a near unanimity among historians that it was unworkable. Cooke remarked that 'as an instrument looking not so much toward a noble and harmonious world as to the actual government of a scattering of small nations, it is quite as impressive as the Charter of the United Nations, another document of dubious practicality' (1974: 131). The Articles presented a document, hoping to begin 'a firm league of friendship'. It was a document 'to substitute both Crown and Parliament' (ibid.). However, there were inherent weaknesses. For instance, the Congress lacked the power to raise federal taxes to maintain the central government. It could not regulate shipping and lacked any overriding authority essential for effectiveness. The consequences were grim as within four years after the War of Independence, the nation was near bankrupt and lacking in strong leadership. The functioning of the confederation clearly exhibited that there was no nation called the United States of America; instead, it was the Disunited States of America.

In the spring of 1787, the Founding Fathers met at Philadelphia to make the Articles work, despite their overall suspicion of democracy. Furthermore, Patrick Henry (1736–99) refused to attend the meeting as he 'smelt a rat in Philadelphia tending towards monarchy' (cited in Cooke 1974: 132). The assembly consisted of some of the most principled and enlightened people, whom Jefferson called 'demigods'. It was a group of 55 men, who represented the elite of government, business and law, with more than half being lawyers. The Articles of Confederation were grossly inadequate, and it was decided that they had to be replaced with a more effective and workable document. They were greatly suspicious of monarchy and the standing army. For eight weeks, the assembly deliberated and found a parliamentary system to be unworkable, given the wide geography and 150 years of practice of different types of government. The dilemma facing the Founding Fathers was, as J. R. Pole remarked, that 'the convention had no power to give anything to the states, the problem was how to take existing power away from them and yet secure their consent' (ibid.: 134).

Consequently, the most difficult part was chalking out a workable balance of power between the central government and the States. Three different perspectives on this can be analysed through the different views of

Hamilton, Mason and Madison. Hamilton advocated a strong and powerful central government. He preferred an aristocratic government with lifetime executives, and senate members who were all property-owning with a right to veto the laws of the States. Mason stood at the opposite end; he advocated the weakest possible central government and a continuation of the structure of confederacy. Against the background of the failure of the Articles he had few supporters, and sensing the lack of support, he emphasised individual rights and argued for the inclusion of the Bill of Rights, to be patterned after the Virginia Declaration of Rights that he had authored. His propositions were, however, rejected. Subsequently, though, the first 10 amendments of the constitution did incorporate the Bill of Rights. Madison was convinced about the inadequacies of the Articles and explored the possibility of the new system tackling an unprecedented situation. He was also convinced that reconciliation was impossible, given the 'aggressive sovereignty' of the states. Through a deep study of confederations, both ancient and modern, he managed to convince the delegates that no confederation had ever succeeded in resolving conflicts between the national and provincial set-ups.

To sort out the mess, Madison concentrated on the purpose of government itself and found that meaning lay in acting 'upon and for individual citizen', which was his own novel innovation. Another related concern was the doctrine of majority tyranny and the need for minority rights. The enduring dimensions of the US Constitution were thus taking shape. Madison reasoned on the basis of a comparative survey of other systems, reinforced by a liberal scepticism of human nature. He even anticipated the rise of political parties and did not decry factions, either. Factions, according to him, were the natural result of disagreement, and as such an instrument for expressing one's liberty. The only check necessary was to see that no faction becomes tyrannical. To achieve this, the largest share of powers should be left to the states and the national Congress should represent all types of men, interests and factions. Wheare (1963: 11–12) was of the opinion that if residue is left with the general government and if the powers of the regional governments are specified, then it is not a federal government. He considered the Constitution of the United States the embodiment of the federal principle because it 'names certain subjects over which the general legislation has control and it provides that powers not so delegated to the general government remain with the states'. Conflict is endemic, according to Madison; he only cautioned against the overwhelming presence of a single ideology or any one faction. Balance was the key to Madison's scheme and a precaution against one powerful interest grabbing all the power; for this, he proposed that separate branches of government be responsible to separate constituencies, accepting that a collision of interest is natural and healthy. He argued that ambition must be countered with ambition. The interest of man must be connected with the constitutional rights of the place.

Madison, in contrast to Hamilton and Mason, provided a balanced arrangement of power sharing, both within the central government and between the centre and states. Equal representation in the Senate boosted the morale of the smaller states, while the democratic spirit of representation was preserved in the House of Representatives. As an assurance to the states, all residual powers were earmarked for them, which meant that there was no attempt to curtail their powers. Even after Hamilton realised his scheme had been rejected, he wrote four essays with a plea to the states to ratify the constitution. Ratification by states was achieved, although by a thin majority in some states like Virginia. The first modern, democratic federal system emerged, and with minor modifications, has survived for more than 200 years. In essence, American federalism as laid down in the Constitution is the brainchild of Madison; however, it was accepted by others and was an example of compromise. It is this spirit of accommodation and compromise that lies at the heart of any successful constitutional order and is the basic precondition of an enduring federal order.

ESSENTIAL PRE-REQUISITES FOR SUCCESSFUL FEDERALISM

Dicey (1908: 141) identified two basic requirements for the formation of a federal state: (*i*) a group of countries connected closely by geography, historical antecedents, race, or similar attributes of a 'common nationality'.

An earlier common sovereignty is also an advantage for a federal formation. (*ii*) It must exhibit a sense among the people that they 'desire union and must not desire unity'. As a consequence, a federal state has to reconcile national unity while preserving the rights of the component states. This is done through the promulgation of a constitution that elaborately divides the powers between the two different set-ups. National concerns are placed with the central government and regional concerns are left to the states. This fundamental idea of a federation is expressed in the Preamble of the US Constitution, which begins with the famous phrase, '*We the people of America*'. The Tenth Amendment makes it more explicit by stating that the powers belong to the people. A slightly amended phrase finds expression in the Swiss confederation. A federal constitution has to be rigid as it prescribes the distribution of powers which are defined and demarcated. A Supreme Court, as custodian of the constitution, is also an essential requirement of a federation. The Supreme Court is the source of ultimate power in a federation, but is of no use in a unitary system. The smooth functioning and long-term survival of a federation depends on the wilful observance of Supreme Court judgements. The appointments of judges must not be left to the judiciary and it is the court, and not the legislature, that is the arbiter of the constitution.

Dicey (1908: 144) summarised the essential basis of a successful federation thus: a federal system

> can flourish only among communities imbued with a legal spirit and trained to revere the law. Federalism substitutes litigation for legislation and none but a law fearing people will be inclined to regard the decision of a suit as equivalent to the enactment of a law. The main reason why the United States has carried out the federal system with unqualified success is that the people of the union are more thoroughly imbued with legal ideas than any other existing nation.

Dicey (1908: 150) mentioned three weaknesses of federalism: (*i*) a federal government is inherently weaker than a unitary one; (*ii*) it tends to be more conservative because of the rigidities of a federal constitution and the reverential attitude of the people towards the constitution; and (*iii*) federalism means legalism, and 'a special danger arises lest the judiciary should be unequal to the burden laid upon them'. He also notes the many similarities between the American and the British political system, in spite of the wide difference between a unitary and a federal system and between a written and an unwritten constitution, because of the common inheritance of a common law tradition. In this sense, Dicey anticipated the findings of Almond and Verba's (1963) notion of civic culture.

IS FEDERALISM AN IDEOLOGY?

Division of power and protection of minorities are important aspects of federalism. 'Federalism' means certain types of governmental mechanisms and political processes, leading to the question of whether federalism is a political doctrine or an ideology. Burgess and Gagnon (1993: 3–13) distinguished between federalism as an ideology and federation, which is a description. While conceding that federalism is not an ideology like liberalism or socialism, he stated that it is still an ideology for two reasons: it is a prescriptive guide to action, and philosophically, it is a normative prescription of an ideal type of political organisation. Smith (1995: 4), like Burgess, also considered federalism an ideology as it believes in 'diversity through unity'. King (1982: 75) considered federalism a sub-category of pluralism. However, Forsyth (1981) believed it was illogical and impractical to categorise federalism as an ideology as, like feudalism and capitalism, federalism is more than a political ideal; it is also inapplicable in actual political and economic structures.

The crux of the matter is that federalism, like political parties, is an innovation of modern times to deal with the problems of mass democracies. Both flourish and survive within the larger framework of liberal democracy. A one-party system is inconceivable in a democratic order; similarly, the ingredients of a federation are only possible within a liberal democratic framework. While a unitary state can survive for a considerable period as a non-democratic one, a federal state can only survive as a liberal democracy. This is exemplified by the fact that both the erstwhile Soviet Union and Yugoslavia were technically federal states, but collapsed like houses of cards as they were federal in form but not in spirit. Federalism is the practical application of the liberal doctrine of limiting state power, and dividing it constitutionally in larger formations. In this sense, federalism is an application of liberalism in practice.

Preston King (1982: 94) detailed certain general characteristics of a federal system: (*a*) primacy of the territorial representation; (*b*) representation on the basis of at least two sub-national levels, that is, regional and local; (*c*) participation of the regional units in the decision-making process at the federal level electorally; and (*d*) alteration in the previous three arrangements through only extraordinary constitutional measures, and not through a simple majority vote or an executive decision. The last point is the most important as both division of power, and regional autonomy and representation are constitutionally guaranteed. The centre does not have the right to abolish or alter the boundaries of a provincial unit. This also means the supremacy of a written constitution and an arbiter mutually binding the union, states and individual citizens, like the Supreme Court. A formal role of the states in the amendment process is another protective measure to balance the power between the centre and the states. In the US, the most successful federation, a constitutional amendment requires a two-thirds majority in both houses of the Congress, as well as ratification by three-fourths of the states.

Regional participation in the policymaking process at the national level is a pre-requisite for a successful federal enterprise. Dual voting of citizens, at the regional and the central levels, is one important device. Moreover, the upper chamber is designed to reflect this power-sharing arrangement and protect the smaller states. As Dahl (2001) observed, the composition of the US Senate is based on undemocratic principles, but is good for US federalism. The arguments for differentiated citizenship derive inspiration from this constitutional arrangement, but are flawed in that they transfer a political arrangement to the social sphere where the large parameters for determining social stratification and inequality operate.

TYPOLOGY OF FEDERAL AND UNITARY SYSTEMS

In the contemporary world, most states are unitary with sovereignty lying exclusively with the central government. Regional and local authorities may make policies and implement them, but only at the behest of the central government. Since authority is centralised, the central government can abolish or alter the set-ups at the lower level. The saying that the British parliament can do anything except 'make a man a woman and a woman a man' exhibits the power of the central government in a unitary system. Unitary states have a long lineage of kingship, for example Britain, France, Denmark and Japan. Unitary forms are also common in smaller democracies which are homogenous, like the Scandinavian countries. With a tradition of highly centralised and personalised presidential rule in Latin America, the smaller nations are unitary. Unicameralism is also a feature in many unitary systems. A unitary system is supposed to be more efficient and orderly. Here, again, the record is a mixed; many unitary states have the same forces of bargaining and distribution as in federalism.

Broadly, unitary states can be divided into three types: (*i*) Territorial decentralisation, in which the central government is situated away from the capital in the sense that the bulk of government activity takes place outside the capital. It is supposed to be a system in which local government officials perform their jobs better because of their knowledge of the local area, and the central government concentrates only on policy formulation and not on execution. (*ii*) A decentralised polity, implying delegation of authority and power to local authorities. However, the policies are formulated at the national level. (*iii*) Devolution, which is similar to a federal structure with decision-making power delegated to the local level. Great Britain is a good example of this model, making it a unitary system in name, while in practice it functions like a centralised federation. The trend in unitary systems is to have multilevel governmental structures with intermediate levels of functional categories. In Europe, the EU policy of distributing funds directly to regions has encouraged regional groupings within the unitary systems. Regional governments have also been authorised to legislate on areas of competence. The trend in many unitary systems is to settle for regional government, rather than self-government.

K. C. Wheare (1963: 10) stated that a federal state is based on a doctrine of divided sovereignty, which is manifested in two ways: (*a*) division of powers between two sets of government, and (*b*) within the designated sphere, each acts independently and equally. But within this broad characterisation are many different types of federal arrangement. Wheare admitted that there were systems that are federal in name only, as the federating units are not equal or independent. These are termed **Quasi-federations** as one tier, normally the central one, can intervene in the jurisdiction of the other (the states), resulting in the latter's subordination and dependence. Such a system resembles the unitary one. India and Canada are examples of quasi-federations.

Federalism is also incompatible with an overdeveloped and authoritarian regime. The communist states, the erstwhile USSR, Czechoslovakia and Yugoslavia were termed 'pseudo federations' as behind the facade of formal division was a highly centralised and sophisticated control of power, both ideologically and coercively, making federalism inoperative. **Dual Federalism,** also referred to as **layer cake federalism**, is one in which there is proper division of power and separate authority, with rough parity between the two tiers of government. The term was used to describe the federal evolution in the US till the New Deal legislations, assuring that each level performed their functions allocated by the Constitution. This may be described as the ideal type of federalism. It continues to have considerable appeal among a large section of Americans even today. However, in reality this dogged independence is rarely practised as the basis of a successful federalism is interdependence and not independence.

Cooperative Federalism, also referred to as **marble cake federalism,** is one where there is functional cooperation, partnership and interdependence between the national government and the states, with emphasis on collaboration rather than conflict and separateness. Since its inception, the German Federation has been based on this principle. In the US, since the New Deal, cooperative federalism has replaced dual federalism. With increasing intervention in states and regulations like the minimum wage applicable throughout the nation, the federal government has been playing a pivotal role even in domestic policies, which traditionally were reserved to the states. The balance of power is so much in favour of the central government that it is even described as 'coercive federalism'. **Creative federalism**, also known as **picket fence federalism,** predominated during 1960 to 1980 in the US. This relationship was characterised by overloaded cooperation and cross-cutting regulations. **New Federalism** signifies the revival of the old dual federalism, and was initiated by Ronald Reagan with his overall attack on big government and the growing welfare budget. Rejecting the neo-Keynesian consensus developed since the New Deal legislations, Reagan, as a believer in the New Right philosophy of limited government, introduced the concept of new federalism, which attempted to transfer the responsibility of managing and funding welfare measures from the federal to the state governments.

Federalism in Canada functions on the basis of a federal power-sharing arrangement between the English-speaking and French-speaking Canadians; it has, however, met with only limited success. The attempt, termed **'asymmetrical federalism',** to grant greater autonomy to French-speaking Quebec with a special status has not succeeded yet. The term **bargaining federalism** is used in the context of the post-communist Russian federation to refer to a powerful centre, which controls the purse and has the power to fix developmental priorities as part of a planned national development. The units bargain to receive more central allocation and financial grants than the others. This system underlies intense rivalry and also an absence of well-laid out guidelines and framework for a division of resources between the centre and the states. **Judicial federalism** refers to a federal arrangement in which the Supreme Court, as in the US, normally supports the central government to further reduce the powers of the states. The same is true of Australia. On the other hand, Canada has moved away from centralisation to decentralisation. Even in the US, with the resurgence of the New Right regime beginning with Reagan, the Supreme Court has tilted more towards the states than the centre. The financial balance is also in favour of the states.

Competitive Federalism means that regional or local governments compete with each other. One of the most important features of such competitive federal structures is regional autonomy. Regions have the right to autonomously decide on the structure and scope of public goods provision, with public goods financed completely out of the tax prices paid by residents of the region. Competition takes place through residents 'voting with their feet' for the jurisdiction that best matches their preferences. **Fiscal federalism** is a system of transfer of payments by which a federal government shares its revenues with lower levels of government with the purpose of enforcing national rules and standards. There are two primary types of transfers: conditional and unconditional. A conditional transfer from the centre to the state or province involves a certain set of conditions, like spending instructions. The Canadian Health Transfer is an example of this. Unconditional grant is usually a cash or tax point transfer with no spending instructions. The federal equalisation transfer is an example of this.

CONCLUSION

A federal system is based on a constitutional division of power. Federalism arose out of the failure of the confederation to provide stability. A confederation, with its emphasis on the primacy of the federating units, results in a very loose and negative federation with a toothless centre. The anarchists led by Pierre Joseph Proudhon (1809–65) advocated this type of arrangement. The major drawback of the confederation theory is that it is unworkable; it retains independent states and hopes for an ideal, unanimous decision-making process, which is practically impossible. The US tried a con-federal arrangement twice, first in the form of a continental congress (1774–81) and then under the Articles of Confederation (1781–89).

In recent times, the Commonwealth of Independent States (CIS), which replaced the USSR in 1991, is an example of a con-federal arrangement. It comprises 11 of the former Soviet Republics, with Georgia and three Baltic states having refused to join the Confederation. However, its executive authority had neither permanence nor direction. It was more of a regional organisation, as a forum for debate, discussion and arbitration. But confederations have little chance of long-term survival. A confederation inevitably moves in two diametrically opposite directions: either towards a federation, as happened in the case of the US, or collapse due to centrifugal forces and disintegration, as has happened in the case of the CIS.

Wheare (1963) made an interesting distinction between constitutional provisions and the actual practice of government. The Canadian central government has the right to veto over provincial legislation, which has been used rarely, maintaining the autonomous status of the states. On the other hand, in Australia, like the US constitution, the independence of the states is guaranteed; however, the authority and power of the government of the commonwealth of Australia is so pervasive 'that in practice the states of Australia are little more than the administrative agencies of the commonwealth'. Wheare concluded that although Australia is constitutionally federal, it is unitary in practice. While the Canadian constitution is quasi-federal, in practice it is federal, more than that of Australia. As such, like any other concept in political science, federalism is also to be tested in practice, as its theoretical postulates could be at variance with reality.

With regard to unitary constitutions, Wheare (1963) pointed to its widespread practice and even questioned the purpose behind its classification. As far as the erstwhile USSR constitution is concerned, Wheare pointed out that although it was described as federal in practice, it was a 'unitary constitution with a wide measure of decentralization'. Wheare also added that apart from actual practice, the Stalin Constitution of 1936 conferred enormous powers to the central government, as well as a wide grip over the finances of the constituent units. 'The federal element, even in the law of the constitution is insignificant.' It is an irony of history that in the great ideological debate of the late nineteenth and early twentieth centuries, between the anarchists led by Proudhon and Bakunin and the Marxists led by Engels and Lenin (1870–1924), considerable attention was paid to the best ways of managing a political order. The anarchists favoured decentralisation and accepted a confederation as the essential minimum of a necessary evil—the state—whereas the Marxists wanted total control with the help of democratic centralism managed by professional revolutionaries. Both models were inadequate and impractical, but when the Soviet Union disintegrated, it had no alternative but to fall back upon the anarchist ideal of a confederation.

It is generally perceived that a unitary system is better for smaller states and federalism is preferable for larger ones. However, small states that are heterogeneous would be more stable under a federal set-up. A good example of this is Switzerland. Another case is that of Sri Lanka where the Tamil minority, after a civil war that lasted more than two decades, sought a federal structure with devolution of powers. At present, Sri Lanka is a unitary state. If the overdeveloped Pakistan state had been federal with a power-sharing arrangement, it could have prevented its own disintegration and the subsequent emergence of Bangladesh.

Nigeria is a federal state, but has been characterised by instability and backwardness. The federal structure in Nigeria came up in 1914 after an amalgamation of the Northern and Southern protectorates. The legislative powers are shared between the federal state and federating units. A federal structure was adopted to bridge differences in culture, region, language, customs, traditions, and the like among the different ethnic groups so that no one ethnic groups dominates. The idea is to protect the diversity and pluralism of Nigeria and ensure that every ethnic group is independent and autonomous. Despite the federal structure, there is inter-ethnic rivalry over the question of leadership of the country.

In the contemporary liberalised and globalised world, a decentralised federal system can manage better than rigid, centralised ones. We find that even in smaller European countries like Spain and England, there is now a larger acceptance of federal principles, although on paper they remain unitary. This is because the homogeneity of even small nations is now over-stretched. Britain has to contend with Scottish and Irish sub-nationalism, while Spain has to deal with the Basque and Catalanian sub-nationalisms.

In the contest between nationalism with its doctrine of self-determination and secession, and federalism with its plank of power-sharing and 'unity in diversity', the latter is more acceptable; even if the world is divided into 1,000 nations, a large number of minorities would still be present in many of them. As such, in today's world (which is akin to a global village), federalism is a better option than nationalism when it comes to offering a feasible solution to ethnic problems.

There are many examples of successful federalisms; however, there are also cases of failed federalisms. The West Indian federation of 1962, the Central African Federation of 1963, the withdrawal and expulsion of Singapore from the Malaysian Federation in 1965, and the break-up of Yugoslavia in 1992 are some recent examples of failed federalism. However, an analysis of the failure of particular federating processes would show that in all of them, federalism was present only in form and not in spirit. As such, these particular failures do not indicate that federalism as an ideal is still in an experimental stage. With a constitutional division of powers, checks and balances, and with the Supreme Court as the arbiter, federalism has maintained its unity and has evolved a complex mechanism of resolving conflicts while guaranteeing the rule of law and human rights in both fractured and cohesive societies.

NOTE

1. Huntington points out that American political institutions have been imported from Britain, with the exception of Federalism. Federalism has made it possible to overcome the traditional hostility to a centralisation of authority. Furthermore, as modern societies are complex, there will be diffusion rather than a concentration of powers. England, Australia, Canada and New Zealand are examples of centralised parliamentary systems, while the American presidential system is a decentralised one.

9

PARLIAMENTARY AND PRESIDENTIAL SYSTEMS OF GOVERNMENT (WITH SPECIAL REFERENCE TO INDIA)

(We) have all derived from the British Parliament and we still continue to derive from its proceedings, from its history . . . (and) from its traditions.

Rajendra Prasad, cited in Austin 1999: 11

Considering the unusually lengthy and relatively (speaking in colonial terms) successful experience India had with representative government, it is not surprising that Indians should have favoured a parliamentary constitution.

Austin 1966: 40

Some critics of Prime Ministerial system view the lack of separation between the prime minister and the legislature as a dangerous concentration of power since both are controlled by the same party.

O'Neil 2009: 152

The universal acceptance of representative liberal democracy after the collapse of communism settled one major theoretical issue, as liberal democracies are broadly divided between presidential and parliamentary systems. This vital question of choice assumed unprecedented significance in the contemporary world as more and more countries move towards democracy, characterised by Huntington as 'the third wave'. This has also intensified the debate concerning the desirability of the two models. In countries as diverse as Argentina, Brazil, Chile, India, South Korea and Turkey, concerned citizens, policymakers, public figures and constitutional experts have intensely debated the related merits and suitability of different constitutional arrangements in the specific contexts of their countries.

The **parliamentary and presidential systems of government** focus on the nature of the political executive at the apex of the government, which is in charge of directing the nation's affairs, supervising policy, mobilising support for its goals, and providing leadership during crises in democracies. As liberal democracies rest on the principle of constitutional limits of authority, the executive's term, rules of succession and powers are clearly specified. In addition to parliamentary and presidential systems of government is the **semi-presidential government,** wherein exists a dual executive, a mixture of the two pure types. A powerful elected president coexists with a prime minister accountable to the legislature.

CHARACTERISTICS OF A PRESIDENTIAL SYSTEM

The presidential system has at its apex an independent chief executive with the dual task of executing and initiating policies. As Head of the State and the government, the president is constitutionally independent of the legislature, with respect to both the duration of his tenure and his political policies. He is the real executive who actually exercises the powers vested in him by the Constitution. He is checked, assisted and supervised by an independent legislature. Normally, in such systems the chief executive is chosen for a fixed term through a direct national election. He can be removed from office only in very exceptional circumstances, through extraordinary legislature or a judicial procedure. The president wields enormous powers and enjoys important privileges. He has the power to veto legislative bills and also enjoys important responsibilities, such as initiating budgetary legislation, foreign treaties, and other crucial policies. He also enjoys emergency and war powers. He appoints major executive officials who hold their offices at his will. To limit the abuse of power in such systems where the president enjoys considerable power—as exemplified in the well-known statement that, except for a few dictators, the US President is the most powerful elected head—there are special constitutional provisions prohibiting presidential re-election. In the US, the President can serve only two terms,[1] whereas in Costa Rica and Venezuela Presidents are prohibited from serving two terms in immediate succession.

The United States is a classic example of the presidential system. Other countries which follow different variants of the presidential system are Costa Rica, France, the Philippines, Uruguay and Venezuela. The framers of the US Constitution adopted a Republic with the President as the chief executive. The three branches of the government, the legislature, executive and judiciary, are independent of each other, with some overlapping in certain areas.[2] The Congress passes the laws, but the president can veto them; the president nominates certain public officials who must be approved by the Congress. The laws made by the Congress and the executive actions are subjected to judicial review.

CHARACTERISTICS OF A PARLIAMENTARY SYSTEM

The other major model is the parliamentary system, broadly classified into **Majoritarian Parliamentary** systems (Australia, Canada, India, Ireland, Jamaica, Japan, New Zealand, Sri Lanka, United Kingdom and Germany) and the **Representational Parliamentary** system found predominantly in Continental Europe (Austria, Belgium, Denmark, Finland, Italy, Netherlands, Norway, Sweden and Turkey).

A distinctive feature of the parliamentary system is, in Bagehot's (1867) classic analysis, the distinction between the 'efficient' and 'dignified' aspects of government; the former that works and rules, while the latter that excites and commands the reverence of the people. The cabinet, prime minister and ministers represent the efficient leadership, while the monarchy is the dignified element. The former is the head of government while the latter is the head of the state.

In parliamentary systems, the head of the state is either a monarch or a president. Besides Britain, in Belgium, Denmark, the Netherlands and Spain, the head of the state is a constitutional monarch. In Canada, a former British colony, the governor-general stands in for the monarch. In republics, the head of the state is the president, directly elected as in Ireland or elected by parliament as in Israel, or through an electoral college consisting of the national legislature plus representatives of state/regional legislatures, as in Germany and India. The presidents, whether appointed or elected, are, like the monarchs, honorific.

In the parliamentary system, the individual chief executive is the leader of the majority party in the legislature and is accountable to the national legislature. Although the Prime Ministership is the most important office, there is a collective responsibility of the Cabinet. The prime minister continues to be in office as long as his party remains the majority party in the legislature. The details vary widely from country to country, but the most important common point in all parliamentary democracies is the dependence of the prime minister and the Cabinet on a legislature majority for their survival.

A. V. Dicey (1885) pointed out that parliamentary sovereignty lies within the ambit of the supremacy of the law. He cited two reasons as to why parliamentary sovereignty would not be arbitrary; first, the will of parliament can only be expressed through an act passed after a formal and deliberate process involving the two houses and the monarch. The act is also subject to judicial interpretation. Second, the parliament has never attempted to exercise executive power.

Political parties play a crucial role in a parliamentary system of government. There could be a single party system as in Britain or coalition governments as in continental Europe, which follow a system of proportional representation. Britain follows the first past the post system[3] which normally results in single party dominance, with exceptions such as in 1852–55, 1915–16, 1916–22, 1931–40, 1940–45 and 2010–15, when there were coalition governments. India too follows the first past the post system, but the first national-level coalition government was from 1977 to 1979, with Moraji Desai as Prime Minister. From 1996 India has had a coalition government[4] at the centre. At present, however, there is a one party majority government in the Lok Sabha, although the central government is a coalition as the government is that of the NDA and not the BJP.

DIFFERENCE BETWEEN PARLIAMENTARY AND PRESIDENTIAL SYSTEMS OF GOVERNMENT

In a presidential system, there is a separation of powers. The executive and legislative arms have equal status, and are separate and independent of one another. In a parliamentary system, there is no separation of powers. The executive is accountable to the legislature. In the presidential system, the President is the Head of the State as well as of the government, while in a parliamentary set-up there are two executives—Nominal or Titular, and Real. The former can be the President (as in India), the Monarch (as in Britain), or the Governor General. The Real executive is the prime minister and the cabinet. In a presidential system, the President is the chief executive of the state, exercising all the powers vested in him by the constitution. In a parliamentary form of government, executive powers are vested in the nominal head, while they are exercised by the real head. The head of the state exercises his powers on the advice tendered by the cabinet, headed by the prime minister. In a presidential system, the president is assisted and advised by a cabinet chosen by the president; its tenure also depends on the president. In a parliamentary system, the cabinet is the real executive, with the prime minister as the first among equals. The president and the cabinet do not attend the sessions of the legislature and cannot be removed through a vote of no confidence in a presidential system. Even an adjournment of a censure motion cannot be brought against them. In a parliamentary system, the prime minister and cabinet are members of either house of the parliament. If the prime minister is not a member of parliament, s/he is given a specific period of time within which to seek membership of either house of parliament. By convention, it is expected that the prime minister be a member of the popular house, that is, the lower house of parliament; however, there are exceptions to this rule. The prime minister and cabinet members attend the sessions of the parliament, answer questions, place bills before the parliament and make statements relating to their policies. A vote of no confidence, an adjournment motion and a censure motion can be brought against them.

In a parliamentary system, the Head of State is not responsible to the Parliament, and neither is s/he a member of the parliament. The sessions of the parliament begin with a speech delivered by the Head of the State. In a presidential system, the president is elected for a fixed tenure and can be removed from office through an elaborate and cumbersome impeachment process. In a parliamentary system, the prime minister and cabinet remain in office for as long as they enjoy the confidence of the parliament, namely the lower house.

France is a **semi-presidential system** as there is a prime minister and a National Assembly, which resembles the British House of Commons more than either chamber of the US Congress. The President has the power to dissolve the National Assembly; however, once dissolved, it cannot be dissolved again within a year. If the electorate returns the same representatives, then the President has to mend fences with those with whom he had crossed swords. It is significant that Sri Lanka, which has been following the French model, is now switching over to the pure parliamentary form; the French model has proved weaker since the President may have to cohabitate with a parliamentary majority that is different from his own political background.

PARLIAMENTARY SYSTEM IN INDIA

Periodically in India, a well-known political leader, political scientist or political commentator will point to the desirability of introducing a presidential system instead of continuing with the present parliamentary form. It was Congress leader R. Venkataram who first demanded the introduction of the presidential system in 1967 after the Congress debacle in the polls. Since then—and increasingly so from the 1990s—similar demands have usually been made when a political party fails, or is uncertain of mustering a clear majority in the parliament on its own. The underlying assumption of such a suggestion is that the parliamentary system followed for the past five decades has not succeeded to the extent desired, and that this relative failure is enough reason for advocating an alternative structure conceived as more effective and democratic than the existing one.

India opted for the Westminster model of a majoritarian parliamentary system after Independence. This was not unexpected as the Government of India Act of 1935 had provided the necessary grounds for the practice of the British model in India. The acceptance of a liberal democratic framework was expected in India, as almost no other nation gaining independence in the aftermath of World War II was 'institutionally as well prepared as India for self-government' (Huntington 1968: 85). This favourable situation was created by the existence of two vital institutions: a well-organised political party in the form of the Indian National Congress and an experienced civil service.

In fact, the founding fathers of the Indian Constitution showed considerable wisdom and foresight in choosing the majoritarian parliamentary system for India. The acceptance and near continuous functioning of the parliamentary system is one of the positive aspects of India's post-independent evolution. This has nullified the popular European perception of Oriental despotism, as well as the arrogant claims of Churchill and his ilk that parliamentary democracy can be practised successfully only by the British. In 1947, before the declaration of India's independence, Churchill remarked that political power was being handed over to a few 'men of straw' who may not be able to administer the country properly. However, by 1959 one could see a noticeable change in this attitude when John Stratchy commented that the institution of parliamentary democracy was 'a remarkable, if precarious achievement' in India. But the continued operation of the system for the past five decades does not mean that there are no problems or shortcomings; in fact, there are a number of them.

First, there is the question of cost. In India, when the parliament is in session, the expenditure is a staggering Rs 2.5 lakh per minute, according to 2015 estimates. The second point concerns the quality of parliamentarians. Third is the important role of interest groups and pressure groups, which undermine the very basis of representative democracy. Fourth is the vexed problem of the legislative's relationship with the executive and the judiciary, especially in times of one-party domination. The fifth point concerns the vital role and control of the media. The sixth pertains to the problem of financing elections, and seventh is the inability and slackness of the system as compared to the presidential system. The eighth pertains to the weakness of the party system. The ninth point is an important factor, especially for the developing world; this concerns the capacity of the parliamentary system to bring about basic structural changes.

In order to remedy these problems, the presidential system is advocated as an alternative to the parliamentary model, as it is supposed to be free from such evils. However, a close examination of the system brings out a number of shortcomings, which are just as acute in a few key areas here as they are in the parliamentary system. First, the presidential system is as expensive as its legislative organs are not abolished but separated from the executive; the other important components of the parliamentary system, like the Cabinet and political parties, continue, although in a much more personalised form. The primary system in the US for presidential candidates, which has democratised the entire system to a very large extent, is also expensive, and since legislative aspirants operate from different constituencies at separate elections most of the time, the expenses multiply. The administrative expenditure for running the presidential system is similar to that operating within a parliamentary system.

In 1840 in the US, the Federal judiciary employed around 150 persons, including the judges. In 1994–95, this number had increased to 26,000. The legislative branch, the Congress, has created its own, very large, group of specialists. The number of Senate employees per Senator today exceeds the total membership of the entire US Congress. In 1840, a Congress of 223 Representatives and 52 Senators employed a total staff of 57; in 1994–95, 425 Representatives employed over 12,000, and 100 Senators employed more than 7,000. The sheer size of its employees makes the Congress larger than 99 per cent of all business firms in the US. If this is the case in the US, which has a philosophy of limited government, one can safely project a much larger number in countries like India, where the government plays and will continue to play a pivotal role. Besides the question of costs and numbers, there is also the role of specialists in a democratic country.

> Whatever they may claim, however, specialists are not neutral, purely apolitical purveyors of knowledge; they are political actors with their own views and agendas. To pursue their agendas, they need and usually acquire some measure of autonomy and authority. Because experts are difficult to control without expertise, like lawyers, experts create a demand for the services of others experts. And so it goes (Dahl 1993: 451).

In the American presidential system, both nomination and election are lengthy, time-consuming and expensive processes, and if this system were to be followed, the costs would multiply in poorer countries like India. Second, the operation of pressure groups and interest groups assumes a formidable significance in the presidential system as is evident from the campaign money, which comes from particular interests. In the US, interest group politics began with the establishment of the Republic. Tocqueville had taken note of them as associations to achieve well-defined goals, including political ones. These associations were interest groups (Dahl 1993: 451). But whereas the number and diversity of interest groups have increased, there has been no corresponding growth in the strength of integrating institutions. The theory of separation of powers does not provide for any constitutional process of resolving conflicts. Neustadt (1990) pointed out that the American system is not one of separation of powers; rather, it is a system of separate authorities sharing power. An exclusive authority to govern, which is also really accountable, does not exist, and this leads to inevitable divisions and deadlocks in even the American system. There is a propensity to avoid dealing with difficult issues, resulting in parochialism and incoherent, inefficient and particularly targeted policies instead of clear policy preferences. This lacuna may become serious in countries like India where the contradictions are major, and the strict separation of powers may lead to severe constitutional crises. The president, being directly elected, can claim legitimacy in a plebicitarian sense (or in the sense in which Rousseau used the term). An identical claim may be made by elected members of legislative organs as well, leading to a crisis situation.

Third, the most important argument in support of the presidential system is that it provides for, and indeed achieves, executive stability. One major argument in favour of this system is the fixed term of the Chief Executive.

> Following British political thinker Walter Bagehot, we might say that a presidential system endows the incumbent with both the 'ceremonial' functions of a head of state and the 'efficient' functions of a chief executive, thus creating an aura, a self-image, and a set of popular expectations, regardless of the victory margin, that are all quite different from those associated with a prime minister, no matter how popular (Linz 1991: 13).

In reality, though, this has plenty of drawbacks. It breaks the continuity of the political process. In case of an unexpected event, like death or impeachment of the incumbent, succession is automatic and the successor may be temperamentally different, leading to a lot of uneasiness. Moreover, in a presidential system, Vice Presidentship is by and large insignificant and may not appeal to many ambitious and competent politicians. It should also be noted that in the politically volatile late twentieth century, a fixed term may be detrimental to the democratic process itself; change and adaptability are important qualities of a successful statesman, both of which are denied in the theory of a fixed term.

Perhaps the biggest drawback of the presidential system is that it reduces the political process to a zero sum game in which the winner takes all, even when he polls a minority of votes. This is detrimental to the ideals of democracy, which lays emphasis on sharing power. This is more so for modernising and developing societies, where the distinction between classes, gender, educated and uneducated, rural and urban is pronounced, as is regional differentiation with uneven development; in such a context, a strong president would be able to represent only a few interests and would divide and polarise rather than unite and strengthen the political process. With growing ethnic, tribal and linguistic consciousness, a charismatic leader or strong symbolic presidential authority may become ruinous. In the mass societies of today, which are inherently plural, a successful political process needs to be accommodative and participatory, and in this crucial area the presidential system is grossly inadequate as it restricts politics instead of expanding it. It polarises politics rather than accommodate regional aspirations, extreme ideological parties and minority organisations. In the Indian context, it is often argued that the British parliamentary system was adopted 'without adequately realising that in a heterogeneous society like India's a strong central authority is needed to hold the people and the territory together' (Pathak 1993: 36). The greatest advantage of the presidential system is that it preserves national unity in a vast state with large ethnic, religious, regional and linguistic diversities, in which the president becomes the embodiment of the national outlook (ibid.: 36–37). One can refute these arguments along these lines:

> One general recommendation that can be made concerns the traditional categories of constitutional engineering. Unlike consensual plurality, electoral systems, and unitary forms of government, a better institutional framework is offered by their opposites: parliamentary systems (or semi parliamentary systems with a plural executive such as in Switzerland), list systems of proportional representation, and, in case of societies with geographically concentrated segments, federal systems (Lijphart 1989: 224).

The proponents of the presidential system often forget that the only successful example of this model is the United States. Its very uniqueness exhibits its serious limitations, as both in political evolution and societal formation the United States is a nation without a parallel. However, it is generally conceded that the political process is not integrative. As a result, some even advocate a switchover to the parliamentary system. As the Canadian Ambassador to the United States, Gotlieb, remarked,

> Washington is a mass of moving charged particles, some more powerful than others but all with power of some kind. Even the president is just another particle, though one with a charge that changes its magnitude from time to time. Senators, representatives, columnists, congressional staffers, lobbyists, lawyers, even hostesses are all a part of a 'system' that seems to lack any well-defined systemic properties (cited in Dahl 1993: 448).

Equally important is the fact that separate elections for the president and the legislature create minority presidents. A survey carried out by G. Bingham Powell, Jr. in the 1970s revealed that a majority of presidential systems saw a divided legislature/executive for over two years in the decade. It also pointed out that majoritarian parliamentary systems 'were the most effective at avoiding minority governments as well as providing for executive stability' (1982: 63). In presidential systems, the average durability was 36 months, as compared to 33 months in majoritarian parliamentary systems and 22 months in representational parliamentary systems. On balance, the majoritarian parliamentary system emerges strongest if both indicators of executive stability and avoidance of minority governments are taken into account. Added to these is the important fact that there is considerable violence in the presidential system; in sharp contrast, representational parliamentary systems reflect the least average violence, followed by the majoritarian system.

Fourth, the more ethnically divided countries are likely to have majoritarian legislatures, which makes the presidential system inappropriate for countries like India. 'The experience of India and of some English speaking countries in the Caribbean show that, even in greatly divided societies, periodic parliamentary crises need not turn into full blown regime crises and that the ousting of a prime minister and cabinet need not spell the end of democracy itself' (Linz 1991: 12). Fifth, the argument concerning the weaknesses of party systems in parliamentary democracies is also not vindicated as the party system has an independent dynamic of its own and is not linked closely with either system. The two classic examples of stable party systems, the United States and Britain, follow two different models, thereby showing that weaknesses can be combated in both. Moreover, it is generally conceded that in the more personalised politics of the presidential system, the party system is likely to be weaker. The argument that the endemic problem of defections can be checked under the presidential system also comes from an erroneous understanding of policies and decision-making in the presidential system. An organised group of legislators in a divided house can stall the entire proceedings and can always demand their price. As Neustadt (1990) mentioned in his classic study of presidential powers in the United States, to be in that high office need not mean power as in the American context, power flows from manipulative skills in the Congress and other areas of interest group activity. Such manipulative skills ensure that policies of defection will be more prominent in the presidential type than in the parliamentary one, with its fixed tenure of office.

Sixth is the important point that functional differentiation is a part of the modernisation process in which the United States presidency, which combines the functions of a head of state as well as of the government, is an anachronism amongst modern constitutional practices. 'The Presidency is indeed, the only survival in the contemporary world of the constitutional monarchy once prevalent throughout Medieval Europe' (Huntington 1968: 65). In the modern state, the theoretical assumption is that a large representational assembly performs governmental functions constitutionally. But in actual practice, leadership and direction comes from a small body like the cabinet, the presidium, or the collective executive. In contrast, the divisions in the United States system, with its three clearly distinguished organs followed by further sub-divisions, is more like the division that existed in pre-modern medieval Europe. The only person who unites all three functions is the president, a combination which 'is a major source of his power, but also a major limitation on his power, since the requirement of one role often conflict with the demands of another'; also, this 'combination of roles perpetuate ancient practice' (ibid.: 67). In this context, it may also be pointed out that whereas the United States constitutional set-up faces little challenges and strains as it deals with a society of minor contradictions, the Indian political scene reflects major conflicts and contradictions, which further weaken the case for the presidential system here.

Another argument in favour of the presidential system is that it would enable the infusion of able persons in service of the nation, which we lose because the parliamentary system is unable or unwilling to accommodate them. This leads to the triumph of mediocrity. However, this in itself is an elitist idea inappropriate for the democratic age; it may also be added that for elite accommodation, the parliamentary system, with its larger legislative and executive arena, offers a more plausible alternative than the presidential one. It is no accident of history that all plural societies have had parliamentary democracy. Even the special form of presidentialism recommended by B. K. Nehru for ethnically heterogeneous societies is more complicated and cumbersome than the existing parliamentary system. Broadening of the societal base and increase in people's participation is more easily achieved in the parliamentary than in the presidential system (Nehru 1992: 138).

India, with its diversity and plurality, is a nation in the making. For orderly, balanced and peaceful development and for creating trust amongst the people, there can be no substitute to parliamentary democracy in India. The working of parliamentary democracy has disproved J. S. Mill's contention that representative democracy is only possible in a small, homogenous state. It has also nullified predictions of India breaking up.[5] The parliamentary system has enabled India to have a peaceful transition to power and has allowed all different ideologies and points of view to be represented in the decision-making process. In the larger context, it is now generally admitted that India is just one of few developing countries that is both stable and viable. Moreover, compared to other contemporary democracies under the parliamentary system, India has fared well with regard to ensuring popular participation, stability, and in containing violence. Here, it may also be pointed out that the American army administration in Japan had opted for the parliamentary system as being more appropriate for Japan, rather than their own presidential system (Robinson 1996: 193).

Despite this consolidation of the parliamentary system, some trends in recent years have led to anxiety about its feasibility and continued relevance. The first is the virtual collapse of the Congress system as the one-party dominant system with inner party democracy. Coalition politics is the second feature, in view of the fact that no single party has been able to win a majority. In this context, it is important to point out that the strength of a polity does not depend on the formal stability of the superstructure, but on the efficient and impartial functioning of basic institutions. On this front, we have not fared well because our political structure continues to remain oligarchic. The Westminster model has allowed the perpetuation of power by political parties who could not muster more than 50 per cent of the votes. This model has led to a disproportionate share of power as it endorses the dictum 'Winner takes all', thereby giving the ruling party 70 per cent of seats while securing 40–50 per cent of the votes. This asymmetry is to be corrected by giving representation to the poor and underprivileged through a variety of political groupings. With increasing elite accommodation of these relatively deprived sections, Indian democracy is being strengthened by the emergence of a large number of political parties at the national level. This in itself allows for power sharing, which is imperative in a pluralist democracy like India.

The need of the hour is to strengthen the existing parliamentary system rather than switching over to the presidential system. The parliamentary system in India has ensured participation, stability and minimal violence, and with some reforms, it could become more vibrant and meaningful. These reforms include the public funding of elections, checking electoral malpractices, fixing a ceiling on election expenses, and making political parties more democratic and accountable in their functioning. Moreover, as Wolin (1986: 192) rightly pointed out, 'a democratic vision means a genuine alternative'. The mechanism of parliamentary democracy guarantees that alternative, and hence our endeavour should be to make it the essence of our core political culture. The Indian political system is 'not just a system providing means of competition and conflict but also a coalitional arena in which both ruling and oppositional groups can enter their diverse claims' (Kothari 1970: 421).

The appropriateness of the parliamentary system for India can serve as an example to other developing countries. First, for stabilising democracy, a basic precondition is the actualisation of social and economic rights. A comparative analysis of Costa Rica, India and Turkey revealed that Turkey was the least stable[6]; it also had the least egalitarian set-up. In contrast, India is more egalitarian, both in terms of distribution of income and land. Her record is also better than Costa Rica's as the Indian government has been able to maintain progressive taxation and relative economic security by keeping inflation below 10 per cent. This relatively better performance is largely due to the continuance of the parliamentary system for over five decades.

Second, Arat (1992) made an interesting distinction between early developers in the West, which successfully followed a policy of gradual change in both the political and economic spheres. However, for late developers the gradualist strategy was not feasible as in the twentieth century, governmental legitimacy largely depends on the creation of an egalitarian society. Arat also endorsed Pateman's (1989) critique of civic culture with its emphasis on a minimal role for citizens, especially in the context of the developing world, arguing that the stability of the democratic system is threatened if the government fails to maintain parity between civil/political rights and social/economic rights. The parliamentary system with its wider network of participation and representation is more conducive to the realisation of social and economic rights, rather than the presidential one. Third, in sharp contrast to consensual democracies of the West, democracies in the developing world remained divided and polarised for a considerable period of time; because of this key factor, the parliamentary system would be more stabilising as it would accommodate divergent interests, aspirations and regional groupings. The wide variety of state governments in India testifies to this, and proves that for healthy state formation in the developing world, the parliamentary system has much to offer.

Fourth, it is often argued that the developing world needs strong states. But as Duodo (1994: 8) has shown, the main cause of alienation among Africans is the unitary structure of state power. This is because even civilian rulers spend more state money in ethnic areas of their own origin. Such monopoly of power which benefit a few and disadvantage the many undermines the very concept of a strong state, the inappropriateness of which has already been demonstrated by Fukuyama (1992). The solution to this problem calls for decentralisation, the formation of effective and financially independent local governments, and wider participation of the people. For all of this, the parliamentary system offers more opportunities.

CONCLUSION

In developing countries like India, where no single authoritative voice is accepted as final in any major segment of activity, a plural executive is always better than a singular one. It is estimated that the late Prime Minister Jawaharlal Nehru, in spite of his tremendous popularity, commanded only 25 per cent of electoral support. In such a scenario, the presidential system is likely to further erode the unifying basis of the Indian state by increasing discord, disharmony, frustration and alienation, rather than ensuring stability. Former prime minister Manmohan Singh, in a press conference held in 2014, acknowledged that the parliamentary system is best suited for India, and that the presidential system would be counter-productive. A presidential alternative would widen the gap of credibility and legitimacy, which already faces a crisis of governability (Kohli 1990). The idea of India, as described in the Indian Constitution within the framework of the parliamentary system of government, has withstood the test of time, and peaceful changes in government have blunted the arguments of both critics and occasional sceptics about the efficacy and suitability of this system of government for India.

NOTES

1. In 1951, a constitutional amendment limited presidential terms to two. George Washington had set a precedent by choosing to step down upon completion of two tenures in office, which was followed until Franklin Roosevelt, who served four terms from 1933 until his death in 1945.
2. The phrase 'separation of powers', which describes the relationship between the President and Congress in the American system, is misleading. Hague and Harrop (2001: 238) prefer to call it separation of institutions rather than that of legislative and executive powers. 'President and Congress share the powers of the government: each seek to influence the other but neither is in any position to dictate' (ibid.). According to Jones (1994), this relationship is subtle, intricate and balanced. It reflects a successful attempt by the founders to build checks and balances into the American government.
3. The first past the post system (FPTP) is also referred to as the Winner Takes All system. It is followed in the UK, the US, India, New Zealand and Canada. It usually results in significant differences between the party's total share of votes and its share of seats in the parliament. This is because there can only be one winner in each constituency, even if the difference in votes won is small and elections are decided by the number of seats

rather than the total number of votes they receive across the country. The winning party usually wins more seats than the votes polled. FPTP usually results in single party majority governments. This was the case in every FPTP election in New Zealand from 1935 to 1993. This was also the pattern in Britain, although in the 2010 elections, a conservative/liberal democrat coalition government with more than half the seats in parliament formed the government.

Under the FPTP, the difference in vote share among the stakeholders is proportionately represented in the seats secured. For instance, David Cameron's Conservative Party secured 47 per cent of seats with a vote share of 36.1 per cent, while the Labour party polled 29 per cent of votes but secured 40 per cent of the seats. The Liberal Democrats secured 23.9 per cent of votes but just 8.8 per cent of seats. Hence, Nick Clegg argued that the FPTP is inherently unfair and defective, and as the voice of the majority, goes unrepresented in parliament.

Two questions lie at the heart of the debate. The first is the legitimacy of the system, which virtually assures that the winner takes all; second, the marginalisation of smaller parties, neglecting their concerns in the important decision-making processes. As far as the first point is concerned, the fact remains that both in the US and Britain, and even in India, it rarely happens that the winner gets more than 50 per cent of the votes (with the exception of the 2008 US presidential election). This means that the government is formed on the basis of a win, even if the winner has secured less than 50 per cent of the votes. This also throws up a question concerning the essential legitimacy of a representative government. In a fragmented party system, the percentage of votes required to win in the FPTP is much less. There have been examples (as in India) where an elected MP or MLA has won by polling merely 12 per cent, and has become a minister. This leads to the second important point—the increasing plural nature of modern mega democracies and the need for a different power sharing arrangement than that ensured by the rigid and over-simplified FPTP system. This argument is reinforced by the Continental European experience, where coalitions and delayed governmental formations are accepted as normal and routine. Unlike the British system, the parliament is supposed to be hung all the time, and instead of being alarmed or characterising it as unhealthy, it is accepted as an essential reflection of societal plurality. In Europe, a coalition government is accepted as an essential component of the political process because politics, after all, reflects the cleavages and faultlines of a political union. Since this is accepted as given, delay in government formation does not lead to alarm, nor does it disrupt normal economic and political activities. In Denmark, it took eight months and in Germany, 40 days after elections to have a government in place. Although elections are more frequent in Europe than in England, the fact is that elections in the Continent are less intently fought and are more in the nature of a cabinet reshuffle. The same people return to parliament and the Cabinet has familiar faces; however, this is seen as representing political reality and continuity than the FPTP system, where the winner takes all.

Other arguments against FPTP are that it encourages tactical voting, as voters vote not for the candidate they most prefer, but against the candidate they most dislike. It restricts voter choice, which is taken care of by the introduction of the NOTA in India. FPTP encourages the emergence and continuation of a two-party system and is usually disadvantageous to third parties in a system dominated by multiple parties. This also works in its favour, as it might result in a single party government with a decisive leader, rather than relying on other parties for support. It ensures a clear winner; avoids messy coalitions and hung parliaments; and encourages the victory of 'centrist parties', unlike the PR system which may allow fringe fundamentalist and/or extremist parties with less favoured policies to be in parliament. Moreover, FPTP allows the voter to reject unpopular governments. Its advocates are elected on a manifesto which they are expected to implement, while other systems are more likely to produce indecisive outcomes, with the government decided through horse-trading and political fixes with manifesto pledges being ditched and promises broken. These were the reasons why, in the nation-wide referendum held in Britain in 2013, the alternative vote was rejected and FPTP continued. Other arguments in favour of FPTP is that it is simple to understand and easy to administer as the declaration of results is faster.

4. From 1999 to 2014, India saw two broad alliance groups—NDA and UPA rule at the centre. The NDA was led by the BJP while the UPA was led by the Congress. In 2014, the NDA came to power, but the BJP had a parliamentary strength of its own.
5. Harrison argued persuasively in *India: The Dangerous Decades Ahead* (1960) that India may not survive as a single national state and if it does, is likely to be authoritarian. He believed that the decline of English would strengthen regional languages and encourage regional aspirations, loyalties and regional elites. As a result, the central government would find it increasingly difficult to separate decisions pertaining to economic development from parochial demands.
6. In 2015, Turkey rejected outright the presidential system and endorsed the parliamentary system.

10

CONSOCIATIONAL DEMOCRACY AND POWER SHARING

Consociationalism is the most influential contribution to comparative politics.

Bingham Powell 1979: 25

The primary characteristic of consociational democracy is that the political leaders of all significant segments of the plural society cooperate in a grand coalition to govern the country. It may be contrasted with the type of democracy in which the leaders are divided into a government with bare majority and a large opposition.

Lijphart 1989: 25

Arend Lijphart's typology of democratic systems has been perceived as one of the major contributions to comparative political science in the last decades. His differentiation between consensus and majoritarian democracies has been widely adopted and expanded by other researchers. However, it has also been fiercely debated.... that the typology is a useful tool to categorize established democracies but is incapable of capturing patterns beyond the scope of the original sample. This is due to Lijphart's inductive approach that cannot sever the intricate connection between culture and institutions built into the typology. Moreover, this connection makes it difficult to predict differences in policy performance.

Bromann 2010: 1

Homogeneity as a basis of stability is an old theory in Political Science. Consociational democrats regard Aristotle's (1979: 181) remark that 'a state aims at being, as far as it can be, society composed of equals and peers' as the guiding spirit. The need for social homogeneity and political consensus to ensure a stable democratic order is also a well-established fact. In contrast, sharp social divisions and wide political disagreements in a plural society are seen as the major causes of instability and in the failure to create an enduring democracy. However, Lijphart, the main theorist of consociational democracy, demonstrated that while it may be difficult to set up stable democracies in societies with wide cleavages, it is not impossible to achieve one through proper elite accommodation and power sharing mechanism. In 'a consociational democracy the centrifugal tendencies inherent in a plural society are counteracted by the co-operative attitudes and behaviour of the leaders of the different segments of the population' (Lijphart 1989: 1).

Lijphart identified four features shared by consociational systems[1]: (*i*) a grand coalition government (between parties from different segments of society); (*ii*) segmental autonomy (in the cultural sector); (*iii*) proportionality (in the voting system and in public-sector employment); and (*iv*) minority veto. Consociational democracy as articulated by Lijphart refers to segmented societies, where the behaviour of people is bound by close social ties based upon language or religion, which determines patterns of work organisation, marriage and recreational life. In such societies a political system operating on the principle of simple majority rule would not work because members of each group would be apprehensive of the other group taking too much advantage of the opportunities for power offered. Also, in such societies the need has been for institutions that allow the various groups in a plural society to share and enjoy power, and co-operate in a grand coalition to govern the country. This is the opposite of majoritarian democracy, which integrates minority groups and aims at the distribution of individual rights. Consociational democracy, on the other hand, accommodates minorities by granting them collective rights. It is similar to corporatism; while this is more applicable to an economic arrangement, consociationalism refers to divided segmented societies.

Consociational democracy is a model that is both empirical and normative. It explains the factors behind the political stability in a number of small but plural European democracies, like Austria, Belgium, The Netherlands and Switzerland. But this theory has a larger importance in the context of the evolution of democracy in many other plural societies in the world, and because of this contemporary relevance, the theory's importance is not merely historical but also practical. For instance, in a study of 114 countries by Norling and Williams, Dahl (1971: 231–45) found that about 58 per cent had a low degree of sub-cultural pluralism; they are polyarchies or near polyarchies. Only 36 per cent could be classified as moderately plural and 15 per cent of these were cases of marked or extreme pluralism. In fact, outside the ambit of Western democracies there is a vast arena where a variety of sharp cleavages have led to political instability, with oscillations between democracy and dictatorship in many cases. Lijphart argued that the success of these smaller European countries in establishing stable democracies in spite of these wide cleavages could serve as a model for other nations wishing to build enduring democracies. Examples of consociational democracy can be found in Europe. Switzerland has been characterised as consociational since 1943, Belgium after World War I, Austria from 1945–66, and The Netherlands from 1917–67. Czechoslovakia was consociational from 1989–93. India has been one since 1947, Colombia from 1958–74, Malaysia from 1955, and South Africa since 1994; while these can be considered successes from a normative point of view, Cyprus and Lebanon's experiments ended in civil war. Some scholars actually consider the European Union a consociational democracy.

Consociational democracy provides for a government by grand coalition of all the groups, with provision for minority votes on crucial policy matters. It also ensures proportional representation in the cabinet and civil services on the basis of ethnicity. Rough parity is also to be maintained in financial allocations while ensuring the cultural autonomy of all groups. In the context of Lijphart's empirical study, the politics of accommodation is between Catholics and Protestants and between the liberals and social democrats. A realistic accommodative political process can achieve the goal of peace and stability. Consociational democrats like the classic pluralists consider their theory a realistic way to accommodate unavoidable conflicts, as maintaining peace and stability is the overriding concern. Both the Catholics and Protestants have an elitist bias as leaders play a crucial role in promoting two balancing acts: (*i*) catering to the special interests of the constituents while (*ii*) negotiating with and accommodating other groups to maintain peace. The similarity between Lijphart's 'cross-cutting cleavages' and Truman's 'multiple group membership' is clearly established. In this sense, consociationalism is an offshoot of classical pluralism that deals with a different situation with multiple cleavages; as classical pluralists did not have to deal with this, classical pluralism was more concerned with dealing with issues like the tyranny of the majority and fear of mob rule. Although there are many similarities between classical pluralism and consociational democratic theory, there are some differences as well. For instance, social democratic values and their link with the Catholics are much bigger and less homogenous than the special interest groups that the pluralists highlight, like the chambers of commerce or neighbourhood groups. Lijphart believed that parliamentary democracy was easily compatible with consociational practices and structures. Pluralists, especially in the US, see their views as compatible with presidential federalism, as articulated by Madison. Lijphart also shared the classical pluralist belief that there has to be a degree of commitment to common belief structures among divergent groups—like nationalism and even loyalty to a king—whereas for pluralists, republican values reign supreme.

Lijphart portrayed a model of democratic governance where 'the political leaders of all significant segments of the plural society co-operate in a grand coalition to govern the country', and contrasts it with an 'adversarial' or 'government-versus-opposition' model (1989: 25). Anticipating criticism that involving segmented leaders in major policy decisions can lead to the veto power being misused, in turn leading to stalemate or partition, Lijphart argued that there were ways and means of counteracting these tendencies; and in any case, under 'the unfavourable circumstances of segmental cleavages, consociational democracy, though far from the abstract ideal, is the best kind of democracy that can realistically be expected' (ibid.: 48). The commonality between pluralism and consociational democracy is reflected in Dahl's (1989: 264) acceptance that the theory is applicable to societies; he views divisions as 'strong and distinctive subcultures'.

Some major criticisms of consociational theory pertain to its neglect of the need for an opposition space in a democracy, because the grand coalition theory leaves no space for the emergence of a legitimate opposition. Two others are that such an arrangement leads inevitably to a limited government with limited powers, which is unable to tackle the manifold problems of complex modern societies, and that it leads to immobility. Another criticism is that the very formation of a grand coalition is impossible in a context of severe divisions as it will lead to a situation where group interests would predominate. Another argument states that while consociational theory will definitely be attractive to minorities, it will not be so for majorities, who logically prefer a majority rule. As such, 'there are consociational features adopted occasionally by states, but few full-blown consociational regimes. Grand coalitions and minority vetoes are particularly scarce' (Horowitz 2004: 15). Barry (1991: Ch. 5) points out a contradiction in consociational theory: consociational arrangements and measures of mutual accommodation among group leaders are usually required for and devised in deeply divided societies, and when consociational democracy is feasible, it is no longer needed. Barry (1975: 504) also pointed out that 'the relevance of the "consociational" model for divided societies is much more doubtful than is commonly supposed'. Lijphart (1989: 30) agreed that 'a moderate attitude and a willingness to compromise' are required for consociational arrangements, and maintained that the very prospect of joint participation in government stimulates these attitudes by providing 'an important guarantee of political security' among parties 'that do not quite trust each other'.

However, it can be said that within the larger framework of pluralism, consociational democratic theory has to be understood in the context of the refinement of pluralist principles in societies with great cleavages, mutual suspicion and distrust. Where democracies are supposed to be inherently fragile, the consociational model holds out a promise of stability with institutionalisation, accommodating the aspirations and needs of different segments within a larger collectivity. The theory is also realistic in its acceptance that it is not applicable to societies like Northern Ireland, where sub-cultural hostility and religious and social divisions, coupled with a highly developed sense of historical identity, leads to a lack of consensual culture among political elites. The major barrier to peace here is also the lack of inter-elite cooperation. Instead of creating a grand coalition, the elite enhances inter-communal hostility. Lijphart considered Northern Ireland a major aberrant to the framework of accommodative consociational politics. However, such cases are exceptions rather than a rule, and the historical success of this model in Europe and the continued success of pluralistic politics in many parts of the developing world—for example, in Lebanon for a considerable period and the continued success in countries like Malaysia and India—proves the practical relevance of this theory for stabilising democracy in plural societies.

POWER SHARING AS A MODEL TO CEMENT MAJORITY-MINORITY CONFLICT

A satisfactory solution to the problem of minorities plays a crucial role in the formation of successful mega-nations in the contemporary world. The minority—or rather, the feeling of a minority—can be based on language, race, ethnicity or religion. The composition of the mega-states also varies widely. The Chinese have a predominant Hun majority of 92 per cent, while two other equally large states—India and Indonesia—consist of many ethnic groups. India is composed of 72 per cent Indo-Aryans and 24 per cent Dravidians, but only 28 per cent are *Hindustani*. Indonesia comprises 39 per cent Javanese, 16 per cent Sundanese and 12 per cent

Indonesian Malay. Africa has a stupendous problem as two-fifths of its population are minorities, whereas in Western democracies and Latin America, minorities constitute only one-tenth of the population. The erstwhile communist world had no visible minority problem; however, the myth of a communist solution exploded with the disintegration of the Soviet Union and Yugoslavia.

Minority consciousness of race, religion or culture normally crystallises with a feeling of deprivation and exploitation, and through the presence of a permanent majority and minority. However, minority discrimination was not always a fact of contemporary history; the apartheid regime in South Africa insulated and pampered the white minority population, raising their standard of living to that of any First World nation, while leaving the majority black population in despair and hopelessness. But such a situation continued to be highly unstable as the exploitative and wealthy minority feared a perceived or actual retaliation. One of Nelson Mandela's spectacular achievements, one that has been continued by his successors, was to limit such retaliation to a minimal, manageable level.

As solutions to the problem of minorities, various alternatives—autonomy, self-government, secession—have been suggested or tried in various phases of modern history. A unitary structure emphasises assimilation or genocide, the latter practised in the pre-democratic period to eliminate the aborigines in Australia and Native Americans in the North and South Americas. The process of assimilation normally generates a serious backlash. Neither genocide nor forced assimilation, which result in the control of one ethnic group over another, has any place in contemporary norms of societal and state formations.

The trend in the modern world has been to emphasise reconciliation and integration based on a policy that would not obliterate but accommodate a plurality of cultures, and ethnic and religious minority groups. The policies of Affirmative Action and Reservations in the United States and India, respectively, are contemporary and successful examples of processes of accommodation. Outside mediation has also been successful in Africa. Within the ambit of one person one vote, institutional protection for minorities has been provided in Zimbabwe and post-apartheid South Africa.

However, the most practical solution to the problem is power sharing, which assures each segment of society, big and small, an assured voice in the decision-making process and a rough parity in the share of public resources. Switzerland and Belgium are good examples of this model. The philosophy of power sharing and special protection of minorities is based on a shift from the first past the post system, which means that a simple majority normally based on a minority of votes polled leads to a situation where the winner takes all. Hypothetically, in such a system one ethnic group, which constitutes more than 50 per cent of the population, can rule and favour its own interests at the cost of other minority group(s); this would be rejected by the minorities. However, if a constitutional arrangement or practice accepts genuine and not merely cosmetic or symbolic power sharing, giving the minority a genuine voice in decision-making, it is likely to ensure genuine loyalty and erase feelings of exclusion or a desire to secede. The problem of minority alienation can then be effectively tackled. Such an arrangement will not create a permanent majority or a permanent minority.

Case Studies

This hypothesis can be tested by some contemporary, successful examples of power sharing, which are compared with some failures of constitutional arrangements where such power sharing did not exist. For instance, the United States has successfully practised a constitutional arrangement for more than two centuries, whereas Russia collapsed twice in the same century, first in 1917 under the Tsar and then in 1991 under the communists. The US, with its European roots, emerged as one nation, incorporating first the idea of the melting pot and later on, multiculturalism. Russia, on the other hand, under both Czarism and Communism, with its three-fourth Slavic population dominated by the Eastern Orthodox Church, was composed of many other ethnic minorities. The latter retained their identities more starkly than was the case in the US. Unlike the theory of the melting pot practised in the US, Russia exhibited a system of brutal might where the distinct nationalities felt repressed. Russia's acquisition of territory was forceful, unlike the territorial expansion of the US, which was mostly voluntary. Russia continued to be divided by territorial ethnicity, language and religion, but the US developed a shared belief structure based on constitutional democracy and equal opportunities under capitalism. The success of the US is the success of democracy, whereas the Russian failure is the failure of autocracy.

Another comparative study can be made of the splendid success of Singapore and the relative failure of Sri Lanka. Singapore is a soft authoritarian unitary structure that emphasises economic modernisation and the development of human resources. Ethnic identity is subdued due to its present-day prosperity and future promises. While Chinese, Malay and Tamil are given equal status as official languages, it is English that is the lingua franca. It has been able to unify different nationalities without encroaching on their relative autonomy, thus building a new kind of nationalism despite being divided along racial, linguistic and religious lines. Sri Lanka, on the contrary, is endowed with good natural resources and acquired independence almost a decade and a half before Singapore; however, its per capita income is poorer than Singapore's and its growth rate has been only 50 per cent of Singapore's over the past 25 years. Like Singapore, it is a unitary state, but its effort towards a united nation-building exercise has yielded little success. It is predominantly a Sinhalese state (the Sinhalas comprise three-fourths of the population) with continued centralised abuse of power and discrimination against minorities. Its habit of giving predominance to its own language and religion through the help of state power ultimately resulted in a bloody civil war between the Sinhalese majority and the Tamil minority, which lasted more than two decades.

Switzerland is another interesting example of successful power sharing in contrast to Yugoslavia, where an absence of power sharing has led to its failure. Switzerland, which prides itself on being the oldest democracy with the highest per capita income, no civil strife and no foreign wars, is composed of two major religious beliefs and four different languages. But in spite of the wide differences, the Swiss have a remarkable feeling of oneness and of belonging to one nation. In contrast, Yugoslavia, which was the least repressive communist state, non-aligned in foreign policy (like the Swiss policy of neutrality), and one of the richest, disintegrated like the Soviet Union. Its disintegration proves that unity imposed from the top does not endure for long. The Swiss confederation was consolidated from below and like the United States, became more centralised in the nineteenth and twentieth centuries. Yugoslavia, however, never enjoyed free choice and its unity was imposed from above after World Wars I and II, first by a king and then by Tito. Its unity essentially depended on a strong centre under a strong leadership. Unlike Switzerland, which had strong cantons, in Yugoslavia the local units were artificially created and imposed from above. Yugoslavia witnessed three clashes of civilisations—orthodox Christianity versus Islam in Bosnia and Albania, and Western Christianity in Croatia and Slovenia. Switzerland has been part of a single Western civilisation.

The disintegration of Yugoslavia proves that peaceful existence for long intervals is also no sure guarantee of continued existence, as nationalist passions based on past injustices and imagined or real deprivations may lead to uncontrollable violence and total annihilation. In contrast, Switzerland evolved out of a shared culture, with German, French and Italian recognised as official languages without altering linguistic boundaries. Yugoslavia, on the other hand, followed the Soviet model of centralised control, which greatly hampered its commitment to power sharing. Unlike the Germans who constitute three-fourths of the population in Switzerland, the Serbs in Yugoslavia comprised two-fifths, which meant that their security and identity were less secure. In spite of being smaller in percentage, the Serbs were over-represented even in non-Serbian areas within the Communist Party, the armed forces, the secret police, and the entire government bureaucracy. The Serbian minority in non-Serbian areas used intimidation and force to overawe the majority, making retaliation inevitable. In sharp contrast, there was no rigid overlap between ethnicity, religion and wealth in Switzerland. There are both Catholics and Protestants among the Germans (unlike in Canada, where the majority of Francophones in Quebec are Catholics). In Yugoslavia, all languages were equal, but for the Army. Serbo-Croat was compulsory. It was a stratified structure in which each ethnic group felt discriminated. The poorest republics perceived the taxation structure as benefiting the centre. Christians and Bosnian-Albanian Muslims feared one another.

Similarly, ethnic Albanians and Hungarians feared Slavic dominance. The Serbs felt that the borders were carved in a way that took their legitimate share away; all others, though, feared Serbian domination. The Swiss actualised power sharing, not only in the federal government, but also in private organisations like the National Soccer Association. The federal government's executive body consists of seven members, of which four are German-speaking and two or three are either French or Italian-speaking; this rotates each year, thus ensuring collective decision-making. The Swiss legislature, like the Senate of the United States, assures two seats from each canton in its upper house. In Yugoslavia, Tito's new constitutions of 1963 and 1974 tried to weaken central power by promising a loose confederation and an executive more like that of the Swiss, while in reality the domination of the top leadership of the Communist Party stressed unity, resulting in the emergence of strong leaders like Milosevic. A long-time communist, Milosevic championed Serbian nationalism, leading to the demise of Yugoslavian federation, at terrible human and economic cost.

In South Asia, the advantage of power sharing is clearly manifested in the internal evolution of India and Pakistan. India has negated Harrison's (1960) prediction that it would break up through a large and diverse model of power sharing within the ambit of democracy. However, a delayed constitution in Pakistan in 1958 and shorter interludes of democracy among long spells of rule by the army led to the secession of East Pakistan (now Bangladesh). Not only do *Muhajirs* dismiss the two-nation theory as a big joke, but the overall Punjabi domination in the army and other important spheres of state power has also created a feeling of discrimination. It is also interesting to note that the democratic process in India led to Annadurai's DMK giving up the plank of secession after the Indo-China war of 1962. Now, increasingly, the insurgency movements of the Northeast are coming to the fore, with a conviction that Indian democracy is maturing and moving towards a pluralist politics based on power sharing.

Preconditions for Power Sharing

On the basis of this study of how plural societies are managed successfully through power sharing, we can mention certain basic requirements of successful management. First, there has to be a satisfactory sense of participation, equal opportunities, and trust in mutual benefits among all members of society. The decision-making process must not only avoid any tyranny of the majority, but must also appear to be just. Second, there is a need to accept the multiple identities of citizens and accommodate diversity. Third, the question of affluence is an important factor, and there is a need to demonstrate that democracy is as much a necessity for economics as it is for politics. If the size of the cake grows, as has happened in China, then basic needs like education, healthcare and infrastructure can be tackled more quickly and much better. It also leads to a majority middle class, which has been the case in all well-established democracies; this, following the Aristotelian prescription, is the surest stabilising factor for a decent plural society. Similarly, the emergence of a sizeable Black middle class in the US has strengthened race relations. It can be reasonably argued that if pre-independent India had had a comparable middle class amongst the Muslims as amongst the Hindus, composite nationalism would have triumphed over the two-nation theory.

Fourth, the past histories of most countries have innumerable instances of conflict and discrimination, as equality and democracy are modern concepts. The past should be forgotten and there has to be elite accommodation from all segments—as has happened in the United States, which has had five southerners as Presidents in the twentieth century. Fifth, transparency in the decision-making process allows different needs and interests to be articulated by different groups, thus leading to a proper filtering of societal demands into the political system, and thereby ensuring durable policies. A lack of such transparency was one of the major reasons for the failure of the Soviet system as even within the Communist Party, only 2 per cent of its members had faith in the efficacy of communism. Sixth, there is a need to properly understand the feelings of minorities with regard to their language, culture and religious beliefs. This is to demonstrate compassion rather than sympathy, which is the surest antidote to feelings of separatism. Seventh, there is a need to cultivate a high level of tolerance, with an emphasis that in this age of democracy, the lack of it will be detrimental to economic development; also, stifling dissent will retard innovations and creativity. Eighth, there is a need to establish institutions of secularism, for example, implementation of the rule of law, and access to resources, education and justice to every single citizen.

Minorities also have an important role to play in actualising the doctrine of power sharing. They must uphold their primary interest, but must not be over-ambitious and demand a share larger than their due. Similarly, minorities must protect and enhance their own culture and heritage but not decry the majority belief structure, as that would mean a lack of respect for the majority, thereby encouraging majority alienation. Pedigree is important, but there should be a realisation that isolationism and self-sufficiency are least feasible in this age of globalisation and internationalisation of the means of production, distribution and exchange. It is no accident that the most affluent countries of Europe—Finland, Sweden, Denmark and Norway—continue to flourish within their own cultures and languages, but for international dealings, use English as a medium of communication. The same is the case with the Japanese and Koreans, and with the majority of successful intellectuals and entrepreneurs within the Indian middle class, who master both their mother tongues and English. The minority must also mobilise the international community for support in case of severe repression; however, such support should be sought only after exhausting all the domestic opportunities.

CONCLUSION

Conflict between a majority and a minority is not insoluble, as has been demonstrated through the experiences of the US, Switzerland, Singapore, and also India. What is required is the creation of a consensual basis of politics based on a genuinely pluralistic framework of power sharing, as that seems to be the only democratic mechanism that does away with a permanent majority and a permanent minority. Long ago, Pericles had said that the basis of democracy is that even if a few originate policy, all are able to discuss it. But in the mega-societies of today's democracies with all their complexities, such discussion can only lead to consensus if the entire mechanism of policy formulation and execution exhibit power sharing by all significant groups in society, including minorities.

NOTE

1. O'Leary modified Lijphart's idea of a grand coalition and demonstrated that what matters for a democratic consociation 'is meaningful cross-community executive power sharing in which each significant segment is represented in the government with at least plurality levels of support within its segment'.

11

CORPORATISM

Corporatism can be defined as a system of interest representation in which constituent units are organized into a limited number of singular, compulsory, non-competitive, hierarchically ordered and functionally differentiated categories, recognized or licensed (if not created) by the state and granted a representational monopoly within their respective categories in exchange for observing certain controls on their selection of leaders and articulation of demands and supports.

Schmitter 1979: 13

Corporatism is based on a body of ideas that can be traced through Aristotle, Roman law, medieval social and legal structures, and into contemporary Catholic social philosophy. These ideas are based on the premise that man's nature can only be fulfilled within a political community.... The central core of the corporatist vision is thus not the individual but the political community whose perfection allows the individual members to fulfil themselves and find happiness ... The state in the corporatist tradition is thus clearly interventionist and powerful.

Hewlett 1980: 25

Corporatism, in its broadest sense, is a means of incorporating organized interests into the processes of government. There are two faces of corporatism, first authoritarian corporatism is an ideology or economic form closely associated with Italian Fascism. It was characterized by the political intimidation of industry and destruction of independent trade unions. Secondly, liberal corporatism (societal corporatism or neo corporatism) refers to the tendency found in mature liberal democracies for organized interests to be granted privileged and institutional access to policy formulation. The mechanisms through which this is achieved vary considerably, as does the degree of group integration. In contrast with the authoritarian variant, liberal corporatism strengthens groups in relation to government, not the other way round.

Heywood 1997: 257

The question of political representation is a contested one. The controversy has ancient roots, but it became important with the consolidation of mass democracies in the West when it became clear—in spite of Rousseau's criticism that British people were free once in five years—that there was no possible alternative to representative assemblies to represent the mass of people and take decisions. Pitkin, in her classic study *The Concept of Representation* (1967), detailed four types of representation: (*i*) authorised, where a representative is legally empowered to act for another; (*ii*) descriptive, where the representative stands for a group by virtue of sharing similar characteristics, such as race, sex, ethnicity or residence; (*iii*) symbolic, where a leader claims to stand for national ideas; and (*iv*) substantive, where the representative speaks to advance a group's policy preferences and interests. Pitkin admitted that all four have ambiguities and complexities.

CORPORATIVIST VIEW OF REPRESENTATION

The dominant view of modern theories of representation, emphasising 'one person one vote' territorially, has been challenged by a group-oriented functionalist view of corporatism. Since there is no clear definition of this view of representation, it is better described. Some see corporatism as a state-specific phenomenon, shaped by particular historical and political circumstances. Austria, Sweden, the Netherlands, and to some extent, Germany and Japan, are countries in which governments have generally practised a form of economic management. Many see corporatism as a general phenomenon that grows from tendencies implicit in economic and social development. Even the US, which is described as a pluralist democracy, has regulatory agencies with quasi-legislative powers. The term 'corporatism' simultaneously designates a particular interest group structure, characterised by monopolistic, centralised and internally non-democratic associations, and a particular policymaking process known as 'concertation' or 'social partnership' (Baccaro 2003: 683). It rejects the liberal view about the inevitability of conflict and argues that it is both desirable and possible to lay out a consensual basis of politics by ensuring the functional representation of numerous professional groups. It emphasises the associational character of modern life based on division of labour and functional categories like peasants, craftsmen, shopkeepers, industrialists, lawyers, bank employees and doctors, which are all self-governing, essentially distinctive in their function, and can act as mediators between the government and the members. Modern equal citizenship and modern equal representation are replaced by group identity and occupational membership, changing the entire connotation of a liberal theory of citizenship based on territorial representation.

> Corporatism is more than a peculiar pattern of articulation of interests. Rather, it is an institutionalized pattern of policy formation in which large interest organizations cooperate with each other and with public authorities not only in the articulation (or even 'intermediation') of interests, but—in its developed forms—in the 'authoritative allocation of values' and in the implementation of such policies (Lehmbruch 1979: 150).

Lehmbruch offered a historical-sociological definition for corporatism. According to him, there are three basic types of corporatism: 'liberal corporatism (for example, the kind operating in democratic industrial countries), statist corporatism (for example, the fascist, authoritarian, and clerico-authoritarian variety) and traditional corporatism (for example, the guild systems of medieval cities).'

While Corporatism refers to the emergence of state-sponsored, monopolistic legal associations for different groups in society, Pluralism recognises the other side's right to live and tries to provide for the co-existence of both sides while allowing each the right to pursue its own interests. Dahl points out that pluralism is not only a Western bourgeois concept, but can also be implemented in communist regimes, for instance, during the decentralised socialist Tito rule in Yugoslavia or in Chile. Almond criticised the corporatist model for mobilising people and groups under state control, preventing them from following their own interests freely.

MODERN CORPORATISM AND THE MEDIEVAL GUILD SYSTEM

According to Morall (1960), with the decline of the feudal order in the nineteenth century, the Western European monarch was compelled to move towards a system of representation. The basis for such a system was provided by corporate organisations which came up with increased urbanisation; and with the prime attention of each 'to safeguard its autonomous existence' (ibid.: 60). However, a clear distinction between feudal and corporate ideas is yet to emerge. 'The thirteenth century,' remarked Morall, 'saw no absolute incompatibility between the kind as feudal overload and the kind as public head of the whole political community' (ibid.: 61). In such a situation, the process of representation was slow and uneven.

Plena Potestas

This is the most important innovation in the medieval representational system, which continues even today. Roman private law recognises an agent or protector to conduct a case and accept the final judgement, which is followed by the corporate bodies. The first clear example comes from Italy, where Roman law had the deepest and largest impact. The other countries of Western Europe followed it too, 'and by the end of the thirteenth century we find representative assemblies on a national basis becoming familiar in England, France and the Spanish Kingdoms' (Morall 1960: 64).

This corporate representation proved immensely beneficial to the king for a number of reasons. Representative assembly eliminated the long and acrimonious process of dealing with a large number of groups. Ignorance or lack of consent was eliminated by the principle of Plena Potestas, binding all to the decisions. The Roman legal norms helped to create a situation where decisions were taken by the majority. Again, the practice of Roman private law applied to political representation; 'closed the door against attempts by a community to disclaim responsibility for agreements reached between its representatives and the central authority of the realm' (Morall 1960: 65). But it was far from a democratic act as it 'was not an assertion of embryonic democracy so much as a device of the monarchy to obtain a guaranteed assent of the realm to its demands' (ibid.). Medieval representation had no consent clause and there was no right to refuse a king's policies. It was 'self-government at the king's command' (White, cited in ibid.). This medieval representational system was the most successful and endured the longest in England, because England had self-government for a long time.

MODERN REVIVAL

Corporatism in modern times originated in Germany in the nineteenth century. It rejected the early liberal constitutionalism as it had evolved in the Anglo-Saxon world, and was based firmly on the primacy of the individual. Corporatism was the answer to early industrialisation and class conflict. It questioned the core liberal values of individual representation, primacy of civil liberties, free competition and liberal democracy. The key word for a corporatist political order is harmony. It is the group as a functionalist category, rather than the individual, that is projected, with corporate organisations mediating between the governmental apparatus and society. Medieval corporatism evolved in very different forms. Johannes Althusius (1563–1638) was the first to elaborate a comprehensive theory, a 'consociationalist' constitution. It was written at a time when the medieval order itself was facing serious challenge from absolute monarchy and indivisible territorial sovereignty. Antony Blake considered Althusius a great theorist of corporatism, with 'perhaps the most substantial exposition of guild ideas ever known. The commonwealth consists of all the different associations with a defined territory as an apex body. It was a social contract which creates a common power, a one person or one Assembly of persons that may reduce all their wills, by plurality of voices unto one will' (Black 1984: 441). Czada (2011) is of the view that Althusius propagated the idea of shared sovereignty, which stands at the opposite end of Hobbes' unitarism and Jean Bodin's (1530–96) theory of monarchical sovereignty. Althusius believed in corporative autonomy or recognition of groups, making him a precursor of modern federalism.

An interesting aspect of early corporatism is that, unlike its later variants, it did not merely emphasise the collective, but also stressed individual autonomy. Both Althusius and Marsilius of Padua propagated a decentralised polity as well as popular sovereignty. However, the fact remains that medieval corporatism had an organic view of life that often blurred the distinction between the collective and the individual, state and society, politics and religion, and the public and private spheres. Being a philosophical defence of the medieval guild system, the corporatist theory of society perceived a static social order with individual activity and choice restricted to a narrow sphere, characterised by delicate social balancing and clearly drawn boundaries.

Within the larger framework of the medieval guild system, corporatism performed several functions in economic, cultural and religious life, as well as in the crucial area of political life. With emphasis on division of labour and professional expertise, they set the standards for prices and wages, and education and work. It also provided for the care of widows and orphans, representation on town councils, choosing officials for courts and the town militia, and maintained social cohesion and charitable institutions like hospitals, orphanages and housing for the poor. Medieval European corporatism is comparable to what Tagore perceived as the function of society in the Indian context, as outlined in his *Swadeshi Samaj* (1904). The rise and consolidation of the modern state and capitalism made medieval corporatism irrelevant, when the functions that it performed were taken over by the state and became subject to state prerogative, governmental administration and the market. Corporatism has always had an uneasy relationship with the market.

As an ideology, corporatism received great support from leading theorists in the nineteenth century. Similar to the anti-machine movement, it provided an ideological framework to deal with the early phases of unregulated capitalism and all its horrors (as exemplified in the writings of Charles Dickens [1812–70] and Victor Hugo [1802–85]). In any era of quick and unprecedented change, there is always a glorification of a golden past, contrasted with the uncertainties of a fast-changing world. Like the security provided by the Indian joint family system, the traditional social security provided by a more static order is defended as both desirable and feasible. What further added to this thinking was class conflict, an inevitable by-product of liberalism and the market economy, both of which it rejects.

The most important and immediate catalyst was a counter-revolution to republicanism. German romanticism recaptured a sense of community in order to promote the general interest of the entire community by bridging the gap between atomised Hobbesian individuals on the one hand and the state leviathan on the other, through functionalist communal organisations. Two important considerations strengthened this school of thought: (*a*) social stability, caricatured by revolutionary theorists as merely transitional; and (*b*) genuine concern for traditional craftsmen, small businesses, workers and industrialists, who were being pushed to the edge by the market and new innovations.

Adam Muller

The French Revolution had a substantial impact on East Germany and Austria. The first major theorist of corporatism was Adam Muller (1779–1827). He rejected French egalitarianism and Smith's *laissez faire* economics, as well as Hume's objection to mercantilism. Resurrecting a powerful state, he developed a scheme to adjust the interests of all economic groups subordinated to the state. Reviving the medieval guilds, he tried to prove their necessity in a modern class state. The function of modern corporatism was primarily two-fold, regulating the production and coordination of class interests. He believed that modern units modelled after feudal classes could create a harmonious society. Each corporation controlling specific functions in the important social, economic and cultural spheres would coordinate the entire lives of all citizens. Muller was firmly opposed to Smith; Smith was purely materialistic, a liberal political economist and partisan, as he depicted an individualistic side to society and a British life that had no universal validity. Smith propagated economic individualism and free trade, which Muller opposed. Rejecting Smith, Muller, like Fichte, emphasised the ethical elements in national economy and autarchy. In his *Address to the German Nation*, written in response to the French occupation, Fichte praised the 'German spirit', whose ideals transcended the selfish aims of Western culture. He described Germans as the only Europeans capable of profound and original thought. He proposed a 'closed communal state' that would conduct foreign trade through state monopoly, aiming at the highest degree of autarchy. Fichte, like many subscribers to corporatism, recognised unrestricted international commerce as a potential threat to domestic regulation and 'ethical markets'.

Although Muller was inspired by a feudal past, he was not reactionary. He was attempting to link the political with the social sciences, while rejecting revolutionary ideas and radical politics. He disagreed with the distinction between constitutional and civil (common) law, placing his faith in an all-powerful leviathan. He idealised medieval feudalism as the basis on which modern political order should be modelled. The exit of Metternich ended any serious discussion of his theory. However, towards the end of the nineteenth century, Muller's ideas were revived in France, Austria, Italy and Germany with the rise of Christian syndicalism, dialectically linked to the rise of revolutionary syndicalists like Georges Sorel (1847–1922) and the consolidation of socialist political parties in West Europe. He influenced thinkers like Othmer Spann (1878–1950) and Guiseppe Toriollo (1845–1918).

According to Hegel, civil society comprised three different but interrelated aspects: the system of needs, the administration of justice, and the need for police and cooperation. Regarding the first, Hegel stated that these were the particular needs of particular individuals, existing in contrast to universal principles. They were subjective needs. Hegel argued that the needs of animals were limited in scope, whereas those of human beings multiplied. Division of labour was one major means for their attainment, as through this division an individual's work became simpler and his skill increased with the growth in output. Individuals become interdependent, leading to a 'dialectical advance' as self-interest generates a situation where everyone else's needs are also satisfied. The cumulative effects of particular motivations result in a universal minimum in which each person's enjoyment leads to similar enjoyment by all others. Through education and the skills of multitudes of people, the general wealth of civil society also increases.

Civil society was inevitably divided into classes and estates. This division was bound to take place because of the presence of different skills, outlooks, interests, ways of life and opportunities, and other factors such as risk or fortune. The three broad groupings—the peasantry, business class and the universal class of bureaucracy—mediated between the family and the state. As the state was large and impersonal, an individual's public spirit and communitarian feeling had to grow within the ambit of civil society. Hegel's corporation was the mechanism through which this could be achieved—by the flowering of professional associations and voluntary organisations. Like de Tocqueville, Hegel accepted freedom of association as a key right in the modern world. Corporatism was an essential requirement for actualising freedom. He went to the extent of arguing that freedom of association was more important than freedom of speech and opinion, as the former could further different human capacities and allow an individual to identify with groups of one's choice. Associations helped to prevent not only the over-centralisation of the state, but also the fragmentation of the market at a particular level. They also provided for the development and recognition of particular skills, abilities and talents. People learnt how to cooperate, and gain from such cooperation. Membership entailed the acceptance of a code of conduct, which inculcated a sense of discipline. Next to the family, it allowed for the growth of pride and integrity, giving the individual dignity.

Another important aspect of corporatism is the welfare functions it undertakes for the underprivileged. The state, in Hegel's theory, was not a welfare state, and nor was Hegel an advocate of a planned economy. But he opposed social indifference to poverty and the idea that people should fend for themselves. Concerned about social stability, he suggested that a safety net be provided by the corporation for all those who suffer in the market. However, he had recommended foreign markets, believing that domestic problems could be solved by external involvement. For him, society consisted of three classes: the agricultural, governmental and business classes. The last incorporated all craftsmen and producers. The corporation also played the role of mediator between the state and civil society by facilitating political representation for its members. Like other political thinkers of his time, Hegel opposed universal franchise, arguing that it would lead to fragmentation and apathy. But he was also conscious of the need for representation, and preferred corporate representation in legislative assemblies or states. Representation is not geographical, but interest-based, and participation in the political process would protect those interests better. Hegel's idea was very similar to Burke's theory of representing interests. For Hegel, a kind of functional representation led to class cooperation and harmony. This political recognition was essential to preventing the formation of an organised group of disgruntled people against the state.

> The consideration behind the abolition of Corporations in recent times is that the individual should fend for himself. But we may grant this and still hold that corporation membership does not alter a man's obligation to earn his living. Under modern political conditions, the citizens have only a restricted share in the public business of the state, yet it is essential to provide men—ethical entities—with work of a public character over and above their private business. This work of a public character, which the modern state does not always provide, is found in the Corporation (Hegel 1969: 278).

In the twentieth century, corporatism was viewed with suspicion because of Italian Fascism, and also because the military and authoritarian rulers of South America used this term in the context of total governmental control and direction of business enterprises and labour movements, to secure unity, discipline, order and efficiency in order to crush any opposition. It was supposed to create a state-supported consensus between different and even conflicting social groups by controlling market competition. Hegel's corporatism, though, was very different. It is more akin to the idea of liberal corporatism, that is, self-regulation by quasi-autonomous social groups within the ambit of constitutional government. It was still not democratic, as by preferring organised groups and the elite, it would negate the representational process. For Hegel, corporatism was a natural conclusion to the design of his theory of the state.

> Hegel's purpose was to find a middle ground between Hobbes and Robespierre, between the market place and citizen virtue. Hegel believes he has found such a middle ground in the existing class structure, with its corporations and professional associations comprising civil society. These institutions help to prevent further atomization and particularization but also seek to connect the individual with some wider and morally satisfying forms of social life without merely submerging his identity or 'personhood' within them. They provide, as it were, a 'second family' (Smith 1989: 250).

Cole stressed the associational and functional nature of all kinds of organisations. A genuine democracy was supposed to be based on a system of coordinated functional representation. Representation as such had to be 'specific and functional' and not merely 'general and inclusive'. The present parliament 'professes to represent all citizens in all things, and therefore as a rule represents none of them' (Cole 1920: 108). This theory of representing functions is similar to that of Burke, who wanted to institutionalise an anti-democratic oligarchic power structure with a natural aristocracy at the helm. Cole, on the other hand, wanted democracy to be alive in every sphere of social, economic and political activity. There were significant differences between the Webbs (Sydeny [1859–1947] and Beatrice [1858–1943]) and Cole with regard to the theory of representation. For Sydeny Webb, 'the supreme paradox' of democracy was reflected in the fact

> ... that every man is a servant in respect of the matters of which he possesses the most intimate knowledge, and for which he shows the most expert proficiency, namely the professional craft to which he devotes his working hours; and he is a master over that on which he knows no more than anybody else, namely, the general interests of the community as a whole. In this paradox ... lies at once the justification and the strength of democracy (Webb 1920: 108).

However, for Cole, the failure of this was manifested in its acceptance by all classes, depriving the ordinary worker and average citizen of any meaningful role in determining their social environment. The individual, 'in learning to control his own industry would learn also to control the political machine' (Cole 1917: 185).

Durkheim's essential assertion was that the existing societal bond was of a 'collective consciousness', which is an essential prerequisite for individual happiness and maintenance of order. His theory came in response to Spencer's assumption of the social bond that emerged from his methodological individualism, that is, it was individual-centric and based entirely on interaction by individually motivated actions.

Durkheim and Spencer belonged to two different and distinctive schools of thought. Spencer was a product of the British tradition, influenced by Hobbes, Locke, Smith, Hume and Mill. Durkheim was firmly placed in the French tradition, which was influenced by Montesquieu, Rousseau and Comte. Durkheim's thesis was rooted in a collective sentiment based on structural functionalism. Communal solidarity leads to common societal practices, while Spencer's methodological individualism led in an opposite direction. The controversy centred mainly on Durkheim's *The Division of Labour in Society* (1893). However, Perrin (1975, 2005) argued that 'Durkheim's criticism is not based on Spencer's original writings but against general ideas that Durkheim assumes Spencer maintains'. Later, Perrin even claimed that 'Spencer and Durkheim differ very little in their conceptions of the causes of an expanding division of labour'. His argument was that while they did differ with respect to the effects, Durkheim's explanation was not an improvement on Spencer's (Perrin 2005: 801).

For Durkheim, altruism and social cohesion were core values that he mentioned while distinguishing himself from Spencerian Utilitarianism, which considered them dispensable in social life. Rejecting Spencer's theory of explicit contract, Durkheim highlighted unintentional and non-contractual facts as being intrinsic to the entire process of an exchange relationship. The important hidden factors could be religion, morality or law, or a combination of the three. Durkheim, like Muller, assumed that medieval contractualism was still applicable in modern altered circumstances, and refuted the assertion that contract could replace status, as self-interest weakens the social bond. He distinguished between an individual and a social being, the latter being a higher reality. Moral ideals cannot be reduced to a part of utilitarian ethics and individual reasoning is subordinated to the social one. A common consciousness is vital for social cohesion in order to avoid anarchy. This social realism is clearly manifest in all our actions. The uniqueness of individuals is restricted as both for happiness and livelihood, group identity is a prime necessity. While society is an arrangement amongst individuals, the collective, too, has its own dynamics. Durkheim acknowledged the presence of a collective mind, without which an individual's survival is impossible. However, his thesis cannot be tested empirically; the only plausible defence he could provide was his personal conviction.

Durkheim wanted to provide a scientific framework for sociology, but in placing the societal whole before the individual, he clearly established his value preference. He was suspicious of any individual-based study. Hegel and Spencer were both satisfied with contemporary reality and did not worry much about social cohesion. But Durkheim, like Weber, was aware of the unsettled nature of European society and the possibility that an irrational action would upset the entire social stability. Durkheim's transformative criticism of Spencer is comparable to Marx's attempt to revise Hegel by projecting the future along very different lines. Durkheim's emphasis was on the variety and relativity of social formations; for him, Western European liberal society was one such social formation, with future development remaining uncertain.

CRITIQUE OF CONTEMPORARY INDUSTRIAL SOCIETY: DURKHEIM'S STUDY OF SUICIDE

Durkheim's celebrated work *Suicide* was published in 1897, in which the major faultlines of modern industrial society became apparent. His theory established a close link between *laissez faire* economic doctrine and quick change, and the larger societal failure to inculcate the quality of restraint and limits in individuals. When unlimited desire remains unfulfilled, it leads to relative deprivation, which in turn leads to suicides. Earlier stable societies did not face this problem, as there was always a balance between desire and attainment.

But the contemporary world has no such boundaries, and this leads individuals to hopelessness and desperation. Cohesiveness and societal hierarchy lie shattered. Material well-being and earning increasing amounts of money become the motto, said Durkheim. 'The appetite which industry brings into play finds themselves freed of all constraining authority. This apotheosis of material well-being, by, so to speak sanctifying them, has placed economic appetites above every human law' (Joll 1981: 135).

Durkheim launched a frontal attack on liberal economic philosophy and its endorsement of a capitalist industrial society. However, he was also optimistic of matching human desire to reasonable expectation. Human beings should realistically assess the situation, rather than fantasise about or hope for *El Dorado.* Paradoxically, he was disturbed by the free enterprise doctrine and was a critic of contemporary economic, social and political developments within the liberal framework; yet, he remained a firm believer in reason and progress and, as Joll pointed out, 'he explicitly stated that the motive for his sociological writing was his desire to contribute to the moral constitution of the Third Republic' (Joll 1981: 136).

The new anthropological discoveries supplement Durkheim's claim, as they demonstrate that all societies need not develop in one single direction. By implication, the liberal perception of industrial society is only one of many possibilities. Durkheim, like Otto von Gierke (1841–1921), proposed the establishment of corporatist associations to deal with the problems of disorder, social anomie and isolation, created by the division of labour and erosion of traditional bonds of solidarity.

FASCISM AND CORPORATISM

Mussolini coined the terms 'fascism'[1] and 'totalitarianism'. The communist thesis stating that its rise and consolidation were signs of the imminent collapse of capitalism, in a context where social democrats were looked upon as lackeys of capitalism, facilitated the consolidation of fascism. The communist elite was convinced about Nikolai Bukharin's (1888–1938) thesis of the final crises within capitalism and the collapse of communism. It did not occur to the communists of the time that there was a fundamental difference between liberal democracy and fascism; and fascism rejected both the major tenets of liberal democracy and communism. Mussolini projected fascism as a new development in history. It was a doctrine with universal application and was supposed to herald a new civilisation. However, the theoretical basis of fascism was worked out only after Mussolini came to power; Joll believed that this was to acquire some 'intellectual respectability' (1981: 344–45). However, fascism was a new phenomenon in the West and in the background of fear, revolution and uncertainty, it tried unsuccessfully to bring in an enduring sense of national community and solidarity.

The lynchpin of this new formation was the corporate state. It was popularised because (*i*) its philosophical roots could be traced to a non-liberal and non-Marxist tradition, where the state is glorified as a protector and builder of the human collective; and (*ii*) it could build a collective consciousness of all the people. Such a functionalist and collectivist category tried to do away with the main plank of liberal democracy, the one person one vote. The social and political existence of each individual in modern mass society is to be expressed only through a corporation.

'Corporate state' was a valued phrase in both fascist Italy and Nazi Germany. Professional and economic bodies were supposed to be the pillars of the state. Rosenberg considered it a process of creating a new kind of man (Joll 1981: 345). 'Fascism is a religious conception in which man is seen in his immediate relationship with a superior law and an objective will that transcends the particular individual [and] raises him to conscious membership of a spiritual society' (Rosenberg, cited in ibid.: 348). In the fascist state, the newly and hurriedly formed corporate organisations remained a facade, used more for publicity and the creation of a support base, behind which the totalitarian state existed with its repressive apparatuses and total control of education. Arendt believed that fascism's success lay in its ability to create 'mass organizations of atomised isolated individuals' (cited in ibid.: 345).

The corporativist ideology that flourished beyond Italy and Germany was both anti-communist and anti-liberal, and a convenient and popular attempt at legitimisation. However, penetration into and attempt to control all facets of life in which corporativist ideas were used as a tool highlighted the clear distinction between traditional corporativist ideas and fascism. As Nolte[2] demonstrated, the fascism that developed in Europe in the 1920s was distinctly different from other forms of authoritarianism; similarly, fascist corporativism was a unique and historically determined phase. Linz (2000: 220) supported this historically specified fascist corporativist thesis. He also described corporatist authoritarian regimes as those in which corporate institutions are used extensively by the state to co-opt and demobilise powerful interest groups.

Authoritarian Corporativism

Bolivar dismissed US constitutionalism as a suitable model for Latin America. Except for Chile, which had a long history of constitutional regimes, the continent was a favourite ground for experimenting with various forms of corporativism, before the dramatic shift described by Huntington as the 'democratisation of Catholicism' swept through the continent in the 1980s. In Latin America, there were many experiments to represent interests, primarily to reduce conflict between labour unions and the state. Given the widespread patron-client relationships and acute inequality, corporativism became a tool for authoritarian regimes to control social and economic unrest and postpone democracy for as long as possible. Later, these models were adopted and practised in a number of countries in Asia; however, the term 'corporativism' was avoided because of its link with authoritarianism in popular perception.

Corporativist Constitutionalism

This is rather an exception than the rule. Croatia, which has a long corporativist tradition, contains in its constitution provision for a second chamber, corporative representation of trade unions, employers and farmers organisations, educational institutes, craftsmen and freelance professionals, etc. Another example is Hong Kong, where nearly half the legislative members have been elected by functional constituencies defined by professional occupations or economic sectors since 1985. The crux of corporativist evolution is found in a retarded party system which hinders the proper functioning of a constitutional government, and is detrimental to the realisation of elementary civil and political liberties.

CONCLUSION

Corporatism provides a critique of the liberal individualistic tradition that began with Smith, extending it to the economic arena. It could never provide a coherent alternative to liberal capitalism, and remains at best a critique rather than an alternative. Its popularity was more or less restricted to Germany, made possible both by its history and its economic evolution.

NOTES

1. Fascism, which rose first in Italy, had a number of reasons for its success: (*i*) the effect of World War I; (*ii*) the imperfect functioning of parliamentary government before, during and after the War; (*iii*) the continuing division between a prosperous, industrialised North and an impoverished agricultural South; (*iv*) a weak party system that allowed rule by personalities rather than the leaders of parties, accompanied by widespread corruption; and (*v*) instability due to the introduction of proportional representation, which subsequently took place in Germany as well. The five governments between 1918 and 1922 reflected a parliamentary paralysis. In the beginning, Mussolini's party was a minor constitutional force; however, they controlled the streets violently. In the background

of massive post-war unemployment and industrial and agricultural discontent, there were some improvements. Mussolini captured power not against parliamentary democracy, but rather, by 'inventing a communist threat from Bolshevism and putting fascism as an alternative saviour'. Interestingly, Mussolini had no programme to place before the parliament. His immediate aim was to attain power and subsequently, he moved cautiously to assume total power.

In the first ever genuinely democratic elections in Germany in 1919, the Social Democrats emerged as the largest single party and its leader, Ebert, wanted to achieve socialism through parliamentary means. But the communists, influenced by the success of the Bolsheviks and led by Liebknecht and Luxemburg, occupied all the larger cities of Germany. The government could defeat them only with the Freikorps, private voluntary regiments raised by anti-communist ex-army officers. Had the communists supported the Social Democrats, the history of Germany would have been very different. Germany under the Weimar constitution passed through three distinct phases: 1919 to the end of 1923, an unstable period; the end of 1923 to the end of 1929, which saw an industrial boom and massive US assistance, a golden period; and the last phase, October 1929 to January 1933. In the background of world economic crisis, which had a disastrous effect on Germany with 6.5 million unemployed by 1932, the Republic was on the verge of collapse. Given the humiliation of the Treaty of Versailles, little respect and no tradition of a democratic government with proportional representation, no party could win an overall majority; also, the disbelief of the communists and nationalists in the republic and an increased threat of a civil war all hastened the end of the republic. In this situation, and with growing economic instability, Hitler offered an attractive alternative. The Nazis increased their electoral support, offering national unity, prosperity and full employment, the overthrow of the Versailles settlement, a private army (a feature of all parties), and the storm troopers (which could provide jobs to unemployed youth). Wealthy landowners and industrialists supported them because of their hostility towards the communists, and the clear difference between the ineffective governments of the Weimar Republic and the efficient Nazi government. Once in power, Hitler emulated the one-party state model of Soviet communists and Italian fascists. However, despite their virulent anti-communism, the two models of fascism had many structural and ideological differences. Many other countries facing serious economic crisis followed this model in the 1920s and 1930s—Japan, Spain, Portugal. In the 1940s, many South American politicians were influenced by them, mainly in Argentina and Brazil. But these later versions were markedly different from the Italian model.

2. Nolte distinguished fascism from other reactionary movements and considered it anti-traditional and anti-modern, rejecting both communism and liberal democracy.

12

AUTHORITARIANISM AND MILITARY RULE

Military coups are inconsistent with competitive democratic theory . . . they inevitably damage the very facets of civil and political life that make competitive democracies theoretically attractive.

Karsten 1989: 4

The countries of the world display a much greater diversity of authoritarianism than they do of democracy, since the former lacks any universal rules or norms other than the preservation of power.

O'Neil 2004: 119

Military intervention is universal in its mildest form; in its most manifest expression, it is symptomatic of the profound malaise which some societies experience. Yet military regimes do not provide a cure to the malaise which is at the origin of their existence. Where military personnel take over power, they do not provide more than that, at best, a temporary often illusory solution.

Blondel 2014: 368

Even when liberal constitutionalism was on its ascendant in the eighteenth century, there was a lot of suspicion about democracy and the ability of ordinary people to be responsible citizens in a liberal democratic order. Macpherson (1966, 1973) pointed out that 'democracy is a good thing'. Today, politicians and political theorists of all hues, including Marxists, profess their commitment to liberal democracy and its principles. From being a contested and derogatory term, democracy in its earlier libertarian form has come to occupy an unrivalled, pivotal position.

But even in the contemporary world, there are a number of regimes that are not democratic and that can be described as authoritarian. Freedom House (https://freedomhouse.org/), which brings out an annual survey of democratic nations, still believes that the majority of the world's population, that is, about 60 per cent, live in countries which are either 'partly free' with severe limitations on personal liberties and democratic rights, and 'not free', with a complete absence of both personal liberties and democratic rights. These categories provide examples of different varieties of authoritarian rule.

DEFINITION OF AUTHORITARIANISM

Unlike democracy, which can be precisely defined, the wide variety of authoritarian rules means that authoritarianism can be better described than defined, with reference to the common characteristics that do not allow it to be termed 'democratic'. Hobbes described the quest for unlimited power as the essence of human nature, and authoritarianism champions the enjoyment of such power by one or a selected number of people, who simultaneously deny that same power to the overwhelming majority of the population. This enjoyment of power by a small number of people denies the very framework of rule of law or the constitutional mechanism of checks and balances. Power and authority are always extra-constitutional and arbitrary.

The people by and large have no role in selecting and/or removing those leaders who wield all the power at their will. Since the latter can dictate policies, they are called dictators. The total elimination of civil and political liberties makes their leadership more autonomous. Freedom of speech or assembly is either severely restricted, or not allowed at all. Political activity is strictly limited and restricted by the top echelons in authority. Although many communist regimes claimed that restrictions on social and political freedom enhanced equality, in actual practice it denied both political freedom and equality. Boris Pasternek's (1890–1960) masterpiece, *Dr. Zhivago* (1957), explains this phenomenon graphically.

IDEOLOGIES AND AUTHORITARIANISM

Authoritarianism does not form a linear set of principles or ideologies; on the contrary, a wide variety emerges. Many of them are invented after the capture of power to justify the action. Two dominant forms of authoritarian rule that evolved in direct opposition to liberal democracy were communism and fascism. Although the theoretical underpinnings of these two doctrines were antithetical to one another, both were united in their opposition to liberal democracy. Arbitrary rule or justification after the seizure of power is not only the dominant pattern of authoritarian rule, but also often has ideological underpinnings. The liberal constitutional state is often portrayed as weak and unable to perform the important functions of a state; here, even the curtailment of individual freedom and abrogation of a constitution is justified.

AUTHORITARIANISM AND TOTALITARIANISM

Both 'authoritarianism' and 'totalitarianism' (see Chapter 6 for totalitarianism) are used to describe a non-democratic and repressive regime. But it is better to treat totalitarianism as an autonomous category within the larger framework of authoritarian regimes. Totalitarianism was invented in the twentieth century when the ideological polarisation between liberal democracy and its rivals, fascism and communism, had reached its peak. Within a well-cultivated ideological basis, both fascism and communism wanted to complete the transformation of the human character, state, society, economy, and the entire ideological basis of the modern, liberal democratic order. To achieve this, a great degree of terror, state power and secret organisation is supplemented by the mass mobilisation and deification of its leaders. The cleavage between the ruler and the subject is projected as just and ordained, and no deviation is tolerated. Ideology provides the real strength to the regime, and to proclaim and continue rule on the basis of one sole ideology, violence and terror invariably become the essential mechanisms, with no consideration for constitutional checks and balances. Totalitarianism, by its very nature, rejects any opposition or obstacle, and will attempt to reach its goal with all the essential ruthlessness and violence. The purpose of this terror is to destroy the very essence of individual personality and creativity. However, the mere use of violence does not make a regime totalitarian; what does so is its capacity for an all-comprehensive totalitarian ideology, under which every single individual is subordinate to the state. The ideology can be of either the radical right or the radical left, but both proclaim a complete rupture from the present, made possible through the cleansing force of violence.

As Hobbes said, the primary human desire is the desire for power, and there are plenty of examples where leaders have sought the use of terror for complete control. Many such attempts fail, while a few succeed. The two best examples of modern totalitarianism are Hitler's Germany and Stalin's Soviet Union. Although the aims of these rules were diametrically different, when it came to using terror and maiming and killing people, their records are similar.

FACTORS LEADING TO AUTHORITARIAN RULE

There is no unanimity amongst social scientists with regard to the causes of authoritarian rule. In many cases, the reasons may be circumstantial and local. However, it is still possible to identify the broad but differing perceptions of scholars about these causes.

Economic Factors

Most scholars accept the pivotal importance of economic factors. However, in liberal and communist perceptions, the causes are diametrically opposed. Liberalism insists on the centrality of the market in the evolution of both liberal democracy and authoritarianism. For liberals, the presence or absence of the market is the key factor in understanding the evolution of these two forms of governance. The existence of the market allows the slow and definite development of a substantive middle class, which in turn allows both the generation and distribution of wealth. This provides more educated and competitive manpower; the widespread distribution of wealth works as a bulwark against an individual or small group, until the latter usurp all the powers of the state and create obstacles to middle-class prosperity. Liberalism welcomes a weak state and a strong, self-perpetuating civil society. Consequently, the middle class with its economic strength influences the political process. Meade's term property-owning democracy, or George W. Bush's ownership society, explains the societal basis of democracy.

Where the middle class forms a small segment of the population, poverty and inequality are widespread and this facilitates authoritarian rule. It can take either form: (*i*) to protect, by any means, the wealth of the few, or (*ii*) to forcibly distribute the wealth of the few to the majority. However, since the size of the cake is small, forcible redistribution of wealth and lack of further wealth generation creates more poverty than before.

Communists hold the opposite view as for them, it is capitalism that is the basic cause (rather than the solution) of authoritarian rule. The theory of widespread wealth created by the market is a myth for them as in capitalism, wealth is created by a surplus, accumulated through the exploitation of workers. According to this theory, the small middle class would gladly embrace authoritarian rule to protect their own wealth. Following Lenin's theory of imperialism, the argument is that wealthy nations that reject authoritarianism at home endorse the same in the colonies or poorer countries, and this constitutes a different form of the same exploitation.

O'Neil has made interesting observations on these contrasting views. He commented: 'ideologies are built around ideals of how the world should be, but in reality, the circumstances are much more complicated' (2009: 125). Giving the example of a free market economy that failed in Germany, which in turn gave rise to Nazism in the 1930s, he stated 'that when members of the middle class believe that economic insecurity, rather than those who hold political power, is the greatest threat to their wealth, they may become the greatest supporters of authoritarian rule' (ibid.). He also pointed out that the thesis that market economy leads to democracy is questionable, as both economic development and capitalism can flourish in an authoritarian regime. A definitive conclusion is yet to emerge. On the other hand, the communist position is equally problematic. The theory of the link between capitalism and authoritarianism is to 'be considered in light of communism's own horrors' (ibid.: 126). However, as Lichtheim (1975) has pointed out, democracy has flourished only in a capitalistic order and the dream of combining democracy and socialism is yet to be realised. This demonstrates that although all capitalist countries need not be democratic, democracy needs a free market to succeed.

Societal Explanation of Authoritarianism

There is widespread literature that disregards the economic factor and considers a particular culture a pre-condition of capitalism and democracy. Culture can retard or strengthen democracy, 'depending on whether the existing culture embodies norms and values that are consistent with democratic practices' (Lichtheim 1975: 126). This view found its strongest support in Weber, and is linked with the Protestant Ethic (see Chapter 5) or Calvinism, with its emphasis on individualism, secularism, tolerance, the consolidation of the nation-state and early industrialisation. Huntington's (1984a, 1984b) phrase 'democratisation of Catholicism' proves that overemphasis on the specificity of culture as an obstacle to democracy is grossly overstated.

Gramsci's Analysis of Fascism

Unprecedented violence has been used by both totalitarian fascism and communism to retain uncontested power. However, Gramsci provides an interesting and alternative view about the success and limitations of fascism. Nolte was among the earliest to dissect fascism (see Chapter 11). One of Gramsci's significant contributions is his analysis of fascism. In his paradigm, Italy, like Spain, Portugal, Poland and the Balkans, occupied a mere peripheral status in the capitalist world. The other European nations were characterised as advanced and transitional. This created some problems for Italy; for instance, the political connotations of different classes remained confusing and vexed. This weakness stemmed from the fact that Italy, like Germany, entered the capitalist phase not through class conflict or a bourgeois revolution, but through the impact of a foreign war. As an inevitable consequence, Italy reflected a very imperfect capitalist order in which the hegemony of the dominant class was only partially successful, leading to perpetual hegemonic crises.

The phenomenon of fascism has to be understood as a device that could contain the capitalist crisis, but only with machine guns and revolvers. As such, the hegemonic crisis continued. Gramsci characterised fascism as a passive revolution which was congenial to Italy's situation, as it enabled it to modernise and restructure the economy within capitalism with massive state support. This gave rise to a situation that was just the opposite of the modernisation process initiated in the Soviet Union after the proletarian revolution. Fascism was not mere Bonapartism, as Trotsky believed; rather, it is a new organisation with mass support from the petty bourgeoisie. Gramsci contended that this happened for the first time in history.

Fascism could contain but not solve the Italian crisis, and the consequent static equilibrium could usher in true hegemony. Gramsci predicted a 'long life' for the fascist regime, but denied that it constituted an epoch. His analysis was vindicated by history when, within eight years of his death, fascism was wiped out not only from Italy, but also from all of Europe. While analysing fascism, Gramsci developed three general concepts—Caesarism, war of attrition and passive revolution. Caesarism referred to a situation when some previously dormant or unknown forces capable of asserting domination intervene politically and restore a static equilibrium in a hegemonic crisis. Variants in this intervention could be progressive (Caesar and Napoleon I) and reactionary (Napoleon III and Bismarck). 'Caesarism always involves a perpetual struggle for the hearts and minds of the population beyond that usually associated with processes of legitimization in normal politics' (Adamson 1980: 629).

For Gramsci, such a struggle represented a War of Attrition. Fascism was an example of this. He contrasted this with a War of Movement, which means seizure of power through military confrontation. An example would be the Bolshevik coup of November 1917. The rise of fascism demonstrated that such methods were outmoded and the War of Position, whether won by incumbents or insurgents, became decisive. Discussing the process by which the War of Movement becomes a War of Position, Gramsci stressed their differences, and on this basis criticised Trotsky's theory of permanent revolution.

The third concept, passive revolution, does not launch frontal attacks 'because they possess either substantial hegemonic force without a capability for domination or like Caesarism, a capability for domination without substantial hegemonic force' (Adamson 1980: 629). The passive revolution of the Christians under the Roman Empire is an example of the first type, and the Italian Risorgimento is an example of the second.

TYPES OF AUTHORITARIANISM

As there is no one single denominator for consolidating authoritarianism, there is no single model of authoritarianism either. There are a number of variants and some of the more prevailing ones are given below.

Individual and Personal Rule is one of the most prevailing modes and one that has ancient roots. Describing such a rule, Hegel said that in such regimes there is only one person who is free; such rulers derive their authority in a number of ways, like charisma and/or tradition. Such a ruler is considered above both society and the state. It is bereft of any clear-cut ideological basis, and in some cases the basis may be a patrimonial authority (a term that Weber used). The authority of such a rule is derived from the support it receives from a section of people who benefit from this rule. Often, such a rule could be a Kleptocracy[1] or Neo patrimonialism.[2]

Military Rule is the most prevailing authoritarian rule in the twentieth century. Widely prevalent in Latin America, Africa and Asia, military intervention normally follows widespread public unrest, and even violence. Military intervention is justified as restoring order and stability. Military rule, though arbitrary and normally conservative, may even enjoy widespread popular support in the hope that it would end political instability, corruption and bring in professionalism in administration. There is a huge literature on the subject, and as Clapham and Philip commented, 'the basic problem about military regimes is not one of how they can gain power but of what they do with it' (1985: 1). They compare military coup to an election victory by which a new government is installed, with both opposition and support determining its political options. The most important problem is retaining power; military rule is often compared to riding a tiger, with the most crucial and unpredictable movement being dismounting. S. E. Finer (1962) stated that military intervention depends on two factors: opportunity and disposition. All armed forces have the opportunity to intervene, but few have the disposition to do so. Finer was sceptical of the military in politics, particularly with regard to the processes of change that regimes undergo: their breakdown, and in rare cases, their transformation into civilianised rule.

However, military regimes do not follow a universally acclaimed pattern and their differences and typologies differ as much as they do in liberal democratic and non-military authoritarian regimes. The most important question revolves around the structure of civil society and the nature and composition of the military, and the intricacies in the relationship between the two. The general pattern is reflected in (*a*) unity of the military command structure; (*b*) differentiation of the military from civil society; (*c*) level of perceived response from the civil society; (*d*) level of autonomy of political organisations; and (*e*) the level of political culture.

Types of Military Regimes

Veto Regimes is military rule against a strong, well-established civilian political structure.

Moderate Regimes, which Huntington (1957) called the guardian type, reflects a high degree of both unity and differentiation, with a great deal of autonomy and little threat from civil and political organisations. The coexistence of unity and differentiation makes it perennially unstable.

Factional Regimes are different from moderate regimes, reflecting military intervention more in the nature of a personal intervention by a disgruntled officer. They are highly unstable.

Breakthrough Regimes lack an ideal type. Huntington (1957) characterised them as highly ideological reformative military action with a flexible pattern of co-option from the civil and political arena to perpetuate its rule.

The 1950s and 1960s saw the largest number of military regimes, mostly in the long independent nations of Latin America which had a low degree of political development, although some were comparable to more developed nations in the area of human development. Military regimes were common in Africa and Asia. Succession and a peaceful transfer of power normally elude such regimes, and some of them oscillate between periods of civilian rule and army rule. In the 1950s and 1960s, theories of the army as moderniser were popular amongst a section of modernisation theorists. Now, though, with greater consolidation of democratic regimes and their spread even in Latin America, such studies have only a historical importance in today's comparative politics. They have been replaced by a more focused study on the imposition of democracy by force.

FORCED DEMOCRACY

Military intervention by one country in another is a coercive tactic to compel a policy that otherwise would not have been followed. This is very different from a peacekeeping mission, which tries to maintain peace in a civil war situation, normally at the invitation of both parties in conflict. This is also in sharp contrast to the long tradition established by the 1648 Treaty of Westphalia—the doctrine of non-interference in the domestic affairs of another country. However, at the suggestion of the United Nations, the Security Council can now recommend military intervention to maintain international peace and security. The sudden disappearance of a superpower competition and the phenomenal increase in civil conflicts has led to US-UN interventions, ignoring the sanctity of state sovereignty. The ground reality also reflects a change: from 90 per cent countries being authoritarian, the current situation is such that most nations are now democratic, with the promotion of democracy even by force seeming legitimate and fair. This attempt to spread democracy by any means is a successor to the Containment Theory, propounded to contain the spread of communism and slowly enlarge, in a geographical sense, the free community of market democracies.

This massive effort to introduce democracy has been undertaken by a large number of organisations, and the programme includes strengthening the rule of law and human rights, getting international electoral observers to monitor free and fair elections, improving financial management and accountability, decentralisation, and devising ways and means to establish civilian control of the military and improve electoral systems. It also actively supports efforts to improve the quality of legislatures, political parties, media, education and the image of the police. This impetus is in line with the nation-building exercise that began after World War II with the building of democracy in Germany and Japan, and the non-communist but not necessarily democratic regimes like Vietnam, Korea, and most of Central America. Initially, the policy thrust was anti-communism and anti-Soviet, which led to the support of authoritarian forces and even dictatorships in China, Saudi Arabia and Uganda. The US government's support to these regimes did not form the basis of any reform plank or democratic initiative. However, this limited anti-communist role changed to a pro-democratic one in Panama, Somalia, Haiti, Bosnia and Iraq. In the latter, there was a marked attempt to have at least a rudimentary democratic order, in stark contrast to the Cold War era when containment of communism was all-important. The US defeat in Vietnam further reduced the enthusiasm to expand democracy.

The initial success of the Allied powers in installing democracy in Germany and Japan was facilitated by three factors: (*i*) the unconditional surrender of both Germany and Japan; (*ii*) a high level of development in education and highly industrialised societies; and (*iii*) a firm commitment to create democracies in these countries (von Hippel 2000). An added factor was the long tradition of political parties, which included the Social Democratic Party (SPD) in Germany, and the practice of the Weimar Constitution of 1919–33 (which many consider the finest ever democratic constitution), and the different ideological party formations in Japan. This commitment came from the common interest of the US, Britain and France to see that these two erstwhile enemies did not re-emerge as powerful, aggressive nations. A stable, democratic Germany and Japan was a vital component of Allied policy, which was not the case in Panama, Somalia, Haiti and Bosnia. However, it should also be noted that the enormous cleavages and disparities in both education and wealth between the governing elite and the masses were more pronounced in these countries than in post-War Germany and Japan. In spite of this in-built advantage, both Germany and Japan secured huge assistance from the US in all key areas of security, trade and political relations, which allowed both to enjoy unprecedented prosperity within a short period of time.

Hippel drew attention to many total collapses of states in the contemporary world, which undermined many democracies. A state collapses when both its repressive and ideological apparatuses disintegrate and the central authority is unable to check rampant corruption, violent ethnic conflicts and large-scale territorial disputes. A partial explanation for such collapses is rooted in colonial rule, when territorial lines were drawn between rival colonial powers without any consideration for ethnicity, religion, language and natural geographical boundaries.

Apart from internal factors, the international situation and behaviour of the major powers add to state collapse through mechanisms of support and withdrawal. In these fault lines, rogue regimes capture and continue power by winning elections, but without initiating the expected political reforms. Fundamentalist groups win elections in many such volatile situations (for instance, Algeria in 1991), nullifying a basic presumption of constitutional democracy—that extreme forces are forced to operate only on the fringes as democracy, with its politics of compromise, leads inevitably to moderation.

In such unstable and volatile situations, Western intervention is normally (with the exception of Iraq) taken as a last resort, with three broad aims: (*i*) re-establishing internal security, allowing for normal human activities; (*ii*) a longer effort to empower the different segments of civil society; and (*iii*) to find ways and means to strengthen democracy. Apart from reinforcing the formal institutions of democracy, the reform agenda includes proposals like police and judicial reforms, which indirectly strengthen democracy. Reform of the police is crucial for ensuring both public safety and gaining popular support. Changing the image of the police—from organised state-supported gangsters to a force which provides security to ordinary people and not only to a privileged lot—is an essential step. The most important step is the commitment to deal with complex problems deftly and comprehensively; as Hippel (2000) points out, this is what made the emergence of stable democracies in Germany and Japan possible. Similar successes will multiply only if that commitment is repeated. Whatever the net result of these efforts, one thing looks increasingly certain—the Westphalian state system, which allowed insularity to all important states, is coming to a close due to a global capitalistic system and the willingness of the US to intervene decisively, with or without UN support, in a variety of situations, ostensibly to promote democracy. This policy of installing democracy by force has a strange parallel with Brezhnev's doctrine of limited sovereignty, invoked to justify the right of the erstwhile USSR to intervene in its satellite states of Eastern Europe. The essential difference is that while Brezhnev confined it to the Soviet sphere of influence, the US seeks to encompass the entire world.

This policy shift, however, has met with severe criticism from some new liberal/conservative commentators like Zakaria (2003). Continuing the theme propounded by Huntington (1968) concerning the distinction between order and disorder, which is more important than the ideological divide between liberal democracy and communism, Zakaria makes a sharp distinction between liberal constitutionalism and democratic disorder. While not an opponent of democracy, Zakaria is concerned about its excesses and points out its 'dark sides'. Using a framework that draws heavily from the past, he argued that the success of the West is not due to democratisation, but rather, to the consolidation of liberal constitutionalism and capitalism. Tocqueville had taken note of the role played by independent, that is, non-state, groups and associations in American democracy. These developments created a solid foundation for the eventual flowering of liberal democracy; without the evolution of such a societal framework, the long-term survival of democracy is doubtful. The absence of democracy then leads to illiberal regimes. Although Zakaria began with the past, his major concern is with contemporary 'illiberal democracies', which 'mix elections with authoritarianism'. The major reason for this degeneration is the absence of both liberal constitutionalism and capitalism. The absence of any such tradition in the Middle East means that the West should not try to force democracy in a hurried manner in this area.

Zakaria's argument centres round the presumption that constitutional liberalism has less to do with the exact procedure of selecting governments than with objectives like the protection of individual autonomy by providing a bulwark against any coercion perpetrated by the state, church or society. This is a restatement of J. S. Mill's famous dictum that a liberal society, anchored in the rule of law, is a precondition for a liberal state. Even in the democratic US, Zakaria advocated that important decisions should increasingly be taken outside the democratic process to insulate them from short-sightedness and the political manipulation of pressure groups. He also delved into the well-known theory of democratic expansion and the link between prosperity and democracy. He pointed out that in the contemporary world, a per capita income of US$ 6,000 (preferably US$ 9,000) is the minimum necessity for the long-term survival of democracy. This wealth, however, has to be earned and not merely accrued due to bountiful natural resources, as that discourages incentives to grant liberty to its people. These are 'trust-fund states', where the problem is easy wealth and not poverty. Zakaria is convinced that only market capitalism can lead to a successful democracy. However, in even Western democracies, increasing democratisation has created a vast army of particular interests in the political space because, 'by declaring war on elitism, we have produced politics by a hidden elite, unaccountable, unresponsive with any larger public interest' (2003: 198). The solution to excessive democratisation is the delegation of power to institutions like the Supreme Court and the Federal Reserve Board.

There is a striking parallel between Zakaria's prescriptions of reform and the classical elitists. The only difference is that classical elitists viewed elite rule as inevitable, whereas Zakaria considers such rule desirable. He forgot, as Miliband had pointed out, that even in Western democracies today the ruling class has a privileged position, and so the proposal for further restriction is unnecessary. What is required, instead, is greater expansion to include the under-privileged and the under and non-represented. Moreover, elite rule without popular control will become something like the Soviet *nomenklatura*, or what Djilas called the 'new class' or the *nomenklatura*. The period that Zakaria glorifies is one of oligarchy, and not democracy. Even US exceptionalism was the rule of a few over the many (exemplified in *Uncle Tom's Cabin*), which Thoreau had protested. With a pronounced Western bias, he ignores the possibility of consolidating democracy through other routes. He also ignores the fact that democracy is feasible even in trust-fund societies (the precedent had been set in Mussadeq's Iran). Zakaria's confusion arose because what he considered liberal constitutionalism is actually democratic constitutionalism, which Jefferson had described as a rule under a constitution, and not the will of a single or a few individuals.

One Party Rule is when other parties are excluded/debarred from contesting for power. This is another form of authoritarianism and is inevitably associated with the totalitarian regimes of both the left and the right (see Chapters 6 and 11). However, the possibility of a one-party state becoming a democratic one has been debated. Macpherson (1966) pointed out that one party system in the Third World in general and the Solidarist model[3] in Africa in particular resonates with Rousseau's ideas on democracy. This is another model of democracy, besides liberal democracy and the communist variant. Lively (1975: 45) pointed out that one party system is incompatible with responsible government since it does not allow for the possibility of cogent alternatives. A rule by one party, to be elective both with regard to persons and opinions, has to allow factions, and unless party membership is co-terminus with a democratic electorate, it cannot be responsible to all competent citizens, but only to party members.

Quasi-Democracies are those where people have the right to vote, where elections are free and fair with a competitive multiparty system, but which lack democratic legitimacy. Singapore and Malaysia are seen as quasi-democracies. Despite full literacy, a majority middle class, and being among the wealthiest countries, Singapore is not among the open, free and democratic countries of the world. It has been ruled by the People's Action Party (PAP) in the nation's 50-year history without much dissent or opposition. In the early 1990s, the late Lee Kuan Yew attributed the electoral success of the PAP to the consistent double-digit growth rate, which the PAP government has been able to maintain. Contrary to Lee's claim, however, the PAP has been the ruling party for five decades only because the country's election process is highly unequal, with the odds stacked against the opposition parties.[4]

As Slater (2015) argued, most of Asia's democracies came about because authoritarian rulers wanted to keep ruling without remaining authoritarian. It began in the late 1940s in Japan, where conservative politicians stuck with democracy, even when Cold War considerations made the US stop caring much about it, because it delivered them landslide victories. Taiwan had followed suit by the 1980s, and the island remains wealthy, stable and democratic. South Korea democratised at nearly the same historical moment. Its old ruling party currently continues to hold power some 30 years later, just as the old Kuomintang does in Taiwan. Taking a leaf from Japan, South Korea and Taiwan, Lee Hsien Loong, too, should shed authoritarianism and embrace democracy. If he starts the process, history will remember him for something other than being the son of Lee Kuan Yew. Singapore awaits its Prague Spring.

FALSE DEMOCRACY

The term 'False Democracy' was coined by Owens (1987) to explain that development is not about economic and social progress, but also carries political connotations of freedom and democracy. According to his definition, most democracies in the developing world are false because they are top-down, centralised and externally imposed; in this category, he includes India, Kenya, Tanzania, Philippines, and some Latin American countries. True democracy, on the contrary, is indigenously derived and provides ordinary people access to the system and its resources and public organisation, establishes the rules of law, and realises political freedom. The basic malady of most development strategies is that their focus is limited to the economic and social aspects of life. Local institutions that are absolutely essential to sustaining proper development by securing the participation of common people are generally ignored. The utmost need is the establishment of community-based organisations to pursue economic, social and political development, as development is a composite process.

A notable distinction between industrialised and developing countries lies not in their capacity to generate GNP, but in the fact that in the former, the government has been at least partially reformed. In contrast, in the developing world, only a handful of governments has treated economic development as part of the political reform process. What is ironic is that all such reformed governments are authoritarian. Certain essential reforms are needed to involve the poor in the development process, which are fundamentally non-ideological and feasible in any political system—democratic, fascist, communist, or authoritarian.

Critical of the trickle-down theory of development, Owens pointed out that not only does development mean broad-based economic growth, but it must also be linked with one's own improvement and productivity. Development is not a process where a few experts exclusively handle a few technical subjects, but is one in which the poor are involved and where the pace of change does not depend on the dictates of the government, but on the capacity of ordinary people to absorb innovations and change. This failure of the trickle-down approach can be best demonstrated by the role of technology. Reliance on large-scale, high-cost technology where the production units are small, capital is scarce and unemployment is massive is bound to be counter-productive. In the developing world, the use of modern technology is always restricted to a minority; the key factor is the availability of access to modern technology. Such technology caters to the elite. The solution lies in accepting an integrated approach with the application of appropriate technology. Western technology should be limited to the modern industrial sector, while an alternative approach emphasising improved tools and techniques for small production units and low-income categories should be implemented. Decentralised structures are necessary because they lead to accountability of members, provide access to the law, bring integrity into public affairs and secure the rule of law. Surprisingly, however, none of these reforms have been initiated in false democracies. This demonstrates that economic and social rights can be created without creating political rights, and that the presence of just, formal political rights is no guarantee for the realisation of economic and social rights. In the developing world, Owens contended, purposeful political distinctions do not relate to the form of government, but to those who have created economic and social rights for the masses.

The tragedy is that the bulk of governments in the developing world remains unreformed and underdeveloped. As an example of an unreformed government, Owens cited the case of Bangladesh, which is widely believed to be a 'basket case', that is, saddled with economic difficulties and unable to pay its debts. Bangladesh's tragedy does not lie in its overpopulation, but in its unreformed and underdeveloped government. While the technology to turn it into a rice-exporting nation is available, her farmers lack adequate access to it. The ideal situation is a combination of political rights with economic and social rights; however, the first ceases to have any meaning if the second is not realised. Economic and social rights can become a reality for the majority if there is active local participation, with local institutions to cater to their needs. Meaningful development does not merely mean the establishment of sophisticated macro-developmental institutions with well–publicised, huge financial institutions, modern technological information, and health systems accessible only to few urban, well-connected people. With such limited access, state agencies cease to hold meaning for most people. The privileged appropriate all the benefits of economic development. The dual societies of the developing world do not create a mechanism by which the majority automatically benefits and thereby develops a stake in the system. The rural masses need access to essential areas like land, easy credit, nearby markets, appropriate and inexpensive technology to fulfil their needs and aspirations, sympathetic and honest government agencies to handle local issues, a voice in the political decision-making process of the country, and legal redress to the poor. Creating access means giving power and respect to people who have for long been exploited and powerless. It begins with involving the poor in the workplace and allowing them to be a beneficiary of their own labour. Since benefit increases with increased productivity, a manifold increase takes place in production in such a decentralised developmental exercise, in which ordinary people are assured of resources, a responsive, local public organisation and legal protection. The challenge before all developing countries is creating economic and social rights for the poor.

Another rampant problem is the existence of widespread corruption, an endemic sickness in the developing world. Embezzlement, fraud, bribery, pay-offs, nepotism, extortion, blatant violation of constitutional and legal rules to favour someone special, and brutal and violent suppression of documents to conceal the truth are common occurrences in many countries. The most important motive behind corruption is of course unreasonable personal greed, a desire for a standard of living which the limitations of a modest income are inadequate to meet. The easiest way to enrich oneself is through this unearned income, which in many instances is accepted as a matter of right. The consequences of corruption are devastating as corruption, as a system, evokes its own rules of obedience and success. Subservient behaviour acknowledging a patron-client relationship, which looks upon independent initiative, risk or innovation with utmost suspicion, is perpetuated. The first casualty of systemic corruption is the denial of just reward and meritocracy, the twin principles by which a well-ordered society maintains upward mobility and efficiency. Lipset's (1979) survey of American workers showed that 80 per cent of them accepted that the system treated them fairly, and the reward they received was appropriate to their skills and qualifications. This was in sharp contrast to Tucker's (1987) survey of political culture in the heydays of Soviet Communism; he found that only 2 per cent of Communist Party members had faith in the efficacy of communism. The overall societal consequence of corruption is equally devastating. The forced satisfaction of personal greed leads to denying the poor access to resources, becoming a part of a fruitful public organisation, and enjoying the guarantee of the law. In the absence of such essential institutional support, corruption becomes the most important reason for the perpetuation of abject poverty in the developing world.

A fair and free government is a modern innovation, and the remedy for corruption is intrinsically linked to the process of democratisation. The government is supposed to maintain public standards and investigate and prosecute the corrupt. In developed countries, ordinary private citizens can initiate action against governmental corruption without fear of reprisal, including arbitrary imprisonment; this may not be possible in the developing world, which makes their democracies false. Owens conceded that in the developing world, some authoritarian and former countries had demonstrated considerable advancement over the pre-industrial order for the mass of ordinary people. By today's yardstick, virtually all pre-modern governments were corrupt. According to pre-democratic perception, few groups of people—kings, the nobility and aristocrats, supported by religious leaders, dignitaries, scholars and lawyers—comprised the ruling class. With government function being extremely limited and most of the time given over to self-preservation, the overwhelming majority accepted this situation as inevitable. To minimise corruption, one needs to reform the imperial and oppressive nature of government and make governments transparent, accountable and responsive, so that instead of lording over the citizens, they would serve the people. To begin with, it is important to empower the ordinary citizen and transfer capital to the rural hinterland, along with a judicious mixture of sophisticated Western and indigenous technology. There is a need to adapt technology to daily use and improve the skills of ordinary people, thus ensuring individual well-being, dispersed economic prosperity and an end to the present dual society. Real—and not merely formal—political stability calls for a need to tackle problems of mass poverty, deprivation and unemployment, and guarantee a reasonable growth rate. Otherwise, development and affluence will remain confined to a minority, with the vast majority remaining untouched and breeding an alienated political culture that translates itself into apathy and, ultimately, disorder. The problem in most parts of the developing world is essentially economic, rather than political. If South Korea can boast of a majority 61 per cent middle class within three decades of development, there is absolutely no reason why other developing and underdeveloped countries cannot aspire for the same.

Furthermore, there is a need to ensure strict compliance to the rule of law for all to ensure that the rich and famous do not buy justice. Most parts of the developing world vindicate Rousseau's indictment of eighteenth-century French feudal society—that the law was a very good thing for property owners and a very bad one for the property-less. A strict compliance to law enabled the success of capitalism over communism, for it established and protected the citizen from the coercive state apparatus. In the former communist countries, the *nomenklatura* were a law unto themselves and were pre-modern, securing the privileges that positions of power gave them. The elite in the developing world is similar to the erstwhile *nomenklatura*. Besides the right contacts, the latter also have the money to twist the system, skilfully evading legal norms. Unless this scenario changes, democracy in most parts of the developing world will remain bereft of its most important ingredient—the rule of law.

Sen (1990) argued that the acceptance of democracy with fair and free elections, a multi-party system, alert and active opposition political parties and groups, and a free and vibrant press form the foundational arrangements in a democratic system. This can prevent the occurrence of periodic famines and abject poverty because leaders who do not pursue the proper policies to alleviate mass deprivation would be shown the door at the time of elections.

Myrdal on Soft State

Twenty years after all of South Asia gained independence from Britain, Myrdal undertook a stocktaking of the area in *Asian Drama* (1968), in terms of their promise and actual performance. He analysed economic problems within a larger demographic, social and political setting, and emphasised the high-pitched aspirations of people after independence and the consequent bitter reality. He contrasted the limited public works of the colonial period with the emphasis on economic development in the political independence phase. Contrasting democracy with authoritarian regimes, he credited the latter with enforcing social discipline through compulsion, mobilisation, acceptance, participation and cooperation, which includes even the poorest. He also mentioned the feeble resistance to and obstruction of many of these measures. Newly emerging democracies like India had a number of shortcomings: deficiencies in government administration, social and economic inequalities, a vested interest in the status quo, and a traditional, stagnant society. In such a situation, which Myrdal termed 'soft state', policies are decided but never enforced as there is a great deal of reluctance in imposing obligations on the people. A rigorous enforcement of obligations is possible with the expansion of education and spread of literacy, neither of which is in much evidence.

The language of the elite is very different from that of the people, which leads to an intellectual and cultural gulf between the classes and the masses. Myrdal situated this in the context of India's outstanding leadership at the time of independence; yet, despite such 'exalted' leadership the essential progressive commitments were ignored and concessions were made to conservative elements in order to maintain stability (1968: 273). Priority was given to immediate problems in post-partition India; while there were plenty of radical principles, the practice was conservative, thereby leading to a big gap between ideals and reality. This stemmed from the unwillingness of the leadership to impose necessary obligations on the people. Democratic governance is based on obedience to rules laid down by democratic procedures, but in comparison to Western democracies and even former communist countries, the level of social discipline is very low, leading to disobedience. In light of the nationalist movement and its ideological legacy, this non-compliance was rationalised through an argument differentiating compulsion and violence on the one side, and change of heart on the other. This resulted in vested interests being safeguarded, which in turn led to Nehru and his team compromising on the process of modernisation in practice by postponing the solving of crucial issues instead of taking hard decisions, thereby helping the conservative forces. Instead of working out the modalities of a social and economic revolution and shifting the power base, the policies strengthened both conservative segments and reactionary forces. The postponement, supposed to be temporary, became permanent. Political revolution also remained incomplete in India as policies were neither devised in the interests of the people, nor controlled by them. A limited mobilisation has retarded both national consolidation and economic development. As a result, the masses do not effectively participate in politics, and this has led to a system of privileges, patronage and accommodation of self-seekers and opportunists. The effectiveness of governmental action depends on the enforcement of policies at the lower levels—states, districts and localities—but with no dedicated workers and no contact with the people, implementation suffers and party plutocracy is perpetuated.

Myrdal's central argument was that overemphasis on political stability leads to stagnation and a hierarchical power structure, which tries to initiate rapid change from the top. This, according to him, is a hopeless quest. Development and change requires a change in attitude, without which any development or transformation of social institutions becomes impossible. It is because of mass deprivation that Third World democracies, in sharp contrast to Western democracies, have been unable to extend the benefits of development to the poorest sections of society. The dynamics of Western democracy culminated in Britain's 1945 Labour Party victory, which created the welfare state. The overall acceptance of this social welfare philosophy was vindicated by the fact that even the efforts of the new right to roll back the 'nanny' welfare state did not lead to any substantial reduction in social welfare measures. However, the inability of Third World democracies to either institutionalise democracy or create a more egalitarian structure has resulted in an authoritarian attack on democracy in the developing world.

CONCLUSION

Morris-Jones (1971, 1978) offered an effective answer to those Third World elites who claimed that the backwardness of their people is an obstacle to democracy. In reality, they are alarmed at the prospect of democracy being used by the poor against the power and privileges of the minority. He also pointed out that the cultural argument emphasising the authoritarian tradition of the Third World countries is aimed at halting any progressive or democratic change. With regard to the elitist argument that democracy is an impediment to eradicating poverty, he asserted that even in Western Europe, 'the most substantial erosion of mass poverty took place only after liberal democracy has been extended far enough to create strong pressures from the ranks of the disadvantaged' (1978: 150). Democracy is not a hindrance but a very important tool for progress, and a means to bring about important structural changes like land reforms, which would accelerate economic development.

NOTES

1. Kleptocracy, alternatively cleptocracy or kleptarchy, is derived from Greek *(kleptēs*, or thief and *kratos*, meaning power, rule), and hence 'rule by thieves' is a term applied to a rule wherein officials or the ruling class, collectively called kleptocrats, extend their personal wealth and augment political power by systematic embezzlement of state funds and resources at the expense of the people. Kleptocracy is usually associated with dictatorships, oligarchies and military juntas. It is common in developing countries, whose economies are based on the export of natural resources.

2. Neopatrimonialism is a term that Eisenstadt (1973) coined. He derived it from Weber's patrimonialism to describe a system of rule wherein administrative and military personnel are responsible to only the ruler. Patrons dole out state resources to secure the loyalty of the people, their clients. Such a system undermines the political system and the rule of law.
3. The Solidarist philosophy that Julius Nyerere, the first President of Tanzania and one of the most well-known leaders of Africa, propounded was a model of democracy in the Rousseauean sense, applicable to societies that are relatively homogenous and lacking in both experience and institutions of conventional parliamentary system. The primary reason for this was the increasing consolidation of power by the majority party after independence. This is exemplified by Tanzania. Nyerere was not a Marxist, nor did he believe in a one-party state of the Leninist type. He was a Roman Catholic and believed in social democracy. However, he was aware that a multi-party system would not work in the newly independent countries. The Solidarist one-party state, according to Nyerere, was democratic, with open membership and no restrictions on personal freedom. He understood the importance of a legitimate opposition in a political system, but pointed out that this could not work in newly emerging nations like Tanzania. He asserted that democracy did not require organised opposition; what it demands is not the actual existence, but a theoretical acceptance of the idea. The central fact that he emphasised was the internal backwardness of the newly emerging nations. Since classes were not well-developed, class politics had to be ruled out. Added to this was an important fact, namely the common aspiration for development. In the absence of a differentiated industrial society like Europe and America, the introduction of a pluralist system was not possible in Africa. There was no organised group that could exercise hegemony over others. The challenge of development needed a firm, strong and centralised control from above, a fact that Western societies never had to contend with.

   In the African context, the task is to democratise society from the top. Independence enhanced the role of the state. Mobilisation of resources and the exercise of authority increased state authority. National consolidation took place through the active participation of the state. The backwardness of traditional societies did not allow for the immediate adaptation of a Western-style parliamentary democracy. However, this did not mean that democracy was absent. The absence of viable class divisions ensured equality, and since traditional African society is democratic with a history of free discussion, the government was established with the approval and participation of people. Unlike the erstwhile Soviet system, which had a low level of discussion compatible with its totalitarian political structure, Africa had an indigenous democratic experience. This experience was linked with the African version of socialism—*ujamaa*—with the following features: (*a*) in traditional society, mutual respect exists with a recognition of the place and rights of each member of the family; (*b*) a belief in communal life exists with a theory that all goods are held in common; inequalities exist, but are not marked and offensive to social cohesion; and (*c*) every single person has an obligation to work. However, there were two inadequacies in the pre-colonial situation: an inequality between man and woman, and a low standard of living. It was optimistically hoped that the use of technology and increase in economic activity according to the three basic principles of traditional life would eliminate these within a short period. Such a philosophy fitted perfectly well with a Solidarist one-party democracy. In reality, the *ujamaa* movement suffered from economic difficulties like low productivity and limited output, and the dual strategy of public sector and cooperatives as well as private enterprise led to tension in the implementation of democratic and socialist principles.

   In view of this, Nyerere's call for a multi-party democracy in the early 1990s acknowledged the fact that the specific conditions faced by newly independent countries in the post-independence phase no longer existed, and the one-party state reflected this extraordinary circumstance. This acknowledgement indicates the entry of the Third World into the modern age of multi-party democracy.
4. Since 1959, the ruling PAP has continued its hold over 90 per cent of seats in Singapore's parliament; the remaining seats are mostly filled by unelected, 'non-constituency' MPs and 'nominated MPs' to create the illusion of an opposition within the parliament and show that PAP policies are the result of serious partisan debate. In reality, it is a pliant opposition. To be an opposition party member is the most Herculean task in Singapore's political landscape. Many have been slapped with lawsuits, which are pursued determinedly to bankrupt and disqualify

them from political candidacy. Joshua Benjamin Jeyaretnam, the Worker's Party leader, and Chee Soon Juan, the Singapore Democratic Party leader, were bankrupted in 2001 and 2011, respectively. Moreover, the PAP has 'punished' entire constituencies in the past by diverting funds from infrastructure projects, and then accused the opposition of mismanagement. Political manipulation of the legal system impacts freedom of expression in Singapore. The *Public Order Act* requires that persons engaging in political discussion must register with the government and the *Public Entertainment and Meetings Act* permits the assemblage of four persons with police permission at all times; in normal democracies, this is usually invoked during tenuous law and order situations. Editors and mediapersons are pressured to register as members of political bodies if their columns are about national policies.

Singapore is designated 'Partly Free' and received an overall freedom rating of 4.0 on a 7-point scale by Freedom House's *Freedom in the World Report*, which has been keeping track of political rights and civil liberties since 1972. Singapore is judged less harshly than many other authoritarian systems, and is termed a soft authoritarian state. The PAP has consistently resorted to electoral gerrymandering; elections are completely controlled by the government and lack in transparency. There is no independent body to monitor this blatant gerrymandering. Constituencies are created and reshaped to the advantage of the PAP. The opposition is usually up against announcements of boundaries late in the election cycle. In 1988, the PAP created the Group Representation Constituencies (GRCs), which requires six candidates per party, making it virtually impossible to win. In February 2011, the PAP's Electoral Boundaries Review Committee decided to convert the Single Member Constituencies of Nee Soon Central and Nee Soon East, where the Workers' Party had had enough support in the 2006 elections to become a GRC. Even if the opposition had won the GRC—as happened with the surprise victory of the Workers' Party in 2011 in Aljunied GRC—the PAP simply redrew the boundaries of that GRC in the next election cycle.

13

CLASSICAL ELITISM, DEMOCRATIC ELITISM AND PLURALISM

The three C's—group consciousness, coherence and conspiracy (the last term meaning a 'common will to action' rather than 'secret machinations')—are clearly necessary features of the concept of an elite.

Meisel 1958: 48

Elites have been regarded as the chief threat to the survival of democracy.

Parry 1969: 13

The term 'elite' connotes exclusiveness in combination with special skills or resources; not every minority or interest group can be described as an elite.

Goodwin 1992: 226

Image 13.1: Vilfredo Federico Damaso Pareto (1848–1923)

Source: https://commons.wikimedia.org/wiki/File:Vilfredo_Pareto.jpg.

The dawn of the twentieth century saw many writers who were dissatisfied with the metaphysical preoccupations of political thinkers and influenced by new scientific and psychological theories that viewed politics realistically. These writers, referred to as classical elitists—Pareto, Mosca and Michels—perceived politics as a study of power and of the elite groups who control the process of decision-making. A study of the nature of power and its acquisition and maintenance, and the interplay between the elite and the masses through different tools like force, myths and symbols is also undertaken. Elitists claim that their approach has the same objectivity that exists in natural science, a fact strikingly absent in previous thinking about politics. Mosca pointed out that past thinkers were more concerned with making recommendations about politics than with discovering the principles according to which political systems work. The classical elitists were interested in how control is maintained. According to Michels, the elite are concerned with power, while for the masses material conditions are important. The masses are satisfied if their material demands are fulfilled and are reverential towards the elite, whom they perceive as culturally superior. According to Pareto, the elite control the masses through myths that convince the latter they are worthy of ruling, while for Mosca, political rule rested on a political formula; historical myths are inspired by illusions. All revolutions result from sentiment and not reason: people have to be convinced that things will improve.

For the elitists, a ruling elite was inevitable regardless of the form of government (which includes democracies). They were sceptical about the feasibility of real democracy, in the full sense of government by and for the people.[1]

The elitists also believed that the governing elite came from a particular social group and reacted to the Marxist notion of the ruling class—the idea that an economic group also rules politically. An elite emerges because it is organised, while the masses are not. There was no uniformity of political convictions between the three scholars. Mosca was a conservative who feared the tyranny of both the sovereign and the people; Pareto attacked liberalism, pacifism and ideas of human solidarity;[2] and Michels was sympathetic to both syndicalism and socialism.

The *Oxford English Dictionary* defines an elite as a 'select group or class' and 'elitism' refers to a theory or perception that an elite rules in every society in different forms. The elite may be different in different fields of human endeavour; yet there is always a distinction between the leader and followers. Most of the contemporary world views the idea of elite rule as ominous, with exceptions like Jose Oretga y Gasset (1883–1955), who in *the Revolt of the Masses* (1930) praised elitism and deplored the mass mediocrity of democratic society. He maintained that it was the duty of the masses to follow the elite and that a properly constituted mass and elite were key to a nation's well-being. These propositions were empirically tested during the behavioural persuasion in politics in the 1950s and 1960s, and the general conclusion was that elite groups dominated local politics, thus vindicating the major thrust of classical elitism.

CONTEXT OF THEORISING: CLASSICAL ELITISM

The late nineteenth and early twentieth century saw a steady expansion in state activity and executive power, even in democracies. Dicey (1908) took note of this when he remarked that in England, since 1870, there have been revolutionary changes with legislative collectivism displacing individualistic liberalism as the basis of government action. The organisation of bureaucracies with 'careers open to talents' meant that civil service was now open to anyone with talent, and was no longer dependent on influence or patronage. Bureaucracy referred to certain procedures and deliberately constructed rules, on basis of which government power was exercised. It also meant hierarchy and responsibility flowing from the top to the bottom, enabling a more efficient organisation of state power than before in history. The trend towards a stronger executive also coincided with the extension of franchise in many European countries. From the 1860s, the general contours of democratic politics were being laid down. A result of the extension of franchise was the emergence of mass parties. Taking advantage of an expanded electorate, parties opened membership to all those who had the right to vote and were willing to subscribe to the party's aims. In the mid-nineteenth century when the process of democratisation was consolidating and expanding, elitist reaction to it was also being consolidated, as reflected in the writings of the classical elitists. Dismissing the idea of popular representation as fiction, they argued that there was nothing called majority rule. In every society it is an elite that rules, controls key resources and takes major decisions. The elite theorists rejected both the contention of majority rule of liberal democratic theory and Marxism's classless society, considering elite rule inevitable in all societies.

Elite theorists dismissed past theorising as ideologies (Mosca 1939: 6), offering laws and facts in its place. Mosca's historical method in political science was based on 'the study of the facts of society', and 'those facts can be found only in the history of the various nations' (ibid.: 41). In a similar vein, Michels' iron law of oligarchy was 'inevitable' and 'an essential characteristic of all human aggregates', and 'historical evolution mocks all the prophylactic measures that have been adopted for the prevention of oligarchy' (1962: vii). The elitists had no intention of making any ethical comment on the phenomena they described.

Mosca rejected the Rousseauean myth of popular sovereignty. A government in a democracy is certainly *of* the people, it might even be *for* the people, but it is never *by* the people, but by the ruling class. This is also true of socialist society, and faith in a classless egalitarian society is a pious hope, akin to religion, with which to deceive the lower classes while bolstering their confidence. Pareto expressed this caustically when he remarked that 'it is, paradoxically, precisely the inequality of men which prompts them to proclaim their equality' (1966: 164). The belief that they were exposing hidden truths in ideologies gave their writings an air of confidence and reinforced their conviction that all statements must be empirically verifiable, as that distinguishes science from religion, truth from metaphysics in philosophy, and myth from reality in politics.

The classical elitists were as concerned with refuting Marx as they were with establishing a neutral political science. The later elitists, Burnham and Mills, attempted to synthesise facets of Marxism with those of elitism. The classical elitists attacked Marxism's claim to being a science, dismissing it as an ideology. Pareto tried to prove that Marx's analysis was false by stating, point for point, the Marxist account of economy, politics and ruling to establish Marxism as an ideology or a religious myth, rather than a science. The elitists accepted the Marxist critique of liberalism, but while Marxism used it to prepare the basis for revolutionary action on behalf of the working class, the elitists gave it a middle-class twist. While Marx saw history as a conflict between economic classes, the elitists (with the exception of Burnham) did not see politics as a reflection of the economic class structure. While not denying the importance of economic factors, they stressed that through political means, the elite controls, accommodates and/or even counteracts economic forces. While for Marx the tension was between the class that owns the means of production and that which does not, the tension for the elitists lay between the dominant political elite and any rival elite that might issue a challenge for power. The mass of people remains unorganised and becomes politically significant only when the elite unifies it. The elitists attacked Marxism on three points: (*i*) to prove that Marxism was not a science of society and a guide for action; instead, is was a time-bound ideology for the working class in capitalist societies; (*ii*) they dismissed Marx's prediction of the future as classless and egalitarian as baseless, and underlined the inevitability of hierarchy in society; and (*iii*) they disproved that economics was the determining factor in politics and history (Parry 1969: 28).

Pareto was an Italian economist, sociologist and philosopher, and one of the founders of modern sociology. His '*Treatise of General Sociology* (*The Mind and Society*) is the grandest of all the classical elitist doctrines—a gargantuan retort to Marx' (S. E. Finer 1966: 77). For Pareto, the elite are neither a product of economic forces nor the result of their organisational abilities; they are the outcome of certain human attributes that are constant throughout history. His first definition of the elite was with reference to achievement and not morals; it is skills and not virtue that is the reason for elite rule. In every field there are some more talented than others, and this explains why they rise to the top. The persons with the highest indices in each field of human activity are clubbed together and described as the elite (ibid.: 248). The elite exist in every profession and in all spheres of human endeavour.

The elite are subdivided into those who directly or indirectly play an important part in government—termed the 'governing elite'—and those, like top sportspersons or performers, who form the 'non-governing elite'. However, Pareto abandoned this definition as being impractical for sociological research. Only under theoretical conditions of perfect competition can those with the highest ability reach the top in their field. In practice, this does not happen. Factors such as wealth, birth and corruption frequently advantage the less-skilled, who then establish themselves right at top, particularly in less technical and rational activities like politics. Instead, Pareto used a simpler distinction between the elite (governing and non-governing), defined as those who, regardless of ability, occupy leading positions, and the non-elite. Paralleling the Marxist view of history as class struggle, Pareto saw the history of every hitherto existing society as the relation between its elite and non-elite, and the psychological make-up of the elite. For Pareto, most human activities are 'non-logical'.

Pareto discerned a number of human instincts and the residues they reflect, and subsuming them under two classes, offered the key to the explanation of society, including that of elite domination and elite replacement. Class I residues reflected the 'instinct of combinations', the impulse to put together ideas through the use of imagination. Arts, ideologies, and political coalitions and manoeuvrings would all stem from this active inventive instinct. Class II residues reflected the instinct of 'the persistence of aggregates', or the desire to consolidate what is established. These instincts are of permanence, stability and order, and in a political sense stand for solidarity, order, discipline, property or family. These are in no way to be identified with traditionalism.

Borrowing from Machiavelli's two types of elite—the *foxes* and the *lions*—he explained the nature of governing elite structures; these two elites represented two different methods of governance. The foxes governed by consent since they were intelligent, cunning, enterprising, artistic and innovative, while the lions were persons of strength, stability, integrity and unimaginative capacity, who used force to achieve and maintain their position. Lions were defenders of the status quo with a commitment to public order, religion and political orthodoxy. The qualities of the lion and fox are mutually exclusive and history is a process of circulation between them.

Politics requires both the lion and the fox—partly by force and partly by consent. At any time, the style of governing would depend on whether the governing elite is composed predominantly of those with fox-like qualities or those with lion-like qualities. The non-elite were predominantly the Class II type—impassive and unimaginative, but with strong attachments to political ideals which fulfil their desire for stability. This explains the appeal of religion—from Christianity to imperialism to socialism.

The fox elite govern by securing consent with the help of ideologies that attract the masses, devise policies to tackle immediate crises, and satisfy the demand of the moment. Material interest is placed before the pursuit of ideals. The ideal politician is a 'wheeler-dealer' or political fixer. Usually the fox elite abstain from using force to tackle political problems. A misplaced humanitarianism leads to compromise and pacifism, which weakens the regime. The lion elite usually do not seek consensus and rule with the help of force. They suppress opposition and dissent. Public order, rather than private satisfaction, becomes the main goal of the government.

The ideal, for Pareto (as it was for Machiavelli), was a balance between the two, which rarely happens. The balance in history has swung from one elite type to another. He pointed out that a circulation of individuals between the upper and lower levels of the same profession and a circulation between the governing and non-governing elite, with different groups of persons moving into positions of political authority, takes place all the time. This ceaseless process of elite renewal, circulation and substitution highlights the fact that the elite rules in all organised societies, even though the composition of that elite may keep changing. Pareto argued that oligarchy and elite circulation between governing and non-governing elites have been borne out by historical experiences.

Pareto's typology of political systems was two-fold. All were oligarchies, but in some elites, Class I residues predominate while in others, Class II residues prevail. He also recognised the existence of mixed types, with either a Class II elite being infiltrated by persons of Class I residues, or a Class I elite being backed by a proportion of Class II elements. These mixed regimes may eventually revert to one or the other 'pure' type, and can be regarded as sub-types. Pareto offered a number of examples for this model. However, there is an inadequacy. It suggests a similarity between regimes that are otherwise different, but does not explain their differences, which are at least as striking. His faith in the uniformity of human nature led him to classify the Athenian democracy of fifth century BC as belonging to the same type of mass democracies prevalent in modern Europe, because both were dominated by Class I elites. By focusing on this one similarity, he ignored the enormous differences between the two systems—in their political institutions, scale of functioning, degree of bureaucratisation and economic structures.

Pareto's defence of the inevitability of elite rule was based on the psychological premise concerning the fundamental inequality of human beings. He projected his theory as historical; however, in reality it was profoundly ahistorical. He interpreted all of human history in terms of the circulation of elites and rejected the egalitarian basis of democracy as fallacious, as the capacity to rule is distributed unevenly. A point that Pareto made—and which Schumpeter echoed—is that outside the ambit of purely economic relations, human behaviour is fundamentally irrational. He rejected the notion of responsible self-government as an impossible dream, considering democratic procedures ineffective. He stated that elites would be part of any given society. However, the nature of the elite would be different in different societies and different times, reflecting the changes in society and technology.

Pareto rejected the Marxist propositions that the state was a mere tool of the dominant economic class, and that 'the history of all hitherto existing society is the history of class struggle'. He dismissed the pluralist contention that the state was a coordinator of national interests in a plural society, and discarded the liberal assertion of majority rule and people's sovereignty as expressed through democratic institutions and procedures.

Mosca was more historical and sociological in his analysis than Pareto, as is evident from his explanation of elite rule. Accepting Aristotle's division of governments into monarchic, oligarchic and democratic, he pointed out that the reality behind every governmental system was the rule of the few over the many—the fact that a small ruling class wielded real political power in society. Aristotle's typology was an instance of political myth. The starting point in *Ruling Class* (1896) is the argument that:

> In all societies ... two classes of people appear—a class that rules and a class that is ruled. The first class, always the less numerous, performs all political functions, monopolizes power and enjoys the advantages that power brings, whereas the second, the more numerous class, is directed and controlled by the first, in a manner that is now more or less legal, now more or less arbitrary and violent, and supplies the first, in appearance at least, with material means of subsistence and with the instrumentalities that are essential to the vitality of the political organism (1939: 50).

Neither one person nor the mass of people, whom Aristotle referred to as the 'one' or the 'many', could ever rule. On the one hand, a single ruler required the help and support of advisors and administrators, and on the other, a people could act politically only under the direction of a small group of leaders. Mosca drew evidence for this proposition from all periods of history.

The ruling class monopolises and enjoys the benefits of power and uses both legal and capricious methods to sustain its domination. The elite, as compared to the masses, is organised with a certain unity, a point subsequently reiterated by Mills. 'A hundred men acting uniformly in concert, with a common understanding, will triumph over a thousand men who are not in accord and can therefore be dealt with one by one' (Mosca 1939: 53). In modern society the elite, consisting of leaders, trained administrators and technicians, rule because of wealth, knowledge and bureaucratic skills, along with their intrinsic unity. This is supported by evidence from all periods of history and from all over the world. The ruling class possesses some resource or attribute that is valued and influential in that particular society, and that it utilises to its advantage and power. For Mosca, elite rule was not only inevitable in all societies, but the elite would also be composed of the middle class.

For Mosca, the key to elite control was the capacity of the minority for organisation. The elite's position came about because its members possessed, either in fact or in the estimation of others in society, some attribute which society valued. This attribute might be wealth, a concern for the public good, military prowess, or status in a religious hierarchy. Elite control depends on the capacity of the minority to weld itself into a cohesive force with a common front vis-à-vis others in society. A minority had advantages, according to Mosca, simply because it is a minority. A small group is more readily organised than a large one, with simpler internal channels of communication and information. Its members can be contacted more speedily, formulate policies rapidly, and agree quickly and demonstrate complete solidarity in its public postures. It can respond to altered circumstances and changed situations better than a large one. The most important quality of elite leadership is that the majority looks to the elite for the right 'cue'. Despite the numerical strength of the majority, it is the minority which is the stronger of the two. The majority, unorganised collection of people will remain a large aggregation of individuals without a common purpose, and without the means of coordination and communication skills that a minority can easily command. 'The power of any minority is irresistible as against each single individual in the majority, who stands alone before the totality of the organized minority' (Mosca 1939: 53).

Mosca's ruling class, or the 'political class', is divided into a higher and lower stratum. In view of the consolidation of party machinery in his days, he considered the innermost core of the elite as comprising of party 'bosses' who direct the party's electoral campaigns and thereby control the parliament. He called them the 'grand electors' as they would get the vote delivered in the electoral area where they held power; most importantly, though, they picked the candidates and determined the range from which the electorate would make its supposedly 'free choice'. It was not the electorate who chose the representative; instead, 'his friends have him elected' (Mosca 1939: 154). According to Mosca, 'a candidacy is always the work of a group of people united for a common purpose, an organized minority which inevitably forces its will upon the disorganized majority' (ibid.). The party bosses operate behind the scenes without any constitutional or legal basis and are in no way accountable to the electorate.

Mosca concluded from his earlier writings that a person of principle or integrity would not stand for election, and that representatives would usually be of mediocre ability. The assembly would be lowered in quality and would rarely represent the complete range of interests amongst the ruling class. Meisel (1958) believed that Mosca was faced with a dilemma: of failing to reconcile this tendency with the faith he had in the middle class as a source of political regeneration. Mosca never resolved this dilemma and quietly dropped the idea of the decline of political leadership from his later analysis in *The Ruling Class*. In his later writings, the elected political leadership assumed greater importance. In the meantime, he also reassessed the value of representative democracy in general.

Despite asserting that a ruling class would dominate every society, Mosca distinguished between political systems on the basis of two factors: the direction of the flow of authority and the source of recruitment to the ruling class (1939: Ch. XV). Political systems can be compared along these two axes. There are two principles according to which authority flowed and two tendencies determining elite membership. Authority in any political organisation either flows downward—the autocratic principle—or upward, the liberal principle. In the autocratic principle, officials are appointed and granted authority by some higher official. In the liberal system, rulers are authorised by those ruled—usually by means of an election. Autocracy and liberal are the ideal type systems of authority to which any given society will conform to a certain degree. Many societies will be a mixture of these principles. Mosca cited the example of the USA, where the chief executive derives his authority from the liberal principle of election, but where he then appoints other executive heads according to the autocratic principle.

Recruitment of the ruling class will display either an 'aristocratic' or a 'democratic' tendency. When new members of the ruling class are recruited from the descendants of the existing ruling class, it is aristocratic in nature. When the ruling class is renewed from the lower class of those ruled, it is democratic. Both tendencies are ever present in political systems but vary in intensity over time and place; sometimes the aristocratic tendency is predominant while at others, the democratic is. In their extreme forms, both tendencies have their limitations. An overwhelmingly aristocratic society will be stifled in due course, with its ruling class losing touch with the needs and interests of society. Where the democratic principle predominates, it smacks of a revolutionary situation. A ruling class hardly exists as it is in the process of being replaced from below. In course of time it might stabilise and allow for a gradual infiltration by persons from the lower class. This would allow the ruling class to renew itself and keep in touch with the needs and interests of society, thus preventing any decline in the quality of leadership the ruling class provides.

The two principles of authority and the two tendencies of recruitment can be combined in any one of four ways, offering the basis for a comparative political analysis. An autocratic system of authority most often combines with an aristocratic method of recruitment into the ruling class; hereditary monarchies are examples of this. Some autocracies display a democratic tendency in recruitment; Mosca cited the examples of the mandarinate of China and the Roman Catholic Church. The Polish constitution is an example of a liberal society with an aristocratic tendency. The modern representative democracy of Britain is an example that combines the liberal principle with a democratic tendency. Mosca viewed the last example as an illusion. Implicit in his argument was the belief that the overall trend of political systems would gravitate to either the aristocratic-autocratic or the aristocratic-liberal type. Although Mosca began by refuting Aristotle, he ultimately echoed him when he pointed out that a balance between the principles and tendencies is desirable—with enough democratic openness to refresh the ruling class and enough aristocratic restrictiveness to ensure stability, a liberal system of elective authority but an electorate confined to the middle class, led by the 'little nucleus of sound minds and choice spirits that keep mankind from going to dogs every other generation' (1939: 429). In his later writings, Mosca took a more favourable view of representative governments as they permit the electorate to balance the liberal authority of parliament against the autocratic authority of the bureaucracy.

Mosca rejected Marx's explanation of the ownership of the means of production being the source of power as one-dimensional, pointing out that military force, priestly status or administrative expertise could be equally compelling reasons for political domination. In every case, the elite tries to convert itself into a form of hereditary rule by using its power to perpetuate itself. As a minority, it has the advantage of being cohesive. In liberal democracies, there is manipulation as party elites control free elections and official positions, despite their being filled through open examinations. Therefore, official positions routinely favour the established ruling class. Besides, with the help of violence and manipulation, the ruling class rules through ideology or some other means convincing to the majority of the people. In highlighting the role of ideology in perpetuating elite rule, Mosca preceded Gramsci, who developed his theory of hegemony with the capacity of the state to control the ideological apparatus (Mukherjee and Ramaswamy 2000).

Political change comes about as a result of conflict between a ruling class that tries to retain power and new forces, also led by minorities, seeking to dislodge the ruling class. Elites lose power because of their failure to assimilate new social forces by opening their ranks to new people, or by adapting their policies and ideas. A reclusive and immobile elite gradually loses its political and social hold over society and may be overthrown. Mosca predicted that elites would always dominate society, including communist society. Djilas' *New Class* (1957) vindicated Mosca's thesis, for in the former communist societies there existed the *nomenklatura*, those who enjoyed privileges and special status because of their position within the hierarchy of the Communist Party.

Change is always cosmetic as it never ushers in political equality. For Mosca, elite dominance with the consequent rigid division of society could be explained in terms of social development. Masses are disorganised whereas the elite are organised, although they may not be exactly cohesive. This unity will guarantee their survival in even the democratic electoral process. The survival of the elite from one period to another depends on their acquiring new skills. In modern industrial society, wealth, knowledge and bureaucratic skills dominate. Even within the elites, there are two categories: a higher stratum of leaders who control the machinery of the state, and the second stratum of trained administrators and technicians. The second layer is equally important and must not be relegated to a secondary position, as it is essential for the survival of the state. Mosca was more favourably disposed than Pareto towards representative democracy. He saw the possibility in competition to restrain the rulers. However, his general conclusion was that the democratic ideal was largely a myth, similar to Pareto's main argument.

Michels, Mosca's disciple, tried to apply many of Mosca's theories. In his famous work *Political Parties* (1911), he developed the argument that society in general and all organisations are subject to oligarchic domination: 'who says organization says oligarchy' (1962: 364). This is the *iron law of oligarchy*, which he applied to one of the most democratically organised political parties—the German Social Democratic Party (SPD). 'Every party organisation represents an oligarchical power grounded upon a democratic basis.... The formation of oligarchies within the various forms of democracy is the outcome of organic necessity, and consequently affects every organisation, be it socialist or even anarchist' (ibid.: 365). He never offered a precise formulation of the law of oligarchy, but its meaning is clear. In any organisation of any size, leadership becomes necessary for its success and survival. He considered 'leadership as a necessary phenomenon in every form of social life'. The nature of organisation is such that it gives power and advantages to a group of leaders who cannot be checked or held accountable by their followers. This is true even when the leadership is elected. Organisational and psychological factors are responsible for this.

There are two reasons why leadership becomes autonomous: first, an organisation of any size and complexity requires skills and expertise, thus making it virtually impossible for ordinary members to supervise the specialists who take decisions on behalf of the party on their own initiative. The need to compete and win elections and also provide stability to the organisation makes the leader influential. The second is the psychological need of the masses to be led, as they are disorganised and incapable of collective action unless led by an activist minority. Changes in leadership are less due to elite displacement and more through a process of absorption of new members into existing oligarchic organisations.

Michels, like Mosca, predicted that leaders of the new socialist parties, who are proletarian in origin, would rapidly become 'bourgeoisified' once in positions of power. He demonstrated that power breeds power, a central theme of elitism. The leadership controls the party funds and party channels of information, mainly its newspapers. It selects parliamentary candidates and dispenses patronage. Michels analysed the impact that the party's role in the entire political system had on its internal power structure. Power is necessary for the party's electoral success, which needs the support of voters who are not party members, but may be committed to the party principle; this means that the party would have to moderate its ideology and provide an assurance of stability. This would strengthen the hands of two groups within the party: the expert party bureaucrats more interested in power than in principle, and the elected parliamentary representatives of the party, whose election gives them added weight within the party but who owe their electoral success to their appeal to the electorate at large, rather than to the narrower party membership.

Party leaders owe their position within the party largely to their support outside the party. This forces the party to adopt a hierarchy that mirrors the hierarchical power structure in the political system as a whole, with 'shadow' ministers supported by an efficient bureaucracy, leading to the triumph of oligarchy with a proven leadership that is 'stable and irremovable'. This process takes place in even proletarian parties as within them, too, a proletarian elite emerges, which ceases to be proletarian except in origin as it exchanges manual labour for desk work and wages for salary. These organisational factors are reinforced by psychological ones. The majority are apathetic towards public matters as most people are concerned with politics only if it affects their private interests. They possess no knowledge about the workings of the political system. Within the party organisation, too, only a small group is active and truly influential. The majority are glad to have others take on political responsibilities. Apathy, submissiveness and deference are the reasons why the interested few, who have also organisational ability, can lead. The majority will never rule despite the formal apparatus of universal suffrage and the myth of majority will. In reality, in any democracy it is a powerful oligarchy that rules; however, democracy allows the emergence of a number of rival parties—each led by an oligarchy—whose competition ensures a certain indirect influence to the people whose support they must cultivate. The democratic tendency cannot prevent, but can restrain the oligarchy.

> The great error of socialists, an error committed in consequence of their lack of adequate psychological knowledge, is to be found in their combination of pessimism regarding the present, with rosy optimism and immeasurable confidence regarding the future. A realistic view of the mental condition of the masses shows beyond question that even if we admit the possibility of moral improvement in mankind, the human materials with whose use politicians and philosophers cannot dispense in their plans of social reconstruction are not of a character to justify excessive optimism. With the limits of time for which human provision is possible, optimism will remain the exclusive privileges of utopian thinkers (Michels 1962: 482).

Michels failed to distinguish between technical expertise and political leadership. He extended the existing elite critique of Pluralism and Marxism that stated that direct government by the masses was impossible. Applying this argument to political parties, he alluded to the inevitability of first, bureaucracy, and second, oligarchy, due to their technical and administrative functions. Unlike Pareto and Mosca who advanced a general framework for studying politics, Michels restricted his enquiry to politics alone.

MODIFICATIONS OF CLASSICAL ELITISM

James Burnham (1907–87), in *Managerial Revolution* (1941), provided an economic approach to elitism, arguing that the rise of professional managers has created a new class that can replace the old ruling class of capitalists. The managerial class is in the process of establishing control across all capitalist states; this implied that the manager and technocrats would increasingly gain prominence over the owners of capital. Burnham was among the first theorists to understand the indispensability and relative autonomy of the technologists in the modern industrial revolution. He presented refined versions of the arguments proffered by Saint Simon. Fascinated by the emerging captains of industry, Saint Simon clubbed them together with scientists and artists, whom he collectively called *industriel*, as pre-eminent and independent within society. The *industriel* would be entrusted with the task of directing public fortune, ensuring the economy of public expenditure, restricting arbitrary power and promoting public good. According to him, they had the greatest capacity for positive administration; however, he was ambiguous about how they would gain political power.

Burnham assumed that the capitalist system was on the decline and would be replaced by a society controlled economically and politically by the managerial elite. He assumed that politics would always be a matter of struggle between groups for power and status, and that in all societies, a small group would inevitably control the ultimate decision-making. The shift in the composition of the elite, wherein the new elite replaces the old one, leads to social change. The need of advanced industrialised societies for technical training and expertise makes the prospect of an egalitarian classless society inconceivable. This was proved by the failure of the Bolshevik revolution in Russia.

According to Burnham, the basis of elite power is control over the chief means of production, which gives a group a dominant position in any society. There are two aspects of control: the controlling group will prevent others from gaining access to the means of production, and it will receive 'preferential treatment' when the product—in money and goods—is distributed (1941: 56). These two forms of control normally go together. Burnham believed that it was a sign of stress if control over access did not bring with it preferential treatment and status. In normal circumstances, '... the easiest way to discover what the ruling group is in any society is usually to see what group gets the biggest income' (ibid.: 57). Burnham, like the Marxists and elitists, saw power as cumulative; control of production gives rise to political power and social prestige, as well as to wealth. State institutions are gradually integrated with the prevailing system of economic control. The laws of the state help to sustain the dominance of the owners of the means of production by protecting existing property relationships. Under capitalism, according to Burnham, a separation is maintained between the state and economy—the state does not intervene in the capitalists' enterprise but establishes a legal framework within which a capitalist economic system can succeed. As a last resort, control of the means of production does not depend on legal forms, but upon the nature of economy. The success or failure of the elite to perpetuate its power depends on whether it can monopolise the instruments of production.

For Burnham, capitalism faced a crisis as capitalists, as the formal owners of productive forces, became increasingly divorced from the actual operations of production. Originally managers of their enterprises, the capitalists gradually left this activity to professional managers, concentrating on financing rather than on the production process. The final stage in the decline of the capitalist class was its gradual retirement from even financing to become a 'leisured class', spending the profits from their enterprises without contributing to production. The productive process in the meantime came to be controlled by the managerial class—a skilled technical elite with counterparts in the state bureaucracy—whose position was dependent not on the capitalist finance structure, but on the technical nature of modern production. The capitalist class was not overthrown in favour of a classless society, but was replaced by the technically indispensable managerial elite. Economic control made political control possible.

Burnham predicted that governments in all contemporary societies would be increasingly controlled by the executives rather than the legislatures, and would be managed by bureaucrats, whether the civil service in

Britain, the state planners in the former USSR, or the military-industrial complex in the US. Capitalist dichotomy between the state and economy would cease as industry became increasingly state-run and as managerial personnel and state bureaucracies became interchangeable with the government. Managerial control of the state and state control of the economy would ultimately lead to a new elite domination.

A very different theory emerged in C. Wright Mills' (1916–62) hard-hitting classic, *The Power Elite* (1956), written in response to what many in the media depicted as the Great American celebration, namely that American society had become relatively classless and pluralistic, with people exercising power through their political parties and public opinion. Mills challenged this view by studying the social backgrounds and career paths of the people who occupied the highest positions in the three major institutional hierarchies in post-war United States—the corporations, the executive branch of the federal government, and the military. He concluded that in all of these, the members of this leadership group consisted of white Christian males who came from 'at most, the upper third of the income and occupational pyramids'. Mills criticised American pluralism by arguing that far from being an independent arbiter of the national interest, a power elite of politicians dominated the state, military and corporate bosses, who shaped public policy to suit their own ends. Mills' theory involved a three-level gradation of the distribution of power. At the top were those in command of the major institutional hierarchies of modern society—the executive branch of the national government, the large business corporations and the military establishment controlling political power, means of production and death, respectively, reinforcing Eisenhower's conception of the military-industrial complex.

The pluralist model of competing interests, according to Mills, applied to the middle level—the semi-organised interplay between interest groups and legislative politics that pluralists mistakenly consider the feature of the entire power structure of the capitalist state. At the bottom exist the politically fragmented masses (1956: 167–68). Mills' account explained the close nexus between economic elites and governmental elites: the corporate rich and 'the political directorate'. He asserted that the growing centralisation of power in the federal executive branch was made visible by the presence of a large number of 'political outsiders' from the corporate world (ibid.: 235). Notwithstanding this, Mills declared that it would be misleading to consider that 'the political apparatus is merely an extension of the corporate world, or that it had been taken over by the representatives of the corporate rich' (ibid.: 170). He tried to distinguish his position from what he termed the 'simple Marxian view' that considered the economic elite the real holders of power, and therefore used the term 'power elite' rather than 'ruling class' as that implied too much economic determinism (ibid.: 276–77). Mills was less deterministic than Marx, but considered his analysis compatible with the Marxist view despite the fact that he, unlike the Marxists, refused to accept that history was the by-product of social forces; instead, he insisted that it was repeatedly made by individual human beings. Furthermore, he also maintained that political, military and economic elites were considerably autonomous units, often in conflict, and rarely acted in total unison.

Mills, like Burnham, was of the belief that the elite and its status and composition were derived not from psychology or the skills of its individual members, but from the social and economic structures of that particular society. Positions of power are attached to certain roles in society. While for Burnham it was the means of production that was the source of power in society, for Mills, power stemmed from a wider set of institutions that are pivotal in society. The uppermost ranks of the hierarchy in these institutions constituted the 'strategic command posts of the social structure' (Mills 1956: 4). The closeness of the links between the institutional hierarchies determined the cohesiveness of the elite. 'If these hierarchies are scattered and disjointed, then their respective elites tend to be scattered and disjointed; if they have many interconnections and points of coinciding interest, then their elites tend to form a coherent kind of grouping' (ibid.: 19). The national elite existed because of the contact maintained among themselves by the leaders of the hierarchies. Institutional proximity is at its strongest where individuals 'interchange commanding roles at the top of one dominant institutional order with those in another' (ibid.: 288).

Mills' account, according to Miliband, lacked details, ruling out room for debate, even though the background thesis was reasonably satisfactory. Miliband praised Mills' account for its richness and intricacies, and its readability. Applauding it, he said, 'it is one of the very few books to glitter among the grey mass of what, in the United States, passed for social analysis in the frightened fifties' (1968: 5). He agreed with its general thesis that in the contemporary US, some small number of people enjoyed enormous power, which was both unchecked and irresponsible. However, he rejected Mills' dismissal of organised labour as the leader of an alternative political order. Dahl's criticism (1968) of the analysis was on the grounds of insufficient data. He noted that a theory that could not be converted to empirical evidence could not claim to be scientific. The burden of such proof had to be provided by the theorist and not by his critics. The argument that '*A* is more powerful than *B*' is both ambiguous and meaningless without specificity. No comparison is actually possible when two actors are performing different functions. Any ideal of political equality is utopian, and the absence of political equality does not mean the existence of a ruling elite.

Parsons (1957) praised Mils' copious data and agreed that Mills had put it to good use; however, he rejected Mills' claim as the data was not sufficient for empirical grounding. He argued that Mills had ignored two very important developments: first, the dynamics of a maturing industrial society, and second, the altered position of the United States in the world in the context of the relative decline of Western Europe, rise of Soviet power and independence of the colonies. The combination of all these factors had led to an enormous enhancement of American power in a short time and given their profound repercussions, the old political institutions have disappeared. In an essentially non-political and individualistic society that places primacy on economic values of production, this increase in the relative importance of government and its power creates a great degree of tension. Ignoring these important developments, Mills made large generalisations on the basis of short-term experience. Parsons argued that the structure of American political leadership was far from settled. Mills provided a very selective treatment of a complex problem. Without dismissing power as illegitimate, one should accept it as an essential and desirable component in a highly organised society. However, it is clear that power can be abused and needs many safeguards and controls. Mills was partly pre-liberal, anti-capitalist and pro-socialist within the Jeffersonian tradition; however, such loose identities were no longer enough for serious model building. According to Sweezy (1956), the book's greatest merit was its graphic description of those who really ruled America. He considered it an authentic voice of American radicalism, but also criticised Mills for blurring class relationships and the dynamics of the class system in aspects such as the loss of high-class status and the process of co-option from mass society, which created a leadership void in the underclass. In short, even admirers on the left like Miliband and Sweezy did not consider Mills' account a rigorously worked out and empirically verifiable thesis of power in contemporary US.

Bell viewed Mills' work as a kind of romantic protest against life today. With regard to the complex, modern industrialised society leading to bureaucratisation, he believed that this need not be inevitable. In a society with mass education, an elevation in standards of living and multiplicity of choice, the

> ambiguous use of terms like 'bureaucratisation' and 'power elites' often reinforces a sense of helplessness and belies the resources of a free society: the variety of interest conflicts, the growth of public responsibility, the weight of traditional freedoms, the role of volunteer and community groups, etc. Like the indiscriminate use by the Communists of the term 'bourgeois democracy' in the thirties, or by Burnham of 'managerial society' in the forties, or the term 'totalitarianism' in the fifties, *particular and crucial* differences between societies are obscured. This amorphousness leads, as in the case of *The Power Elite* with its emphasis on 'big' decisions, to a book which discusses power, but rarely politics (Bell 1968: 224–25).

Zweigenhaft and Domoff (1998), in their study of the power elite after a gap of 40 years, revealed that the power elite in contemporary US is more diverse when compared to the 1950s, although the core group continues to be wealthy Christian males, most of them still from the upper third of the social ladder. High social origins continue to be a distinct advantage in making it to the top, and in general it takes about three generations to rise from the bottom to the top in America. Although women and minorities have found increasing representation, they continue to remain under-represented.

DEMOCRATIC ELITISM

Joseph Alios Schumpeter (1883–1952), in *Capitalism, Socialism and Democracy* (1943), tried to make democracy compatible with elitism. Pointing out the inadequacies of classical democratic theory, he said that it set impossibly high standards by stating that it has to reflect the will of the people. This was a highly unrealistic assumption as it was based on an idea of people as homogenous, whereas all large societies are characterised by a multiplicity of conflicting wills. Another fallacy was the assumption that it depended on a high level of rationality, whereas in public affairs people's behaviour is likely to be irrational (although it could be the reverse in private matters). He took no account of political leadership except to state that all governments take decisions independently of the people's will. However, in spite of this profound scepticism, Schumpeter believed that democracy had a great deal of descriptive content and much to be recommended for. The presence of competing parties offering alternative programmes means that the role of the people is limited to choosing the government. The difference between governments in a democracy and a non-democracy is that in the former, competition exists and provides a minimal degree of accountability. This necessitates some basic freedoms, as competitive party democracy requires the formation of associations and propagation of ideas.

Schumpeter defined democracy as a political method to arrive at political, legislative and administrative decisions. He placed in certain individuals the power to decide on all matters, as a consequence of their successful pursuit of people's vote. 'Democracy is the institutional arrangement for arriving at political decisions in which individuals acquire the power to decide by means of a competitive struggle for the people's vote' (Schumpeter 1976: 269). Schumpeter's account is known as democratic elitism (Bachrach and Baratz 1962) because he reasoned that free elections introduce an element of competition among elite groups. He believed that powerful social forces limit participation in politics and that liberal democracy, at the very best, is a restrictive endeavour to select decision-makers and ensure their legitimacy through elections. He shared Marx's view about the inevitability of the collapse of capitalism (due to its own internal contradictions) and argued that large corporations did dominate the production and distribution of goods. However, he rejected Marxist class analysis and theory of class conflict. He considered it appropriate for socialists to develop a suitable model of democracy to fulfil the requirements of big government in the context of planning. He rejected the idea of the common good, as developed in classical democratic theory, as both misleading and dangerous, for people have different wants and different values. There rarely exists an agreement among individuals and groups about ends; even if they do agree, there will be disagreements about the means to be employed to realise that given end. Modern societies are economically and culturally diverse and there are bound to be different notions of the common good. He declared common good as an unacceptable element of democratic theory. In complex, modern societies, people's wills are conflicting and divergent (1976: 252ff).

Schumpeter believed that the decisions of non-democratic agencies could sometimes prove more acceptable to people than democratic decisions. In this context, he cited the example of the religious settlement which Napoleon Bonaparte had imposed on France at the beginning of the nineteenth century, observing that this example was far from isolated: 'If results that prove in the long run satisfactory to the people at large are made the test of government *for* the people, then government *by* the people, as conceived by the classical doctrine of democracy, would often fail to meet it' (Schumpeter 1976: 256). He explicitly rejected the classical theory of democracy and held that people were, and could be nothing more than, 'producers of governments', a mechanism to select 'the men who are able to do the deciding' (ibid.: 296). Hence, he disproved the notion of 'popular will' as a social construct with no rational basis, as a 'manufactured' rather than genuine popular will. 'Popular will' was therefore the 'product and not the motive power for the political process' (ibid.: 263). He offered three arguments against popular participation: the incompetence of typical citizens, the tendency towards irrationality on the part of ordinary citizens, and the opportunities that public participation allowed for special interests to pursue their own aims.

Democracy merely legitimised competition among governing elites, for he accepted the inevitability of hierarchy and considered the democratic process a procedure that was 'simply an institutional arrangement for reaching political decisions, not an end in itself' (Schumpeter 1976: 126). He drew an analogy between political behaviour, where leaders competed for people's votes, and market behaviour, the vote having the same importance as money in the market. He saw a division between political activists and a passive electorate as the key to a strong, efficient government and the defence of liberty. Viewed from this perspective, democracy and socialism are compatible, provided that the conditions for its successful functioning are met. These are:

1. The calibre of politicians must be high.
2. Competition between rival leaders (and parties) must take place within a relatively restricted range of political questions, bound by consensus on the overall direction of national policy, on what constitutes a reasonable parliamentary programme and on general constitutional matters.
3. A well-trained independent bureaucracy of 'good standing and tradition' must exist to aid politicians on all aspects of policy formulation and administration.
4. There must be 'democratic self-control', i.e. broad agreement about the undesirability of, for instance, voters and politicians confusing their respective roles, excessive criticism of government on all issues, and unpredictable and violent behaviour.
5. There must be a culture capable of tolerating differences of opinion (1976: 296).

Thus, Schumpeter's conceptualisation of democracy left out the two pillars of the classical theory of democracy—popular sovereignty and public good. He cautioned against the collapse of democracy when ideologies and interests are held resolutely, for then people would be unwilling to compromise. Such a situation would indicate an end of democratic politics. His account of democracy had some definitive advantages over other theories: it provides an efficient criterion for distinguishing democratic governments from others, acknowledges fully the centrality of leadership, establishes the importance of competition in politics, and even if imperfectly, shows how governments are created and destroyed. The theory clarified the nature of popular wishes without exaggerating their significance. Schumpeter pointed out that his theory explained the relationship between democracy and freedom. If freedom meant 'the existence of a sphere of individual self-government, then the democratic method required that everyone is in principle, free to compete for political leadership. This is possible only if there is considerable amount of freedom of discussion *for all*' (1976: 270–71), and that entailed both freedom of speech and freedom of press.

> Schumpeter's theory of democracy highlights many recognizable features of modern Western liberal democracies: the competitive struggle between parties for political power; the important role of public bureaucracies; the significance of political leadership; the way in which modern politics deploys many of the techniques of advertising; the way voters are subject to a constant barrage of information, written materials and discussion; and the way, despite this barrage, many voters remain poorly informed about contemporary political issues and express marked uncertainty about them (Held 1987: 178).

There are some fallacious assumptions in Schumpeter's analyses. He seemed to suggest the presence of only one well-developed classical theory of democracy; this is not the case as there are a number of models within it (Held 1987: 179). Schumpeter defined democracy with reference to procedures, practices and goals prevalent at that time in the West, and did not take into consideration the theories that criticised reality—visions of human nature and of social arrangements that explicitly rejected the status quo and proposed alternatives (Duncan and Lukes 1963). This criticism would have been more substantive had it been validated by empirical evidence or through a well-argued logical construction. Schumpeter's basic contention was that the tall claims of classical democratic theory were inoperative in the actual functioning of liberal democracies. His argument that his theory of democratic elitism was akin to a competitive market economy, thereby providing it with legitimacy, can be questioned on two grounds: (*a*) the motivation of each individual voter differs; the different motivations could be tradition, apathy, coercion, pragmatic acquiescence, conditional agreement, normative agreement or ideal normative agreement; (*b*) The manipulation and distortion of political will by the holders of political power point to the complexities of the close relationship between legitimacy and power, which Schumpeter overlooked. However, with regard to both criticisms, Schumpeter was on firm ground. Vis-à-vis the first, his theory emphasised the atomisation of individual behaviour, and with regard to the second, his procedural theory sought to provide a functioning model of a competitive party system where these larger normative questions were of little relevance. Macpherson (1977: 89) considered it appropriate to describe Schumpeter's model as 'oligopolistic', for

> there are only a few sellers, a few suppliers of political goods.... Where there are so few sellers, they need not and do not respond to the buyers' demands, as they must do in a fully competitive system. They can set prices and set the range of goods that will be offered. More than that, they can, to a considerable extent, create ... (their own) demand.

Mills' famous gloss of Schumpeter's argument revealed the workings of an industrial-military-political complex in American national politics. The power elite in the US is far more powerful than the other elites, which explains the promotion of the arms race, although Mills insisted that the power elite submitted to the control of the intellectuals. This, however, questioned Schumpeter's belief that elites were periodically responsible to the people through elections. Bachrach and Baratz (1962), reacting to the elite perception of treating people passively and considering them incapable of making judgements or exercising power, pointed out that 20 per cent of the 'apathetic voters' in the US in the 1950s and 1960s came from the poorest strata of society. Instead of revising the democratic ideal, Bachrach and Baratz (ibid.) considered it necessary to reform social conditions.

Schumpeter influenced and inspired the analysis in Downs' *An Economic Theory of Democracy* (1957), which studied democracy from the perspective of an economist. Assuming that human beings were rational, they would choose the least costly means to achieve their ends or goals. Downs made this assumption about political actors, both voters and politicians. The rational voter would vote for a party and a politician from whom he hopes to gain the maximum. Likewise, the rational political party would try to maximise its vote in order to stay in office, or to gain office. Democratic politics is about the competition for power between rational actors; this view reinforced Schumpeter's view of politics as a competitive struggle through fair and free elections.

PLURALISM

The Pluralists accept diversity and contend that the modern liberal state is too complex for any single group, class or organisation to dominate society. Pluralism affirms the separation of state and civil society and distinguishes economic from political power. It considers the political system all-inclusive, operating on the basis of consensus by taking into account everyone's interests and ensuring the satisfaction of all as part of a larger group or association. It differs from elite theory, which establishes a dichotomy between the ruler and the ruled. The classical theory of democracy posits the existence of a common good that the democratic system throws up, while pluralists accept that the existence of groups of particular interests does not necessarily indicate the absence of a general interest.

> Just as elitism was a reaction to the naïve expectation of early democrats, so pluralism was a reaction against the 'ultra-realism' of the elitists. Where elitism sees rule by a minority, pluralism sees rule by *minorities*.... Pluralism is

> a midway position between elitism and democracy. Unlike elitism, it claims there is no single, dominant elite. But unlike a 'majority rule' view of democracy, it accepts that the majority does not govern. What we have is government by the many, rather than government by the majority (Hague, et al. 1992: 14).

The classical theory of democracy perceives individuals as isolated and discrete, and not as members of one or several group(s) that overlap. This is unrealistic in view of the multiple identities of a person in modern society. Pluralism, like Madison's theory, is preoccupied with factions and pressure groups, for it considers society essentially heterogeneous and pluralistic with diverse aspirations, interests and wills. It accepts Madison's concern with factions and their modern counterpart—interest groups and pressure groups—as a natural corollary of free association in a world where most desired goods are scarce and where the complex industrial system fragments social interests and creates a multiplicity of demands. Like Madison, pluralists accept that the basic function of government is to protect the freedom of factions to advance their political interests, while preventing any individual faction from encroaching on the freedom of others. However, they differ from Madison in that they do not regard factions as a major threat to democratic associations, or as a source of instability, or as undemocratic in nature. They consider the existence of diverse competitive interests the basis of democratic equilibrium and essential for the favourable development of public policy. Pluralists combine Locke's individualism and Dewey's participatory ethic with Burke's concern for continuity and stability.

Pluralists view politics as an arena where conflict is resolved between the different groups representing all the dominant interests in society. They view conflict as 'democracy's lifeblood' (Lipset 1973: 83), as 'whatever the explanation for conflict may be its existence is one of the prime facts of all community life' (Dahl 1967: 6). Accepting conflict as given, they prescribe democratic forums to accommodate it. While conceding that some marginal groups might be left out, they assert that all major streams are usually represented. They also argue that certain groups may try to establish close links with particular departments in the government, which may lead to a neglect of other interests. Truman (1951: 10) acknowledged that institutionalised relationships could develop between an agency and its attendant interest groups, and this could lead to other interests being ignored. However, Wilson (1977: 45) pointed towards the existence of Whitehall pluralism, that is, even if one department ignores the interests of a particular group, it is not necessary that others would ignore them as well. Their views could be taken up 'by the fact that other departments have checks and have different departmental views accordingly'. Pluralists perceive the state as a balancing factor between departments representing a range of interest groups. Thus, interest groups are accepted as the basic building blocks of the theory. For pluralists, 'interest' refers to 'subjective interests', or what Truman called 'attitudes'. Authority is distributed within the government (Eckstein 1963: 392), which means that the state is not controlled and dominated by any single interest.

Yet, the state is seldom neutral but mirrors the range of group pressures it faces as 'policy arises from the interaction of various social elements' (Easton 1965: 172). The state attempts to make policy by bargaining between a range of conflicting interests, and the government takes into consideration the interests of 'unorganised and potential groups', which do not need 'organized expression except when these needs are flagrantly violated' (Truman 1951: 448). Politics is a constant process of negotiation; new issues emerge all the time, which ensures the peaceful resolution of conflicts (Dahl 1967: 24). It is thus contended that an explanation of the actual process of politics refers to an analysis of groups. In his influential study of New Haven, Connecticut (1961a), Dahl found no single group to be predominant in the city across all policy areas such as education, urban redevelopment and political nominations. 'In each issue area different actors appeared, their roles were different and the kinds of alternatives which they had to choose among were different.' Dahl concluded that as far as key decisions were concerned, there existed no cohesive ruling elite.

Policy emerges from constant conflict and exchange between different groups, with the government being regarded as just another group. Only by organising themselves into groups could individuals have their interests represented in government. The state is a distinct organisation that makes policies in response to the innumerable groups exerting pressure on the government. It is accepted that conflict between groups is pervasive within liberal democracy; however, this conflict rarely threatens the stability of the system. A consensus, defining the limits of political action and the framework of policy outcomes, ensures political stability.

Pluralists understand power as the capacity to achieve one's aims despite opposition. They concede the existence of several inequalities in society, and that not all groups have equal access to all types of resources, let alone equal resources. However, nearly every group has some advantage that could be utilised in the democratic process to make an impact. Since different groups have access to different kinds of resources, the influence of any particular group would generally depend on the issue at hand. Pluralists perceive power as non-hierarchical and competitively arranged, and embroiled in an 'endless process of bargaining' between many groups representing different interests. These groups, in the long run, change their concerns and shift their positions. Both at the local and national levels, political decisions do not reflect a unified public opinion on basic issues, as Locke, Rousseau and Bentham had presumed. Policymaking in today's complex world emerges from the intense lobbying of different interest groups, with policy ultimately reflecting the inputs of all such divergent groups. Political outcomes come about through mediation and adjudication between the competing demands of groups. There is no powerful decision-making centre in the pluralist model. Since power is dispersed throughout society, there is a plurality of pressure points, a variety of competing policy-formulating and decision-making centres. Equilibrium in society is achieved because of the existence of diverse interests and overlapping memberships, which unleashes competing forces without any one force wielding excessive influence (Truman 1951: 503–16). These varied groups sustain democratic goals and help citizens to advance their own interests.

The key questions for pluralists are: Who are involved in the decision-making process, and who can be seen to influence outcomes? Polsby (1960) advised a researcher to study behaviour either first-hand, or from documents, informants, newspapers, and other appropriate sources. Pluralists lay stress on the actual process of decision-making and by ignoring untested concepts like false consciousness, hegemony and a dominant ideology, they developed a theory of power that is empirically verifiable. Their notion of 'modern society and polity as fragmented, diverse and democratic' is 'more accurate about the distribution of power than found in monolithic Marxist and elitist theories' (Smith 1995: 214). Their equal emphasis on democracy and pluralism has led to the theory being called the democratic pluralist view. Modern pluralism has some similarities with the early pluralist view, expressed at the beginning of the twentieth century by Ernest Barker, Mary Follet, Harold J. Laski, A. D. Lindsay and Robert MacIver—for example, the associational nature of modern society and acceptance of authority as federal in character. However, the major difference between the two is that while the essential focus of early pluralism was more Aristotelian (in their emphasis on different associations), modern pluralists emphasise interest and pressure groups.

The key characteristic of pluralism is that different minorities make or influence decisions in different areas. Groups with a special interest in particular areas are allowed their say on that topic, but rarely go beyond it. For example, teachers would want a say in the education policy and generals would want to express their preference in defence matters, but neither would impose on the other's terrain. Pluralism believes that well-informed views are given special weight.

POLYARCHY

Specifying the exact nature of pluralist democracies, Dahl argued that (*a*) if competitive electoral systems were characterised by a multiplicity of groups with strong views on different subjects, democratic rights would be protected better and extreme political inequalities certainly avoided; (*b*) There is empirical evidence to suggest that certain policies in the US and Britain fulfil these conditions. Dahl was convinced that power was distributed and shared by many groups in society representing diverse interests; these particular interests are defended through the government, thereby creating a proclivity towards a 'competitive equilibrium' that benefits citizens in the long run. At a minimum, 'democratic theory is concerned with processes by which ordinary citizens exert a relatively high degree of control over leaders' (1956: 3). This control is maintained by two methods: regular elections and political competition among parties, groups and individuals. He dismissed the concerns of Madison, Mill and Tocqueville regarding the tyranny of the majority as misplaced, for a tyrannous majority is impossible as elections express the preferences of divergent competitive groups rather than the wishes of a strong majority. He agreed with Madison about the existence of factions, believing it possible to deal with their effects rather than eliminating them. Madison believed that attacking factionalism would be improper and wicked, and that the government's first objective is the protection of human diversity, which makes different kinds and degrees of property possible. And property is a fundamental right.

Polyarchy or pluralist democracy is rule by a series of minorities—some self-interested and others disinterested—within the boundaries stipulated by consensus, with none able to dominate but all possessing space for manoeuvre and bargaining. This emphasis on consensus is in contrast to Schumpeter's view of democratic politics as ultimately managed by competing elites. The pluralist system is a decentralised one, aiming to arrive at compromise rather than truth. Competition among groups safeguards democracy and establishes the democratic nature of the system. Democracy establishes not a sovereignty of the majority, but a rule by 'multiple minority oppositions'. For Dahl, the difference between dictatorship and democracy is that between 'government by a minority' and 'government by minorities'. The greater the presence of competing interest groups, the more secure the democracy. Furthermore, he pointed out that change in size from city-states to modern nation-states inevitably led to a shift from a monist to a pluralist democracy. This change in scale is crucial to understanding present-day democracies. In the modern context, the very essence of democracy is realised by polyarchy, which stipulates the presence of a large number of organisations and associations. These enjoy relative autonomy both in relationship to one another and with regard to governmental power and jurisdiction. The institution of polyarchy distinguished a democratic regime from an authoritarian one.

The preconditions for a functioning polyarchy are consensus on the rules of procedure, consensus on the range of policy options, and consensus on the legitimate scope of political activity, which act as buffers against oppressive rule. The greater the level of consensus, the more secure is democracy, and the society enjoys protection from tyranny through non-constitutional provisions. Dahl also accorded importance to principles like the separation of powers and the system of checks and balances, for these are pivotal in deciding the importance of the benefits and burdens that groups face in a political system (which is why they are so bitterly fought over). However, compared to non-constitutional rules, the importance of constitutional rules for the successful development of democracy is less. Dahl believed that democracy was safe for it brings about moderation and agreement and maintains social peace (as long as the social preconditions are secure) (1966: 134–35, 151). He did not consider the equal distribution of control over political decisions or equal political weight for all individuals and groups necessary for a successful democracy (ibid.: 145–46).

In *A Preface to Economic Democracy* (1985: 54–55), departing from his earlier works, Dahl addressed the economic sources of inequalities in political resources, mainly 'ownership and control of firms' that contribute to creating great differences among citizens in wealth, income, status, skills, information, control over information and propaganda, and access to political leaders. These differences generate significant inequalities among citizens in their capacities and in opportunities to participate as political equals. Contrary to Madison, he argued against property being a fundamental right and devoted half the book to describing a 'self-governing equal order', a kind of workers' self-management, stating that it would achieve economic egalitarianism that would be conducive to democracy. In *Democracy and its Critics* (1989: 333), he once again cited the problems that economic inequalities posed for democracy, but maintained that its prospects were 'more seriously endangered' by political inequalities 'derived not from wealth or economic position but from special knowledge'.

He contended that common goods were the informed interests that individuals shared, and that 'the rights and opportunities of the democratic process are elements of the common good' because informed people would realise that these were necessary to gain the enlightenment required to know where their own interests lay (ibid.: 306–08). He pointed to the conflicting visions of what American society was and ought to be. It was the first and 'grandest attempt to realise democracy, political equality and political liberty'. The other vision is of 'a country where unrestricted liberty to acquire unlimited wealth would produce the world's most prosperous society' (ibid: 162). He proposed a system of self-governing firms, partly to expand the number of politically active people, both in the workplace and in the broader political arena, through the resources and experiences gained in the firms. In this way he addressed the critiques of pluralism that stated that it sanctions a narrowing access to democratic politics to those who have the time and resources to be part of interest groups.

Macpherson (1977: 87–88) and Held (1987: 204–05) criticised pluralist theory for sanctioning apathy. The pluralists, however, did not see this as a criticism, as they believed that a certain degree of public apathy was unavoidable. Many considered apathy desirable as they shared Schumpeter's view that widespread political participation unduly constricted political leaders and endangered social and political stability (Lipset 1973: 14–16). The pluralists even went to the extent of asserting that it was all right if some people had no interest in politics as, being members of larger groups, their interests would be taken care of either way.

CONCLUSION

Democratic elitism and pluralism viewed politics as one of the major activities of modern society. They did not undermine the value or seminal importance of politics, only attempting to situate it in the context of modern societal factors where economics usually predominates over politics. However, both were conscious of the determining importance of democratic politics in managing the complexities of modern societies. Pluralists were conscious of the shifts in the scale of democracy, from city-states to contemporary mega-nations. While governing the large nation-states of today, power and authority over public matters have to be distributed among a plurality of organisations and associations that are relatively autonomous in relation to one another, and often, even in relation to the government. The institutions of polyarchy distinguish themselves from authoritarian regimes. As Dahl said as a criticism to unrealistic projects like deliberative democracy: 'if the most relevant and likely alternative to polyarchy in the modern world is not city-state democracy, but an authoritarian regime, then even from a democratic perspective, the untidy systems of polyarchy and pluralism begin to look much more charming' (1986: 242). It is surprising that he excluded the role of the Church in the US as a platform from which the underprivileged and unorganised individuals could acquire political skills (Verba, et al. 1995). However, in explaining how group competition could form the basis of a realistic and functioning democratic order, Dahl and his associates have provided an irreplaceable framework of analysis.

NOTES

1. This scepticism led Pareto and Michels to sympathise with Fascism. More importantly, Schumpeter's restatement of democracy as a system of competing elitism stemmed from this scepticism.
2. The fascists claimed inspiration from Pareto and Mussolini attended some of Pareto's lectures; however, Pareto was a supporter of *laissez faireism* and his elitism had no racial element.

14

POLITICAL PARTIES AND PRESSURE GROUPS

Like other human organizations, parties deserve neither praise nor criticism which they periodically receive. It may be unrealistic to expect parties to unite a divided country, genuinely represent social and economic development. The oscillation between cynical criticism and exaggerated hopes may simply reflect the failure of observers to recognize that a human institution can only achieve limited results in a short period of time.

Blondel 1963: 162

The development of modern democratic states has been paralleled by the emergence of mass political parties.

Axford, et al. 1997: 372

Duverger's law occupies pride of place . . . as one of the major statements in electoral studies research and the canonical statement of the role of electoral systems in general.

Bowler 2006: 579–80

In the contemporary complex world, it is difficult to imagine any viable and legitimate political order without political parties. However, despite the pivotal role of political parties today, their origins are recent—they date back to about 200 years. It is also interesting to note that in the initial period of consolidation of the liberal constitutionalism, political parties were seen as undesirable. George Washington (1732–99), the first American President, was distressed at the rise of factionalism in his administration and warned against the growth of political parties. Similar sentiments can be found in the writings of Jefferson. Such sentiments, however, were short-lived. Washington's exit from the political scene ended the dream of a party-less democracy.

Another important characteristic of political parties is that their growth was extra-constitutional, as no liberal constitution mentions political parties. Political parties rise and decline and new formations emerge over time and place when apocalyptic changes alter the course of politics, or when new issues become political at one particular place and time. It is because of this inherent elasticity that political parties need a democratic set-up in order to bring about essential changes peacefully, without the system either breaking down, or collapsing.

THE FIRST POLITICAL PARTIES: WHIGS AND TORIES IN GREAT BRITAIN

As in many other crucial areas concerning the modern evolution of liberal constitutionalism, the political party in its rudimentary sense arose in Great Britain. After the English Civil War ended in 1644, there emerged a group of members of the House of Commons and the House of Lords who wanted the Parliament to be stronger than the King. This logic of collective action originated in their dislike and fear of the Catholics, and their support and sympathy for the Puritan non-conformists. United in their opposition to the Court Party, they assumed the name Country Party; their opponents nicknamed them Whigs, after some Scottish Puritan Outlaws. The opposite camp was called the Court Party as it consisted of supporters of the King and endorsed the divine rights of the King. They disliked non-conformists and favoured the Church of England with its ceremonies and Bishops. The Whigs considered them supporters of the Catholics and nicknamed them Tories, after the Irish Catholic Outlaws.

The Whigs and Tories were the first political parties, and with their share of treasury benches and the opposition, politics assumed the form of a dual party system. However, after the Glorious Revolution of 1689, the predominance of the Whigs increased phenomenally and Great Britain became a one-party dominant system. Later, the Whigs transformed themselves into a liberal party in the nineteenth century, which culminated in the Prime Ministership of William Gladstone (1809–98), while the Tories became the conservative party, culminating in the Prime Ministership of Benjamin Disreali (1804–81). The early party system led to the institutionalisation of liberal democracy with the enactment of the Habeas Corpus Act of 1679. This act was largely the work of Lord Ashley (1621–83), the Earl of Shaftesbury and founder of the Whig Party in 1681. All modern democracies have provisions for Habeas Corpus (a writ issued to bring a person who has been detained into court, usually to see whether the decision is lawful) in their constitutions.

In the nineteenth century, the Unionists grew out of the Tory party to protect the interests of the country gentry and the merchant classes. The name Conservative Party has been used since 1830. Its nickname, Tory, continues even today. After the Reform Act of 1832, the Whig Party changed itself into the liberal party, championing electoral parliamentary and philanthropic reforms. As a consequence of the widening franchise, brought about by the 1832 Act, the middle class entered the otherwise aristocratic Whig Party. By 1839, the label 'liberal party' had begun to be used, and the first liberal government was formed in 1868. The liberal party disintegrated in the 1880s mainly because of its inability to solve the Irish question, and with the consolidation of franchise for the working class, the Labour Party emerged as the dominant party in 1901, replacing the liberals. However, the liberal party still continues in Great Britain, and after merging with the social democratic party in 1988, is now called the Social and Liberal Democratic Party.

DEVELOPMENT OF PARTY SYSTEM IN THE US

In the US, the political party emerged in its rudimentary form when Washington relinquished his Presidency after completing two terms in office, leaving behind a convention that was broken only with Franklin D. Roosevelt (1882–1945), prompting a constitutional amendment limiting presidential terms to two. John Adams (1735–1826) and Hamilton were the leading federalists, while Jefferson represented the opposite spectrum. In the 1726 elections, Adams defeated Jefferson in a closely contested election. It was at this time that two competing congressional party groups emerged, representing two different perspectives—a strong national government against a weak central government, with states' rights predominating. While the former championed commercial interests, the latter defended agrarian interests.

In the elections of 1800, the Federalists supported Adams but were defeated by Jefferson and his party, the Democratic-Republicans, by a wide margin. However, despite the crucial role that the Democratic Party played in his election, Jefferson continued to view the party as a temporary arrangement to mobilise support, and not as a permanent feature of the democratic electoral process. Given the widespread hostility towards party politics, there was no prevalent party identification. There was no conception of a broad-based party organisation, and what really mattered were legislative caucuses. These anti-party origins of US democracy continued with a loose party system reinforced by the prevailing overall anti-political sentiments, with predominance given to economics over politics. This explained Dahl's assertion that it was absolutely all right if somebody took no interest in politics.

A proper party system emerged in the US in 1824 when Andrew Jackson (1767–1845) ran for the Presidency, and in the absence of a clear winner, the House of Representatives chose John Quincy Adams (1767–1848) as President. This incident changed the nature of political parties. With the decline of the Federalists and the survival of Jeffersonian Republicans, Jackson began to build a national political party system which led to the ushering in of the Democratic Party. To attract the newly enfranchised voters, Jackson introduced patronage and the spoils systems, which continue even today. The Whig Party was subsequently formed in the US to oppose this Jacksonian coalition.

Jackson won the Presidency in 1828 and organised the first party convention in 1832. In order to attract voters' support, the Whigs fielded war heroes; this trend continues even today, with Eisenhower being an example in more recent times. They created local party organisations and decided to contest both state and local elections, thus inaugurating the two-party system in the US with the broad support of the people. This system continued till 1860 and after that, in the context of the debate on slavery, the Whigs declined and a third party emerged, Abraham Lincoln's (1809–65) Republican Party. Ever since then, the two-party system has continued in the US.

FUNCTIONS OF POLITICAL PARTIES

Political parties perform a wide variety of functions. They build channels of communication between the people and decision-makers. In doing so, they filter, combine and structure the demands of the people to the authorities, communicate new demands and convey a loss of support to the government. Political parties can be classified under three dimensions: number of parties; relative size of the parties; and the ideological dispersion of political parties in the political system. Political parties are integral to politics in four main ways:

> (1) Ruling parties offer *direction to government*, performing the vital task of steering the ship of the state. (2) Parties function as agents of *elite recruitment*. They serve as the major mechanism for preparing and recruiting candidates for public office. (3) Parties serve as agents of *interest aggregation*. They transform a multitude of specific demands into more manageable packages of proposals. Parties select, reduce and combine interests. They act as a filter between society and state, deciding which demands to allow through their net. (4) To a declining extent, political parties serve as a *point of reference* for their supporters and voters, giving people a key to interpreting a complicated political world (Hague and Harrop 2001: 167).

The origins of political parties can be traced back to the democratic revolution of the late eighteenth and early nineteenth centuries. This evolution took place in three ways: (*i*) the association of like-minded representatives in the legislative organs to promote common policies and coordinate political activities; (*ii*) through the process of electoral support for parliamentary candidates; and (*iii*) extra-parliamentary considerations, like planning a revolution or achieving parliamentary representation, like the British Labour Party and the contemporary Green Party. States parties could also originate to overthrow a particular regime, for example, the Bolsheviks against Tsarism and nationalist parties like the Indian National Congress or the African National Congress, which came about to gain independence and fight colonial regimes.

Political parties are biased as they are committed to one ideology, and oppose the ideologies and programmes of their rivals. Their membership and programme reflect fundamental social divisions like class, religion, region and nationality. They might highlight a wide range of concerns or be more specific in their policy orientations, for example, some espouse the causes of the environment or prohibition. They represent the interests of members and supporters and serve as a source of recruitment of political leaders. They structure elections and provide coherence to the process of choosing legislators. They organise campaigns, present candidates, publicise issues, and offer alternative programmes in a competitive electoral process. Even in a non-competitive process like the erstwhile Soviet Union, the electoral process received formal prominence with the leading role of the Communist Party. Political parties help in policy development. European political parties are ideologically coherent and strongly disciplined. In contrast, the party system is weak in the United States and hardly exists in many parts between elections. In Great Britain, both leading parties—the Conservatives and Labour—and their think-tanks, the Adam Smith Institute and the Fabian Society, respectively, offer detailed policy alternatives. Through the mechanism of a shadow cabinet, the British party system tries to develop reasonable expertise in particular areas of governance. Political parties also perform socialising and educative functions. In a competitive party system, political alternatives are projected, whereas in non-competitive ones, involvement is emphasised.

Party structures reflect three levels of organisation: legislative structure, national organisation, and a locally arranged constituency level, which is normally geographic. The Soviet Union followed a unit based on the workplace. Guild socialists in England, under the leadership of Cole, proposed functional representation (see Chapter 11), but there were not many takers for this proposal. Political parties are the key institutions of the modern state. Easton placed the operations of political parties in an intermediary position between the public and governing authorities, aggregating and structuring demands and indicating support for the authorities. However, political parties do not only mediate, but also provide the personnel for key public offices. In this sense, they are more than intermediary organisations.

PRESSURE GROUPS AND POLITICAL PARTIES

Pressure groups are organised interest groups that are not actively involved in the political process. Their involvement in politics is to represent the interests, values, beliefs and concerns of their members and supporters. They promote and protect interests through political channels. Pressure groups are not just selfish; they could also promote impersonal objectives like prevention of cruelty to animals, the plight of the homeless, protection of tribal rights (in case of displacement), and abolition of capital punishment. In this sense, new social movements are also pressure groups of a kind. Pressure groups represent particular self-interests, like those of ex-servicemen, dairy farmers, university teachers, petrol pump owners and automobile manufacturers. Apart from the political process, pressure groups also use other channels and methods to advance their cause, for instance the media, the judicial process, strikes, boycotts and civil disobedience campaigns. They can even take recourse to extreme steps like terrorism. While pressure groups have a political end to achieve, they need not use political means exclusively, as some operate outside the political ambit. Cause groups are a type of pressure group that promote causes, issues or ideas, and do not represent organised occupational interests.

Like political parties, pressure groups are of different types and sizes:

(*i*) The degree of politicisation differentiates them. Some are exclusively political, for example, those against nuclear weapons or in favour of quotas for women in national legislatures. Others may be non-political or be involved in politics minimally, like the professional associations of architects or chartered accountants.

(*ii*) Pressure groups differ in territorial scope, like national, regional or local.

(*iii*) They differ with respect to resources, size of membership and prestige, organisational skill, leadership and success.

(*iv*) Pressure groups could be either permanent or ad hoc. The latter are normally issue-based, like the suffragists.

(*v*) Pressure groups also differ on strategies. Some are promotional, like the group for Equal Rights amendment in the US. Others are defensive, like those financing church schools. However, many are both promotional and defensive.

(*vi*) Pressure groups differ mainly in their primary concern and might follow contradictory agendas, like trade unions, industrialists' associations, farmers and consumers.

Like political parties, pressure groups emerged along with modern complexities, industrialisation and democracy. With enhanced state intervention, increased economic and technological specialisation, and conflicting interests resulting from a multiplicity of interests, pressure groups have become an important component of the modern democratic process of decision-making. Since gain and loss emerge from political and economic decisions, pressure groups aim to protect particular interests and enhance gains and minimise losses. The increased role of specialists and secretive government deals like defence purchases have led to the rise of lobbying and institutionalisation of pressure groups. In contrast to liberal democracies, where autonomous pressure groups have legal sanction, the one-party communist system rejected such groups as illegitimate and superfluous. Negating the legal and political sanction given to groups to organise politically, articulate freely, and demand and petition the legislative representatives—which makes pressure groups not only agencies of representation, but also channels filtering public demand and feedback in liberal democracies—the absence of competing political parties in the erstwhile communist system meant that there was no autonomous development of pressure groups.

However, the inevitability of conflicting interests led to clandestine networks channelling interests in the communist system. The marked hostility shown to pluralist or group-based politics led to restrictions on group activities, and alienation of the nomenclature from the people led to a total collapse of the system. Since dissent was never made respectable, channels of feedback were completely closed. In the absence of pressure groups in the communist system, the only possibility was mass protest organisations like the Solidarity of Poland. In liberal democracies, the most important targets of pressure groups are public opinion, election campaigns, political parties, the media, legislature, civil service, ministers and opinion-makers.

Pressure groups also help to bring new issues into the political process in the form of new social movements like, for example, environmental protection and conservation. This is in contrast to the older, original pressure group politics, which was dominated by selfish and particularistic interest groups. In recent years, political parties like the Greens have emerged from social movements. However, in even this changed context, the wide diffusion of older pressure group politics remains, through separate identities like the Campaign for Nuclear Disarmament (CND), Greenpeace and Amnesty International.

Political parties differ from pressure groups in four crucial areas: (*i*) they try to influence a very wide range of policies, whereas pressure groups have a more limited ambit of a single or few issues. (*ii*) Political parties aim to influence or formulate policy through participation, or in coalition, whereas pressure groups try to do so without assuming governmental authority. This is why pressure groups lack the legitimacy of political parties. (*iii*) Political parties put up candidates for elections, which pressure groups seldom do. (*iv*) Pressure groups are much more cohesive than political parties and unlike the latter, do not have identifiable factions.

Like political parties, pressure groups operate in the open political system; also like political parties, there is a continuous rise and fall of particular pressure groups. Within the flexibility of a liberal democratic order, pressure groups help political and legal institutions to adapt to new demands and circumstances. While the clandestine nature of some pressure groups leads to public suspicion, no modern political process can do without them. As such, pressure groups are a necessary evil.

CRITICISMS OF POLITICAL PARTIES

Political parties have been criticised in a number of ways.

(*i*) There is a conservative rejection of political parties, which are perceived as obstacles to the rationalisation of the social and economic structure. There is a rejection of popular participation as necessary for successful modernisation. Political parties are perceived, as Washington and Jefferson did, as divisive and as perpetuating conflicts, as irrational, corrupt and inefficient, and as lacking the qualities of governance.

(*ii*) The second category accepts participation, not with the help of political parties but through the medium of a plebiscitarian model. It is a romantic portrayal of direct democracy, something that Rousseau advocated. Here, parties are no longer considered necessary intermediaries between leaders and people; rather, they are believed to be obstacles to the expression of the general will. However, exponents of this view have no answer to the important point that in the modern complex world, it is not possible to locate general will. They also highlight the negative aspects of political parties: they promote corruption and administrative inefficiency; divide rather than unify society; lead to political instability and indecisiveness in policy formulation and execution; and follow particularistic policies and are prone to being influenced by external powers and agencies.

However, as Huntington (1968) pointed out, these criticisms are not against political parties as such, but against the weak and imperfect ones. He also pointed out that the elite attempts to prevent the formation of political parties, trade unions and farmers' associations in an effort to restrict and eliminate politics. Such a situation is inevitably unstable, and in the absence of an organisation, leads to uncertainty and turmoil. Such suppression usually occurs in areas with a substantial level of political consciousness and activity, where forced passivity and long suppression leads to an authoritarian rightist political control. A state without political parties reflects a static traditional society. In a context of modernisation, a philosophy of no parties leads to an opposition to the parties themselves. Hostility and instability are the inevitable consequences of an order without parties; such an order is usually conservative and prone to coups. The stability of a political order depends on the strength of political parties. A strong party system channelises mass support in an institutionalised manner. Huntington asserted that the oscillation between democracy and authoritarianism, and the possibility or absence of coups also depend on the presence or absence of a strong party system. A strong party system allows the ordered accommodation of new groups and demands within the political process. A pluralistic, open party system is the only mechanism for managing the complex mega societies of today, as it bridges the urban-rural divide and halts, even if temporarily, the personal ambitions of unscrupulous, charismatic, or military leaders.

Political parties remain the key agency organising political participation. Huntington observed that political participation without proper organisation degenerates into mass movements, while organisations without participation degenerates into personalised cliques. States without a healthy system lack the institutional mechanism to generate, sustain and absorb change. These varied functions of political parties in a modern state led Duverger to remark that a regime without parties is bound to be conservative.

IRON LAW OF OLIGARCHY

Oligarchy, in contrast to democracy, demarcates rule by a few from that of the many. Michels (see Chapter 13), in *Political Parties* (1911), propounded the doctrine of the 'iron law of oligarchy': 'he who says organization says oligarchy'. He deduced this from an examination of the structure and function of the German socialist party, the SPD. Behind the formal democratic organisation of the party, there is concentration of power only in a handful of party leaders. Robert Mckenzie, in *British Political Parties* (1955), proved that the perception of the conservative party as elitist and leader-centric and the Labour Party as having a high level of internal democracy was a myth. He argued that despite their different structures, ideologies and value systems, the distribution of power in these two parties was virtually identical, as both were dominated by a small group of parliamentary leaders. Both accounts vindicate Ostrogoski's (1902) view that the increasing influence of the party machine had relegated the representation of individual interests to the background. The growing importance of the government had led to parliamentarians and those holding state power becoming more important and influential than party workers and organisational office bearers.

In the US, the doctrine of machine politics, which evolved in the early twentieth century, led power brokers to exercise a decisive advantage in nominating candidates. But protests and clashes at the Chicago convention of the Democratic Party (1968) spearheaded a reform movement that attempted to curb the powers of local party leaders and strengthen the role of ordinary members. The primary system largely tackled this problem through a process wherein candidates were selected. However, attempts to democratise the Labour Party in Great Britain led to a split in the party, and to the emergence of the Social Democratic Party. The successive defeats of the Labour Party led to a reintroduction of centralised leadership, which helped it to regain power.

PARTY SYSTEMS

Party systems are important for comprehending the functions of a political system. Duverger distinguished between one-party, two-party and multiparty systems. Sartori (1976, 2005) emphasised relative size, depending on electoral and legislative strength. A fragmented party system exists in countries like Russia, which is making a quick transition from a rigid one-party system to a multiparty one. The modern party system is usually classified under the following categories: One-party system; Two-party system; Dominant party system; and Multiparty system.

The One-party System was articulated and defended by Lenin in *What is to be done*? (1902). With total control and no scope for dissent, the communist party, the vanguard of the proletariat, controlled by a small number of professional revolutionaries, ruled the country through a highly centralised mechanism—democratic centralism. Another variant of the one-party system was the Solidarist model that emerged in the post-colonial systems of Ghana, Tanzania and Zimbabwe. Macpherson (1973) characterised these systems as modern expressions of Rousseau's general will. The most important theorist of the one-party state was Julius Nyerere, who repeatedly emphasised its open nature and distinguished it from Lenin's model. He took recourse to the exceptional situation of post-colonial Africa to defend his thesis; however, in the mid-1980s he abandoned his formulation and embraced multiparty democracy as the best model, even for Africa.

The Two-party System occurs where two parties are the key players; they have a rough parity, with equal opportunity and prospects to form a government. While minor parties do exist in such systems, the two parties enjoy a decisive advantage in legislative and electoral strength. The rule is by one party and not in coalition, and opposition space is occupied by the other party. Both parties are electable and the opposition is a 'government in the wings', endorsing the notion of the 'Shadow Cabinet' in Britain. Although the Conservative Party proclaims itself the natural party of governance and has ruled Great Britain more often than the Labour Party in the past 100 years, Britain is considered a two-party system. The United States is another example of the two-party system. According to Duverger, the first past the post system resulted in a two-party system.

A Dominant Party System is one where a number of parties compete; however, normally a single party rules without interruption. Sweden is a classic example of this system, and Japan is another. In the early years after independence, the Congress Party was dominant in India. Since different views and groups are inevitable in our times, in such a system, factions within the dominant party replace the competitiveness of the two-party system. Stability and predictability are the two defences of the models. Its biggest shortcoming is that it blurs the distinction between state and government, which leads to slackness and laxity in administration.

A Multiparty System is when more than two parties compete for power; the governments are normally coalitional and elections are frequent. In such systems, however, elections are like cabinet reshuffles, and usually the same parties and leaders return to power and continue with the old portfolios. European democracies, to a large extent, exemplify this model. Multiparty systems usually thrive in cases of proportional representation, where it is difficult for any single party to win a majority of seats in the legislature.

CLASSIFICATION OF POLITICAL PARTIES

There are many classifications of political parties, but Duverger's (1951) classification is considered the most authoritative and influential. Epstein (1980) elaborated on Duverger's thesis, and Sartori (1976, 2005) offered another formulation. Besides these, there is the notion of a catch-all party. Duverger's typology of party organisations has two dimensions: the structure as direct or indirect, and the basic elements of the party. This demarcation is based on a 'horizontal plane' of unitary organisations—the direct structures—while indirect structures are confederations of different bodies. The latter are uncommon and are usually found in socialist and catholic parties. However, a large number of political parties contain both characteristics, for example, the British Labour Party. The basic elements of the party are found in the 'vertical plane', that is, the units from which the parties consolidate. Both direct and indirect parties are composed of the caucus, the branch, the cell, and the militia.

The **Caucus** is the early form of the party. It manifested in legislative assemblies during the pre-democratic period and the transitional phase of early democratisation. It is a small organisation of like-minded people, and expansion is possible only through tacit co-option or formal nomination. It is a group of political elites, with the leader controlling the areas of influence after co-opting similar leaders throughout the nation. Caucus parties are highly decentralised, with a loose organisation.

Branch is based on mass membership. Recruitment is attempted to enhance resources, but not at the behest of the local elite, or to use Duverger's term, the notabilities. Branch parties are closely interlinked with central control and regulation. Caucus parties emerged in the pre-democratic legislative organs whereas Branch parties were created mainly outside the parliamentary arena, by those excluded from parliamentary politics.

Cell is an invention of the communist parties. Here, quality was more important than numbers and admission was centralised, unlike the Branch parties. The key organisational unit was not linked to geography, but to the workplace. Given the primacy of the urban proletariat and the rejection of the rural peasantry, it focused on organising the proletariat. Elections formed only a small part of this set-up. It also developed the concept of 'whole timers', giving life and meaning to Lenin's doctrine of professional revolutionaries.

The **Militia's** origin is linked to the fascist and other extreme right-wing groups that arose between the two world wars. Its functions centred on activities that had little or no link with electoral politics. It was a private army with recruitment made along military lines, both in composition and structure. A pyramidal structure emerged, which was instrumental in forming larger groups.

Duverger argued that the branch party was better than the caucus party. Competition for votes forced caucus parties to transform themselves into branch parties, or at least assimilate most of their features. The cell and militia parties were highly ideological, and remain on the fringes in liberal democracies. Duverger's argument was not that all political parties would eventually have a similar organisation, but that the logic of electoral politics would compel parties to modify their organisations in order to make them as competitive as possible. The fundamental sociological difference between a cadre party and a mass party continues even today. Cadre parties are usually the older eighteenth-century parties, consolidating around the political ideologies of liberalism and conservatism. Mass parties are a creation of the twentieth century; these were consolidated with the extension of franchise. Social democratic parties arose once workers were given the right to vote, whereas enfranchisement of women gave a fillip to Christian democratic parties. Mass parties are larger, with dispersed middle-class financial support, whereas cadre parties are more restrictive, depending on the larger donations of select individuals.

Electoral competition was key in Duverger's theory of party organisations, but Epstein (1980) believed that party organisations were shaped in response to competition for votes. He also questioned Duverger's European bias. Duverger considered the American party system a continuation of the caucus system, as American parties had never encountered a challenge from a socialist party. Epstein, in contrast, thought that the American party system was best suited for modern election campaigns, as in this age of television, mass media and opinion polls, there is no need for a great number of party members to mobilise votes. Interest groups and individual donations are more important than mass membership. A large party membership is also a hindrance to flexibility. Epstein concluded that in liberal democracies, the determining factor would come not from the left but from the right, as practised by the Republican Party in the US. Epstein ignored the differences in the political evolution of Europe and the US, a fact cogently dissected by Duverger.

Sartori's (1976, 2005) classification was based on the two assumptions of party fragmentation and ideological distancing. Party fragmentation is based on the number and relative size of political parties in the legislature. Ideological division relates to left-right ideological differentiation, the attitude of parties towards the regime, and other parties towards the system. In his formulation, ideologically motivated extreme parties were likely to be anti-system, whereas centrist parties would not hold such extreme positions. His model was based not on the competitive party system, but on the direction of party competition, which could be either centripetal or centrifugal. In centripetal systems there is a strong pull towards the political centre, and parties cannot take up a hard line. In the centrifugal competitive system, the political centre is weak, and that encourages parties to espouse extreme positions.

A two-party system is characterised by low party fragmentation and minor ideological distancing between parties in a centripetal order. A political party taking an extreme position would lose electorally and be forced back to the centre. A polarised multiparty system is the opposite—it is characterised by a weak centre and the existence of extremist parties. The lack of an alternative weakens the centrist parties during times of governmental unpopularity. Two other subdivisions of the model are the moderate and the multiparty system. The former reflects a moderate level of party fragmentation and centripetal competition. Such systems have three to five parties. The latter formation reveals a high level of party fragmentation, with no centripetal competition. The parties do not take up extreme positions. Such situations arise when there are two identifiable sub-cultures, which appeal to group solidarity but also cooperate in government formation. This prevents a movement towards extremism. Sartori also mentioned a special category found in the early period of democratisation, an atomised multiparty system in which 15 or 20 small parties competed. Such systems were temporary as they either collapsed or led to a more stable party system.

Sartori's was a wide and generalised survey and provided a framework for evaluating party systems. However, because of its generalisations it ignored many particularistic characteristics of nations, and did not provide a proper mechanism for the systemic shift of political parties and systems. As a starting point, though, Sartori provided a plausible scheme for studying the wide variety of contemporary party systems.

CATCH-ALL PARTY

In the post-World War II period, in the early 1950s, the consensual nature of Western democracies emerged in the writings of Dahl (1956) and Lipset (1973). Bell described this phase as the post-industrial society. In 1956, the Milan conference proclaimed the end of ideology in advanced capitalist countries. In response to this changed situation, the relationship between political parties and their support bases underwent a critical scrutiny. Lipset and Rokkan raised these issues and in 1966, Otto Kinchneiur coined the phrase 'catch-all party'. Epstein endorsed this idea a year later. The catch-all party thesis rejected the notion of a loyal electorate based on ideology, as popularised by the organisational network of political parties. Different methods aimed at broadening and widening the support base have altered the earlier limited mobilisation of political parties. The means have become different and the appeal is now to all social groups, hence the phrase 'catch-all'. In the altered situation, the existing party system would also become weaker, making transformation easier. The party leadership would make increasing use of electronic media, further weakening the parties. Both European and American parties would look similar and the need for new parties would be grossly reduced, as parties would adapt to new situations quickly. Catch-all parties seek to govern in the national interest rather than as representatives of a single social group. They are dominated by leaders who appeal to the people directly.

Alan Ware (1996) gave four reasons for the emergence of this view: (*i*) a reduction in cleavages in the Western capitalist order; (*ii*) no emergence of new social cleavages that would allow new parties to crystallise; (*iii*) a reduced attraction to ideologies in mobilising the electorate; and (*iv*) the ability of parties to transform quickly. However, catch-all parties underestimate the continued strength of ideologically rooted social democratic parties, as well as the emergence of new parties like the Greens. The catch-all party thesis ignored the fact that new issues would always emerge, and new political formations would also emerge accordingly. American exceptionalism is conditioned by the fact that it is a society of minor contradictions. But even in the US, a Perot could be a spoiler.

CADRE AND MASS PARTIES/CAUCUS AND MASS PARTIES

This is the most fundamental distinction among political parties. Cadre parties usually denote communist parties, with trained and professional party members with a high level of ideological commitment and doctrinaire discipline. Their distinguishing feature is their reliance on a politically active elite that offers ideological leadership to the masses. A mass party has a broad membership and wide electoral base. Caucus parties, also known as elite parties, existed in the nineteenth century when suffrage was restricted to a few people, and were led by elite 'notables', aristocrats, or wealthy public figures. Mass parties emerged in the twentieth century because of the universal franchise. Parties broadened their social bases and electoral appeal through large memberships.

LEFT AND RIGHT PARTIES

Parties are also classified on the basis of ideological orientation. Left-wing parties refer to the progressive, socialist and communist parties with a commitment to change, while right-wing parties generally prefer to maintain the status quo, stressing on continuity. This distinction is seen as at 'best simplistic and at worst deeply misleading' (Heywood 1997: 233). Most parties tend to have left and right-wing factions within themselves. The notion of left and right-wing parties originated with the seating arrangement in the French Assembly after the 1789 revolution—the revolutionaries were placed on the left and the reformists on the right. The emergence of new political issues such as the environment, animal rights and feminism and the blurring of old class polarities have rendered irrelevant the ideological divide between the left and the right (Giddens 1994).

THE SPOILS SYSTEM

This is generally linked to US political evolution, but is practised throughout the world. It means the practice of appointing loyal party members in power to public offices. It was a part of US political culture from its very inception, but was legitimised and practised widely by Andrew Jackson in the 1820s. The phrase 'spoils system' was coined by William Manch in 1832. It reached its peak between 1860 and 1880 and declined after the Civil Services Act of 1883, which insulated most important positions from the spoils system through a recruitment process based on merit.

CONCLUSION

Criticism of political parties is not new; this distrust could be found from the beginning of modern mass democratic politics. In recent years, the emergence of a large number of anti-political movements indicates a protest against traditional centres of power and a distrust of political parties in general in liberal democracies. The collapse of the Soviet Union has discredited the model of communist dictatorship under the one-party system. However, the other one-party solidarist system that emerged in Africa in the wake of decolonisation has moved towards a multiparty democratic model.

As we have seen, most criticisms of political parties are against weak party systems; such criticism is valid against any weak organisation. Modern political democracies cannot function without political parties and as such, the quest is to make parties more democratic and accountable. The emergence of the primary system in the US is an example of this broadening base of political recruitment in the US. Moreover, in a competitive world capitalistic system, efficiency, innovation and an effective, reformed state are prime necessities for success; in this process, the existing political parties need to change, otherwise new political formations and parties would emerge, relegating the fossilised ones to history.

15

NEW SOCIAL MOVEMENTS

> *A social movement is the organized collective behaviour of a class actor struggling against its class adversary for the social control of its historicity.*
>
> Touraine 1981: 77

> *The sociology of social movement is recent—barely half a century old.*
>
> Wieviorka 2005: 1

> *Social movements are forms of collective action that emerge in response to situations of inequality, oppression and/or unmet social, political, economic or cultural demands. They comprise an organized set of constituents pursuing a common political agenda of change over time.*
>
> Batliwala 2012: 3

In the vocabulary of Political Science, the word 'movement' is described in a number of ways. For instance, Aristotle considered a movement an unfinished act.[1] The term 'social movement' came into circulation in the late eighteenth and early nineteenth centuries, during great social, political and economic upheavals, mainly within the broad parameters of liberalism and socialism. The German sociologist Lorenz von Stein used this term in his work *History of the French Social Movement: From 1789 to the Present* (1850). For him, social movements were a dynamic force in society, dialectically posited against the state. The state, in his opinion, was a static legal expression, whereas a social movement was a forceful expression of antipathy towards the state. It was a societal phenomenon transcending the state's judicial and administrative apparatus. However, while Stein (ibid.) described social movements, he did not provide a clear definition. A universally accepted definition of social movements still eludes the subject.

ORIGIN OF SOCIAL MOVEMENTS

As exemplified in Stein's approach, social movements, like political parties, are of recent origin. They originated in the late eighteenth century in England and the United States, and then spread throughout the world. The origin suggests an intrinsic link between the democratisation process and the emergence of social movements. The biggest impetus for their emergence was the industrial revolution, which transformed the old static society into a dynamic one. The British movement to abolish slavery and extend franchise rights is an early example of social movements. Bentham played a key role and his importance, according to Bronowski and Mazlish (1960), can be gauged from the fact that his popularity and influence is comparable to that of Mahatma Gandhi. However, the first documented social movements were linked to the French Revolution of 1789 and the Polish Constitution of 3 May 1791.

The labour and communist movements, which originated with the industrial revolution, also began as large social movements. With their total distrust of the state, both Marxism and Anarchism originated and continued throughout the nineteenth century as social movements. This was reflected in the fact that Marx never thought in terms of a political party, instead advocating the spontaneous solidarity of the entire working class. However, after Marx's death in 1883, these movements gravitated towards the formation of communist parties and social democratic parties. The movement for the rights of women crystallised into the Christian Democratic Parties, while the fight for workers' rights led to the formation of social democratic parties in Western Europe. The same processes took place in most West European countries after Napoleon's exit. In Czarist Russia, there was a belated outburst of social movements in the context of the Russian Revolution of 1905. This outburst so impressed Lenin that, despite inventing the Communist Party in 1902, he practically abandoned it between 1905 and 1917 when the Czarist state collapsed. Between World Wars I and II, the Italian fascists and German Nazis described themselves more as parts of a movement rather than as being political parties.

In the post-World War II period, Western European nations led by England initiated radical reforms that saw the establishment of the welfare state. In the context of the Cold War and the fear of a total annihilation of civilisation, a massive social movement emerged in Great Britain, the Campaign for Nuclear Disarmament (CND), under the leadership of Bertrand Russell. It was followed by a massive peace movement in Germany. In the 1970s, the issues of women's rights, participation, peace, civil liberties and the environment were taken up by what is referred to as the New Social Movements. The background for these was provided by the emergence of a post-World War II generation of post-materialists, who took up causes that did not involve their own economic interests, but were larger issues affecting the entire society. The most important aspect of this evolution was the emergence of the green movement, which ultimately led to the formation of various environmental groups in Western Europe, forcing all other major political parties to move towards a policy of sustainable earth. However, the green movement, like its predecessor the peace movement, was essentially restricted to Western Europe.

After the collapse of communism in the 1990s, a new philosophy of universalism emerged, which prescribed the need to think globally but act locally. With the emergence of a communication revolution, the philosophy of a little village as the description of earth emerged, and issues of elementary civil and political rights, environmental issues and new 'isms' involving liberalisation and globalisation within a world capitalistic system came to the forefront. Contemporary new social movements can be broadly classified under two categories: (*a*) the ones that continue with post-materialist concerns and are confined mainly within advanced capitalism; and (*b*) large forums like the World Social Forum, which takes up issues that are not only post-materialistic in nature, but also those of the developing world involving tribals, displaced persons, developmental issues, and the preservation of ancient heritage and culture.

FACTORS LEADING TO THE CONSOLIDATION OF SOCIAL MOVEMENTS

Just as the invention of the printing press had facilitated the emergence of modern nation-states, the process of modern urbanisation and communication helped to build social movements. The emergence of cities following the industrial revolution led to interaction between people who had much in common economically, culturally and socially, and with a common political programme which facilitated the emergence of mass social movements. The process of democratisation and the spread of education also created a new consciousness. People realised that they could succeed only through a massive show of strength. As democracy was essentially a game of numbers, various social movements emerged to articulate their demands and aspirations forcefully, so that their collective voice could have an impact on the political process. It all began with the debate and pamphlets in the late eighteenth century in the wake of the American and French Revolutions, discussions in pubs and cafes, in the consolidation of mass sports like football (which have both a social and a political dimension), and subsequently with the emergence of the fourth estate, the free press, which enabled the articulation of particular social goals of different segments of society. In the contemporary world, the Internet has become a major means of consolidating large social movements.

Social movements like free trade unions and the free press are essentially by-products of the democratic process. Since they are essentially voices of dissent, authoritarian regimes suppress them brutally. However, social movements with a clear programme towards democratisation, like the Polish Solidarity, became the catalyst which initially challenged communist totalitarianism, and later became the most important factor in ending it. However, social movements in the real sense can only flourish in a democratic set-up.

Civil Disobedience and the New Social Movements

Ever since Henry David Thoreau (1817–62) popularised the concept of civil disobedience in the wake of the American Civil War, its relationship with social movements has been taken for granted. Even Mahatma Gandhi's (1869–1948) civil disobedience movement and Martin Luther King's (1929–68) Civil Rights Movement are cited as important examples of social movements. Civil disobedience can be a weapon that social movements wield; however it is rarely used as the base, purpose and method of social movements are much less restricted than the ambit of a civil disobedience movement. Civil disobedience is a weapon of mass struggle involving a very large segment of the population on issues that are not contested, for example Gandhi's salt satyagraha (and unlike divisive issues such as globalisation). Moreover, in the context of Gandhi, civil disobedience was organised under a political party, whereas social movements reject any definite affiliation with political parties. Similarly, violent struggles for independence from colonialism cannot be identified as a social movement as social movements can only flourish in a democratic or democratising order.

Social Movements and Pressure Groups

Social movements also differ significantly from pressure groups. Pressure groups or interest groups employ clandestine tactics like lobbying decision-makers, whereas social movements are a form of extra-parliamentary mass struggle to apply pressure on important policy shifts. In this, social movements, like citizenship itself, are in conflict with the market, whereas pressure groups are an extension of invisible market activities. Pressure groups are normally a movement from above, whereas social movements come from below, and try to broaden the participatory base of democratic politics. Pressure groups try to bypass the democratic process itself.

Social Movements and Political Parties

Although some social movements lead to the formation of political parties, a wide gulf exists between the two in their organisation, nature and function. Political parties follow what Michels (see Chapter 13) called the 'iron law of oligarchy', that is, a hierarchical organisational structure, with a few persons taking most of the important decisions. In a social movement, the organisation is loose and decentralised with considerable popular participation. Political parties usually have rigid memberships, while social movements are more open and relaxed. A political party by its very nature is an umbrella party, with factions dealing with a large number of domestic and external issues, some of which even appear contradictory. In the case of social movements, like pressure groups, the focus is normally limited and cohesive. The functions of political parties revolve around providing alternative programmes and candidates, and organising and financing elections. Social movements, on the other hand, may support or oppose particular candidates or parties during elections, but are not involved with the electoral process. In the context of the mass, indirect democratic process, social movements try to fill the void left behind by larger political groups, and supplement them. In this manner, social movements perform an important function in modern democracies by reducing the gulf between some under-represented or unrepresented groups and the political process, through their efforts to influence policy formulations and execution. In a weak political party system, social movements perform the vital function of reducing the alienation between the rulers and the ruled.

TYPES OF SOCIAL MOVEMENTS

Like political parties and pressure groups, there is a wide variety of social movements.

(a) **Reformative Social Movements:** Such movements concentrate on legal, constitutional, electoral and panel reforms. The classic example of such a movement is the British Fabian Society (1884), which popularised the phrase 'inevitability of gradualism'. A reformative trade union movement may press for increasing rights of workers and enhancement of their pecuniary benefits; and an environmental movement would pressure for more regulations like limiting fuel emissions, a cleaner environment, etc. There can also be single-issue movements, like the women's right to vote in the nineteenth century, abolition of slavery, ending capital punishment, or having the right to abortion. Single-issue reformist movements end with the attainment of their goal. Reformist social movements normally use peaceful and constitutional means to achieve their goals, coupled with mass campaigns to garner popular support for their cause.

(b) **Radical Movements:** Unlike the reformist ones, radical social movements try to bring about fundamental changes within a limited time period. The nineteenth-century Japanese Meiji Restoration is one example, by which Japan changed itself from a traditional agrarian to a modern industrial society within two generations.

(c) **Rigid Movements:** These are movements to ensure compliance to particular norms and values. By their very nature, they attract a small number of adherents and followers.

(d) **Traditional Movements:** These emphasise the maintaining of traditional functions, mainly when traditional values are threatened. The anti-machine movement in England at the onset of the industrial revolution is a classic example. In the Indian context, Gandhi tried to initiate a social movement by modernising traditions.

(e) **Group-based Movements:** This could be a think-tank or policy-oriented movement advocating specific policy changes. Anti-immigration, changing the political system, and advocating withdrawal from international organisations like the UNESCO are some examples. Many such groups, which are more organised than other social movements, operate both within and outside political parties.

(f) **Individual-based Movements:** These movements target the industrial behaviour pattern and also act as recruitment agencies to train the under-privileged for public office. They are primarily religious movements and are plentiful in the US.

DIFFERENCE BETWEEN OLD AND NEW SOCIAL MOVEMENTS

The old social movements originating in the late eighteenth or early nineteenth centuries were mainly addressed to an identifiable group, and were primarily concerned with economic issues. They involved groups like the working class, the peasantry and property owners. Each group tried to secure certain guarantees to ensure their economic security and advancement. The enclosure movement, the 10-hour working day movement, minimum wages movements, and prevention of child labour in industries are some examples of these early movements.

The new social movements have a very different perspective. Habermas (1981, 1987) stresses a break with the past with the commitment to newness. This perspective is not a cost-benefit analysis of the welfare state, but is rather a deeper involvement with questions of human well-being and issues of life and death. It is post-materialist concerns that ignite new social movements and not older concerns of distributive economics. He was emphatic about the 'newness' of the new social movements. There has been a transformation from an old political framework determined by economic and social security to a new politics, whose prime concern is with equal rights, quality of life, individual self-realisation, participation and human rights. Habermas called this basic transformation a silent revolution.

The agents of transformation are also different. The old politics and social movements were spearheaded by employers, workers and middle-class traders. The new politics and new social movements gather their most important support from the new middle classes, the post-World War II younger generation and groups who have a more formal education. The focal points of the new social movements are opposition to nuclear weapons, environment protection, peace—issues not specific to any one particular place, but to all of humankind. At the local level, they champion participatory politics and alternative projects concerning living a good and worthwhile life. In their projection, minorities comprise the elderly, people of alternate sexualities, religions and races/ethnicities, and the handicapped. These movements are for emancipation and autonomy. They are not like the class struggles of yesteryears, but are struggles for regional, linguistic, cultural and religious autonomy or independence. New social movements, unlike traditional ones, subscribe to a common ideology. Their organisational structures stress decentralisation and participatory decision-making and they practice 'new politics', namely innovative and theatrical forms of protest politics, moving away from established parties, interest groups and representative processes.

THE SCOPE OF NEW SOCIAL MOVEMENTS

New social movements may be broadly classified under three categories:

1. **Trans-national and Global Movements:** These try to revive the optimism of the early nineteenth century, best exemplified by Marx's assertion in *Communist Manifesto* (1848): 'workers of the world unite'. Both Marxism and Anarchism had global aims and objectives, and the First (1864–76), Second (1889–1916), Third (1919–43) and Fourth (1933–38) Internationals were established to achieve these global aims. However, this early optimism was belied by the rise of aggressive nationalism in Europe, which resulted in two devastating world wars that originated against the background of acute rivalries between great powers. Some new social movements have attempted to revive the international dimensions of the social movements of the early nineteenth century and propagate world solutions to the problems facing humanity. The collapse of communism and the arrival of a world capitalistic system have given an impetus to such movements. The World Social Forum is a good example of such movements.
2. **Localised Movements:** These have a restricted and localised agenda. They organise to highlight local issues like a clean and safe neighbourhood, and to protect the local natural setting, culture and lifestyle. Normally, such groups advocate a great degree of autonomy and decentralisation at the local level so that appropriate solutions could be found locally.
3. **Multilayer Movements:** These are modelled after the catch-all parties and take up problems at all levels, involving people from all walks of life. In this sense, they deviate from other new social movements whose support bases are more identifiable. Multilayer movements accept the complexities of contemporary technological society and understand that no single mega-solution can be sought to tackle the manifold problems besetting today's economies and polities. They try to comprehend local, regional, national and international concerns and work out multilayer solutions to deal specifically with each, and integrate them into a feasible unity.

FACTORS LEADING TO THE ESTABLISHMENT OF SOCIAL MOVEMENTS

Like political parties and pressure groups, social movements also have a lifecycle. They originate at a particular time and place, grow to maturity and eventually change form because of altered circumstances or failures, and some of them cease to exist. The logic of collective action to further a cause consolidated after the triumph of liberal individualism, which ushered in the democratic age. The associational nature of civil society activism in the United States, noted by Tocqueville, reflects this new urge to unite for a particular cause. The realisation of individual rights secures civil and political liberties, but with regard to social and economic concerns, the individual voice is ineffective and needs a collective voice to articulate their needs and grievances. In the wake of the industrial revolution, social movements primarily focused on human misery and issues concerning poverty. Charles Dickens' (1812–70) novels and Victor Hugo's (1802–85) writings highlighted the miserable cleavages and inhumanness that existed when wealth was unevenly divided. The majority faced innumerable economic hardships. The new social movements are a post-welfare state development, and an altered economic scenario led to a shift from the material to post-materialist concerns.

The most important reason for the emergence of social movements is a climate of deprivation, when a large number of people feel that unless and until there is a united struggle their voices will not reach the decision-makers. However, even in such a situation a catalytic agent is required to start the movement. Smelsar (1962) termed this an 'initiating event'—when a particular event, or individual or group act brings all those who want action under one umbrella organisation. Subsequent support by influential public figures and organisations allows the movement to gain legitimacy and popularity beyond the people who initiated it.

In the initial period, support comes from the really committed, who earnestly believe in the cause. But once the movement gathers strength and popularity, a very large number of people want to be associated with it, not out of conviction but for the convenience and recognition that comes with belonging to a well-known group which, though non-conformist, is considered respectable. This second category, however, will be the first to dissociate itself from the movement in the event of a crisis or failure. A third category of people may join the movement for purely tactical reasons.

THEORIES OF SOCIAL MOVEMENT

Social movement theories are a by-product of the complexities of contemporary society. The prevailing social structure is intrinsically linked with social movements, and the theories explaining them are derived from the general framework of societal understanding. The four dominant theories are: collective behaviour theory; resource mobilisation theory; new social movement theory; and the action identity approach.

Collective Behaviour Theory

This emphasises the abnormal nature of social movements. It is a semi-national response to structural strains between important societal institutions. The disequilibrium between these institutions leads to an imbalance in the entire social system. This rigid and orthodox approach was popularised by the structural-functionalist approach of the Chicago school, comprising Ralph Turner, Lewis Killian, Talcott Parsons and Neil Smelsar. Smelsar, in his *Theory of Collective Behaviour* (1962), discussed the problem of social movements in detail. The emergence and articulation of a movement develops in stages: (*a*) generalised belief, (*b*) structural strain, (*c*) precipitating factors, (*d*) mobilisation of participants, and (*e*) mechanisms of social control.

A good, orderly and healthy society holds no attraction for social movements. A derivative account of collective behaviour theory is found in notions of mass society and mass deprivation. Hannah Arendt (1951) and William Kornhauser (1959), reflecting on the emergence of social movements, point out that a healthy society manifests itself through the presence of strong class and group affinities, which maintain societal cohesion. In such a situation, manipulation of people is not possible. However, under conditions of urbanisation and industrialisation, such bonds are shaken, leading to an atomisation of individuals. These atomised individuals are then mobilised by a strong elite or a charismatic leader. According to Arendt (1951), totalitarian movements are a consequence of this process of atomisation. Gurr (1976), analysing why men rebel, added the theory of mass deprivation to the collective behaviour approach and equated social movements with an underdeveloped or some form of revolutionary activity. As such, for Gurr, a social movement is some form of revolution, or a failed or aborted revolution.

Resource Mobilisation Theory

In contrast to collective behaviour theory, resource mobilisation theory accepts social movements as a rational and unique action plan in the context of new issues, situations and opportunities. They are innovations resulting from the opportunities provided by democratic politics. Like pressure groups, they operate both within and outside the party system. They are neither exceptions nor irrational, but are an important component of the political process itself. They reflect the broadening of democratic participation. The important exponents of this approach are Zald and McCarthy (1987).

New Social Movement Theory

This was popularised by critical theorists like Habermas (1981, 1987) and Offe (1985), who emphasised the new values approach that follows the traditional Marxist categorisation of contradictions to analyse a social phenomenon. New social movements are an inevitable and desirable product of late capitalism, a super bureaucratic society. A post-industrial society is a highly regulated society with a tendency towards conformism. This conformism creates a divide between human existence and the urge for autonomy, freedom and identity. Post-industrial society gives rise to new contradictions that differ from the earlier ones; the latter, by their very nature, were economic in content and manifestation. Habermas (1981, 1987) analysed these conflicts not in their material reproduction, but in the new contradictions that arose in areas of culture, societal fragmentation and new mechanisms of socialisation. Significantly, political parties and other organisations do not absorb or channelise these conflicts in advanced capitalism, thereby giving birth to the new social movements.

The new social movements reflect two new contradictions: of contemporary society and animosity between the individual and the state. The contradictions are of a different nature in the post-materialist world, reflecting needs that are also post-materialistic. These are the needs for higher aesthetic values, self-realisation and creativity, and lead to a transformation of class interests into the larger category of universal human interests.

Action Identity Theory

This theory considers social movements as part of the normal process. Social movements prevent stagnation and provide a framework for social emancipation; they are instruments of protest against the cognitive rules imposed by a ruling class hoping to dominate the socio-economic reproduction process within rigidly defined social norms. Post-industrial societies are not free of class, and it is the regulations imposed by the ruling class that are challenged by social movements. Social movements are 'class counter-actors'.

Its major argument is that the established industrial capitalist order had over time been replaced by a post-industrial programme society, which has completely altered the old class relations and conflicts. Following in the footsteps of Marcuse, Touraine repeated Burnham's theory of managerial revolution (see Chapter 13) by arguing that in the programmed post-industrialist society, the dominant class is technocracy, in which the traditional agents of change in classical Marxism, the workers, are unable to alter the status quo. The reason for this transformation is the fact that contemporary conflict is sociocultural and not socioeconomic.

The struggle is to control knowledge and investment. In this advanced capitalism, 'the organized collective behaviour [is] of a class actor struggling against its class adversary for the social control of its historicity' (Tourraine 1971: 378).

AN EVALUATION OF DIFFERENT APPROACHES

The different approaches of social movements, like the different approaches to comparative politics, emphasise the different aspects of a general social theory. One major problem of all social movements is that they restrict their attention to particular types of movements, projecting them as prototypes of a feasible universal model. All of them suffer from localism, which makes them inoperative in a universal sphere.

The biggest problem of the collective behaviour approach is that it ignores the causes of social movements. While the approach is useful in comprehending the stable and orderly stages of societal evolution, it is inadequate when it comes to understanding process of change in a turbulent period.

The resources mobilisation approach, in contrast, deals satisfactorily with the formation of social movements as a consequence of change and the emergence of new issues. It also explains social movements as a process of social renewal and adjustment; the collective behaviour approach is virtually silent on this issue. However, this approach deals with issues connected with social movements in a generalised fashion; it does not focus specifically on the wide variety of social movements. It fails to explain the emergence of self-destructive movements like fascism or communism, or analyse the antipathy between social movements and the political system, which leads to explosive situations (like revolution).

The new social movement approach deals with the contradictions of only post-industrial societies. This contradiction is between the individual and the state; the group or class is irrelevant here. But it does not explain how such extreme individualised problems can consolidate into social movements.

The action identity approach accepts the difference between industrial and post-industrial societies, but does not reject the class question. Reiterating Marcuse, it asserts that while classes in the post-industrial order are very different from those in the industrial past, classes in the traditional sense do continue to exist. However, this approach fails to achieve a balance between these two contradictions.

Mamay (2007) discovered differing perceptions in the study of social movements. The collective behaviour approach concentrated on studying totalitarian social movements like fascism or communism. On the other hand, the resource mobilisation approach analysed the movements for citizen rights of the 1960s and 1970s. Special interest groups like feminism or minorities was their focal point. The action identity approach of the late 1960s and 1970s concentrated on anti-nuclear mobilisation and student and urban protest. New social movements studied new values like ecological, anti-nuclear and feminist social movements. According to Mamay, differences arise because they each exaggerate or underplay some aspects, which leads to very different conclusions.

As a consequence, the collective behaviour and resource mobilisation approaches do not take cognisance of the prevailing differences between societies while explaining social movements. Peculiarities and differences are ignored. The new social movement and new values approaches do not link the origin and purpose of social movements with either conflict or the absence of conflict.

Canel (1992) analysed social movement theories from both a North American and a European perspective. The purpose of these paradigms was to explain the rise and consolidation of social movements in post-industrial societies. This has led to the reformulation of traditional theories of collective action on both sides. Beginning in the 1960s and 1970s, there emerged in both the US and Western Europe a new trend of protests and demonstrations against the state and government policies, and against longstanding social conventions. In contrast to earlier movements, the protestors came together from all classes on issues like anti-nuclear, anti-armaments, and women's movements, and demanded that society accept different lifestyles like homosexuality. The last point broadened J. S. Mill's assertion in Victorian England of the need for creating a liberal society.

In the US, early reactions to social movements labelled them abnormal and irrational. This was followed by the resource mobilisation theory, which linked success with resources, both human and material. It emphasised strategies like the pressure groups, and stressed on the political process and not civil society. The political process approach, as the name suggests, focused only on the political sphere. Social movements were treated as a variant of mass politics. The state occupied central focus and the success or failure of social movements was linked to the state's willingness to either allow or crush them. Opportunities become more important than resources.

The debate in West Europe began a little after the US debate. The West European debate had a very different orientation and perception, which crystallised because of the wide gulf in both political history and political theory between the US and Europe. The subject matter of the debate was similar; however, instead of the US propensity towards analysing strategies or elements of success or failure, the Europeans were interested in their origins.

The initial reaction to social movements came from critical theorists with a Marxist bent. These theorists saw no value in the US project of resource mobilisation as contemporary social movements were not about negotiations or strategies to gain political advantage; the basis of these movements is to be found in civil society, not in politics. The new social movement arose from this perception of the contradictions within democratic post-industrial societies. It was a revolt against technocracy and the market.

Due to their very different contexts, the social movement theories originating in the US and West Europe differ in substance and orientation. While both were advanced industrial societies with well-established democratic systems, the difference arose because of their different historical antecedents. The US had no tradition of social democracy, mainly because there were no major contradictions in a nation that had never experienced feudalism or the pain of industrialisation; the emergence of social movements here could not be explained by societal changes, leading to the emphasis on mobilisation of resources and political representation. Western Europe, in contrast, developed a social democratic consensus which led to the initiation of the welfare state, a powerful trade union movement and a corporatist tradition that linked trade unions with the state. Fault lines and changes in society and culture dominate and form the determinants of the Western European outlook.

THE DEBATE IN LATIN AMERICA

Debate about social movements became an important component of the social science discourse in Latin America, which drew inspiration from US and Western European theorists. This derivative discourse was initiated in Latin America mainly because of, first, the close historical links with Europe, with the majority becoming settlers, and second, a predominantly US involvement with the promulgation of the Munroe Doctrine in 1823. The debate began in the 1970s and became significant in the late 1980s and early 1990s. Many Western issues, for example human rights, women's and gay rights, and the environment were of equal concern to Latin American academicians. However, because of their different historical evolution, they modified and adjusted several Western precepts to their needs and ideological belief structures.

In the background of state repression and the absence of political parties and trade unions under dictatorial regimes, urban movements arose, concentrating on issues connected with rapid urbanisation due to the increasing linking of agriculture and industrialisation. New issues like women's rights, ethnic groups and environmental groups strengthened this initial movement. Given the delayed democratisation and abuse of human rights, social movements, in the absence of political parties and a free press, took up issues of employment and livelihood, human rights, and the rights of marginal cultivators and indigenous people. Many social movements spearheaded the causes of democratisation, rule of law and a constitutional order. While adapting Western ideas, Latin American theorists made their own distinct contribution to social movement theory in a number of ways: (*i*) Unlike the Western preoccupation with post-materialist concerns, they focused on access to and control of resources. In this sense, they were rooted more in older social movements. (*ii*) Their prime concern was with the establishment of political and civil liberties that had been established in the West centuries ago. (*iii*) In the absence of meaningful political participation, social movements originated and consolidated in civil society. (*iv*) Most of them, unlike in the West, were political activists. (*v*) Most social movements have not succeeded because the conditions necessary for social movements to flower are absent in authoritarian and repressive regimes. (*vi*) In the 1990s, social movements paid increasing attention to rural areas with the explosion of the Chiapas peasant movement in Brazil. (*vii*) With the revival of democracy, attention shifted to economic issues—the widening gap between the rich and the poor, and ways and means of empowering the poor.

The Latin American concentration on resources is a revision of an earlier version of dependency theory (see Chapter 16), which also originated in Latin America. It highlighted the question of rural identity and culture, which is ignored in the Western emphasis on the market and state. The most important contribution of Latin American theorists was their focus on the problems of peripheral and subordinate areas under a world capitalist system dominated by the West. The increasing linkage of urban areas with world economic centres and the diminishing authority and power of the national political and economic set-up are reflected in a decline of the collective bargaining capacity of trade unions and drastic cuts in welfare measures; under these circumstances, social movements become the key centres for resistance and renewal.

The Latin American perception is based on a pessimistic articulation of the recent surge of democratic consolidation, and has provided a new dimension to the theory of social movements. It highlighted the presence of an authoritarian power structure devoid of popular participation within a merely formal democracy and pointed out the subjugation of Third World states to the forces of market and globalisation. This has denied equality and liberty to the majority of its people. In the context of contemporary processes of democratisation, globalisation and liberalisation, the Latin American input into social movements have been both original and timely. Although they mostly criticise rather than provide an alternative, no social movement theory can ignore the concerns raised, especially with regard to understanding social movements in the Third World.

CRITICISM OF SOCIAL MOVEMENTS THEORY

The social movements theory—rather, its new variant, the New Social Movements—has been criticised for a number of reasons: (*i*) There is nothing new in these movements as they have existed in different forms since the industrial revolution. Arguments of a turning point are, therefore, a myth. (*ii*) There is no empirical evidence or data to vindicate differences. They are picked up at random and can at best serve as random sampling and not as a theory. (*iii*) The period of observation is very short and cannot arrive at a realistic, reliable framework of analysis. (*iv*) The new social movement theory is blatantly one-sided as it highlights only those issues popularised within a small group of leftist believers. Liberal and right-wing segments are totally ignored. (*v*) The phrase 'new middle class' is described but not defined; as such, it cannot be a yardstick for reliable knowledge. (*vi*) Commentators like Fukuyama (1992) have demonstrated that the old liberal values, rather than new ones, are predominant even in post-industrial societies.

CONCLUSION

The social movement theories cover a broad spectrum of movements and as such function as an umbrella theory rather than a definitive one. There is no unanimity about its nature and role, and its many fragmented streams make it hard to pinpoint which are minor and which are major. Its presence within democratic societies is of a supplementary nature, to be studied and analysed along with the constitutional and legal process. In this, they fall within the category of substantive theories of democracy.

NOTE

1. The dictionary meaning of movement reflects the different meanings attached to it. The *Collins Thesaurus* describes movement as an 'act, action, activity, advance, agitation, change, development, displacement, exercise, flow, gesture, maneuvers, motion, move, moving, operation, progress, progression, shifty steps, stir, stirring, transfer' (1986: 336).

16

DEVELOPMENT

The mainspring of human progress is man's command over the forces of production. As history advances, there occurs a faster or slower growth of productive forces in this or that segment of society, owing to the differences in natural conditions and historical connections. These disparities give either an expanded or a compressed character to entire historical epochs and impart varying rates and extents of growth to different people, different branches of economy, different classes, different social institutions and fields of culture. This is the essence of human development.

Novack 1966: 5

Modernization theory predicted that such developments as economic growth, the spread of science and technology, the acceleration and spread of communications and the establishment of educational systems would all contribute to political change.

Pye 1990: 7

Dependency is a concept popularly used in comparative analysis of the Third World countries in Asia, Africa and Latin America. It evolved in Latin America during the 1960s and later it found favour in some writings about Africa and Asia. Both mainstream as well as progressive writers have assimilated dependency into their interpretations of development and underdevelopment, resulting in considerable confusion.

Chilcote 1994: 235–36

One of the major events that followed World War II was the emergence of the erstwhile European and Japanese colonies as full members of the comity of nations. This also led to the rise of new theories and ideologies of Third World-ism. In the late 1940s and early 1950s, 'Third World' was not merely a geographical description, but was also supposed to be a distinct idea. In the background of the horrors of World War II and the emergence of the Cold War with its competing models of capitalism and socialism, it preferred to follow a third alternative. President Sukarno, in his opening address at the Asia-Africa Conference in Bandung in 1955, remarked:

> What can we do? We can do much. We can inject the voice of reason into world affairs. We can mobilize all the spiritual, all the moral, all the political strength of Asia and Africa. 1,400,000,00 strong, far more than half the human population of the world, we can mobilize what I have called Moral violence of Nations in favour of peace (Harris 1986: 11).

This new ideology and confidence had to deal essentially with the question of national economic development. The most important issue was the eradication of poverty at a time when, in marked contrast to the glittering and ever-growing affluence of North America, Europe and Japan, the Third World countries were terribly poor. To deal with this fundamental and gigantic problem, a new branch centred round development emerged in the social sciences. As political independence by itself was not enough, the acquisition of economic power and self-reliance became the key question.

While seeking a solution to this problem, many intellectuals questioned the assumption that growth in world trading would eliminate both poverty and backwardness. This assumption stated that if the world market could operate freely with competition and without restriction, then each country or region would specialise in the area in which it possessed distinct advantages. If managed efficiently, it would lead to comparative advantage and gradually equalise incomes. This theory was not acceptable because of two reasons: (*i*) it was argued that poverty is not inevitable; and (*ii*) the world market by itself is not adequate when it comes to dealing with poverty and economic development. It has been pointed out that

> in economic development of the advanced countries, government plays a pivotal role by their regular intervention and regulating the market by maintaining the armed forces, prison camps, legal systems, investments and tax policies. The consequence is the idea of the third world as a radical critique of the order of world power that has governed international affairs until that time (Harris 1986: 11).

PREBISCH THESIS

This Third World critique questioned the failure of neo-classical economic theory to explain the continued impoverishment of the poor and raw material-exporting countries. Raul Prebisch (1901–86) argued that while the theory of interdependence and free trade had not worked well in the nineteenth century, it was working well in the twentieth century. In the nineteenth century, division of labour was based on a mutually beneficial exchange of agricultural and industrial goods. But in the twentieth century, because of the altered structure of relationships, a mutually beneficial system was transformed into a means of benefiting the countries exporting manufactured goods. 'Reality is undermining the outdated scheme of the international division of labour' (Prebisch 1971: 1).

One significant difference between the nineteenth and twentieth centuries was that the United States, a huge and more sufficient economy with an abundant supply of raw materials, replaced Great Britain as the centre of trade and commerce. Consequently, its necessity for imports from Latin America was less, and as a result Latin American countries did not have the means to pay for the imports of important manufactured goods. Purchase was therefore made by using limited gold reserves. The 'inner directed development' of the United States led Prebisch to predict a long-term disequilibrium in the world economy.

Along with his emphasis on the dollar problem, Prebisch pointed out that during the Great Depression, prices of agricultural exports had declined more than those of manufactured goods. Consequently, countries exporting raw materials and specialising in one or the other commodity were affected differently by the slump. This led to a growing inequality of exchange between these two categories of producers because the exporters of manufactured goods, whom Prebisch identified as the centres that enjoyed a monopoly over the supply of such goods, could effectively control their prices. On the other hand, there was a greater number of exporters of agricultural goods, the periphery, and competition between them caused prices to drop.

After explaining this slump and the short-term movements, Prebisch analysed its long-term implications. Due to a quicker pace of technical development in manufacturing, the monopoly control of the price of manufactured exports ensured that declining costs of production (resulting from cost-saving technical innovations) benefited only the sellers of manufactured goods, and not the buyers. Significantly, the opposite happened in the case of producers of agricultural goods. 'While the centres kept the whole benefit of the technical development of the industries, the peripheral countries transferred to them a share of the fruits of their own technical progress' (1971: 65). Along with this monopoly over the supply of manufactured goods, a monopoly operated in the supply of labour as trade unions in Europe and America did not allow wages to fall in a slump. This was made possible by keeping the price of manufactured goods high. Again, the opposite is true for agricultural goods: 'the less that income can contract at the centre, the more it must do so at the periphery' (ibid.).

In the periphery, investment of capital helped to perpetuate industrial control over the factors of production by ensuring that all local production installations were geared by the export trade. Local savings and investments remained small because of the workers' inability to raise their share of surplus and because of government inability to tax sectors where excess is located, for example the multinational business houses and local traditional economic groups like trades and landowners. In the periphery, inflation was a persistent structural problem not because of an excess of demand, but because of the rigidities of supply. For instance, in agricultural production a lack of transport infrastructure, inadequacies of labour and the persistent pressure for a balance of payment because of unpredictable changes in raw material prices in the world market can create innumerable difficulties.

Prebisch's solution was unlike the Marxist one, which emphasised only the international; he stressed both the international and national dimensions. In the international sector, the centre countries were to give special treatment to raw material-exporting countries and aid Third World governments trying to reform domestic industry till the point where the nation consumed its own locally produced and manufactured goods, whatever the cost. Only such an effort at import substitution would reduce the dependence on imports and the need to export. At the same time, it would increase both domestic employment and income, leading to a more expanded domestic market and enabling further industrialisation. The 'import substitution industrialisation' would enable the concerned country to retain the benefits of technical progress in the manufacturing sector.

Modernisation[1] theory was a mix of sociological, psychological and economic factors as it believed that modernity included aspects such as value systems, individual motivation and capital accumulation. The theory emphasised the role played by values, norms and belief structures. The important condition for social change and transformation from a traditional to a modern society is traced to a change in values. Society evolves when traditional behaviour patterns are replaced by the pressures of modernisation. While Western societies gradually evolved from within, the developing world could modernise with exposure from the outside. This exposure could take the form of ideas, technology, urbanisation, nuclear family, educational growth, literacy, development of mass media, increased business opportunities, capital for investment, replacement of traditional authority with a rational system of law, and the emergence of a representative national government. This entire process is termed 'modernisation of diffusion'. The development approach of modernisation is diametrically opposite to that of dependency theory.

DEPENDENCY THEORY

Unlike Prebisch, whose cure included both international and national factors involving the centre and the periphery, dependency theorists analysed underdevelopment in terms of international structures and processes, countering the argument posed by the Ricardian theory of comparative advantage. The modernisation theory of the 1950s was severely criticised by the dependency theorists. Scholars from different social sciences have dealt with the theory of dependency, which has also has been described differently. However, in spite of this differing emphasis, there are certain basic elements in this theory, with its most important departures being the total rejection of the modernisation theories of Rostow,[2] Pye and Apter.[3] Dependency theory demolished theories of development in both analysis and prediction and followed the Leninist heritage of Marxism, in the sense that it linked continued impoverishment and underdevelopment to the sustained unequal exchange with the developed West. While Lenin considered imperialism the last stage of capitalism, dependency theorists viewed the link with imperialism as the very basis of the perpetuation of inequality and dependency. Dependency was defined as a 'reflex of the expansion of the dominant nations and is geared towards the needs of the dominant economies; eg foreign rather than national needs' (Bodenheimer 1974: 158).

Dos Santos (1971) listed the different forms of dependency historically: colonial dependence; financial-industrial dependence; and the present form of post-World War II dependence, that is, technological-industrial dependence. He extended the notion of 'dependence' to mean domestic rather than the external condition of a Third World country. Economic development in Latin America differs from that in Europe because the dual nature of its economy neither allows nor encourages the full development of capitalist relations of production, instead basing itself upon slavish forms of work. Dependence, therefore, continues in the transitional colonial stage of economic development, *a conditioning situation* in which the economies of one group of countries are conditioned by the development and expansion of others. Dependence is based on an international division of labour, which permits industrial development in some countries while restricting it in others; growth in the latter is conditioned by and subjugated to the power centres of the world. Under these circumstances no genuine development can be possible, and the peripheral countries' only hope is to break off relations with the capitalist world altogether (as China did) and chart their own course. Domination becomes possible only because internally influential local group leaders hope to gain by it; external domination is not conducive to proper development. The only solution, therefore, is to change the internal structure, which may lead to confrontation with the international structure.

Since the 1960s, dependency theory generalised from the Latin American experience, applying it to the rest of the world. Wallerstein (1974, 1980, 1989) advocated his theory of a world economic system which consisted of concentric rings—the 'core' countries of the West, a 'semi-periphery' and the 'periphery'—a differentiation made possible by history. The core states industrialised first and acquired a decisive advantage over the rest of the world. Peripheral states are those that cater to the needs of the core and are wilfully prevented from developing higher industrial skills. The semi-periphery is the middle category of states that can move in either direction, and may include one-time core states that have lost their status. The whole system reflects an international division of labour. A basic nature of this system is the transference of surplus from the periphery to the core. P. P. Rey (1971, 1973), a French sociologist, added to the idea of dualism by advancing a more refined notion of the 'articulation of modes of production'. He argued that underdevelopment in certain areas of the world was largely due to the nature of indigenous society. In the West, feudalism led to capitalism because of the attitude of the feudal upper class. In the rest of the world, which had not experienced European feudalism, the integration of a society into the world economy through trade and investment results in a strengthening of the existing governing classes, reinforcing their resistance to the extension of capitalism. Caporaso and Behrour (1981) stated: 'dependency refers to a structural condition in which a healthy integrated system cannot complete its economic cycle except by an exclusive (or limited) reliance on an external complement' (p. 48).

In contrast to unconventional theories of development that analysed the causes and solution of poverty and related factors of order and participation within an internal setting, the overwhelming emphasis of dependency theory is on an international setting, which links the issues of underdevelopment and poverty to the dependency syndrome. Domestic variables are the key factors for development theorists, whereas for dependency theorists, analysis is to be found in the international setting, based on a hypothesis that the poverty of poor countries is due to the affluence of rich countries. They also point to historical antecedents showing that indigenous developments in pre-colonial states were deliberately stunted by colonial powers. Accepting the theory of neo-colonialism, dependency theorists argue that dependency and imperialism are two sides of the same coin; imperialism is the view from above, while dependency is the view from below. Political independence for the bulk of newly independent countries is superficial as the economic domination of advanced countries continues through multinational corporations, foreign aid, and technological and cultural dependence. Deliberately following a policy of collaboration between foreign and local capital, a new class and new support base are created in these countries.

Arghiri Emmanuel's *A Study of the Imperialism of Trade* (1969), Samir Amin's *Accumulation on a World Scale* (1970) and Andre Gunder Frank's *Dependent Accumulation and Underdevelopment* (1978) take off from the arguments of Rosa Luxemburg and regard trade rather than the export of capital as the main locomotive of European imperialism, and as the instrument by which the West has exploited other countries and impeded the Third World's growth. Both accept Wallerstein's model of the progressive establishment of a single world capitalist economy, with a core and a periphery, and point out the different specialisations in the centre and the periphery, which perpetuate inequality. They reject the Ricardian model of comparative advantage as impossible, given the basic inequity between the developed and underdeveloped nations. Emmanuel rejected the Ricardian principle which stated that differentiation and specialisation of production between more and less developed countries would be to their mutual advantage. Ricardo's contention hinged on the assumption that the subsistence wages of labour would remain uniform worldwide, but capital would be relatively stationary and profit vary from one country to another. Thus, a commodity will have a duplicate labour make-up wherever produced, but will differ in costs according to its capital component. Since he believed that the value of a commodity lay in its labour composition, it follows that international exchange amounts to inequality of exploitation, that is, trade could not bring about a transfer of real values unless compelled to do so, ignoring market values. Profits vary due to differences in the capital component and environmental factors. Emmanuel argued that unlike the early nineteenth century, money wages are no longer uniform internationally; they now vary by a factor of 30 per cent or more. On the other hand, a great reduction in international transport costs means that the prices of identical goods tend to equalise everywhere.

The rise of multinational companies has made capital mobile. If prices and profits remain the same internationally, the main variable in exchange has to be money wages, since workers are not mobile. Exchange becomes 'unequal' when a low-wage country has to pay more for the goods it imports in comparison to what it receives for the goods it exports. The world is divided into two spheres—the high-wage, high-value economies, and the low-wage, low-value economies. The former exploits the latter not through capital investment but through the terms of trade, resulting in unequal development and a gradual widening of the gap between the two. The solutions to unequal exchange, according to Emmanuel, are first, autarchy, whereby poor countries stop international trading and exchange among themselves, and second, through forming cartels in order to raise traded prices artificially by export duties or by monopoly pricing. P. A. Samuelson (1976) viewed the same Ricardian formula from a different perspective in the context of the England-Portugal trade relationship (which Emmanuel had used) to prove unequal exchange, and showed that by adding profit rates, both countries did benefit in the manner that Ricardo had claimed. He held that a poor country benefits from specialisation and trade, even if the benefit is less than it is for a richer country with higher levels of technology and labour productivity.

It is interesting to note that although dependency theory was Marxist in orientation, it drew intellectual sustenance from the non-Marxist analysis of Prebisch, who was the first to highlight the weakness of Latin American raw material-exporting countries. The terms popular with dependency theorists—centre and periphery—originated with Prebisch. But their attempt to revise Prebisch compares well with Marx's attempt to drastically change the Hegelian paradigm, or J. S. Mill's revision of Bentham.

The second important point is that this theory originated among the radical social scientists of Latin America, where it has the most popular following. Initially, dependency theorists developed their formulations on the basis of the Latin American experience. Later, however, Andre Gunder Frank tried to develop it into a grand theory by emphasising that underdevelopment and dependency were intrinsically linked to the globalisation of capitalism. The basic presumption of dependency theorists was a distinction between un-development and underdevelopment, because the entire evolution of development and underdevelopment followed the mercantilist and capitalist expansion of European nations. A unity of interest grew between the developed metropolis and the satellite countries, with disastrous consequences for the latter. With their explicit commitment to Marxism-Leninism and with examples from countries that are supposed to have broken this chain of dependency, for example Cuba, they rejected many of the accepted propositions under five segments:

(*i*) Refuting the argument that underdevelopment is an original state of affairs involving backwardness or traditionalism, Frank argued that underdeveloped countries possess a history, and that their underdevelopment could clearly be related to the effects of mercantilism and industrial capitalism.

(*ii*) The assertion that these societies reflect duality—one urban and modern and the other rural, backward and isolated—is not vindicated by facts. 'The most feudal seeming regions today,' commented Frank, 'are precisely those that had closest ties to the metropolis in the past'.

(*iii*) Contrary to the belief that an inflow of capital and culture are essential for industrialisation, Frank argued that the greatest period of industrial development in the satellites took place at times when the link with the metropolis was at its weakest.

(*iv*) The existence of a pre-capitalist sector in Latin America was rejected by the argument that such a state would have the same outcome as the overall capitalist state, and that the task is to replace capitalist underdevelopment with socialist development. Here, Frank rejected the two-stage theory of revolution propounded by Marx and Lenin and, following M. N. Roy, prescribed just one revolution.

(*v*) Lastly, Frank rejected the generation of economic development by import substitution because industrialisation through import substitution would lead to long-term dependence on the international system, and result in permanent underdevelopment. Cautioning against growth without development, dependency theorists emphasised structural transformation and the inter-dependence of the bourgeois of the centre-periphery. They also highlighted the existence of an internal colonialism, with Frank charging the Latin American middle class for being the major obstacle to reform. He also blamed the bureaucracy for playing a conservative role in both administration and politics (Frank 1972: 3–17).

Dependency theory asserted that the problem of underdevelopment had to be located in the very nature of contemporary capitalism. To avoid the limitations of bourgeois reform, dependency theorists prescribed the erstwhile Soviet model of industrialisation in which, instead of the consumer, the state determined the priorities. Rejecting the developmental approaches of theorists like Rostow, they tried to demolish the basic assumptions of that theory. Declaring Rostow's first two stages as fictional, Frank remarked, 'Rostow's stages and thesis are incorrect primarily because they do not correspond at all to the past or present reality of the under-developed countries whose development they are supposed to guide' (1972: 346).

While dependency theorists emphasised an international setting, modernisation theorists laid stress on internal factors. There is an in-built pessimism in dependency theorising as in their scheme of things, only a leap towards socialism could deal with the problems of capitalist underdevelopment, and lead to both balanced growth and total national control of production and the allocation of the resultant surplus. However, while class differentiation and income disparity are very visible in the bulk of the developing world, there seems to be hardly any prospect of a socialist revolution; dependency theorists also ignore the important historical fact that socialist countries in the developing world suffer as much from dependency as their non-socialist counterparts. For instance, Cuba reflected a paralysed economy as it imported sugar and rice, and the Soviet subsidy amounted to a staggering $4 billion a year, that is, half of Cuba's national income. Ethiopia and Vietnam had faced virtual famine situations in the recent past, and it was the West that had helped them to tide over their crises.

Through their incorporation into the world capitalist system, the raw material-exporting countries departed from the path of development that called for self-reliance. The loss of self-sufficiency also led to their complete dependence on exports. Since they supplied specific raw materials at a price dictated by the buyers, they were unable to either diversify or increase economic productivity. This was one of the reasons for the serious balance of payment difficulties. It also pointed out the contradictions created by dependency. For instance, it emphasised the increased unemployment and increasing inequalities as important indicators of the growing contradictions. This also limited the size of the domestic market and inevitably undermined the hegemony of the local bourgeoisie.

In spite of the individual variations in dependency theory, there are certain common points. All the theorists agree that the centre-periphery relationship leaves very little possibility for a proper economic development of the periphery. This is because capital investment in the periphery, the very organisation of the world market and the pattern of world demand all benefit the centres, at the cost of the periphery. As a consequence, dependent countries face negative growth rates, resource drain, excessive rates of capital repatriation, huge foreign debts, and unstable boom and bust cycles in their economies, mainly because local economies, instead of solving local problems, are geared towards the world capitalist markets dominated by rich capitalist countries.

What followed was the argument that countries with a very high degree of dependency would have very low rates of economic growth. The satellites would have the highest growth rate in those periods when the link with the centre was the weakest; for example, as Frank argued in the context of Latin America, during the two world wars and the period of the Great Depression. On the basis of the argument of a dual economy, it is also stated that a higher foreign investment led to greater inequality of income and more pronounced foreign indebtedness. Dependency theorists countered the argument of conventional economists that foreign trade and capital could be beneficial. However, they did not deal with the problem of isolationism satisfactorily; for instance, the socialist societies followed an isolationist economic policy geared towards self-sufficiency and independent development goals (see Chapter 4).

Kaufman, et al. (1979) tested the hypothesis of dependency theorists in the context of Latin America, with regard to the relationship between dependency economics and economic growth. The variables included the degree of trade partner concentration, degree of concentration of commodities, and flow of foreign capital and investment. The majority of the indicators showed that the more dependent countries grew faster and not slowly, as the dependency theorists had contended. The link between dependency and economic growth proved significant and demolished one of the major tenets of dependency theory. Their findings also revealed that although dependency produced income inequality, there was a strong negative association between dependency and land inequality, again disproving one of the major contentions of the theory.

THE SOUTH KOREAN EXPERIENCE

The contention of dependency theorists that a dependent capitalist country would be unable to solve the problem of capitalist underdevelopment could be questioned by analysing the situation in contemporary South Korea, which, as part of the gang of four newly industrialised countries (NICs),[4] has achieved spectacular economic success in recent years. 'The most irresistible conclusion from the Korean development experience is that with proper economic policies and a continuation of reasonable international aid levels, most developing countries could sustain growth rates as high as ten percent' (Brown 1973: 265).

Korea's integration into the modern world began with the signing of the Kanghwa Treaty with Japan in 1876. By 1910, Korea had been incorporated into the Japanese imperialist empire, both economically and legally. The Japanese imposed a cruel regime on the Koreans. However, along with this cruel regime it also introduced a modern administration with a monetary system that enabled about 25 per cent Koreans to acquire some formal education. There was also considerable expansion in agricultural and industrial production. Between 1910 and 1940, Korean manufacturing output grew on an average by 10 per cent, which resulted in the manufacturing share of Korean gross product rising from 1 per cent to 15 per cent, while the agriculture sector also changed drastically. Light industry, mainly food processing and textiles, declined as a proportion of the total from 72 per cent to 45 per cent during 1926–39. Chemicals expanded from 6 per cent to 25 per cent and metals from 4 per cent to 10 per cent. Much of this growth was export-oriented, with about two-thirds of the manufacturing outgoing going to Japan and other parts of the empire.

The economy was totally dominated by the Japanese, who also owned most of the capital employed in manufacturing. Most technical personnel also came from Japan. By 1940, about 700,000 Japanese were living in Korea, running the administration and managing some of the largest agricultural estates. Around 17 per cent of the labour was also Japanese. The Japanese colonial administration did not allow the Koreans to create something of their own. Korea supplied Japan with raw materials, foodstuffs and semi-finished manufactured goods. Japanese colonialism followed the classical model and the complete dependence of Korea was clearly visible. But in spite of this total control, by 1940 the Japanese had to employ about a quarter of Koreans in the factories and a million in Manchuria, with another two million living in Japan.

The end of World War II saw the division of the country. The Korean peninsula was partitioned along the 38th parallel into Soviet and American spheres of influence. The end of the War led to the loss of Korea's external markets and raw materials import source. The partition also meant that the heavy industrial and mining North became a part of the Soviet-led socialist system. The light industrial and rice-growing South came under American control. The South comprised two-thirds of the population, half the arable land (including 70 per cent of the rice-growing areas) and the light industrial infrastructure. The American administration handed over power to a South Korean regime in 1949. But the Korean War, the first major open conflict of the Cold War between the Soviet Union and the United States, soon followed. It was a destructive war, killing about 1.3 million people and with an economic loss estimated at around two years' gross product.

One major consequence of the war was that both Koreas had to maintain huge military establishments; for South Korea, defence expenditure comprised one-third of the government spending. Its economy was supported by massive American military and civil aid and severe economic controls. Both industrial production and exports increased, but a period of political instability created a great deal of uncertainty and impacted the economic scene. President Synhman Rhee was overthrown in 1960 and the military seized power in 1961.

The ensuing long-term dictatorship of General Park (1961–79) was the period when the Korean economic miracle began. The major concern was with re-adjusting the economy in light of the approaching date for the progressive decline in American aid. Merely cutting imports was not regarded as a solution. There was scepticism about achieving the target with an annual growth rate of 7 per cent. To encourage exports, a steep devaluation was announced. Restrictions on external trade were eased and tax incentives for exports were increased. This strategy worked and export was accepted as key to growth. This was an alternative to import substitution as the government continued to protect the domestic economy. Success led to confidence and ambition. In 1973, a massive plan for the growth of capital-intensive industries like ship-building, steel, machinery and petrochemicals was introduced. However, the rise in oil prices led to inflationary pressures and the volume of exports declined from 14 per cent in 1978 to 1 per cent in 1979. President Park was murdered in 1979.

The crisis of 1979–80 led to a wide-ranging reassessment of the economic direction. The Fifth Plan (1982–86) blamed the government for the problem as excessive government intervention in the private sector had discouraged both private initiative and efficiency. The inefficiency in the management of heavy industry was pointed out. In 1981, the process of denationalisation of banks began and interest rates were allowed to increase. Subsequently, in 1984, special regulations governing foreign banks ended, and some reduction was introduced in import tariffs. Liberalisation was opted for because of domestic needs. However, this did not undermine access to American markets. The result was that 'the building of an independent national economy—albeit of a special export oriented kind—now had to give way to an increase in the integration of the Korean and the World economies' (Harris 1986: 38).

By any reckoning, the economic success of South Korea is splendid. In 1953, agriculture was 47 per cent of the GNP and manufacturing, 9 per cent. In 1981, this rose to 16 per cent and 30 per cent, respectively.

In the manufacturing sector, the contribution of heavy and chemical industries between 1953–55, as compared to the total industrial output, was 23 per cent, increasing to 29 per cent between 1960–62 and 42 per cent between 1974–76. Expansion was visible in the GNP, manufacturing output and exports. In terms of the gross product, only one year, 1980, showed contraction; since 1962, growth has never fallen below 5 per cent (except in 1980), and for six years was above 10 per cent. Exports rose at an average of 18 per cent. The composition of exports changed drastically between 1960–62. Manufactured goods constituted 17 per cent of exports, which rose to 82 per cent in 1975 and 91 per cent in 1981–82. The population grew from 28 million in 1960 to 40 million in the early 1980s, and the labour force itself underwent significant transformation. In 1960, two-thirds were engaged in agriculture and in 1982, two-thirds were engaged outside agriculture. Within two decades, South Korea went from being among the poorest countries to becoming a prosperous country. Life expectancy increased and universal literacy was achieved. Real wages have increased by some 75 per cent since 1971. The per capita income, which was a meagre $67 in 1962, rose to a phenomenal $5,290 in 1990. One of the most spectacular successes of South Korea was in ship-building, which increased between 1973–83 by 15,000 per cent. In 1973, Sweden's output was 230 times that of South Korea; however, in 1983, South Korea's was five times larger than that of Sweden. Steel production was at 1 million tons in 1973; this rose to 12 million in 1984.

The spectacular success of South Korea, along with that of the other newly industrialised countries—Hong Kong, Singapore and Taiwan—clearly demonstrate that the major arguments of dependency theorists about the peripheral states are not vindicated by facts. During Japanese rule, Korea was a dependent economy and in the post-World War II period it had close links with the United States. As Lim (1982) pointed out, 1963–79 was a period of dependent development for South Korea. Development was achieved through capital accumulation and differentiation in the productive structure itself, and dependency was reflected in the exclusion and repression in social, economic and political spheres. Dependency was also reflected in foreign indebtedness, balance of payment difficulties and trade dependence. Dependency continued during the entire Park regime.

Major changes began to take place with the introduction of democracy in 1987. Hall (1988) pointed to the role of the democratic process in lessening dependency, as increasing democratisation meant that the citizen could use the electoral process to participate in the economic sphere as well. The long denied rights of freedom of association and active participation in collective bargaining were now available.

The contention of dependency theorists that income inequality would increase in satellite states was not vindicated by the Korean experience. By 1970, it had come under the low-income and low-inequality category, with the poorest two-fifths and the richest one-fifth getting 18 per cent and 45 per cent of the national income, respectively. This compared favourably not only with the other developing countries, but also with the developed ones. South Korea combined a fast growth rate with improvements in the lot of the poor.

Foreign savings played an important role in capital formation in the early years of industrialisation. In 1962, when the first economic plan was introduced, foreign savings accounted for 78.3 per cent and domestic savings, 21 per cent. But by 1976, domestic savings were financing 85.7 per cent and foreign savings, only 6.7 per cent. Foreign savings played the role of 'pump priming' to enhance national income. This was absorbed for capital formation as the economy gathered strength. This process was less painful than a policy of doing without foreign savings would have been, as domestic and foreign savings were more complementary than competitive.

A major indicator of dependency is the extent and level of dependency on one or more sources. In the Korean case, two countries, the United States and Japan, dominated it both in participation and influence. They were also important as sources of foreign investment, suppliers of imports and buyers of South Korean exports. Together, these two countries provided the largest share of Korea's imports, which was 67.3 per cent in 1970; this declined to 55.1 per cent in 1986. This proved that Korea was able to diversify during the last two decades. The export share of these countries also decreased from 75.4 per cent in 1970 to 55.6 per cent in 1986. Machinery and transport equipment as the percentage of imports increased from 29.7 per cent of the total in 1979 to 33.4 per cent in 1986. These were clear indications that the transfer of technology that took place in South Korea had started to pay dividends. Both in its rapid urbanisation and fall in the birth rate, South Korea resembles advanced countries more than developing ones. Rural-urban migration had reached an equilibrium with a considerable slowing down of the rural to urban movement, and by 1987, the birth rate had also fallen to 1.21 per cent.

Conclusion

One popular explanation of South Korean success is the prevalence of low wages; however, the basic fallacy of this argument is that wages are low in all developing countries. Another explanation for the South Korean miracle is the civil and military aid that it received from the United States. Between 1953 and 1960, this aid was 9 per cent of Korea's GNP. But the point to note is that a fast economic growth rate occurred only when the aid decreased. As Harris (1986) observed, aid might have been a necessary condition of development, but it was not a sufficient one. The argument that South Korea's success was due to disproportionate foreign investment can also be invalidated by facts, as foreign investment was six times higher in Mexico and 14 times higher in Brazil.

Since 1987, with the acquisition of trade union rights, wages have also risen rapidly, negating the presumption of dependency theory in two ways: (*a*) the ability of the NICs to narrow the gulf between both income and technology confounded the pessimistic predictions of dependency theorists, who saw the development of 'peripheral' or developing countries as being stunted by participation in a world capitalist system dominated by 'core' industrial countries; and (*b*) this development is not negative, as predicted by Gereffi and Evans (1981), who believed that 'dependent development' would inevitably widen income disparities, call for political and labour repression, and increase insecurity in production and employment. 'The evolution of an internationalized high technology industry in the NICs in the 1980s has been accompanied by rapidly rising income without worsening disparities, by diminishing political and labour repression as development has progressed and by the security of full employment' (Fong, et al. 1989: 22).

South Korea's success looks more impressive when analysed in a comparative perspective. Two decades ago, the position of South Korea and Chile were similar with respect to industrial exports, although Chile's total exports were four times larger than South Korea's because of its huge mining exports. But in 1970, South Korea's industrial exports grew to seven times more than Chile's, and by 1982, it was 17 times more than Chile. Chile's GNP in 1965 was $1,904 compared to South Korea's $625, and in 1983, these became $1,879 and $2,010, respectively. For Chile, the average annual growth rate was –0.1 per cent while for South Korea, it was 6.7 per cent. Both in containing inflation and in the educational sphere, Korea's performance was better. South Korea moved towards liberalisation in 1964, while Chile did the same in 1973. South Korea's process was gradual, following the Keynesian developmental perspective, while Chile's shift was sudden and based on a neo-liberal monetarist approach. Chile attempted a market-led liberalisation programme where the state was subordinated to the market, while South Korea's objective of long-term economic growth with industrialisation combined the role of the state with that of the market.

The impressive rise in the literacy rate and discipline, the general desire for a higher standard of living, and the will and confidence to achieve progress were important reasons for South Korean success. These were aided by social factors like a less structured society with no strong regional or religious differences. The South Korean success vindicates development theory more than dependency theory. Both in analysing and predicting Third World evolution, dependency theory mistakenly presumed that the Third World would always remain raw material-exporting countries. The NICs export more manufactured goods than raw materials. Another contention of dependency theory—that the Third World would always remain peripheral and dependent—has also been negated by South Korea and the NICs.

China's recent impressive performance is another example in this direction. Till 1982, its per capita income was lower than that of India; today, however, it is 2.4 times more than India's. It outstrips India by five times in foreign exchange reserves. Even in standardising education, especially technical education and research, its performance has been commendable. One very important reason for this impressive performance is China's integration with the world market, which occurred a full decade before India's integration. In the Indian case, belated liberalisation since 1991 had led to an unprecedented growth rate—between 6–8 per cent—with the projection that it would become a developed state by 2020. Competitive capitalism, with differing comparative advantages of regions and countries, has made doctrines advocating insular sustainability—like dependency theory—obsolete and untenable. Wallerstein was not sure if a radical change in the present world economic system, which he termed geo-culture, could be changed by anti-systemic forces like environmentalism, feminism, the political movements of indigenous peoples, and new kinds of organised labour or student activism. He admitted that the core and the periphery were not static structures; one can move from the core to the periphery, and vice versa. The South Korean success is an example of a movement from the periphery to the core and Wallerstein cited Argentina as an example of a core becoming a periphery. This makes the present world system not only unassailable but also just, in the sense that there is an inbuilt mechanism of just reward with possibilities for upward or downward movement. Amongst the available models, the present system seems the best possible insofar as rapid economic growth, alleviation of poverty and enjoyment of human rights are concerned.

SUSTAINABLE DEVELOPMENT AND ENVIRONMENTALISM

Environmentalism has become a major concern in the post-World War II period, although many say that it can be traced to the period when industrialisation began. Thomas Robert Malthus (1766–1834) drew attention to the fact that populations, if unchecked, grow at a geometrical ratio while food supply increases only in arithmetic proportion. William Godwin (1756–1836) and Marques de Condercet (1743–94) realised that population increase would cancel out the economic gains made possible by science and technology, but saw it as a distant threat. In the 1960s and 1970s, amid growing concerns about pollution, there was a strong realisation that environmental problems were due to a complex interrelationship between humankind, global resources, and the social and physical environments (Turner 1988). This led to a public debate about conventional growth objectives, strategies and policies. In response, some have called for zero-growth strategies (Daly 1977), deriving inspiration from the Club of Rome report *Limits to Growth* (Meadows, et al. 1972). The report's conclusion is similar to that reached by Malthus and provides the foundations for modern environmentalism. Organisations such as Friends of the Earth and Greenpeace were both established in 1969. The first recognised Green political party was formed in New Zealand in 1972. The most famous of them all, the German Greens, first achieved parliamentary representation in 1983. The rise of this movement was attributed to the growth of a generation of 'post-materialists' born in the prosperous welfare states of post-World War II Western Europe (Inglehart 1977). Although human beings have for long interacted with nature, the pressing concerns caused by the modern industrial age are acute and global. The Greens' statement that long-term human survival and the integrity of the biosphere are in danger is due to the fact that the biosphere's capacity to cushion and support is dwindling, thus making environmental issues universal and urgent. Issues like global warming, ozone depletion, acid rain and deforestation are among the foremost concerns of environmentalists. It is the scale and intensity of the issues that characterise modern environmentalism, and science has helped to substantiate many of its claims. Green politics usually stresses no-growth, for they contend that infinite growth in a finite resource system such as the Earth is impossible; also, the capacity of the planet to absorb the waste released by human activity is limited. The Greens propose a 'steady-state' economy, either through the imposition of selective taxation to encourage thrifty resource use and discourage waste, or through a political imposition of resource-use quotas.

The limits to growth argument has been widely criticised, leading to its partial replacement by the view that environmental safety and continuing economic growth need not be mutually incompatible or have conflicting aims. The term 'sustainable development' is used to refer to this new perspective. It became a part of public discussion in 1980 with the presentation of the *World Conservation Strategy* by the International Union for the Conservation of Nature and Natural Resources, which aimed to achieve sustainable development through the conservation of living resources. However, this aim is limited since its purpose is ecological sustainability; sustainability is not defined in the context of social and economic issues. The United Nations Environment Programme employed a broader meaning for the term in the report *Our Common Future* (also known as the Brundtland Report), published by the World Commission on Environment and Development (WCED) in 1987.

In 1983, the United Nations General Assembly established the WCED to promote economic development and environmental safety, following a decision taken at the United Nations Conference in Stockholm in 1972 that drew attention to the issue of global environment. The report supports the idea of assimilating environmental policies with development strategies, thus doing away with the common perception that environmental protection can be achieved only at the cost of economic development. It believes that the pursuit of economic development is perfectly congruous with environmental protection. This link came about for two fundamental reasons—first, since the developing world is concerned with eliminating degrading national poverty, its cooperation will be possible only if there is a clear commitment to the goals of development. Second, since poverty is perceived as a major cause of environmental degeneration, its reduction through economic development will help the environment. The WCED report insists on following three principles:

(*i*) All economic decision-making procedures, whether of states, companies or households, must be committed to better environment management. This implies two things—first, refrain from dumping waste into rivers, seas and the atmosphere, and second, develop new technologies that will reduce the amount of energy and materials used in every sphere of economic life.

(*ii*) Refrain from wasting or squandering environmental resources, thereby leaving the planet a better place for succeeding generations. Rich countries should assist the poor to achieve economic development with minimum damage to the environment.

(*iii*) Sustainability means giving more importance to quality of life than to higher material standards of living. The report defines sustainable development with reference to two key concepts—needs and limitations. With regard to the first, it accepts the importance of giving overall priority to the essential needs of the world's poor. Since needs are socially and culturally determined, the report argues that sustainable development should promote those values that encourage consumption patterns that are ecologically feasible. There is a need to change consumption patterns, particularly in the developed societies of the North. The argument concerning limitation refers to the environment's ability to meet present and future needs, depending on the state of technology and social organisation. The report stipulates a number of social and political changes to achieve sustainable development at the global level—elimination of poverty and exploitation, equal distribution of global resources, an end to the current pattern of military expenditure, new methods of ensuring just population control, lifestyle changes, appropriate technology, and institutionalised changes, including democratisation achieved through effective citizen participation in decision-making. It also implies a concern for both intergenerational (the needs of future generations in the formulation and execution of present policy) and intra-generational (that is, the basic needs of the present generation) equity in resource use. In short, sustainable development aims to remove the disparities in economic and political relationships between the rich North and the poor South.

The report argued that no single blueprint of sustainable development exists, since economic and social systems and environmental conditions vary between countries. It acknowledged that despite sustainable development being a global concern, individual countries are yet to work out their own concrete policy options. The report adopted an anthropocentric position with respect to sustainable development, regarding human beings and their well-being as the ultimate goal of all environment and development policies. In 1989, the General Assembly convened a meeting of the United Nations Conference on Environment and Development (UNCED) at Rio de Janeiro in 1992 (the Earth Summit) to discuss the implementation of sustainable development, thus marking the beginning of environment as an object of public policy. It considered issues such as climate change and biodiversity. The Kyoto Summit of 1997 agreed to cut greenhouse gas emissions by an overall 5.5 per cent (at 1990 levels) by 2012, with varying targets for different countries.

Strategies

Sustainable development can be achieved through four different policy options—the treadmill approach, weak sustainable development, strong sustainable development and the ideal model. The treadmill approach hinges on the belief that if human ingenuity is given the freedom to innovate new technology, it can successfully manipulate environmental systems. In other words, it supports the idea of a sustained growth assessed solely in terms of the gross national product (GNP). Weak sustainable development tries to integrate capitalist growth with environmental concerns, a position adopted by David Pearce in the highly influential Pearce Report (1985). It accepted sustainable development through economic growth by taking into consideration environmental costs. Pearce argued that there were two dimensions to sustainability—first, sustainable development, which 'implies some reasonably constant rate of growth in per capita real incomes, without depleting the nation's capital stock', and second, sustainable use of resources and environment, which implies 'some rate of use of the environment which does not deplete its capital value' (1985: 9). This is the approach favoured by the World Bank and the United Nations, and is associated with environmental management. This view has been criticised for regarding environment in monetary terms and not for its cultural and spiritual worth. Advocates of strong sustainable development, like O'Riordan (1981) and Weale (1992), emphasised environmental protection as an essential precondition for economic development, and this is the position that the WCED report highlighted. The Ideal Model is associated with Naess (1989), Echlin (1993) and Goldsmith (1992). It provides a vision of structural changes in society, the economy and political systems by radically altering the attitude of humankind towards nature. It measures overall growth not in quantitative terms (standard of living), but in a qualitative sense, namely the quality of life, which can be achieved by altering the nature of economic activity. Sustainable development requires the participation of not only national governments but also local ones, just as it needs the involvement of international agencies. The participation of grassroots organisations is crucial, because a radical alteration in lifestyles cannot be imposed from above in an authoritarian manner. Success requires a bottom-up involvement, for that interweaves citizenship and educational aspects of development with material and environmental wealth creation (O'Riordan 1981).

Political Arrangements

There is considerable disagreement about the political organisation in a sustainable society. Some Greens urge the need to 'act local but think global' and emphasise localised production and consumption on the grounds that it uses less resources in comparison to a global economy. Other argue that a decentralised polity is a disorganised one and point to the continuing relevance of traditional political arrangements associated with the state, since even in a sustainable society, decisions about resource use and distribution will have to be made. Still others stress that several environmental problems are global in nature, and need global organisations to solve them.

Criticisms

Lele (1991: 613) pointed out that the main problem with the idea of sustainable development is its effort to unite everybody, from green activists and conservationists to poor farmers in the developing South; however, it fails to provide concrete measures for anyone. Lele questioned the idea that economic growth would reduce poverty and inequality when this has never been the case, and asked how economic growth could contribute to environmental protection. Furthermore, to alleviate poverty, there has to be a concerted effort to redistribute incomes in favour of deprived groups (ibid.: 614). Sachs feared the creation of a new type of elite, global 'eco-crats' (1993: xviii), who have hijacked the environmental agenda from the more radical groups. The eco-crats, unlike the Green activists, do not consider the biosphere a brittle legacy that needs to be safeguarded for successors, but view it as a 'commercial asset in danger' (Lele 1991: xvii), which needs to be managed globally by and on behalf of the rich and the powerful.

Community-based Sustainable Development: Elinor Ostrom's Prescriptions

Elinor Ostrom's (1933–2012) lifelong quest was to find a balance between human interactions and ecosystems by evolving a mechanism of sustainable development. She rejected the models offered by both privately-owned markets and the rigid and remote state control of scarce and life-sustaining resources like fisheries, forests, oil fields, grazing fields, biodiversity, oceans and water bodies, and the atmosphere, which are all common pool resources. In this search for a third way in her seminal work *Governing the Commons: The Evolution of Institutions* (1990), her research was monumental and pathbreaking in development economics. She was a co-recipient of the Nobel Prize in Economics in 2009, and is the only woman to have received the award (although she was not a trained economist; her major discipline was Political Science). She had demonstrated with meticulous care, through the help of extensive fieldwork, that societies have evolved collectively by developing diverse institutions to manage scarce resources and by evolving a collective consciousness that avoids the collapse of the ecosystem through overuse.

Ostrom admitted that not all collective arrangements had succeeded in preventing resource exhaustion through overuse. Her only point was that human interaction with nature is multifaceted and diverse, underlining the fact that no single model can be touted as the panacea for problems that individuals and society face in their relationship with nature. She argued that it was impossible for a single governmental or international agency at the global level to address problems of environmental degradation, as the issue is complex and diverse. She stressed on the need to adopt a polycentric approach that emphasises decision-making by people, the real stakeholders, and stated that local problems, issues and concerns need local solutions involving local people. As a realist, she also rejected the theories of the Deep Greens, arguing that by maintaining the ecosystem, the creation and perpetuation of prosperity is feasible.

Referring to the Buchanan-Tollock Programme and drawing inspiration from Hayekean attention to the importance of local knowledge, Ostrom argued convincingly that private groups have quite often been able to avoid the tragedy of the commons. She pointed to the dangers of grand generalised theories of group and collective action that are referred to as pillars of public policy and criticised three influential models—Garrett Hardin's *Tragedy of the Commons* (1968), the prisoner's dilemma game, and Mancur Olson's *Logic of Collective Action* (1965), based on the problem of free riders and individual rational users of resources, which inherently act against the best interests of the users collectively. Such an assertion is based on the universal acceptance of particular conditions, for instance, (*a*) when individual actors possess high discount rates; (*b*) an absence of mutual trust; (*c*) a lack of capacity to communicate or have effective and binding agreements; and even if it is arrived at, (*d*) the absence of a foolproof mechanism to arrange for monitoring and enforcement, leading to over-investment and overuse.

According to Ostrom, Hardin's thesis was an attempt to create and introduce markets into traditional arrangements that have endured and been sustainable for centuries. Hardin demonstrated the conflict between individual interests and the common good. The commons refers to a shared plot of grassland used by all livestock farmers in a village. Each farmer continues to add more livestock to graze on the commons, because it costs him nothing to do so; as a result, in a few years the soil gets depleted by overgrazing, making the commons unusable. Consequently, the village perishes. Any *tragedy of the commons* is caused by the fact that when individuals use a public good, they do not bear the entire cost of their actions. Each individual seeks to maximise his utility and ignores the costs that others bear. This is an example of externality. Common land, as opposed to public land, is land that is held in common. These lands are generally open, unfenced and remote and are for those locals who are 'commoners', with rights of grazing and gathering fuel wood non-destructively. Hardin's thesis was based on individual rational action which in turn was based on self-interest, and which leads to a depletion of shared limited resources like fishing. He suggested two ways of dealing with the problem—first, governmental regulation, and second, division of resources between the users and privatisation.

Ostrom rejected this solution for a number of reasons: (*i*) fencing would mean that many farmers would be left without grazing grounds; (*ii*) overexploitation can be checked through ensuring fairness in the use of common resources; (*iii*) the tragedy takes place when one or a handful of stakeholders who do not belong to the community's socioeconomic system impose their own will, exerting political power by changing the observed rules to gain advantage for immediate profit. Ostrom's data and examples, unlike Hardin's, were drawn from history and the experiences of real people and communities worldwide. A commonly held critical resource can be both well-governed and efficiently managed through close community engagement. She cited the example of a government protected forest which local inhabitants do not consider legitimate, resulting in a failure on the part of the government to protect the forest. Legislation is not the same as law. Without trying to bring in such counter-productive legislation, a better method of preservation is to protecting and perpetuating common resources through common law. Legislation in conformity with such laws, according to Ostrom, was the safest and time-tested solution.

Both in contemporary theories and in the practice of public choice movement and participatory democracy, Ostrom's views are of seminal importance. With regard to the collective management of shared resources and environmental resource management, enduring cooperative institutions organised, governed and shared by the resource users themselves are the best possible mechanism. The attraction of collective benefit can check the problem of free riders. Opportunism is negated by the viability of the long-term benefits of a common property regime. To give it proper shape, she offered eight principles for governing the commons sustainably and equitably in a community: define clear group boundaries; match the rules governing the use of common goods to local needs and conditions; ensure that those affected by the rules can participate in modifying the rules; ensure that the rule-making rights of community members are respected by outside authorities; develop a system, carried out by community members, for monitoring members' behaviour; use graduated sanctions for rule violators; provide accessible, low-cost means for dispute resolution; and build responsibility for governing the common resource in nested tiers, from the lowest level up to the entire interconnected system.

Ostrom also asserted that rules and principles were applicable not only to common resources, but also to common services like communal property management, community policing and money systems. She suggested discarding the top-down approach to climate change. International initiatives to reduce greenhouse effects would be counter-productive unless such initiatives had a local basis and were supported by local communities. She pointed out that generally, we tend to ignore the actions of citizens and instead look up to the person in Washington who makes the rule. This was the recipe for averting big change, destabilisation and chaos. Ostrom acknowledged that the impressions left by her childhood in the background of the Depression had taught her about the usefulness of self-help cooperatives and barter labour. Local unity is a basic ingredient in such economic arrangements. Forcefully speaking for a polycentric and pluralistic world, she insisted that a wide variety of solutions were required to solve contemporary social and ecological problems. The world today needs a network of social connections and interactions. Ostrom did not reject the role of government, but did reject an over-centralised, prescriptive action and top-down planning. She acknowledged her indebtedness to Lasswell and Kaplan's *Power and Society* (1952) in the *LSE Review of Books,* dated 22 April 2012, as it 'broadened my perspective on individual choice and behaviour in a way that was instrumental'.

Ostrom accepted a diverse world, the existence of multiple values, and the possibility of multiple outcomes. She rejected Hardin's conclusion that 'freedom in a Commons brings ruin to all'. For Hardin, the Commons was comparable to a bank robbery. She rejected theories of environmental degradation and arguments about private ownership, arguing that human beings were not just self-interested, but also capable of considering the larger ramifications of their actions, both for those around them and for the environment in which they operate. Difficulties could be overcome democratically, and through local participation, growth could be both equitable and sustainable. She rightly stated the need for universal sustainable development goals on issues such as energy, food security, sanitation, urban planning, and poverty eradication, while reducing inequality. Beyond the two paradigms of Hobbes' sovereign and Smith's invisible hand, Ostrom found and defended a third way to prove that the 'tragedy of the Commons' is an 'opportunity of the Commons'. She placed her hope not in the state or the market, but in the people, to solve the social dilemmas they confront through various means of self-governance. Ostrom addressed her arguments primarily to policymakers and not to scholars. The task now is to take her findings seriously as her way matters for all of humanity.

CONCLUSION

Economic arrangements are made mainly in the context of command and demand politics, which clearly flows from a developmental perspective. Command politics postpones the immediate benefits of development. The Prebisch thesis and our own Mahalanobis Model are reflections of this perspective, 'a social version of this worldly asceticism that Weber associates with the Protestant ethic and the rise of capitalism in the West' (Rudolph and Rudolph 1998: 215).

Recently, developmental theories that emphasise the future more than the present have been challenged by those who do not merely concentrate on GNP as the index of development. This change comes about with the increasing realisation that the poor are neither benefitting from nor contributing to development. This is reflected in the fact that the economic condition of people who live below the poverty line remains virtually static. The poor lack the resources, educational skills, health and medical care to lead better lives and contribute to economic development. The proposition of 'basic human needs'—employment generation, the physical quality of the life index, literacy, life expectation, empowerment of the poor and women—have attracted the attention of the World Bank in the past few years. In response, the World Bank has begun championing broad issues like environment, healthcare, gender, political decentralisation and local accountability.

Owens (1987) criticised the trickle-down theory implicit in the argument for economic growth, pointing out that development does not only mean broad-based economic growth, but must also be linked with one's own improvement and productivity. Furthermore, development is not only economic and social but also political, which refers to the proper kind of freedom and democracy. By his definition, most democracies in the developing world are false because they are top-down, centralised and externally imposed. True democracy, on the other hand, is indigenously derived, allows ordinary people to access the system, its resources and public organisations, establishes rule of law and realises political freedom. The basic problem with most development strategies is that focus is limited to the economic and social aspects of life. Local institutions that are absolutely essential to sustaining proper development by securing the participation of common people are generally ignored. The notable distinction between industrialised and developing countries does not lie in the latter's capability to generate GNP, but in the fact that in the former, governments have at least been partially reformed. In contrast, in the developing world, only a handful of governments have treated economic development as part of the political reform process; and it is ironic that all such unreformed governments are authoritarian. This proves that certain essential reforms needed to involve the poor and the underprivileged in the development process are fundamentally non-ideological, and are feasible in any kind of political system, whether democratic, fascist, communist, or non-ideological authoritarian.

Owens also insisted that development involve decentralised structures, for that ensures the accountability of members, provides access to the law, brings integrity into public affairs and secures the rule of law. He was surprised that none of these reforms exist in false democracies, which demonstrates that social and economic rights can be created without creating political rights, and that the presence of formal political rights is no guarantee for the realisation of social and economic rights. An ideal situation would combine political rights with social and economic rights, as the first ceases to be important without the second. Owens observed that those countries that have secured social and economic rights are on the right side of history. He lamented the fact that most governments in the developing world are unreformed and underdeveloped. Sen (1990) argued that inhuman miseries like abject poverty and periodic famines could be alleviated if leaders followed the right kind of policies. For Sen, this meant an acceptance of a democracy with fair and free elections, multi-party systems, alert and active opposition political parties and groups, and a free and vibrant press as part of the foundational arrangements. Citing the examples of Sri Lanka and Kerala, he stated that a rise in GNP and production is not enough, as true development means the enrichment of the life of an average person according to the values that one cherishes.

Development theory now accepts that human capital is as important as physical capital. Schumpeter differentiated between political economy and economics, arguing that the former had value and ideological preferences whereas the latter was value-free. The development debate of the past several decades clearly reveals that a meaningful discourse is possible only within the framework of political economy, with a value shift within the developmental paradigm from the narrow basis of GNP growth to concerns about the quality of life and social justice.

NOTES

1. Since the nineteenth century, there has been an assertion that Western societies have progressed successively towards modernisation. Weber contrasted traditional with modern societies; Parsons pointed out that traditional societies emphasise ascriptive statuses, diffuse roles and particularistic values, while modern society values achievement, specific roles and universalistic values. Eisenstadt, reiterating Weber and Parsons, associated modernisation with a highly differentiated political structure and the diffusion of political power and authority into all spheres of society.
2. Rostow, in *Stages of Economic Growth: A Non Communist Manifesto* (1960), identified five stages (see Chapter 5). Rostow's take-off stage is relevant to new nations, when growth becomes a reality. A decade later, he added 'the search for quality' as a sixth stage in *Politics and the Stages of Growth* (1971). Rostow's theory was adopted by many political scientists. A. F. K. Organski examined the role of government through four stages in his *Stages of Political Development* (1965): (*i*) primitive national unification; (*ii*) industrialisation; (*iii*) national welfare; and (*iv*) abundance. For Organski, political development refers to an increased government efficiency in mobilising human and material resources towards national ends.
3. Apter, in *The Politics of Modernization* (1965), distinguished between modernisation and development: 'Modernization is a particular case of development . . . implies three conditions—a social system that can constantly innovate without falling apart . . . ; differentiated, flexible social structures; and a social framework to provide the skills and knowledge necessary for living in a technologically advanced world. Development in general results from the proliferation and integration of functional role in a community' (p. 67). Apter identified

two models: secular-libertarian' or the pluralistic system, and 'sacred collectivity' or mobilising systems. The former is represented by the modern reconciliation system, diverse leadership and power, bargaining and compromise. Sacred collectivity is represented by the modern mobilisation system through personalised and charismatic leadership, political religiosity and the organisation of a mass party. While the US is an example of the first, Mao's China, Nkrumah's Ghana and Nasser's Egypt are examples of the second type.

4. The Newly Industrialised Countries (NICs) of East and Southeast Asia have negated the basic assumptions of dependency theory. By achieving a high standard of living and emerging from the dependency syndrome, they have become integrated with developed nations. With the exception of Thailand, all the new states in this region were colonies. Taiwan (Formosa) and Korea were Japanese colonies from 1895 and 1910, respectively, till 1945. Malaya became independent in 1957, expanding into Malaysia to include Singapore (for two years) in 1963. Indonesia, Sabah and Sarawak were Dutch colonies till 1949. Hong Kong was a British colony till 1997, when it was handed over to China. At independence, they faced the same problems as the new states of Black Africa and South Asia. Yet, by the 1970s and 1980s, they had become the most dynamic economies in the world, originating the concept of the East Asian miracle. They challenged the assumption that it is impossible for ex-colonies to join the ranks of affluent industrialised countries. Since their success is due to the export of manufactured goods, it proves that it is possible for countries with predominantly agricultural economies to discover their comparative advantage in manufacturing and exploit it.

   There are two groups within these countries. The first, comprising Hong Kong, Taiwan, South Korea and Singapore, was the pioneer in rapid manufacturing growth and exports. The others followed in and after the 1970s. Of these four, Singapore and Hong Kong are city-states; however, in spite of the limitations of geography, they have become successful exporting countries. The East Asian miracle, according to the World Bank, is because of high rates of investment, averaging 20 per cent of GDP between 1960 and 1990, and the rising endowment of human capital due to universal primary and secondary education. Governments in these countries are interventionist, yet market-oriented. They pursue sound open market macroeconomic policies, but are prepared to intervene when the market appeared to fail. Intervention took many forms. Except for Hong Kong, the others, in the early post-war years, followed a highly protectionist policy aimed at import substitution, a fact common to almost all Third World countries. However, what makes the East Asian tigers (except Hong Kong) exceptional is the fact that they combine protectionism with export promotion. In this way, they were able to gradually move from highly protectionist import-substitution industrialisation to moderately open competitive economies, thereby maintaining the momentum of industrialisation. Furthermore, the state maintained close ties with the business and technological elite. Their governments were competent and not corrupt, with a bureaucracy that was exceptionally efficient in economic management. This enabled them to judiciously combine interventionist with free market strategies. They were also open to foreign technology, which they welcomed via licensing, training and import of capital goods. Taiwan and South Korea restricted their direct foreign investment, mainly because they were able to raise capital at home or by borrowing, and because they rapidly acquired the necessary know-how and operational skills. With the exception of Hong Kong, all others shifted from import-substituting industrialisation to export-orienting industrialisation, and slowly opened their domestic markets to foreign competition. In short, East Asia was successful because it 'got the fundamentals right' in macro-economic policy—high rates of capital accumulation, limited price distortions and broadly based human capital.

   Private enterprises grew very well. The state also intervened whenever private firms were cautious and business strategies failed. The most important was the adoption of export-push strategies. The distinguishing feature was the quality of their governments and the wisdom of their economic and social policies. The less successful ones were 'soft' states, weak in their ability to govern and devise complex development policies. Their planning was unrealistic and execution unproductive. The state imposed and decided the type of economic activity, with varying degrees of competence. The Gang of Four and their integration into the world economy are now an example for others to emulate. This, however, is unimportant, as given the structural changes in the world economy, one or the other would sooner or later have led the way. Changes in the world economy enabled governments in the

NICs to develop spectacularly through policy and management. Johnson (1982) labelled the governmental system that Japan pioneered from the mid-1920s (later emulated by other East Asian economies) as the developmental state. These states consider national security their topmost concern, possible only through rapid industrialisation. To this end, the state assumes responsibility for deciding national growth priorities, with the help of a powerful economic bureaucracy insulated from democratic/parliamentary and other political interests. An elite core of technically trained members supports the bureaucracy. The state also aims to bring about consensus and cooperation between the public sector, private entrepreneurs and other domestic interests.

17

REVOLUTION

The end of rebellion is liberation, while the end of revolution is the foundation of freedom.

Arendt 1969: 214

The Philosophers have only interpreted the world in various ways; the point however is to change it.

Marx and Engels 1977: 125

Revolutions are popular uprisings involving extra-legal mass action; they are often, although not necessarily, violent. . . . Revolutions differ from rebellions and revolts in that they bring about fundamental change, as opposed to merely a change in policy or the displacement of a governing elite.

Heywood 1997: 198

Revolution signifies a drastic and fundamental transformation. Hence, it is customary to refer to the French Revolution of 1789, Russian Revolution of 1917, Chinese Revolution of 1948, Cuban Revolution of 1959, Iranian Revolution of 1979, and the Velvet Revolution of 1989 that began the process of ending communism in Eastern Europe and also in the former Soviet Union, since these have altered the nature of the social and political systems in which they occurred. 'Revolutions are a form of massive, violent and rapid social change. They are also attempts to embody a set of values in a new or at least a renovated social order' (Dunn 1989: 12). Revolutions are complex events essentially involving three aspects—state breakdown, competition among claimants for central authority, and the building of new institutions, which need not occur in 'clearly separated stages or in a consistent order'. These three factors coalesce with one another to differentiate revolution from forms of political violence (Goldstone 1987: 437). The complexity of revolutions makes it difficult to explain them, although theories attempt to dissect them in terms of causes, the various forms of struggle and possible outcomes. Johnson (1966) argued that revolutions occur in conditions of 'multiple disfunction', when the political system breaks down under competing demands for change.[1]

Plato pointed out that all governments would inevitably go through a sequence of change and degenerate into timocracy, oligarchy, democracy and tyranny. He was convinced that a chain of creation, decay and dissolution gripped the world firmly and only at rare intervals did individuals snatch a brief moment of seeming immortality. Aristotle countered Plato by pointing to change as inevitable. Things change because they have the potential to move towards greater perfection. Change is teleological, which means a movement towards a predetermined end. Unlike Plato, Aristotle perceived multiple reasons for revolutions, other than a regime's prominent deficiency, like extreme inequality. He analysed both general and particular causes of revolutions, along with preventive measures as remedies. He saw order as more important than disorder.

Following Aristotle, Machiavelli discussed social dissension and their causes. He identified (*a*) rivalries among the great, namely the rich and the socially superior, and (*b*) the endemic and natural enmity between the great and the people, or the rich and the poor, as the two main causes of revolution. He accepted conflict as permanent and universal, seeing it as natural, unlike his predecessors who viewed social conflict as unnatural and curable by certain kinds of social and political systems. The basis of social conflict is the permanent struggle between the common man and the powerful and wealthy, although he does not explain this struggle in economic terms. From Polybius, he learnt that conflict is not only widely prevalent, but can also be transformed into an instrument to promote socially useful ends. During the Roman period, theorists were preoccupied with finding justifications, rather than the causes of revolution. Polybius viewed revolutions as a corrective tool for restoring a just and properly ordered society that had been disturbed by tyranny. Nicholas of Cusa (1401–64) and Locke believed that revolutions were justified if monarchs and rulers violate people's trust. Locke was categorical that governments can be altered, amended, changed or dissolved legitimately, and listed five occasions when this was possible.

1. Whenever such a prince or single person establishes his own arbitrary will in place of laws.
2. When the prince hinders the legislature from assembling in its due time or from acting freely, pursuant to those ends for which it is constituted.
3. When by the arbitrary power of the prince, the elections and the ways of elections are altered without the consent, and contrary to the common interests of the people.
4. The delivery of the people into the subjection of foreign power, either by the prince or by the legislature.
5. The person who has the supreme executive power neglects laws already enacted, and could not be executed (Locke 1960: 454–59).

Locke clarified that people could use force against unjust and unlawful authority, and that authority had to be transparent and accountable. He emphatically stressed that a government based on consent, coupled with the right of the people to rebel, is the best defence against rebellion. On the contrary, Robert Filmer (1588–1653) and Jean Bodin (1530–96) maintained that the king derived his powers and authority from god, which were therefore irrevocable and absolute. The Glorious Revolution of 1688 and the American War of Independence of 1776 were understood according to Polybius' explanation of revolutions. Burke, reiterating Polybius, pointed out that tyranny usually leads to revolution. On the other hand, some theorists like Hobbes never justified revolutions because of the chaos and bloodshed it leads to.

THE MEANING OF REVOLUTION IN MODERN TIMES

The meaning of revolution underwent a change with the French Revolution; it was no longer seen as a means to be rid of tyranny, but as a way of establishing a new society. It elicited diverse reactions from the Conservatives, Liberals and the Marxists. Conservatism as an ideology crystallised in response to the French Revolution. Burke's *Reflections on the Revolution in France and on the proceedings of certain societies in England relating to that event* (1790) contains the quintessence of the conservative position. Using the two principles of conservation and correction, he contrasted the English with the French Revolution, for in the former the two principles had allowed a rectification of deficiencies within the existing framework. This balanced the old with the new. In France, a wholesale attack on established religion, traditional constitutional arrangements and the institution of property disturbed the sources of political wisdom that provide a bulwark against sweeping changes. Burke rejected the French effort to start anew on a clean slate by making a complete break with the past. In response to Burke, Paine defended the French Revolution and Enlightenment Liberalism and supported representative government, rule of law and universal suffrage. He rejected Burke's idealisation of the hereditary system of government. Interestingly, Burke supported the American Revolution as it did not redress its grievances by resorting to a doctrine of natural rights. It merely represented the freedom of colonies from British rule, whereas the French Revolution made equality and nationalism the two dominant values. Both these values are possible means of tyranny that can eventually erode the social and moral conditions of the liberty of citizens. Burke also championed the cause of Ireland and spoke against the oppression, exploitation and misrule in India perpetrated by the English East India Company.

Image 17.1: Painting depicting an episode from the French Revolution

Source: https://commons.wikimedia.org/wiki/File:Jacques_Bertaux_-_Prise_du_palais_des_Tuileries_-_1793.jpg.

Tocqueville was alarmed at the attack on ideas of equality of all persons before the law and democracy that the French Revolution unleashed, as that destroyed all class privileges and removed all hindrances to the authority of the state. In *The Old Regime and the French Revolution* (1856), Tocqueville pointed out that revolutions rarely occurred as a result of absolute poverty and gross deprivation, conditions that are often associated with despair, resignation and political inertia. Revolutions occurred when the government relaxed its grip after a long period of oppression. As he put it, 'the most perilous moment for a bad government is when it seeks to mend its ways' (ibid.: 177). Revolution leads to a centralised state as, prior to the revolution, powerful and privileged groups stood alongside the state; after the revolution, however, the state is isolated, garnering all the power. Marx and Engels viewed the French Revolution as a symbol of the demise of feudalism, and the inauguration of a bourgeois society that would eventually be dislodged by the socialist revolution. The idea of a total apocalyptic change, central to Marxism, is derived from the French Revolution.

Theories of revolutionary social change, particularly those deriving from Marx, emphasise the importance of class conflict, political struggle and imperialism as the principal instruments of fundamental structural changes. For Marx, history and historical change represented the unfolding of exploitative relationships between social classes, in which the clash of great social forces is of paramount interest. The unavoidable strife between social classes was determined by whether they owned the means of production, or whether they were mere agents of production. For Marx, political change was an important aspect of social change, and was determined by economic factors. Writing in the background of the optimism of the Victorian age, he provided a blueprint for wholesale revolutionary change.

Marx understood the course of human history to contain a series of major conflicts that he called social revolutions, which originated from objective contradictions or from the strain and disorder that exists in all class-divided societies. While these contradictions are general to all modes of production, they assume particular forms according to historical circumstances. Contradictions ensue within modes of production because of the inevitable tensions between forces of production (types of technology) and relations of production (ownership of property and social class division, whereby one extracts economic productivity from the other). The exploitative nature of these relationships intensifies class conflicts, making social revolutions imminent as the exploited classes acquire a consciousness and unity, which are then visible in struggles against the dominant class. Conditions for social revolution mature when the structures of a new mode of production—capitalism within feudalism or socialism within capitalism—produce a strain that solidifies the revolutionary potential of the working class. Revolution, for Marx, represented a cataclysmic leap from one stage to another and stopped with the attainment of communism, the perfect society. In the *Manifesto*, Marx and Engels prophesied the inevitable destruction of capitalism in advanced industrialised areas through a worldwide proletarian revolution. The overwhelming majority of the working class beyond nations will spearhead this consciously. However, following the abortive revolutions in Europe in 1848, Marx concluded that these were a prelude to a long-drawn one, namely the world proletarian revolution, that would come eventually. Engels, in his significant work *The Peasant War in Germany* (1850), drew parallels between the role played by nobles and burghers in the sixteenth century to crush the peasants' revolt and the alliance between the bourgeoisie and the aristocracy in 1848 against a newly emerging proletariat. He claimed that behind religious struggles lay the different interests, demands and requirements of the various classes. Similarly, the French Revolution of 1789 was more than an intense debate on the advantages of constitutional monarchy over royal absolutism, as the economic concerns of social classes were the key issue.

Taking a cue from Engels' demand for a new mode of struggle as elucidated in the 1895 *Preface to the Class Struggles in France*, Eduard Bernstein (1850–32) insisted on the need for a revision of the Marxist doctrine. His close association with the English Fabians during his exile in England had reinforced his views. The Fabians emphasised gradualism, permeation and constitutional democratic procedures as a means to usher in socialism. While paying tribute to Marx's genius, Bernstein pointed out the open cleavage between Marxist theory and the social, economic and political realities within late nineteenth-century capitalism. Contrary to Marx's predictions, the rate of profit had not fallen, wages had not gone down, the middle class has not disappeared, and there were no signs of an imminent collapse of capitalism. Most importantly, the working class had shown no desire or inclination to bring in a revolution in countries of advanced capitalism. Instead of concentration, there was a diffusion of wealth, making a peaceful transition to socialism desirable. Impressed by the progress of the democratic state, Bernstein insisted that workers could use the ballot box effectively to press forward their cause. In this changed situation, Marx's clarion call for a revolutionary overthrow of capitalism was neither practicable nor desirable. He also rejected a mass strike, and considered Georges Sorel's (1847–1972) idea of a general strike as outmoded in a full-fledged functioning democracy. Bernstein's vision of socialism, realisable through a non-violent, evolutionary, gradualist and democratic method, became the guiding force for not only advanced capitalist countries of the West, but also for the developing world in the latter half of the twentieth century. His most impressive and crucial success lay in promising 'socialism without the tears of revolution' (Dunn 1989: 25). In the scale of history, Bernstein's vision has triumphed over that of Marx.

Within the socialist doctrine, one can see support for both revolution and reform. Babeuf's stress on insurrection and revolution was kept alive by Louis Auguste Blanqui (1801–81), 'thus providing a link between the Jacobin Left and the nineteenth century radicals' (Kolakowski 1981a: 214). Blanqui's rejection of parliamentarism and the majority rule principle and defence of the need for a small, organised, disciplined party to foment a revolution was echoed by Pyotr Nikitich Tkachev (1844–86) and Vladimir Lenin (1870–1924). On the other hand, the earliest advocate of gradual peaceful reform by the state with the purpose of transforming society was Louis Blanc (1811–82), with Ferdinand Lassalle (1825–64) and Bernstein echoing him.

RESTATEMENT OF MARXIST ORTHODOXY

Lenin read Bernstein's *Evolutionary Socialism* (1899) while in exile from 1895 to 1900. Fearing that Bernstein's observations on trade unionism or economism of the working class were true, he insisted on the need for voluntary and decisive individual action with the help of a highly disciplined and organised party that could act as a vanguard of the working class. The party would be based on principles of secrecy, democratic-centralism, specialisation and exclusivity. This all-encompassing and powerful role of the party was the most important post-Marx development within Marxism. Lenin combined Marx's majoritarian perspective with that of Nicholas Gavrilovich Chernyshevsky's (1828–89) theory of elite revolutionism, for Lenin insisted on the need for a conscious party leadership, acting in unison with the masses on the outside. Marx and Engels made contradictory observations, despite Russia being a predominantly agrarian country. In 1875, Engels believed that revolution was imminent in Russia. In 1882, Marx and Engels expressed the hope that an outbreak of revolution in Russia might set into motion similar movements in the West. Lenin, too, hoped in his analysis of imperialism that if Russia, the weakest link in the imperial chain, snapped, it would trigger revolutions elsewhere. In 1885, Engels, in a letter to Vera Zasulich (1852–1919), observed that a Blanquist type of revolutionary change engineered by a band of conspirators could only take place in the highly unstable Tsarist Russia.

Georgii Valentinovich Plekhanov (1856–1918), acknowledged as the 'Father of Russian Marxism', popularised Marxism in Russia. He proposed revolutionary seizure and exercise of power, although he also cautioned against the premature realisation of socialism in a backward region of Europe. Lenin, an already committed Jacobin-Blanquist in the 1880s, read Plekhanov to secure the necessary introduction to Marxism; however, he never wavered from his conviction that terror and violence were the means to realise the dictatorship of the proletariat. Interestingly, Plekhanov censured Bernstein during the revisionist controversy, although subsequently, during the debate on Lenin's proposals within the Russian Social Democratic Labour Party (RSDLP), he insisted that a true revolution would have to be a democratic one. It was therefore not surprising that in 1918, Plekhanov felt responsible for Lenin's actions. With profound anguish and regret, he made a dying confession to an old colleague—that perhaps he had not done the right thing by beginning the Marxist propaganda too early in a country that was pre-modern and backward. This summed up the dilemma and subsequent distortion of Soviet Marxism both at the level of theory and practice.

Sorel concurred with Bernstein that most of Marx's predictions had not materialised, for developments within capitalism and the consolidation of trade unions had raised the standard of living of the workers, thereby blunting the class war. While Bernstein denounced violent revolution in an age of democracy, Sorel endorsed it as the surest way to recapture the essence of Marxism. Its guiding force was the dream of a new civilisation and heroic morality, which would replace the decadent bourgeois one. He insisted on the need for a myth for the masses to revolt, for that would inspire militant consciousness, forge group solidarity and instil the spirit of heroism and self-sacrifice. Equating revolutionary myths with religious myths, he proposed the myth of general strike as the supreme and final aim that would subordinate all other actions. He placed his hope in non-political syndicates that built and sustained consciousness and solidarity among the workers, and rejected political parties and trade unions for these normally frustrate the workers' aspiration for liberation. Sorel supported the use of military and not political violence as the former is free of cruelty, since the wealth of the propertied is left intact. The idea behind the general strike was not to attain political power, but to destroy the existing order without setting up a new authority or a master. It was not conspiratorial, for force and repression were not the means to realise it.

Rosa Luxemburg (1871–1919) criticised Lenin for his rejection of the spontaneity of the working class movement. She desired a dialectical reciprocity between the spontaneity of the masses, the intellectuals and political leaders, a point found in Gramsci and Frantz Fanon (1925–61). She also criticised Lenin's extraordinary faith in ultra-centralism, his implicit contempt for the creativity of the working class and his distrust of spontaneity. She was also critical of Bernstein for equating reform with revolutionary class struggle and digressing from the main essence of socialism by positing social reform as the sole and final aim. She, like Sorel, believed in the need for a myth to create proletarian consciousness.

Mao reiterated the Marxist-Leninist view of revolution as the means of actualising socialism; unlike Marx and Lenin, however, he considered the peasantry to be revolutionary by insisting that the Chinese Revolution had to be conducted under the hegemony of the proletariat. He stressed on the idea of permanent revolution first enunciated by Marx and Engels, which Plekhanov and Leon Trotsky (1879–1940) had also restated.

He contended that the proletariat would bring about a permanence of revolution after the bourgeois-democratic revolution had taken place, with the purpose of overthrowing the bourgeoisie and establishing their transitional state—the dictatorship of the proletariat—to create the material basis of true communism. Unlike Lenin, he insisted on the mass mobilisation of peasants and workers to realise revolutionary goals.

RECENT THEORIES OF REVOLUTION: ARENDT'S *ON REVOLUTION*

Arendt believed that a revolution aimed at freedom by establishing a political realm that was the realm of republican freedom; therefore, being strictly part of politics, it had to preclude violence. She insisted that political freedom should not be confused with liberation, which was the aim of a revolution. However, merely freeing people from tyranny did not establish freedom. She understood revolution in the sense of establishing a new political order, a body politic that provided the framework for the realisation of freedom and not social and economic transformation. She compared the American and the French revolutions, for it was during these two revolutions that the idea of freedom emerged. While the French Revolution is hailed as an important event, the American one remains inconspicuous, and its immediate influence was marginal. However, both revolutions illustrated two different aspects of revolutionary phenomena. Their individual experience provided a clue to the structure of the body politic and society ushered in by the revolution. The French Revolution, with its slogan of liberty, equality and fraternity, could not fulfil its own promise of ensuring freedom, for it degenerated into violence and tyranny. In contrast, the American Revolution succeeded for it established a constitutional structure for realising freedom. Arendt termed it a clean revolution for it did 'not break out but was made by men in common deliberation and on the strength of mutual pledges' (Arendt 1969: 280). For Arendt, the French Revolution was a tale of necessity while the American one was a tale of freedom. The efforts of the French revolutionaries failed because of the social basis of the revolution, its attempt to solve the social question by political means. As a result, they justified tyranny and terror in the interests of social betterment. They overthrew absolute monarchy, but failed to give their republic a stable footing. The power of the state and its police grew, while the freedom of the individual, of the press, of speech, of association and of free enterprise steadily diminished. In contrast, the founding fathers in America were not moved by messianic dreams of solving the social question, and this, coupled with their training in town meetings during the colonial period, had a sobering influence. The result was a constitutional republic that became the basis of freedom and a polity based on free contract, with no need for terror or violence. She described this achievement as 'perhaps the greatest enterprise of European mankind' (ibid.: 55). Furthermore, the American Revolution also demonstrated the importance of moderation and of bringing about far-reaching changes in an evolutionary manner without resorting to violence and messianic zeal.

Arendt admitted that issues like mass poverty cannot be ignored by revolutionary leaders; however, if they were to get carried away by a sense of 'pity' and attempt to end mass misery and poverty, the consequences would be fatal, as was the case of the French Revolution. If the goal of survival replaced the goal of freedom, freedom would become a mere shibboleth invoked more as a routine mechanical symbol, and important concerns like public happiness, public freedom and public spirit would become things of the past. While it is important to take care of human wants, it is equally necessary to restrain men, their passions and to protect zealously their liberties. She saw a certain continuity between the French and the Russian Revolutions. Hegel's 'revolutionary' idea of the 'absolute of the philosophers' as revealed in history was due to the influence of the French Revolution on his thought (1969: 51–52). Marx inherited this idea and transmitted it to Lenin and his successor Josef Stalin (1878–1953). According to her, Hegel introduced—and Marx subsequently restated—the 'most terrible and least bearable paradox in the whole history of modern thought—the paradox that freedom is the fruit of necessity'. Revolutionary freedom was seen, paradoxically, as the child of 'historical necessity'. 'Instead of freedom, necessity became the chief category of political and revolutionary thought' (ibid.: 53–54, 58).

The French Revolution changed the aim from freedom to happiness and that infected and corrupted the entire revolutionary tradition. A similar confusion existed in Marx's thought. Despite Marx's concern with freedom, he 'finally strengthened more than anybody else the politically more pernicious doctrine of the modern age, namely that life is the highest good' (ibid.: 64). The *raison d'etre* of revolution became economic progress. Unlike Fanon, who believed violence was justified since it cleansed like fire and was necessary to regenerate human nature and create a new community, Arendt was a moderate. She nevertheless permitted violence for short-term goals, or if it provided a chance to succeed or helped to 'dramatise grievances'. Her major emphasis is that a successful revolution has to be restricted to the political and should not be extended to the social.

SKOCPOL'S *STATES AND SOCIAL REVOLUTIONS: A COMPARATIVE ANALYSIS OF FRANCE, RUSSIA AND CHINA*

Skocpol offered the most incisive analysis of revolution by historically comparing what she called the 'social revolutions' in France, Russia and China. Social revolutions occur due to two variables. First, there must be a *crisis of state*, often provoked by international factors such as increasing economic or security competition from abroad. This results in divisions within the elite and the army about what to do, weakening loyalty to the regime and creating a revolutionary situation. Second, *patterns of class dominance* determine which group will rise up to exploit this revolutionary situation. Skocpol's approach has three distinguishing features: (*i*) structuralist: the objective conditions necessary for the emergence of revolutionary situations; (*ii*) internationalist: the influence of transnational economic relations and the international structure of competing states on domestic developments; and (*iii*) statist: the analysis of the emergence of revolutionary situations depends on the relationship of the state with its administrative and coercive powers, with military competitors abroad, and with dominant classes losing their solidarity at home.

According to Skocpol, a social revolution is one that involves 'rapid, basic transformations of a society's state and class structures, often accompanied by class based revolts from below' (1979: 26). She termed this kind of change 'structural change' in order to differentiate it from other conflicts and processes that may bring about radical, but not comprehensive change. A revolution is characterised by the coincidence of political and social transformation. By this criterion, the Chinese Revolution and the end of the Khmer Rouge in Cambodia between 1975 and 1979 were social revolutions. However, the Puritan Revolution in England in the seventeenth century and the Portuguese Revolution of 1974 that overthrew Salazar's dictatorship were not revolutions, for these did not undermine the class structures of their societies. The industrial revolution brought about changes in social structures, but without resulting in or leading to political upheaval. Skocpol stated that revolutionary events shared some characteristics with other transformative phenomena like coups or riots, but it is the powerful combination of social and political change that distinguishes them.

Tilly's (1975, 1991) definition of revolution was more cosmopolitan, involving political discontinuity arising from challenges to government control of a single independent political system. It is important to distinguish between political discontinuities on the basis of how far they change the structure of the polity in question; the make-up of the contending forces; and the extent of (social) structural changes that result from the revolution. By this definition, Tilly labelled the accession of Mustapha Kemal to power in Turkey in 1923 and the restoration of the Meiji dynasty in Japan in 1868 after two centuries of rule by the Shogun Gate (military warlords) as revolution. Skocpol, however, characterised these as rebellions or coups, for she was interested only in the structural aspects of revolutionary change and not in the manner in which people view change or contribute to it. She was not concerned with cultural and ideological factors. Gurr (1976) stated that political instability was likely to develop when individuals experienced a sense of relative deprivation, a psychological state which occurs when people perceive a gap between what they have and what they believe they should have—be it in politics, welfare benefits or consumer goods. This perception need not be related to an objective or measurable criterion of deprivation. When there is an intense and widespread sense of relative deprivation, the conditions for violence will be present. Davis (1962) described the dangers that arise when the gap between people's rising expectations and the declining capacity of the government to deliver widens, for it is at this time that a potentially revolutionary situation emerges. However, these accounts leave unanswered the questions pertaining to which segment of the population is likely to rebel. Can collective violence trigger discontent? Why do some discontented people revolt, while others do not? Will revolutionary gaps occur if there are opportunities to express discontent through available political channels? Does the type of value system dominant in society matter?

FUNCTIONALIST ACCOUNTS OF REVOLUTION

Johnson (1966) and Smelser (1963), dominant functionalist accounts of revolution, placed a premium on values as the basis of collective action and examine more closely the conditions in which revolutionary action occurs. These accounts were interested in the causes of what Smelser called disturbance and strain in societies and in how (as Johnson claimed) 'synchronous changes' caused a shift in values, as well as modifications in communities and societies that accelerate revolutionary activity and disturb social equilibrium. During a period of change caused by factors like technological progress, migration or conquest, a system might not be able to sustain its equilibrium, whether culturally, economically, or otherwise. If the changes are sufficiently rapid or intense, there will be greater pressure on political elites to respond; failure to do so may result in an enormous loss of trust in the system and in the perception of the legitimacy of rulers. This 'power deflation', as Johnson termed it, in turn makes it more difficult for the elites to introduce effective measures to stabilise the system. Augmented violence and other forms of coercion, which state elites exercise to demonstrate an appearance of control, lead to further deficits in legitimacy. What is then required is an immediate trigger or accelerator—chance event, a massacre of protestors, or an attempted coup by the military—to accompany a full insurrection. Functionalist explanations of revolutionary change are overly concerned with equilibrium, and have a built-in tendency to interpret all change as causing disequilibrium. They overlook psychological factors relating to the motivations of actors, or treat them in a cursory fashion.

Crane Brinton's *The Anatomy of Revolution*

Brinton discusses the four revolutionary upheavals of recent times—the English Revolution (1688), the American Revolution (1776), the French Revolution (1789) and the Russian Revolution (1917). For Brinton, revolution meant 'a drastic sudden substitution of one group in charge of the running of a territorial political entity by another' (1938: 4). Like Popper, he saw a clear correlation between violence and revolutionary change; while Popper distinguished between holistic revolutionary change and piecemeal social engineering, Brinton distinguished between a peaceful process of transition by elections and a process marked with violence or the threat of violence. A peaceful electoral process is normal within a well-established order, while the consequences of a revolution are uncertain. A revolution is comparable to a disease that brings high temperature in a human body. Disequilibrium, followed by a revolutionary situation, can be created by any one, or a combination of, the following factors: (*i*) rise of new desires; (*ii*) the strengthening of old desires in a different group; (*iii*) a change in the environmental condition; and (*iv*) institutional failure to change.

Brinton's analysis was distinctive as, according to him, revolutions were abnormal and comparable to a diseased human being. In human beings, a complete recovery is equated with a return to normality; similarly, in a revolution, normality is achieved when the body polity becomes comparable to that in the pre-revolutionary phase. It is because of this cardinal truth that revolutions always fail to match the vision of the revolutionaries. This transitory nature of the revolution was seen even after the French Revolution, when the kingdom was restored, which King Napoleon sought to return to and begin a new hereditary dynastic monarchy.

Like a disease, the signs of revolution are manifested earlier, although the process itself takes a long time to fructify. Using the analogy of a fever, Brinton argued that revolutions begin with moderates demanding small and incremental changes, which later lead to violent changes, unleashing a reign of terror (1938: 17). After such a dislocation, there is always a period of recovery. 'The Thermidorian Reaction', the dream of the emergence of a new man, remains unfulfilled, as the earlier normality is restored. The English and the American Revolutions were exceptions; the French and Russian revolutions followed a similar pattern, beginning with moderate revolutionaries, subsequently becoming more radical and leading to a period of terror, and finally ending with a Thermidorian Reaction of a dictatorship.

Brinton also detailed some symptoms that manifest before the revolution. In all the four revolutions that Brinton discusses, serious financial problems existed, although the general perception was that these societies were bankrupt. For instance, France in 1789 was a rich society, but the government treasury was empty. The situation was characterised by uneven distribution and inequality. The people who were taxed most heavily did not have the ability to pay. There was also a widespread belief that legitimate economic activity could not be carried out under the prevailing conditions.

In the context of the American Revolution, American traders were angry with British policy. In France, tax reform proposals threatened the privileged classes, but could not garner the support of the lower classes. In both situations, administrative problems were combined with inefficiency, and an overwhelming feeling of being wronged by the government continued. Failed reform attempts fuelled further frustration. The rulers of all four governments were both ineffective and mean.

Role of Intellectuals

In all four cases, intellectuals shifted their allegiance from the government. They delivered speeches and wrote against the government. Some called for radical reforms, while others were for direct action or seeking an alternative to government in a novel manner. In America, the merchants' committee became a precursor to committees of correspondence. In France, a discussion of Enlightenment ideas eventually led to political action. In Russia, there were many organised groups that wanted a drastic and immediate change; however, they ranged from Nihilists, anarchists, socialists, liberals, and pro and anti-Western (Westernisers and anti-Westernisers) groups. In the pre-revolutionary situation, ideas abound, as without ideas there can be no revolution. But this does not mean that censorship can prevent revolution, nor can ideas be instrumental in motivating revolutions. It 'merely means that ideas form part of the mutually dependent variables we are studying' (Brinton 1938: 49).

Factors of Class Division and Conflict

Both class division and class conflict existed in all four revolutions. Class barriers were perceived as unnatural, while the ruling class remained divided and antagonistic. The French and Russian middle classes hated the aristocracy and believed in its moral superiority. In France, till the middle of the eighteenth century, the middle class was eager to join the aristocracy, but later realised that this was impossible. Enlightenment ideas and the French nobility's refusal to accommodate them widened the gulf. With increased commerce, there emerged a new, prosperous middle class; however, there was no possibility of co-option by the nobility to secure its social and political status.

Formative Period of Revolution

There is always a close relationship between new taxation or an alteration in the familiar one, which leads to a situation where people refuse to pay. However, revolutions are always catalysed by either the revolutionaries defeating the army, or the army joining the revolutionaries and deserting the government. Moderates dominate the initial stages of a revolution; they normally belong to the middle class or the 'liberal nobility'.

But in the crisis stage, the extremists come to the fore. A substantive number of moderates and extremists are intellectuals. However, a revolution is successful only when most classes join it.

Brinton termed the initial moderate period as the 'honeymoon period'. Given the numerous factions in play, this period is short-lived. The moderates are affluent and consist mostly of old oppositionists to the government, for example, Lafayette and Mirabeau during the French Revolution and Kerenesky during the February revolution in Russia. While they have faced all the problems emanating from the older regime, they wield little power and authority to deal with them. The Moderates had often faced foreign or civil wars, and were always divided on how to deal with extraordinary situations. Believing in civil rights like the freedom of speech, press and assembly, they do not want to eliminate or suppress their enemies. They soon face a challenge from the extremists and radicals, who accuse the moderates of betraying the revolution. This radical challenge leads to the establishment of a 'dual sovereignty', for example, the Jacobin club during the French Revolution and the Soviets during the Russian Revolution. The extremists are more organised and disciplined, and tend to discredit the moderates by projecting them with the old regime. One major reason for the failure of the moderates is their incapacity for a centralised strong government. The extremists are always smaller in number and totally devoted to the cause, like the French Jacobins and the Russian Bolsheviks, and are comparable to a militant religious organisation.

Unlike the moderates, the Jacobins and Bolsheviks encouraged terrorism, guerrilla warfare, lobbying, parading, street fighting and propaganda leadership, and inspire unanimous devotion and loyalty. The leaders were activists and authoritarian, for example, Robespierre and Lenin. A reign of terror follows, often caused by war. The radicals come into possession of political knowledge when sharing power with the moderates and their reign of terror signifies the end of constitutional rights. The government becomes highly centralised with dictatorial powers, manifested in the creation of extraordinary courts, revolutionary tribunals, and revolutionary surveillance committees and secret police that spy on its own people.

No effort is spared to proclaim the arrival of a heaven on earth and the beginning of a new age, which is distanced from the past. Traditional vices are no longer tolerated and leaders like Robespierre and Lenin were projected as extraordinary human beings, as personifications of asceticism and devoted to the cause of the revolution. Names of streets, people and places are altered to distance them from the older period. The French Revolution even proclaimed the advent of a republican calendar, which began with the inauguration of the French Republic.

The intolerance of the revolutionaries makes life terrible for the citizens. Thousands are imprisoned and/or killed for the undefined crime of not sharing the revolutionaries' vision. The revolutionaries of the first stage are exiled or executed. While nationalism is always a strong element in a revolution, there is also a desire to export it to other countries. Hostility towards religion is common, with revolutionary symbols replacing old religious symbols and holidays. The terror is also a consequence of acute economic difficulties and class struggle. Brinton saw this period as combining both terror and virtue in the hope of bringing heaven on earth.

A 'thermidorian reaction' sets in after the revolution reaches its peak. In the case of the French Revolution, it began with Robespierre being guillotined on 28 July 1794. This was followed by an amnesty of former moderates and in a total reversal, the most ardent revolutionaries began to be persecuted. Eventually, after the anarchy and abnormality of the revolutionary situation, a strong man such as Napoleon or Stalin would emerge.

Brinton concluded that revolution changes things only a little. Some abuses and institutions are changed only 'slightly, if at all' (1938: 237). Revolution reveals the worst abuses and inefficiencies of the old regime, and 'the machinery of government works more smoothly after than immediately before the revolution' (ibid.: 239). Governments become more centralised and efficient. There is a huge transfer of property through confiscation or forced sale. One ruling class is replaced by another; the new class comprises people who were not part of the earlier ruling class. The revolution leaves behind a tradition, to be emulated elsewhere.

Barrington Moore's *Social Origins of Dictatorship and Democracy: Lord and Peasant in the Making of the Modern World*

Moore's theory of social change explained in detail, and through specific examples, the important structural factors that lay behind the major historical routes taken by important nations of the East and the West while transforming from agrarian to modern industrial societies. He examined the three major routes: (*i*) the emergence of democracy via the path of bourgeois revolution, for example, in England, France and the USA; (*ii*) the rise of fascism, which is imposed from above and leads to a conservative revolution, for example, in Japan and Germany; and (*iii*) the consolidation of communism via a peasant revolution, for example, in China and Russia. The most important factor in understanding the historical process of revolution is the reaction of landed upper classes and peasants to the challenge of the commercialisation of agriculture. Modernisation took three different routes, exhibiting the very different situations of the landed upper class and the peasantry. It was facilitated by the development of an economically independent bourgeoisie; the landed upper classes and the peasantry either supported this group or were annihilated by a revolution (France) or a civil war (the USA). The establishment of parliamentary democracy in England was facilitated by their solving the key agrarian problem, and India's failure to solve its agrarian problems 'constitutes a threat to democracy' (1967: xiii). Even England had faced civil war in its march towards democracy—the 1642 Puritan Revolution. One important feature in all these developments in England, France and the USA 'is the development of a group in society with an independent economic base, which attacks obstacles to a democratic version of capitalism that have been inherited from the past' (ibid.: xv). While trading and manufacturing classes in the cities provided good support, the key role in the emergence of capitalistic and democratic rule in England was played by the landed upper class. The evolution of the peasantry took two different paths: political efforts for capitalism; and/or a marginal or negligible existence, either because of the destruction of peasant society by the advance of capitalism, or due to the absence of a well-fortified peasantry, as was the case in the USA. This process culminated in the combining of capitalism and Western democracy.

The second route was also capitalistic, but instead of moving towards democracy, it culminated in fascism in Germany and Japan in the twentieth century. This is reactionary capitalism in which a coalition takes place between older landed elites and a relatively weak but rising commercial and industrial class; this coalition is directed against the lower urban and rural classes. In such a situation, bourgeois revolution is very weak and can be easily defeated. The third route is very different from both bourgeois revolution and fascism: the emergence of communism. The ground for a communist takeover was facilitated by the continued exercise of power by an agrarian bureaucracy and landed nobility, which forcefully stifled all but the feeblest attempts at commercialisation of agriculture and industrialisation. As a consequence, a huge impoverished peasant population had to live at a subsistence level, and ultimately revolted against the ruling class.

Moore's account, presented with abundant historical facts, had a general framework for comprehending the origins of democracy, fascism and communism. The central variables were: (*ii*) The starting point was the social setting prior to modernisation; (*ii*) Persistence or non-persistence of a strong central authority and its relationship with the landed aristocracy; (*iii*) The landed aristocracy's response to commercialisation, and the form of this commercialisation; (*iv*) The condition of the peasantry, resulting from the landed elite's response to the pressures of modernisation; (*v*) The strength or weakness of the bourgeoisie in relation to the landed aristocracy; (*vi*) The precise nature of the coalition between different classes; and (*vii*) The presence or absence of a successful or unsuccessful revolution and its nature. Isolating particular events and classes is a means of analysing a specific historic situation, and is vital to understanding the evolution. The most important point of departure for Moore was the evolution of Great Britain, which served as an ideal example of a bourgeois revolution culminating in the establishment of parliamentary democracy. Both France and the US were aberrant variants on the same theme, as their passage to democracy was interrupted by violent interludes. As Britain's evolution was smoother, it serves as the ideal type of a bourgeois revolution. However, in the case of fascism and communism, an ideal type does not exist and analysis is restricted to a basic explanation of their divergence and deviation from a model of parliamentary democracy. In other words, it was the absence of conditions necessary for the emergence of parliamentary democracy that led to the consolidation of the two other models of modernisation, fascism and communism.

CONCLUSION

Laski, writing on the centenary of Marx and Engels' *The Communist Manifesto* in 1948, propounded the doctrine of 'revolution by consent', signalling the arrival of the democratic age. Not many today echo Fanon's eulogy of violence as a cleansing force, as the track record of violent revolutions has shown that they lead inevitably to terror, suppression of democratic freedom and institutions, and untold human suffering. It is generally agreed that the ballot box is much more revolutionary and effective as a mode of change than the barrel of a gun. Owing to the universal acceptance of liberal democracy and the spectacular success of East Asian countries, revolutionary theories of social change have ceased to cast their spell. On the contrary, theories that advocate peaceful change, emphasising new social and economic issues, have crystallised in the form of new social movements like feminism, environmentalism, and the movement of indigenous people and marginalised groups and individuals. The potential of all these movements to effect peaceful social change is stronger than yesteryears' insurrections and violent movements to capture state power. This is why Havel proclaimed that 'violence is not radical enough'.

NOTE

1. It is for this reason that the Industrial Revolution and infotech revolutions do not qualify as being 'revolutions'.

18

MULTICULTURALISM

We live in a world formed by technology and trade; by economic, religious, and political imperialism and their offspring; by mass migration and the dispersion of cultural influences. In this context, to immerse oneself in the traditional practices of, say, an aboriginal culture might be a fascinating anthropological experiment, but it involves an artificial dislocation from what actually is going on in the world. The only way that a culture could remain authentic is by adopting a wholly inauthentic way of life by denying the 'overwhelming reality of cultural interchange and global interdependence'.

Waldron 1993: 8

A multicultural society cannot be stable and last long without developing a common sense of belonging among its citizens. The sense of belonging cannot be ethnic and based on shared cultural, ethnic and other characteristics, for a multicultural society is too diverse for that, but must be political and based on a shared commitment to the political community.

Parekh 2000: 225

Multiculturalists tend to be intellectual magpies, picking up attractive ideas and incorporating them into their theories without worrying too much about how they fit together.

Barry 2001: 252

In many well-established Western democracies, issues concerning nationality, ethnicity, religion, language, gender, and the like have come to the forefront of public debate since the last quarter of the twentieth century, by focusing on questions pertaining to recognising cultural diversity, the status and rights of immigrants and, in specific cases, the rights of indigenous people, underlining the need for group representation and rights. Demographic and political changes in these societies in the late twentieth century have necessitated a need to rethink the relationship between culture and politics. The presence of a substantial number of minorities from more than one culture has altered the debate on the ideals of democracy, justice and citizenship. For many, multiculturalism or embracing a diverse and inclusive society was an answer to several of the social problems in Western democracies, thus moving away from the underpinnings of classical political theory which examined questions concerning justice or democracy in a relatively homogenous society with a shared identity, as theorised by J. S. Mill.

MEANING OF MULTICULTURALISM

Multiculturalism is best understood not as a political doctrine with a programmatic content, nor as a philosophical school with a distinct theory about man's place in the world, but as a perspective on or a way of viewing human life. In political theory, multiculturalism is about the proper response to ethnic, cultural and religious diversity. It is not merely toleration, but the accommodation of differences among divergent groups that is the crux of multiculturalism. It is closely associated with 'identity politics', 'the politics of difference', 'differentiated citizenship', 'group differentiated rights' and the 'politics of recognition', as all of these take into consideration the concerns of marginalised groups and disrespected identities and address the economic and political disadvantages that people suffer as a result of their minority status. Besides culture and cultural groups, multicultural claims also include religion, language, ethnicity, nationality, and to a limited extent, race. Multiculturalism focuses not only on the culture of the minority group, but also on the history of group subordination and its attendant experiences.

Multiculturalism believes that cultural diversity needs to be accommodated fairly as public policies have different consequences for and impact on persons from different cultural groups within multinational states. For example, in view of the importance of language to culture and the expansive role of modern states in different aspects of life, the choice of official language will affect people differently. This is also the case with the content of education, personal laws and choice of public holidays, national symbols such as the national anthem, immigration and naturalisation policy, religious freedom, special privileges for minorities or mechanisms for representing minorities. These have increasingly captured the attention of theorists and policymakers in order to avoid policies that entail unfair burdens (Kymlicka 1995b: 1).

The term 'multiculturalism' was first used in Canada in 1971 and then in Australia in 1978. In the US and Britain, it came into vogue in the 1980s. In the US, terms like 'salad bowl' and 'glorious mosaic' replaced the phrase 'melting pot', which symbolises an oppressive white hegemonic culture. Multiculturalism resists homogenisation or assimilation and dismisses the notion of justice as equal rights for all as, first, it overlooks diversity, and second, has the tendency to assume that there is only one correct, true or normal way to understand and structure life and human endeavour. It rejects the idea of 'one person one vote' and insists on the need to take into account differences based on culture, race, religion and ethnicity.

Kymlicka pointed out that the logical conclusion of liberal principles of justice 'seems to be a "colour-blind" constitution—the removal of all legislation differentiating people in terms of their race or ethnicity (except for temporary measures, like affirmative action), which are believed necessary to reach a "colour blind" society' (1989: 141). Multiculturalists consider this move towards a 'colour-blind' society ill-founded, for it is not possible to separate the state and ethnicity. When the liberal state attempts to do so, it unfairly privileges certain ways of life over others. They allege that liberals do not take diversity seriously, despite the fact that liberals value pluralism, with Rawls stressing on 'reasonable pluralism'; this is why liberals defend a neutral public philosophy that entails equal rights for all citizens. Kymlicka (1995a) argued that liberals like Rawls and Dworkin had falsely assumed that members of a political community are part of the same cultural community. He regarded a culture as a civilisation, self-sufficient and with its own social institutions.

Parekh pointed out that multiculturalism is not about difference and identity per se, but about a body of beliefs and practices embedded in and substantiated by culture, in terms of which a group of people understand themselves and the world and organise their individual and collective lives. A culture has a claim to rights if it is vital to the basic interests of its members and contributes to the wider society (Parekh 2000: 217–18). Parekh also pointed out that multiculturalism occupies a middle position between naturalism or monism and culturalism or pluralism. Culturalists like Giambattista Vico (1668–1744), Montesquieu, Herder, and the German Romanticists insisted that human beings were culturally constituted and varied from culture to culture, while thinkers like Hobbes, Locke and Rawls spoke of human nature as unrelated to culture and society.

THEORIES OF MULTICULTURALISM

Kymlicka criticised the earlier models of unitary republican citizenship in which all citizens enjoyed common citizenship rights; this was based on the assumption of a homogenous political community, ignoring cultural and ethnic diversity. He observed that liberalism, with its stress on individual rights, did not pay adequate attention to group rights. He argued that in a multicultural state, a comprehensive theory of justice would have to include both universal rights and certain group differentiated rights, or special status for minority cultures, as the individual's ability to choose a good life necessarily rests within a cultural context. One's ethnic or national culture constitutes a condition of autonomy, and it is for this reason that group rights and differentiated citizenship needs to be guaranteed.

Kymlicka was dissatisfied with post-war liberal political theory, which in his view wrongly assumed that the provision of basic individual rights could resolve the problem of national minorities. He contended that minority rights could not be subsumed under human rights because 'human rights standards are simply unable to resolve some of the most important and controversial questions relating to cultural minorities' (Kymlicka 1995a: 4). These include questions about which languages should be recognised in parliaments, bureaucracies and courts; whether any ethnic or national groups should have publicly funded education in their mother tongues; whether internal boundaries should be drawn so that cultural minorities form majorities in local regions; whether the traditional homelands of indigenous people should be reserved for their benefit; and the degree of cultural integration that might be required of immigrants seeking citizenship. As traditional human rights doctrines offer no guidance on these questions, Kymlicka recommended a theory of minority rights to supplement human rights theory, for he was convinced that this would enable us to confront the burning issues raging in places like Eastern Europe, which was mired in disputes over local autonomy, language and naturalisation. He proposed to develop a liberal theory of minority rights which would explain 'how minority rights could coexist with human rights and how minority rights are limited by principles of individual liberty, democracy and social justice' (ibid.: 6).

Kymlicka, in the course of elaborating his theory, distinguished three kinds of minority or group differentiated rights that were to be assured to ethnic and national groups: self-government rights, polyethnic rights and special representation rights. Self-government rights require the delegation of powers to national minorities, such as indigenous peoples, but are not available to other cultural minorities who had immigrated to the country. Polyethnic rights guarantee financial support and legal and political protection from the state to cultural minorities, for certain practices associated with particular ethnic or religious groups and, in particular, to aboriginal people to enable them to maintain their culture and autonomy. Polyethnic rights might include legislation to prevent the suppression or marginalisation of the cultural identity of minority ethnic groups through deliberate or unthinking discrimination by the majority ethnic population within a country. Special state support for media policies and funding to address the media interests of minority ethnic groups form one particular expression of polyethnic rights. Both indigenous peoples and immigrant minorities might also be eligible for special representation rights, which guarantee places for minority representatives on state bodies or institutions.

Of pivotal importance in Kymlicka's account of group-differentiated citizenship is the distinction that he made between two kinds of minorities: national minorities and ethnic minorities. The former are people whose previously self-governing, territorially concentrated cultures have been incorporated into a large state. These are the 'American Indians', Puerto Ricans, Chicanos and native Hawaiians in the United States; the Quebecois and various aboriginal communities in Canada; and the Aborigines in Australia. Ethnic minorities are people who have immigrated to a new society and do not wish to govern themselves, but nonetheless wish to retain their ethnic identities and traditions.

However, Kymlicka also strongly believed that group-based protection should not violate the rights fundamental to individual well-being. He acknowledged the fact that individuals might need protection from the abusive power of their own ethnic communities. He endorsed group-differentiated rights that provide for the external protection of groups, but does not permit 'internal restrictions' except in cases of systematic and gross human rights violations like slavery or genocide, in which case state intervention is warranted. For Kymlicka, culture was important because it is the context within which individuals learn how to choose; however, its value reduces when it disallows individuals to choose their lives for themselves, thus retaining the overall spirit of liberalism that permits an individual's capacity for autonomous choice. Cultural membership and cultural diversity sustain those options within which autonomous persons can exercise choice. Devoid of autonomy, cultural diversity is neither morally nor aesthetically valuable (1995a: 121–23).

Parekh insisted that cultural minorities must be treated as equal and valued members, as equal respect is central to an individual's sense of dignity that goes beyond conventional notions of non-discrimination and equal opportunity. Minorities should not have to face intended or unintended discrimination in the spheres of employment, housing, education, promotion, and appointment to public offices. Minority communities may be allowed to run their internal affairs themselves, so long as they are not internally oppressive. They should also be free to set up their own cultural, educational and other institutions, organise literary, artistic, sports, and other events, and institute museums and academies, with the help of the state if needed. Cultural differences should also be taken into account in the formulation and enforcement of public policies and laws.

Taylor offered an alternative theory in 'The Politics of Recognition' (1994) by rejecting as inadequate the liberal theory of multiculturalism. Liberalism, in his view, was incapable of giving culture the recognition it required as it emphasised sameness, viewing individuals as the bearers of rights and possessors of dignity, as equal citizens, whereas cultural groups desire a recognition of their distinctness. He rejected Kymlicka's efforts to develop a liberalism that might accommodate difference by granting individuals differentiated rights to enable them to pursue their particular ends. According to Taylor, this solution worked only 'for existing people who find themselves trapped within a culture under pressure, and can flourish within it or not at all. But it does justify measures designed to ensure survival through indefinite future generations' (1994: 62). In this context, he cited the example of the Quebecois, whose aim is the long-term survival of the French-speaking community in Canada. One of the main foundations of Taylor's theory of recognition was the assertion that our sense of our own well-being and moral goals depends critically on how we see ourselves reflected in the eyes of others. Being in a group whose culture is reviled and devalued leads to its members being morally harmed, and hence there is a need for a revaluation and public acknowledgement of the despised group as a legitimate presence in the body politic. While acknowledging the need for 'difference-blind procedures for interpreting and redeeming individual rights' within a liberal polity, he also stressed the need for a common moral purpose forged out of the interaction of the different cultures subsisting within. He also strongly proposed the need for a multiculturalist education to enhance mutual cultural understanding. For Taylor, a multicultural liberal society is one in which individuals were given respect insofar as they followed a particular cultural heritage, as well as a distinctive legal-constitutional regime in which the basic structure of rights and liberties was preserved.

Defenders of the politics of difference desire an extension of democratic processes to give greater scope to the participation of cultural minorities in the shaping and governing of the polity (Marion-Young 1990, 2000; Phillips 1995; Tully 2003; Williams 1998). In *Strange Multiplicity* (1995), Tully recommended a reconstruction of modern constitutionalism to accommodate the wide variety of cultural traditions in order to enhance the quality of liberal constitutional arrangements. Williams (1998) proposed measures like proportional representation, holding reserved seats in legislative bodies for members of underrepresented marginalised groups, redrawing of electoral boundaries when underrepresented groups were concentrated in geographically determined ridings/constituencies, or providing for multi-member districts when appropriate, and providing quotas for underrepresented groups in political party candidate lists.

Marion-Young demanded the guaranteed representation only of oppressed, disadvantaged groups and veto power over policies that affect them. These groups could only be fully integrated through what she called differentiated citizenship. This means that members of certain groups should be incorporated into the political community not only as individuals, but also through their group, and that their rights should depend in part on their group membership: 'group veto power regarding specific policies that affect a group directly, such as reproductive rights policy for women, or land use policy for Indian reservations' (1990: 184).

Marion-Young did not consider the protection of minority cultures a state responsibility, a notion advanced by some liberal multiculturalists like Kymlicka and Raz (1986, 1994), as this was tantamount to confining groups to the private sphere. It failed to publicly endorse their distinct identities. The public sphere is dominated by norms which appear to be universal and culturally neutral, but in reality reflect the cultural values of dominant social categories—middle-class white males. Marion-Young (1992), picking up on Cohen and Rogers' (1992) model of 'associative democracy', proposed that the state ought to be an organisation of oppressed minorities with the idea that they could exercise real power. Arguing within the US context, she (2000) also pointed out that an exclusive emphasis on rational argument further disadvantages minorities who are well-versed in its niceties. She supported forms of communication like rhetoric, storytelling (or testimony, or narrative), and an oral tradition, which are more accessible to disadvantaged minorities.

Phillips (1995) put forward the essentialist assumption of what she called 'the politics of presence', namely representation for the underrepresented (she took the example of women) by reserving places in government bodies for people from marginalised groups, or 'the politics of ideas', ensuring that at least some political party platforms feature marginalised group interests. The second complements the first, and this would ensure the representation of unrepresented segments in government. However, it is possible that representatives would not pursue the specific interest of the group they represent. While party discipline may lead to some accountability, even proportional representation may not lead to electoral success. One solution is including the group list in the list of political party candidates, ensuring the representation of marginalised groups.

Phillips (1995) conceptualised the public and private spheres as interdependent, but distinct. She believed it necessary to integrate the private sphere into the analysis and focus on the gendered nature of power relations within the family, instead of ignoring it as traditional political science has done. Inequities within the family are as relevant to issues of social justice as inequalities in the public sphere. Democratisation of the public sphere, understood in terms of greater participation of women, is possible only if there is prior democratisation of the private sphere. She desired to do so by maintaining the public-private distinction, like Okin (1991) and Marion-Young (1987), so as to preserve the areas of individual decision and privacy. In this context, she mentioned the right to abortion. She also argued for the need to detach the two spheres of gender difference and base them instead on the criterion of right to privacy.

MULTICULTURALISM AND THE COMMUNITARIAN CRITIQUE OF LIBERALISM

Multiculturalism coalesced with the communitarian critique of liberalism. The liberal perspective of the free and equal individual, each pursuing her/his own conception of a good life, with primacy given to rights and liberties over community life and the collective good, is viewed as fallacious as it fails to take into account the fact that an individual's identity is a social construct. Communitarians reject the idea of the individual as existing prior to the community, as well as the idea that the value of social goods can be reduced to their contribution to individual well-being. Traditional liberal emphasis on identical liberties and opportunities for all is replaced by a scheme of special rights for minority cultural groups. Theorists like Kymlicka, however, have justified the claims of multiculturalism within liberalism, based on the values of autonomy and equality. Kymlicka argued that individuals choose within a cultural context from which they derive self-respect, as there is an intimate connection between a person's self-respect and the respect accorded to the cultural group of which s/he is a part. Kymlicka also pointed out that the inequality arising from membership in a minority culture is not chosen, and needs to be redressed. To the query as to whether anti-discrimination laws can address the disadvantages or serious inequalities that cultural groups suffer, Kymlicka and other liberal theorists of multiculturalism pointed out that anti-discrimination laws fall short of treating minority groups as equals, and that states are not neutral with respect to culture. In culturally diverse societies, patterns of state support exist for some cultural groups over others. Furthermore, Kymlicka defended the issue of self-government rights to indigenous peoples and national minorities who have been coercively incorporated into the larger state, while immigrants were voluntary economic migrants who had given up their native cultures while migrating.

Some multiculturalists, writing from a post-colonial perspective, defend tribal sovereignty and argue that if diversity is to be taken seriously in liberal societies, one should recognise 'liberal' as one of many substantive outlooks. Parekh observed that liberal theory could not provide an impartial framework for governing relations between different cultural communities.

CRITICISMS OF MULTICULTURALISM

A major criticism of multiculturalism concerns the problematic view of culture and the individual's relationship to culture. It is pointed out that cultures are not distinct, self-contained wholes; most are the result of long interaction with one another through migration, imperialism, trade and globalisation. Most societies today are cosmopolitan, with cultures that are hybrid in nature.

Waldron (1993) questioned the existence of distinct cultures as most of us are cultural fragments, imbibing from a variety of ethno-cultural sources without feeling any sense of membership to, or dependence on, a particular culture. Defending the cosmopolitan alternative, he argued that most people in the modern world live 'in a kaleidoscope of culture', moving freely from one cultural tradition to another. Cultures can no longer remain monolithic in view of the globalisation of trade, the increase in human mobility, and the development of international institutions and communications. Any talk of pure culture is a misnomer, as that conveys its inability to adapt to changes in circumstances. Waldron (ibid.) also opposed the belief that an individual in modern society chooses from one particular culture, as most choose from a broad spectrum of cultural sources. A liberal conception of the self gives importance to individuals' ability to question and revise inherited ways of life, in contrast to the communitarian perspective that views people as embedded in particular cultures. Waldron rightly worried that this cultural interchange would be decisively hampered if the notion of protecting the 'authenticity' of minority cultures through minority rights was accepted. Glazer (1975) and Walzer (1992) pointed out that the expression and perpetuation of cultural identities should be left to the private sphere; Glazer observed that the response of the state ought to be one of 'salutary neglect' (1975: 25). Protection against discrimination and prejudice is provided to members of ethnic and national groups, who are free to maintain their identity and heritage, consistent with the rights of others but strictly in the private sphere. Kymlicka agreed that cultures are overlapping and interactive, but maintained that individuals belonged to distinct societal cultures and wished to preserve them. This was particularly true with regard to minority and indigenous cultures, which people wished to preserve despite the overall cosmopolitanism within society.

Another criticism alleges that it is individuals and not groups that have rights. Kukathas (1998) pointed out that there are no group rights and that the state, by granting special protection and rights to cultural groups, was overstepping its role. He insisted that states should not pursue 'cultural integration' or 'cultural engineering' vis-à-vis minority groups: rather, they should pursue a 'politics of indifference' as there are groups that do not themselves value toleration and freedom of association, including the right to dissociate from or exit a group. Such groups may practise internal discrimination, but the state would have very little authority to interfere in such associations. Kukathas was convinced that a benign approach would permit the abuse of vulnerable members of groups, tolerating 'communities which bring up children unschooled and illiterate; which enforce arranged marriages; which deny conventional medical care to their members (including children); and which inflict cruel and "unusual" punishment' (1998: 685).

Multiculturalism also faces the charge that extending protection to minority groups could mean reinforcing the oppression of vulnerable members of those groups—what some have called the problem of 'internal minorities' or 'minorities within minorities'. Multiculturalism focuses on inequality between groups in arguing for special protection for minority groups; however, it does not highlight inequalities within minority groups. Feminists like Okin (1991) and Shachar (2001) have highlighted the tension between multiculturalism and feminism. Extending special protection and accommodation to patriarchal cultural communities help to reinforce gender inequality within these communities. Examples include conflicts over polygamy and arranged marriages, the ban on headscarves in France, cultural defences in criminal law, accommodating religious law or customary law within the dominant legal system, and self-government rights for indigenous communities that deny equality to women in some respects.

Kymlicka (1995a, 1995b) addressed the concern about internal minorities by proposing a distinction between two kinds of group rights: 'external protections', namely the rights that a minority group claims against non-members in order to reduce its vulnerability vis-à-vis the economic and political power of the larger society, and 'internal restrictions', namely those rights that a minority group claims against its own members. He argued that a liberal theory of minority group rights could not accept the latter. There could be a democratic rather than a liberal response to the problem of internal minorities. A liberal response begins from the question of whether and how minority cultural practices should be tolerated or accommodated in accordance with liberal principles, whereas a democratic response, with its emphasis on deliberation, asks how the people affected understand and contest practice. By drawing on the voices of the affected parties and giving special weight to the voices of women at the centre of gendered cultural conflicts, deliberation can clarify the interests at stake and enhance the legitimacy of the response to cultural conflicts. Deliberation also provides minority group members with an opportunity to expose instances of cross-cultural hypocrisy, and consider whether and how the norms and institutions of the larger society, whose own struggles for gender equality are incomplete and ongoing, may reinforce rather than challenge sexist practices within minority groups.

Barry (2001) argued that multiculturalism is a fog that blots out recognition of class inequalities and human rights abuses. It is inconsistent with liberalism, disrespectful of liberal values and should be rejected. By replacing the idea of equal citizenship based on equal rights with culturally differentiated rights and modifying the doctrine of equal citizenship, multiculturalists remain insensitive to the abuse of power inevitable in such a policy. Barry considered uniform citizenship and individual autonomy as achievements of the Enlightenment. By criticising the Enlightenment and advocating culturally differentiated rights, these theorists overlook the gross irregularities and inequities that existed prior to the Enlightenment. Barry found an affinity between the anti-liberal rhetoric of the Right and the Left, as emphasis on special interests is part of an old policy of divide and rule, beneficial to those who gain from the status quo. It denies any unified struggle for the common demand of the disadvantaged. The shared disadvantages affecting all, like unemployment, poverty, low quality housing and inadequate public housing, can be tackled only from the point of view of the larger category of the disadvantaged. The particularity of group politics dissipates the political effort to mobilise people on the basis of a broad shared interest. Emphasis on cultural heterogeneity does not lead to the promotion of either liberty or equality. Such policies are the policies of retreat, as group differentiated politics is inimical to the pursuit of a programme of universal material benefit, to which all must have access. He insisted that the politics of multiculturalism undermined the politics of redistribution.

Barry believed that the conflict between culture and law was over-emphasised, as exemptions in the name of culture normally led to side-tracking or breaking the law, while denying individual rights within a group. He additionally regarded multiculturalism and group rights discourses as endangering the protection of individuals' religious rights, which have been hard won over the centuries, in today's liberal societies. Arguing within the framework provided by J. S. Mill, Barry wrote:

> The defining feature of a liberal is, I suggest, that it is someone who holds that there are certain rights against oppression, exploitation and injury to which every single human being is entitled to lay claim, and that appeals to cultural diversity and pluralism under no circumstances trump the value of basic human rights. For [the multiculturalists] a society is to be conceived as a fictitious body whose real constituents are communities (2001: 132–33, 300).

In contrast to 'Enlightenment liberalism' (which Barry defended), Galston (1995) propounded 'Reformation Liberalism', which takes into account diversity and underlines the importance of 'differences among individuals and groups over such matters as the nature of the good life, sources of moral authority, reason versus faith, and the like' (p. 521). Barry rejected Reformation Liberalism on three grounds: (*i*) Liberal theory was based on the primacy of respect for individuals, which included culture, provided the culture was not illiberal by itself and accorded equal respect to other cultures. (*ii*) On the question of liberalism's commitment to diversity as enhancing the range of choices, Barry argued that for liberals, individualism was more important than diversity. (*iii*) Regarding the question of the public-private divide and liberal commitment to non-intervention in the private sphere, Barry pointed out that throughout history, liberalism has challenged both parental and paternal authority, while protecting the individual from the group. On the question of every group having to conform to liberalism, Barry stated that individuals were free to join any group or association; however, such groups are to comply with the legal protection that exists for all those outside the group. Two important preconditions exist: all participants in the group are to be sane adults; and participation should be voluntary (Barry 2001: 148). Groups may then do as they please, provided that those who do not like the way the group functions are allowed to exit without facing undue costs (ibid.: 150). Barry (2001: 208) castigated multiculturalists for supporting national autonomy as

> they see it as a way of enabling nations within which illiberal values are politically dominant to pursue them in ways that violate the constraints imposed by any standard list of liberal rights, such as those embodied in the Universal Declaration of Human Rights, the US Constitution, the Canadian Charter of Rights and Freedoms or the European Convention on Human Rights.

Liberalism guarantees norms and institutional devices to ensure freedom from injustice and oppression, and 'these do not (contrary to a popular multiculturalist claim) prevent different societies from expressing their differences politically' (ibid.: 209). Barry stressed the need to subject minority cultural rights to democratic deliberation. 'If a cultural or a religious minority failed to gain a concession from the political process', it 'could not properly claim that it had suffered an injustice' (ibid.: 214).

Miller (2000) considered identity politics dangerous to the groups it is supposed to serve, as the identities of these groups are more open and fluid than recognised by the advocates of group identity. Identity politics emphasise separateness, creating a barrier for the politics of inclusion. The political mechanism of inclusion is important to reshape the public space as an expression of a shared national identity in a manner that is 'more hospitable to women, ethnic minorities and other groups without emptying them of content and destroying the underpinnings of democratic politics' (ibid.: 80). Miller mentioned J. S. Mill who, despite lending support to the independence movements in Poland, Hungary and Italy, appreciated the role that national identities played in supporting liberal institutions (2006: 534). In *Considerations on Representative Government* (1861), Mill argued that unless the several groups that compose a society have mutual sympathy and trust derived from a common nationality, it would be difficult to have free institutions. There would be no common interest to prevent government excesses and politics would become a zero-sum game, with each group hoping to profit from the exploitation of the others. In such a situation, rule of law usually becomes the first casualty. Miller cited the example of Mazzini, who argued passionately for Italian unity and independence while defending individual rights and a republican government. He observed that liberal thinkers had, by the mid-nineteenth century, 'forged links between individual freedom, national independence, and representative government in opposing the imperial powers of Europe' (ibid.: 534). Miller (1995, 2000, 2001) stated that nationality was important—as it is a precondition for the pursuit of social justice, which cannot be pursued globally (1995, 1999)—and that its recognition need not mean the suppression of other ethnicities or cultures. The pursuit of social justice requires a measure of social solidarity, which means that citizens need to go along with the institutions that perform a redistributive function.

MULTICULTURALISM AS POLICY

Many Western countries have adopted multiculturalism as an official national policy, starting with Canada in 1971, followed by Australia in 1973 and then the members of the European Union. In Australia, the 2006 census stated that more than one-fifth of the population was born overseas, and that almost 50 per cent of its people were either born overseas or had one or both parents born overseas. In Germany in 2013, more than 10 million people or just over 12 per cent of the population were born abroad; in Austria, that figure was 16 per cent; in Sweden, 15 per cent; and in France and the United Kingdom, approximately 12 per cent. Mass immigration has changed European societies, making them more diverse. Argentina does not mention the term multiculturalism, but its constitution explicitly promotes immigration and recognises an individual's multiple citizenship from other countries; as much as 97 per cent of its people are of European descent. In Canada, the policy of multiculturalism was adopted in 1971 and enshrined in its constitution in Section 27 of the Charter of Rights and Freedoms in 1982. The Federal Government in Canada publishes the voters' guide in 27 heritage and aboriginal languages, which include Arabic, Bengali, Chinese, Croatian, Greek and Somali. Jason Kenney, the Immigration Minister, asserted that Canada has done a better job than Europe of integrating immigrants into Canadian society, instead of merely celebrating cultural diversity.

The French policy is closer to America's melting pot. Its policy of cultural and linguistic assimilation led to the disappearance of many languages as the French Revolution attempted to end not only the monarchy, but also regional privileges which included the protection of regional languages and customs. Since the beginning of its history, France has absorbed many cultural groups who have become part of the French population and have followed the rule of French Universalism: the Romans, the Celts, the Franks, the Vikings; at the end of the nineteenth century, the Germans and Belgians; the Italians, Portuguese, Armenians after 1915, Poles between the two world wars, and the Spanish after the civil war. Roughly 25 per cent of its population is comprised of immigrants.

In the United States, multiculturalism is not an established policy; however, it is prominent in the school system with the rise of the ethnic studies programme in higher education. Grade school curricula have also become more inclusive by taking into consideration the contributions of non-whites. Initially, the term 'melting pot' was used to suggest the assimilation of different cultures.

In Britain, multiculturalism emerged in three phases: first, in the 1950s and 1960s with immigration from Commonwealth countries; second, from the 1980s, with the realisation that Britain's racial riots stemmed from the disadvantages faced by ethnic communities. Since then, a multiculturalism that celebrated cultural diversity was actively promoted. The third phase began in 2001 with a shift in government policy away from multiculturalism towards assimilation: the riots in the northern cities of Oldham, Burnley and Bradford; the Home Office commissioned Cantle report; media hysteria over asylum seekers (echoing the earlier New Right discourse of Britain being 'flooded'); and, of course, 9/11. The Cantle report summoned up the language of 'community cohesion' and concluded that Britain's 'race relations' problem was due to the barriers between different cultures and a lack of civic pride, the solution to which was to bring Britain's ethnic minorities into the fold of its national institutions.

POLITICAL BACKLASH AGAINST MULTICULTURALISM

Interestingly, multiculturalism faced its greatest challenge not at the philosophical, but at the political level. Former British Prime Minister David Cameron launched a fierce attack on what he called 'state multiculturalism', claiming that it undermined community relations and encouraged different communities to 'live separate lives, apart from each other and apart from mainstream', and by fostering differences, weakened British collective identity. The prime minister, while speaking at a debate hosted by the Equality and Human Rights Commission, criticised the Archbishop of Canterbury's apparent suggestion that sharia law be extended into the UK, claiming that 'state multiculturalism is leading to schoolgirls disappearing from school in Bradford and being forced into marriage', and called on Tories to promote integration. He considered multiculturalism a divisive concept that entrenched the right to difference instead of the right to equal treatment despite difference. In its place, he proposed muscular liberalism, which is not merely obedience to the law, and is one that is neutral between different values. A genuinely liberal country, according to Cameron, believes in 'certain values and actively promotes them'. He insisted that religious identity should no longer be a barrier to national identity. Nigel Farage, leader of the United Kingdom Independent Party (UKIP) and an MEP from Southeast England, alleged that multiculturalism, which he described as a 'tick box approach' to identity politics, had failed. He posited another idea called inter-culturalism; this claims that while identity might be fluid, Western societies should reject illiberal practices introduced by other cultures, such as female genital mutilation or the forced segregation of women from men.

This was not the first time that multiculturalism was criticised. Similar sentiments had been articulated in the past, too. In 2006, a year after the London bombings, Ruth Kelly, then Labour minister in charge of community politics, asked whether, in its anxiety to avoid imposing a single British identity on diverse communities, multiculturalism had encouraged 'separateness'. In December 2006, Tony Blair's speech (many elements of which were echoed in Cameron's speech) called for tighter controls on Muslim groups receiving public funds, an entry ban on foreign preachers with sulphurous views, a tougher line on forced marriages, and an expectation that all British citizens should support common values. Both Blair and his successor Gordon Brown stressed on the need for Britishness, with the latter even floating plans for an annual 'British Day'. In 2005, then shadow home secretary David Davis called on the government to scrap the 'outdated' policy allowing people of different cultures to settle without integrating, lest the 'perverted values of suicide bombers' take root. Davis endorsed Trevor Phillips, chairman of the Commission for Racial Equality, who in 2004 had considered multiculturalism as belonging to a different era and called for all citizens to 'assert a core of Britishness'.

German Chancellor Angela Merkel announced the failure of multiculturalism, stating that the attempt to build a multicultural society in Germany had 'utterly failed'. As people had failed to 'live side-by-side' happily, there was a need for immigrants to do more to integrate, including learning German. A recent survey also endorsed the anti-immigrant feeling as more than 30 per cent of the people believed that their country was being 'overrun by foreigners'. A study by the Friedrich Ebert Foundation showed that roughly the same number think that some 16 million of Germany's immigrants have come to the country for its social benefits. In a nuanced message, the Chancellor stressed that Germany needed immigrants for their skilled labour, but reiterated the need for immigrants to do more to integrate. Horst Seehofer, leader of the Christian Democratic Union's (CDU) Bavarian sister party, the Christian Social Union (CSU), declared the death of multiculturalism. Thilo Sarrazin, a senior official at Germany's central bank, added to the debate by stating that 'no immigrant group other than Muslims is so strongly connected with claims on the welfare state and crime'. Anti-immigration sentiments result from the high rate of unemployment, despite the economy growing fast.

The German political class accepts that there was a problem in the 1980s. With the birth rate of native-born Germans dipping and Muslim families expanding, multiculturalism was perceived as the solution. Ethnic communities were encouraged to coexist with Germans, although citizenship was still reserved for those who could demonstrate the presence of German blood in their family trees. Only with German citizenship could one become a civil servant. Germany's multiculturalism allowed immigrants entry into Germany, but without the rights and responsibilities of German citizenship. Immigrants could therefore lead their lives in Germany, while preserving their ties to their home countries. Unlike Britain and France, there were no race riots in Germany. The first and second-generation Turkish immigrants in Germany usually saved enough money for a house in eastern Anatolia, where they could spend their old age. But the third generation of Turks, who came of age in the 1980s and 1990s and only knew Germany as home, began demanding more from the state. When all they received in return were welfare payments, discontent rose both among immigrants and German citizens. Germans resented what they saw as a permanent dependent class; Turks pointed to the systemic discrimination and cultural exclusion.

Thilo Sarrazin, in his new book *Germany is Abolishing Itself* (2010), argued that the strong Turkish and Arab birth rates would lead to the dumbing down of Germany. His message struck a chord with a middle class fearful of declining educational standards and with unskilled workers nervous about lower-paid immigrant competition. The political class had mostly shied away from addressing these concerns; the subject has been taboo in Germany's largely conformist media. Former French President Nicolas Sarkozy echoed the sentiments of both Cameron and Merkel and declared the failure of multiculturalism as a policy, and insisted on the need for a French identity. Roger Scruton, in an article titled 'Multiculturalism, R.I.P.' (2010: 24), wrote:

> Our political class has at last recognized that this is a recipe for disaster, and that we can welcome immigrants only if we welcome them *into* our culture, and not beside and against it. But that means telling them to accept rules, customs, and procedures that may be alien to their old way of life. Is this an injustice? Surely not. If immigrants come it is because they gain by doing so.

The political backlash against multiculturalism has fuelled the success of far-right parties and populist politicians across Europe, from the Party for Freedom in the Netherlands to the National Front in France. And in the most extreme cases, it has inspired obscene acts of violence, such as Anders Behring Breivik's homicidal rampage on the Norwegian island of Utoya in July 2011. Critics of multiculturalism allege that Europe has allowed excessive immigration without integrating the immigrants, which has led to an erosion of social cohesion, undermined national identities and degraded public trust. Advocates of multiculturalism, on the other hand, state that this argument has nothing to do with diversity and much to do with racism. Moreover, while immigration was encouraged, very little was done to integrate immigrants into mainstream society. It was in the 1980s, according to Malik (2015), that the question of cultural difference became important. The reasons for this are manifold and complex: the collapse of the left, the weakening of labour organisations, decline of collectivist ideologies, expansion of the market into all corners of life, and the rise of identity politics. All of these have helped to create a more socially fragmented society.

Malik attributes the heightened sense of Muslim identity across Europe partly to international events such as the Iranian Revolution of 1979 and the Bosnian war of the early 1990s, and partly to European multicultural policies. He considers group identities a product of social interaction; with cultural categories receiving official sanction, certain identities came to seem fixed. By channelling financial resources and political power through ethnically-based organisations, governments provided a form of authenticity to certain ethnic identities while denying it to others. Multicultural policies are premised on the assumption that the true loyalty of minorities rests with their faith or ethnic community, instead of seeing them as citizens. This in itself was a fallacious approach as no single group or set of leaders can be said to represent an entire community. For instance, within the white European community there are liberals, conservatives, socialists, and so on; a white socialist will have greater affinity with an immigrant socialist than with a conservative.

CONCLUSION

The melting pot theory never denied the multiple identities of the present-day political community, but restricted them to the private sphere. Like the radical feminism of the 1960s which proclaimed that the 'personal is political', multicultural theorists grossly exaggerated the notions of cultural exclusivity and differentiation. Rorty (1994) warned of the dangers of cultural essentialism and pointed out that given the sanctity of individual rights, an overemphasis on culture can be both coercive and oppressive. A leaf can be taken from Sir Isaiah Berlin's life-long commitment to the idea of a Jewish nationalist homeland or Zionism and that of a Palestinian state within the broader liberal framework of his thought. While accepting that individual well-being demanded common cultural forms and individual identity and self-esteem required the respectful recognition of these cultural forms, he did not advocate special rights for minority cultures, nor insisted on the need for official recognition from the state, ranging from legal exemptions, to self-determination for minority cultures within its jurisdiction. He advocated integration and not assimilation; members of the group would maintain their distinct identity within the family and voluntary associations while accepting the same public rights and duties as other citizens. He subordinated cultural identity and diversity to two values: (*i*) freedom, understood as choice, which implied that people have a right to choose how to live, a right common to all human beings. Cultures also have to promote a diversity of goods. (*ii*) A successful liberal politics cannot flourish in chronic instability, like the Weimar Republic. It requires high levels of trust and cooperation, which is possible only if there exists a common cultural identity within society. Aggressive cultures that encourage divisiveness cannot sustain free institutions.

As Miller pointed out,

> by turning their backs on forms of identity, particularly national identities, that can bond citizens together in a single community, advocates of identity politics would destroy the conditions under which disparate groups in a culturally plural society can work together to achieve social justice for all groups. Minority groups are likely to have little bargaining power, so they must rely on appeals to the majority's sense of justice and fairness, and these will be effective only to the extent that majority and minorities sympathise and identify with each other (2000: 4–5).

Multiculturalism prevents the forging of a common public space that sustains democratic life. It questions the idea of the shared moral values that exist among human beings, despite their cultural differences. Culture, as an important source of legitimacy and political power, is fundamental. For authority to be effective, it has to be rooted in people's experiences and identity. Only then will it win the loyalty of its people. However, power aims at unity while culture is diverse. By emphasising cultural diversity and overlooking the promoting of cultural consensus, multicultural politics is divisive. While banning the full face veil, the European Court of Human Rights (ECHR) in its ruling in 2014 asserted that the 2010 French ban did not violate religious freedom and aimed to ensure respect for the minimum set of values of social interaction in an open democratic society. A full face veil, by concealing identity, goes against the grain of social connectivity and social interaction, as a veiled person can see everyone else but remains unseen, unknown and unidentifiable, and therefore unequal. However, more recently, on 26 August 2016, the anti-burkini decrees were viewed by France's state council, the supreme administrative authority, founded by Napoleon in 1799, as a 'serious and manifestly illegal attack on fundamental freedoms', including the right to move around in public and the freedom of conscience. The state council has ruled that the mayor of Villeneuve-Loubet did not have the right to ban burkinis. The judges stated that individual liberties can be restricted only if there were a 'proven risk' to public order. The French right, led by former president Nicolas Sarkozy, has called for a nation-wide ban on burkinis and three majors have refused to withdraw the bans.

Stressing any one identity to the exclusion of others makes it meaningless as modern societies accept the multiple identities of persons. Here, though, no one identity is decisive and different identities—gender, class, language, religion, region, ethnicity, culture, colour and race—coalesce in a person. It is this spirit of unity in diversity, of the possibilities of various identities coexisting in a person, that multiculturalism overlooks. Cultural exclusivity and differentiation can, beyond a point, be both oppressive and coercive. Within groups, some practices could be discriminatory and oppressive. What is the possibility of redress of grievances available to the individual in such situations? What is the basis of their assumption that the group will protect and advance the rights of its individual members more than the constitutional state? Multiculturalists do not offer satisfactory answers to these important questions.

The guarantee and protection of individual rights, which form the basis of a liberal state, is still an important component of modern democracy. On the other hand, multiculturalism, with its emphasis on cultural exclusivity, tries to bring in marginalised and neglected groups and redesigns the political space by accepting greater fragmentation and then its incorporation. However, in doing so, not only are economic disadvantages relegated to secondary importance, but the attempt to stress and highlight difference also results in a fragmentation of identities, thereby undermining the benefits guaranteed by uniform citizenship based on one person one vote and equal rights for all.

Multiculturalism alleges that democratic procedures in the West are not neutral, but are biased in favour of white, middle-class males and against women and disadvantaged minorities. It maintains that the interests of these groups are best served not through the existing forms of rational deliberation, but by adopting new forms of political communication—greeting, rhetoric and storytelling. That their call encouraging the use of native tongues rather than the official language is fraught with dangers is apparent from the following incident. Sir William Jones, Judge of the Supreme Court of Calcutta from 1783–94, felt the need for a knowledge of Persian and other Indian languages as he realised that court orders translated from Indian languages were often wrong, leading to a denial of justice. While many view English as the common lingua franca in colonial and independent India as privileging the elite, what is overlooked is the continued discrimination and unfairness faced by those well-versed only in their mother tongues. A common language is necessary for justice and to ensure minimal mischief, apart from the fact that such knowledge would help in career advancement, creating a climate of mutual respect that exclusivity denies, and allowing for a greater flowering of talent (as recent Indian writing in English proves).

The resilience of the liberal framework of one person one vote is the pivot of contemporary mass plural democracies, and the notion of the public-private divide allows its proper functioning, securing the foundation of a liberal society.

19

WOMEN AND THE POLITICAL PROCESS

They (Political parties) have tended to see women voters and citizens as appendages of males and have depended on the heads of families to provide block-votes and support for their parties and candidates

Towards Equality 1974: 301

To include women's concerns, to represent women in the public life of our society, might well lead to profound redefinition of the nature of public life itself.

Diamond and Hartsock, cited in Stokes 2005: 1

While the demand for more women in politics has rested primarily on arguments for justice, of women's interests that men cannot safeguard or on a wish to include women's experiences on the political agenda, gender balance in political decision-making is increasingly seen as a pre-requisite for democracy itself

Dahlerup 2009: 16

Liberal democracies, at the beginning of the twentieth century, have become mass democracies after the working class and women secured the right to vote following decades of struggle. Initially, only educated and propertied men had the right to vote; the working class was gradually enfranchised later. Women's suffrage took a longer time to actualise.[1] However, the mere enfranchisement of women, the working class and young adults has not ensured their adequate representation in local or national legislative bodies in many democracies. The attainment of universal adult franchise has led to a greater concern to ensure the proper representation of all segments of society within legislatures. At present, with the exception of Scandinavian countries and Rwanda, women find token representation in the political sphere, and the public domain, although not exclusively a male preserve, is mostly dominated by men. This is because of a continuing traditional, patriarchal notion that views politics as a patron-client relationship, paralleling the father-son relationship. As a result, men are seen as the legal heirs, and it is only in their absence that women are allowed in politics. The maleness of politics also proves that political culture remains essentially patriarchal, gendered and subject non-participatory, irrespective of the great strides made by women in all other walks of life. Gender inequities in the political power structure are symptomatic of the overall bias that women suffer in society.

ORIGINS AND CONTEXT OF FEMINISM

The intellectual and social ferment of the eighteenth century gave rise to feminism, which promised to liberate women from oppression, domination and exploitation. It stands for 'equal rights for women, based on the theory of equality of sexes' (Evans 1977: 39). Like liberalism, the women's question, or quarrel, as it is often called, is a distinctly modern concept, originating in the Enlightenment and the French Revolution. Hubertine Auclert, founder of the first Woman Suffrage Society in France, first used the word in the 1880s in France. The term was then imported into English. The Oxford Dictionary included the term for the first time in 1895.

Feminism developed in three distinct waves: the first wave comprised of Liberal and Socialist/Marxist feminism[2] (late eighteenth century to the 1920s); the second wave was that of Radical Feminism (1960–80);[3] and the third wave was of post-modernist feminism (1980 onwards).[4] Liberal and Socialist/Marxist feminism subscribed to their parent philosophies, applying the assumptions of those doctrines to the women's question. For the most part, feminism developed alongside the notion of democracy. Historically, democracy based on individual rights took shape with the establishment of the liberal state, which emerged from the throes of absolutism in the late seventeenth century. The declaration of a bill of rights drew up a new relationship between the state and the individual. Initially, the formulation of individual rights was defended with reference to reason and property. The central issue was not the rights of everyone, but only those of propertied male individuals, making franchise and participation oligarchic and patriarchal, rather than democratic. In Britain, only 6 per cent of men had the right to vote prior to the 1812 Reform Act, highlighting the anomalous gulf between democratic theory and practice.[5]

The demand for equal political status for women was part of a larger democratisation process that began in the early eighteenth century by re-examining the theories of citizenship and natural rights. It asked: If individuals were equal, rational and sovereign, then why were women excluded? Embedded in the natural rights theory was a duality. While accepting the principles of reason, equality and freedom, it restricted them to men, dismissing women as the 'other' and thereby denying them legal and public existence with no rights to property, inheritance, custody and civil suit. The silence on the part of natural rights theorists on the status, role and position of women gave rise to feminism, in the same way that the failure of liberalism to fulfill its own promise had given rise to early socialism.

REPRESENTATION AND ITS DIFFERENT PERSPECTIVES

Proper representation is the life breath of a true and vibrant democracy. Unless all segments of a society are represented, no democratic system can be stable or legitimate. It is generally believed that through one person one vote, diverse groups within society would be integrated into a shared identity. However, in even advanced democracies like the United States, some groups like the African-Americans, Native Americans, ethnic and religious minorities, and women feel excluded, unrepresented or underrepresented. As a remedy, cultural pluralists stressed the need for the political system to mirror the distinct cultural identities of different people. Marion-Young (1989) observed that members of marginalised groups could be integrated into the political community not only as individuals, but also through the group, that is, their rights would depend in part on their group membership, setting aside the convention of treating people as individuals with equal rights under law. Her concern was with devising ways in which individuals with special needs or interests could attain representation.

Marion-Young (1990: 187) demanded the 'specific representation only of oppressed disadvantaged groups'. Williams (1998: 221–33) proposed measures such as proportional representation, reserving seats in legislative bodies for members of underrepresented marginalised groups, redrawing electoral boundaries when underrepresented groups were concentrated in geographically determined ridings, or providing for multimember districts when appropriate and quotas for underrepresented groups in the candidate lists of political parties. Phillips (1995: Ch. 3) put forward an essentialist assumption of what she called 'the politics of presence', namely representation for the underrepresented (she gave the example of women) by reserving seats in government bodies for people from marginalised groups, or through 'the politics of ideas', which ensures that at least some political party platforms feature marginalised group interests. The second is complementary to the first, as that will ensure the representation of unrepresented segments in government. However, it is possible that representatives would not pursue the specific interests of the groups they represent. While party discipline may lead to some accountability, even proportional representation may not lead to electoral success. One solution is to include a group list in the list of political party candidates, thereby ensuring the representation of marginalised groups. However, one problem remains—group representation that pursues particularistic interests will impede the idea of the common good, with privileged groups influencing particular perspectives. The idea is to channelise and systematise the voices of erstwhile marginalised and unrepresented groups into the decision-making process, within the general framework of the common good.

WHY WOMEN'S REPRESENTATION?

Since the overall statistics on women in politics and decision-making worldwide, even in well-established democracies, continue to tell their bleak tale of underrepresentation and democratic deficit, this has been perceived since the 1970s as a problem that needs redress. Interest has been increasing worldwide on the question of women's representation in national legislatures. It was accentuated after the collapse of communism and authoritarian regimes in the late 1990s, followed by a resurgence of democracy. Increasing attention was paid to the constraints that hold women back from greater political power. Although the number of women has increased in the rank and file of political parties, unions and the civil service, they still account for only a small proportion of the higher echelons that provide a launching pad for higher political office. The problem revolves around two related issues: insignificant women's representation, and the impact of this denial in liberal democracies, especially when women were visibly present in greater numbers in the decision-making processes of erstwhile socialist countries.[7]

The first point was more serious and was linked to the issues of 'democratic justice' and 'symbolic equity'. It maintained that women's underrepresentation reflects the existing unequal sexual division of labour. Reversing the conventional argument, it asked: What is it that makes men so 'naturally' superior in talent or experience that they claim the right to monopolise legislatures? With this question, feminists drew attention to the fact that their position depended on structures of discrimination. If women did indeed form a marginalised group, their claim was placed within a broader claim—legislatures can function democratically only if they act as a public forum, reflecting all points of view. The second point concerned the legitimacy of the wider political system. Women's exclusion might undermine democratic legitimacy and public confidence in the system. To achieve these objectives, a special electoral mechanism would have to be devised, which would guarantee the legitimacy of the wider political system. With sufficient women decision-makers and representatives, public policy would be substantively different. This presumes that women have their own identifiable interests and distinctive values, and their inclusion certainly affects the actions of their representatives.

However, there is a problem with this argument—while there are identifiable women's interests and needs, issues like childcare and domestic violence could potentially exclude single women and perhaps those married women who do not desire children. Therefore, although women's issues apparently look homogenous and universal, substantive differences exist in dealing with particular issues. Moreover, elections are organised on the basis of geographical constituencies; while these might sometimes have a concentration of particular ethnic or religious groups, there are no all-women constituencies. Another way to argue a case for gender parity is by contending that the inclusion of women would challenge the existing dominant interest groups and infuse a new set of values and concerns (Phillips 1995). This contention is diluted in cases where women representatives come from the same political families as the men; it is often seen that a political family uses its women to reserve seats till a suitable male candidate is found. In view of such complexities, it would be worthwhile to consider men and women as complimentary and argue for women's representation on the basis of gender justice and gender equality. With women constituting half of society, it is fair that their representation should also be commensurate to their numbers. Anything short of this violates the principles of equality of opportunity and equality before the law. Critics of differentiated citizenship and the politics of group identity, like Miller and Barry, have warned against fragmentation and its consequences (see Chapter 18).

While gender is an important social division, it cannot be the only basis of the mass political identities that structure political debates and help in the establishment of political parties. The universality of this category makes it less cohesive and hinders collective identification and mobilisation. Besides gender, a person has multiple identities that include social class, ethnicity, religion, language and region (Smith 1971, 1991). These multiple roles prevent the perpetuation of any single identity as decisive; nonetheless, these need to be represented if the legislatures and other decision-making bodies are to act as public forums. The gender question has to be discussed and accommodated within this multiplicity of identities, as there is also a growing realisation that gender is a universal category. The fact is that gender does not exist in a vacuum. It survives and develops within a larger social and economic context, and the larger questions ultimately determine the status, expectation, and retardation or fulfillment of that particular segment. This calls for a delicate balancing between the different sectors of life and activity. A democratic solution to a problem means greater democracy in a social, economic and political sense, along with a commitment to equality.

The workings of a complex and diverse global economy based on sophisticated technology have fractured the single agency of mega categories (which includes women) into a multiplicity of diverse groups. With women increasingly occupying elite economic, political, administrative and scientific positions, the idea of male-centricism in these areas of human endeavour has been rendered obsolete. Furthermore, there is a realisation that meta-theories (patriarchy), group identities ('all women' versus 'all men'), and visions (women's liberation) or grand narratives (feminism) are no longer feasible or sustainable. This is true not only of feminism, but also of any other mega theory like Marxism, which claims to be universally applicable without being specific to any particular situation. The survival of feminism, like Marxism, in this period of universalisation of democracy depends on its capacity to offer something positive to all categories of women, while taking into consideration specific requirements like class, level of development and societal expectation. Accepting the notion of multiple identities, there is a need to meaningfully integrate women's issues with other concerns like environmental protection, human rights, safety nets and basic economic rights within a larger democratic structure.

QUOTA LAW, GENDER AND POLITICS WORLDWIDE

Women secured elementary civil, political, social and economic rights only after a long and protracted struggle in the nineteenth century, generally called the Suffragists. New Zealand was the first country to grant women the right to vote in 1893. In most societies and cultures, women do not enjoy equal status with men, whether in respect to political power, opportunity or influence. The political representation of women in national legislatures and positions of decision-making is uneven. The figure of 30 per cent is widely accepted as the benchmark to ensure a critical mass of women parliamentarians. Forty-five countries out of 190 that have sent data about their national parliaments to the Inter Parliamentary Union have, as of 1 December 2015, crossed this threshold. Only 22 per cent of national parliamentarians are women, a slow increase from 11.3 per cent in 1995. The Nordic countries have the highest percentage of women parliamentarians (41.1 per cent), followed by the Americas (27 per cent); Europe, excluding the Nordic countries, has 25.5 per cent; Sub-Saharan Africa, 23.3 per cent; Asia, 19.3 per cent; Middle East and North Africa, 19.1 per cent; and the Pacific, 13.4 per cent. Rwanda tops the list with 63.8 per cent.

Since 1974, women's groups from all over the world have advocated the need for a quota for empowerment. Till then, they had opposed quotas as they feared proxy representation, rather than the actual representation of women. This situation changed in the 1970s and 1980s when newly formed political parties compelled the traditional ones to adopt a 'woman-friendly' posture. The promise by the Greens in Germany to provide equal representation of women at all levels in the party generated public and visible political dividends. As a result, the German Social Democratic Party (SPD) made a similar commitment, even though it had had full-fledged women's wings since the 1880s. The spectacular results that quotas brought about for Scandinavian women, increasing their representation to well over 30 per cent, encouraged many other countries to follow suit. Quota laws were adopted in Argentina, Brazil, Mexico, Taiwan and Chile. Since the 1990s, the pace of quota adoption has increased, with national-level quotas spread throughout Latin America and, after 1995, in many African countries (Ballington 2004). Australia, Bosnia and Herzegovina, Burkina Faso, Iraq, Niger and Tanzania adopted national-level quotas. By the end of 2005, more than 100 countries had adopted some kind of gender quota. Quotas have proved a powerful predictor of women's representation across 149 countries (Tripp and Kang 2008).

Similar initiatives could be seen in even the long established liberal democracies like the United States and Great Britain. Former US President Bill Clinton, during his two-term presidency, surpassed previous presidents[8] by appointing 592 women to various positions, including even top positions. Ronald Reagan had appointed 277 women, while George Bush Sr.'s was a meagre 181. Not only did Clinton give women access to the corridors of real power, but he also took up issues[9] that were of special concern to them, namely education, health, childrearing, law and order, and equal opportunities and equal pay at work. The crucial fact was not just the increase in the number of women members in the cabinet, but the specific positions that they enjoyed. Thomas Cronin differentiated between the 'inner' and the 'outer' cabinet. The inner cabinet includes the secretaries of state, defence and treasury, and the attorney general, who serve as counsellors to the president. The outer cabinet includes soft departments like housing, commerce and welfare, and their role is one of advocacy rather than counselling. Of the 15 women cabinet members, 13 have been in the outer cabinet. As mentioned earlier, the Clinton cabinet, with 21 per cent women in the first term and 31 per cent in the second term, had the highest number of women. In George Bush Jr.'s cabinet, there were two and three women in the first and second term, respectively, with one holding the important position of Secretary of State in the second term. President Obama has nine women in cabinet-level positions, the highest so far. Zweigenhaft and Domoff (1998), in their study of the power elite in the US in the 1990s (a notion formulated by C. Wright Mills in 1956), took note of this fact and concluded that the power elite had become gender-sensitive and multicultural. It was no longer the all-male enclave of the 1950s.

In Britain, Tony Blair closed the gender gap in voting[10]—the difference between the number of men and the number of women voting for the Labour Party—in the 1997 elections to 2 per cent. In 1992, by introducing all-women shortlists in a percentage of key marginal seats and in Labour seats where Members of Parliament were retiring, the Party increased the number of women Members of Parliament from 21 to 37, that is, by 13.6 per cent. In 1997, this number increased to 45, by 23 per cent. Blair announced initiatives that concerned women, namely health and education. He also stressed on the need to lift children out of poverty, provide financial support to new mothers, and help them rejoin the workforce. Gordon Brown's first cabinet in June 2007 had five women and a further four with the right to attend. The number of women in his final cabinet was down to four in his June 2009 reshuffle. The Conservative Party under the leadership of William Hague had also espoused these concerns. The Cameron cabinets of 2010 and 2015 had four and nine women in cabinet, respectively. Theresa May is the second woman to be Prime Minister of Britain, Margaret Thatcher being the first. May has six women in her government. The Home Secretary is a woman. May herself was the Home Secretary in Cameron's second-term cabinet. According to UK's The Centre for Women and Democracy, Britain lags behind the other Western democracies in terms of women in cabinet. While women in Cameron's cabinet is less than 20 per cent, in Spain women make up 53 per cent, in Sweden 50 per cent, in Germany 33 per cent, in France 33 per cent, and in the USA, 31 per cent. May has not addressed the issue of gender imbalance in Britain. In July 2016, there were 16 women in office either as Presidents (nine) or Prime Ministers (seven). Gender balance in decision-making is one of the goals of the European Union. The road map for 2006–10 adopted by the EU aimed to promote equal representation for men and women as one of six priority areas for action.

DIFFERENT TYPES OF QUOTA LAWS

The International Institute for Democracy and Electoral Assistance (IDEA) in Stockholm, Sweden, one of the main sources of data and research on gender quotas, classified quotas based on the type of document, law or rule that requires the quota to be met. There are constitutional quotas; electoral law quotas; and political party quotas. Electoral law quotas are legislated by parliaments and are not enshrined in constitutions. Argentina was the first country to adopt an electoral law quota in 1990, called the *Ley de Cupos* or 'Law of Quotas' (Bonder and Nari 1995; Gray 2003; Jones 1996). Political party quota is a set of rules or targets mandating that a certain percentage of party candidates must be women. These rules are enforced by the party leadership.

According to the IDEA (2014), 118 countries use some type of gender quotas for an elected office. Afghanistan, Algeria, Bangladesh, Burundi, China, Djibouti, Eritrea, Guinea, Haiti, India, Iraq, Jordan, Kenya, Kosovo, Lesotho, Libya, Mauritania, Morocco, Niger, Pakistan, Palestine, The Philippines, Rwanda, Samoa, Saudi Arabia, Sierra Leone, Somalia, South Sudan, Sudan, Swaziland, Taiwan, Tanzania, Timor Leste, Uganda, Vanatu and Zimbabwe are countries with reserved seats in the lower or upper houses of parliament, or at sub-national levels. Algeria, Angola, Argentina, Armenia, Belgium, Bolivia, Bosnia and Herzegovina, Brazil, Burkina Faso, Cabo Verde, Colombia, Costa Rica, Democratic Republic of Congo, Dominican Republic, Ecuador, El Salvador, France, Greece, Guinea, Guyana, Honduras, Indonesia, Iraq, Ireland, Italy, FYR of Macedonia, Kenya, Kosovo, Kyrgyzstan, Lesotho, Libya, Mauritania, Mauritius, Mongolia, Montenegro, Mexico, Namibia, Nepal, Nicaragua, Palestine, Panama, Paraguay, Poland, Portugal, Republic of Congo, Republic of Korea, Rwanda, Senegal, Serbia, Slovenia, Spain, South Africa, Timor Leste, Togo, Tunisia, Uruguay, Uzbekistan and Zimbabwe have legislated candidate quotas in the lower or upper house of parliament, or at sub-national levels. Austria, Australia, Botswana, Cameroon, Canada, Chile, Côte d'Ivoire, Croatia, Cyprus, Czech Republic, Equatorial Guinea, Estonia, Germany, Guatemala, Hungary, Iceland, Italy, Israel, Malawi, Mali, Mozambique, Namibia, Lithuania, Luxemburg, Malta, The Netherlands, Norway, Philippines, Romania, Switzerland, Slovakia, South Africa, Sweden, Thailand, Turkey, and the United Kingdom have voluntary gender quotas for the lower or upper house of the parliament, or at sub-national levels.

WOMEN'S REPRESENTATION IN INDIA

Post-independent India adopted a democratic system of government patterned on the British parliamentary system and based on universal adult franchise. Besides equal rights of citizenship, Indian women secured equal educational opportunities, equal rights to property and inheritance, and equal pay for equal work. In fact, one of the most defining aspects of modern India has been the position of women—educated, articulate and active in professional and public life—as opposed to their situation in the mid-nineteenth century, when they were uneducated, subjugated and secluded (Forbes 1996). Mydral took note of the relatively impressive strides that Indian women had made in *Asian Drama* (1968)—at that time, women's representation in parliament was 6.7 per cent, as compared to 2 per cent in the US Congress (1962) and 5 per cent in the British House of Commons (1965). The highest number of women in the Indian parliament has been in the current

Lok Sabha (2014–), with 61 members. The lowest tally was in 1977, when only 19 women candidates won. Being a practising democracy is one of India's major achievements. However, one must not be oblivious to the incompleteness of this democratic enterprise, as India is ranked a mere 109 among 190 countries and is at 12.1 per cent in terms of the percentage of women legislators. Pakistan is ahead of India at the 68th position with 20.6 per cent, and Bangladesh is at the 72nd position with 20 per cent. Nepal tops the list in South Asia at the 39th position, with 29.5 per cent. Comparatively, in India, women constitute 22.2 per cent of central ministers and India is placed at the 37th position. Female literacy is a mere 65.46 per cent according to the 2011 census, compared to 82.14 per cent for males.

Why Women's Reservation?

In 1971, the government appointed a committee on the Status of Women to dissect and report on the status and position of women. The report of the committee, titled *Towards Equality* (1974), concluded that women's impact on politics was marginal, despite their being numerically the single largest minority. The committee proposed that each political party set a quota for women candidates as a remedial measure. As a transitional measure, it recommended a constitutional amendment aimed at reserving seats for women in municipal councils and panchayats, which was done through the 73rd and 74th amendments[11] in 1992. However, at the national level, the Women's Reservation Bill continues to be mired in controversy and inaction.[12]

In view of the serious opposition to the bill, in 1999 then Chief Election Commissioner Gill and some Members of Parliament suggested that instead of amending the constitution to reserve 33 per cent of seats for women by rotation, the same could be achieved by a simple change in the Representation of People's Act. Party-wise representation is the method by which most political parties globally have ensured greater representation of women in their national legislatures. However, in India, no political party—including those who favour tabling the Women's Reservation Bill in Parliament—has initiated steps in this direction, in spite of their commitment to women's reservation. As early as 1989, both the Congress and the Janata Dal decided in their election manifestos to set aside 30 per cent of nominations for women in their respective party organisations; however, they have not implemented it yet. Even political parties headed by women, like the Congress and the AIADMK, despite their public posturing, have done little on this issue. The Left parties, the first to promise gender equality in 1967, have done precious little about it. From 1984 onwards, the CPI and CPM have fielded less than 10 women candidates in the general elections. Except for the Samajwadi Party and Rashtriya Janata Dal, every other political party claims to be publicly committed to women's reservation; and yet, most politicians have tried to stall the proposal by any means.

Arguments against the Bill

Opponents of the bill argue that women lack knowledge of politics since the greater part of their adult lives is spent taking care of family and home. The domestic domain is still perceived as a woman's primary responsibility. Second, male politicians believe that women have a lower chance of winning elections. Third, they demand a 'quota within quota' for dalit and minority women.

The first argument is not new. It has been articulated ever since women, the world over, first demanded the right to vote in the early nineteenth century. Since then, women have come a long way and are found in large numbers in the workforce; in some countries like Denmark, Norway, Rwanda, South Africa and Sweden, they constitute more than 40 per cent in legislatures and other decision-making bodies. This proves that with sufficient societal and family support, a woman can manage both the home and public office. Although near equality with men is still far away, even in the West, women's lives have undergone a real change, made possible by better hygiene, medicine, contraception, the emergence of a service economy and (lately) electronics, Enlightenment, education and employment, and of course, feminist theory and action. In India, during the

Gandhian phase of the nationalist struggle, women emerged in large numbers and participated actively. Gandhiji emphasised the need for society to recognise women's equality, dignity and rights, and perceive them as equal partners and participants alongside their husbands and families. The vision and goals that Gandhiji placed before women had their roots in the initiatives taken by Rammohun Roy (1772–1833), Bankim Chandra Chattopadhyay (1838–94), Ishwar Chandra Vidyasagar (1820–91), Swami Dayananda Saraswati (1824–83) and Swami Vivekananda (1863–1902).

The reasons for the conspicuous absence of women in national legislatures are complex, ranging from socialisation, customs, culture, division of labour within the home, to bias and stereotyping. Girls are socialised, both formally and informally, to consider themselves different and separate from boys. Psychologists and sociologists have proved that social forces, rather than anatomy, shape gender; however, girls continue to grow up believing that domestic responsibilities are their primary goal. There is a belief that more women in legislature will lead to changes that will help women to combine their homes with careers in politics. Such women legislators will serve as role models for other young aspirants; often, what keeps women away from successful political careers is the lack of role models on whom to base their lives.

Women candidates face greater problems with credibility for it is assumed (as it is in some professions like medicine and engineering) that men make better political leaders than women. The credibility problem has three aspects: competence, electability and toughness. Men are presumed to be competent while women have to establish their competence. To a large extent, women also internalise this message. Women have to prove themselves capable of raising money and running successful campaigns. The question of electability is circular for women have to prove their capacity to raise money, yet cannot demonstrate that capacity until the money is raised. Women also have a hard time proving they are tough without being labelled an 'iron lady', or as strident. A section of the Indian media had described Indira Gandhi as the only man in the Cabinet, further reinforcing the stereotyped image of women. Usually, women establish their toughness through overcoming personal tragedies; this further reinforces the stereotyped image of women as compassionate and soft. Moreover, women politicians have to convince the general public that their political careers are not leading them to neglect their homes and children, which is still perceived as women's primary duty. Since most women embark on their political careers after their children have grown up, they lose out to men on this score too. Furthermore, more women in politics would mean greater debate and discussion on social issues that are of direct concern to women. They will articulate the woman's perspective on decision-making processes and policies. Men will also become familiar with and sympathetic to the work and responsibilities that women shoulder as mothers, wives and homemakers. Gender parity in legislatures will eventually create a society committed

Table 19.1: Representation of Women in Lok Sabha 1952–2014

Lok Sabha	*Total no. of Seats (Elections Held)*	*No. of Women Members who won*	*% of the Total*
First (1952)	489	22	4.4
Second (1957)	494	27	5.4
Third (1962)	494	34	6.7
Fourth (1967)	523	31	5.9
Fifth (1971)	521	22	4.2
Sixth (1977)	544	19	3.4
Seventh (1980)	544	28	5.1
Eighth (1984)	544	44	8.1
Ninth (1989)	529	28	5.3
Tenth (1991)	509	36	7.0
Eleventh (1996)	541	40*	7.4
Twelfth (1998)	545	44*	8.0
Thirteenth (1999)	543	48*	8.8
Fourteenth (2004)	543	45*	8.1
Fifteenth (2009)	543	59	10.9
Sixteenth (2014)	543	61	11.2

Note: * Including one nominated member.
Source: Election Commission of India.

to gender equality and justice. As part of the larger democratisation of society, it will also enhance the presence of more competent people in the political arena.

The refrain that women have a lower chance of winning elections is not substantiated by facts. An analysis of the success rate of women candidates as compared to men reveals that it has actually been higher in the last three general elections. In 2014, the success rate of women was 9.4 per cent, compared to 6 per cent for men.

The demand for quotas within quotas has been well taken. Unless the poor, the minorities and the underrepresented are represented—and only with the realisation of social and economic rights for the disadvantaged, which would automatically include the poor and the marginalised—can women's representation be meaningful. Otherwise, it would remain a middle-class conclave. This is endorsed by the fact that at present, the most well-known women politicians have inherited political offices in post-independent India because of their family connections, and in the absence of a comparable male figure. With some notable exceptions like Mamata Banerjee (chief minister of West Bengal) and Mayawati (leader of the Samajwadi Party), most women politicians hail from privileged backgrounds and enjoy power by virtue of birth or marriage. They have entered politics only to perpetuate and enjoy the privileges that public office confers. There have been exceptions like Maniben Patel, Mrinal Gore, Margatham Chandrasekhar, Phulreny Guha, Rebuka Ray, Sucheta Kriplani, and Tarakeshwari Sinha; however, their impact has been limited. As a result, women legislators have neglected issues concerning women and have failed to pass any significant legislation that would ensure the well-being of women. This is also because of the absence of an independent women's movement with clear objectives and goals, which uses the political arena to advance their cause. Most existing women's movements are restricted to the urban middle class and, like the Left movement, have failed to transcend the privileged sectional basis of Indian politics.

If genuine representation is indeed the intention, then it should start from the grassroots and provide equal opportunities to all. Competence, capability and merit rather than family connections must be given weightage. However, in a political culture that continues to be oligarchic, patriarchal and subject non-participatory, most women politicians see themselves as temporary, filling in till a male relative is ready to assume political power. This situation can be remedied if the more meritorious from ordinary backgrounds are given an opportunity. An important reason for supporting substantive reservation for women in India is the fact that political recruitment and selection for the higher echelons are done more through contacts than by merit. Political parties have perpetuated the oligarchic and paternalistic nature of the democratic process. In general, they have fielded women who are somebody's wives, daughters, or relatives.

It is rather ironic that India and her neighbours—Sri Lanka, Pakistan and Bangladesh—enjoy the unique distinction of having the maximum number of women heads of government. Significantly, these women have occupied top political offices as a result of an inheritance from their fathers or husbands. All hailed from political families, which allowed their women to assume power only in the absence of a male member, with a view to perpetuate and enjoy the privileges of public office. Even women prime ministers have favoured their sons while deciding their natural successors. Indira Gandhi, who held office twice for a total of 17 long years, did not take kindly to the political aspirations of her daughter-in-law, and preferred her sons to carry forward her dynastic ambitions. Besides, she did not believe that having more women parliamentarians would further the cause of women politically. Like her father, she felt that both men and women would have to proceed together to make the principle of equality enshrined in the Constitution a reality. Surprisingly, Indira Gandhi also spoke frequently of women's primary duties as being that of a mother, a wife and homemaker. She even remarked in 1979 that her greatest fulfillment came from motherhood.

Proposal for Double-member Constituencies

Given the impasse vis-à-vis the women's reservation bill, there is a proposal to raise the present strength of the Lok Sabha by one-third and reserve it for women through double-member constituencies. This, however, appears to be an easy solution, arrived at without much reflection on a long-pending issue. In August 2003, about 11 women's organisations wrote a letter, released to the press by Brinda Karat, general secretary of the All India Democratic Women's Association, labelling the proposal an insult to women and tantamount to 'rank discrimination against women'.

Opposition to the proposal was on the following grounds. The 180 seats reserved for women would be converted into double-member constituencies; this effectively means that a woman representative would be a part representative of her constituency, co-sharing her responsibilities with a male representative, while the other unreserved seats would be single-member seats. If the 180 seats are made double-member, the number of men will increase, while that of women will only be at 25 per cent, contrary to the promise of 33 per cent under the present bill. The idea of converting 180 seats into double-member constituencies goes against the principles of human and gender equality. It gives the idea that women are incapable and incompetent, unable to care for their constituencies on their own, and that is clearly an affront to the intelligence and capacity of women at large, thereby reinforcing the traditional stereotype of women.

Reservation: Party-wise or State-sponsored?

As agents of change, political parties ought to become gender-sensitive. Even after women gained franchise, their position within the parties changed marginally. In the early stages of democratisation, political parties were interested mainly in enlisting men as members and activists. Alan Ware (1996: 80) attributed this to three related reasons. First, most party organisations perceive the family as the key determining influence on a person's vote. As a result, they tend to rely on men to garner support for the party among women. This effort is often supplemented by establishing separate women's sections, although these are peripheral to the power structure of the party and do not function as a medium for women to attain positions of political influence. Second, since positions of influence within the parties are limited, parties do not want problems with regard to internal management by making it easy for women to enter these positions. Conflict within the existing hierarchies could be avoided if women were considered second-class participants. Third, if women did not have access to positions of influence, they would have little incentive to become involved in politics. The cumulative effect of these factors meant that despite enfranchisement, women remained underrepresented within most political parties worldwide, even in the late 1960s.

This situation changed in the 1970s and 1980s when newly formed political parties compelled the traditional ones to adopt a 'woman-friendly' posture. The promise by the Greens in Germany to provide equal representation for women at all levels in the party generated publicity, and garnered visible political dividends. As a result, the SPD made a similar commitment, even though it had had full-fledged women's wings since the 1880s. In certain cases, like the African National Congress in South Africa, women played an important role in bringing down the apartheid regime and even developed a women's charter for the post-apartheid period. In view of this, it was easy to adopt a quota law with the definite aim of ending the tradition of 'male and pale' dominance in all walks of life.

Many point out that the first past the post system that India follows is, in comparison to the proportional representation system, not suitable to secure an adequate representation of women and other disadvantaged segments of society. However, this was disproved by the British Labour Party in the 1997 general elections under Blair's leadership. In India, too, significant advancement is possible if all political parties widen their present narrow social base and secure wider representation of the underrepresented and under-privileged, instead of confining them to marginal and unsafe seats. Till then, since mainstream political parties are either unwilling or incapable of moving in this positive direction, the only option is to have a state-directed, time-bound quota system that would immediately rectify this imbalance and prepare the society for more corrective measures in the future.

Opponents of the women's reservation bill wish to perpetuate the existing asymmetry in politics. In most other parts of the world, greater women's representation is sought not only to recognise them as equal citizens, but also to bring the feminine perspective into the decision-making process. In order to achieve this, two important requirements have to be met. First, political parties and their affiliated organisations ought to reinvent themselves and become more sensitive and responsive to women. They should not use the quota law to appoint token women with little or no power, especially to bodies with no real decision-making powers. If one goes by the impact that quotas have had on Panchayati Raj Institutions, one can see that percentages of women in various levels of political activity have increased from 4.5 per cent to 25–40 per cent. Women leaders at the panchayat level are transforming local governance by focusing on issues of poverty, inequality and gender injustice, and demanding basic facilities like primary schools and healthcare centres.

Second, there is a need to reorient the socialisation process by making equality the cornerstone of our social and political culture. Even while women continue to discharge their primary responsibilities of mother and homemaker, they should not be perceived as confined to these roles alone. Besides facilities like crèches and daycare centres, men should also shoulder domestic responsibilities along with women. A greater number of women in legislatures under a state-directed quota system will lead to an insistence on changes that will help women to balance their homes with careers in politics. They will also serve as role models for young women, and will debate and discuss social issues that are of direct concern to women. An equal number of women in legislatures will eventually create a society committed to gender equality and justice. A politics of exclusion is counter-productive. Rejecting women's reservation on the grounds that women are primarily mothers and homemakers goes again the ideal of equality of persons before the law. Our decision-makers must be reminded of Vivekananda's observation that the level of a civilisation can be judged from the way it treats its women.

Interestingly, although the electorate comprises 50 per cent or more women, they do not automatically support women candidates. This is because political parties rarely field women who have independent work and achievements to their credit. This also explains why women legislators in recent times have not initiated any significant legislation that concerns their gender. Female infanticide, child marriage, dowry deaths, and indignities against women are rampant, giving rise to the view that ordinary women MPs would have been able to understand the problems faced by an ordinary person. In recent decades, the role of women in electoral politics has differed sharply from the active and purposeful role they played during the nationalist movement, and in the immediate aftermath of independence. Merely reserving seats will not be enough unless there is a change in political culture and in the socialisation undergone by both men and women. Women cannot hope for substantive equality, self-esteem or independence unless they have a decisive role in the power structures within their society. Quotas, however, should not allow the development of a ghetto mentality. Despite the 33 per cent reservation for women at the panchayat level for more than a decade, women representatives at the state or national level comprise less than 10 per cent of the whole. Kerala, with its high female literacy, has only two women MPs in the 14th Lok Sabha. All this indicates that the upward mobility of gifted women at the grassroots is virtually non-existent.

Ram Manohar Lohia once remarked that 'caste is class in India'; if unity is to prevail in the uneven Indian society, the women's question has to be understood realistically within the fragmented social, economic, cultural and political structure of India. Unity in diversity has to be brought about by co-option and inclusion, and not by imposition and exclusion. This is as true of women's representation in the political domain as it is of the other marginalised and oppressed groups in contemporary Indian society. Quotas, whether party-wise or state-sponsored, can empower women only when the democratic process is truly and genuinely democratic. This would mean giving every individual access to education, public organisations, and an assurance of speedy justice (Owens 1987). In its absence, democracy functions under the garb of oligarchy, where a few individuals belonging to well-connected families secure the benefits that public office accrue, making the demands for due representation of women in parliament and state legislatures seem more like a search for posts than for empowerment. In this context, the demand for a 'quota within quota' is both legitimate and just; otherwise, the seemingly modern democratic representation will perpetuate the pre-modern and obsolete Burkean concept of virtual rather than the actual representation of women in India.

CONCLUSION

The status and condition of women is key if a society is to thrive and prosper; societies that oppress and disenfranchise their women operate on a system that equates physical strength with social and legal entitlement. Politics becomes feminised not by raising a few women's issues or through token women candidates, but by treating all issues as women's issues and by having a more holistic and inclusive approach and alternative values. In other words, if politics is to be transformed, it must bring in the concerns of all the marginalised and vulnerable, half of whom are women, and who suffer the most.

NOTES

1. This is evident from the fact that the Social Democratic parties and Christian Democratic parties in Western Europe, which owe their popularity and existence mainly to the working class and women, respectively, did not, in the initial years, become catalysts representing these underrepresented sections.
2. Liberal feminism traced women's oppression to unjust laws and women's subjugation in the private sphere, as the latter is insulated from the ideals of freedom, equality and justice. Liberal feminism emphasises equal rights for women so that they can gain access to the public sphere on the same terms as men. It sought to reform the traditional family and accord women dignity, self-respect and independence by demanding the rights to marriage, property, inheritance and custody. Socialist/Marxist feminism aimed to abolish the private domain of the home by communalising its domestic and childcare functions. It considered women's oppression a result of social and economic structures and subordinated the women's question to the aims of the socialist revolution. Both these strands of feminism took the values of the public sphere as the accepted norm, and contended that women must have the right to be like men.
3. Radical Feminism questioned the public-private divide of the first-wave theories. It differed from both schools of the first wave as it hoped to modify both liberal and Socialist/Marxist feminism to include exclusively women's interests and perceptions. It dismissed liberal initiatives to change existing laws as cosmetic, as that conceals and sometimes perpetuates the injustice that exists within the structure of the family itself (which liberalism and liberal feminism is silent on). Similarly, Socialist and Marxist feminists stress on the economic basis of women's oppression and ignore non-economic factors, especially sexual forms of oppression (Benhabib and Cornell 1987: 3, 5, 16–30). Radical feminism criticised traditional political philosophy and the early feminist discourse, as it legitimised male power and overlooked women's lack of political power. In claiming that the 'personal is political', it denied the existence of a separate political realm and insisted that the concept of the political is itself 'male'. The public sphere is the product of the male imagination, reflecting its competitive and inegalitarian values. Matters such as marital relationships, domestic violence and childcare, which are normally confined to the private sphere, should be brought under the purview of the political.

   It challenged the public-private divide from both ends: the devaluation of the public space through the exclusion of women and private concerns, and the bankruptcy of the private because of the exclusion of men from domestic responsibilities, including childcare. It considered the public sphere the structural expression of male gender values—non-nurturing ones—as the basis of male constructed politics. While for the first-wave feminists patriarchy symbolised inequality, excluding women from citizenship, second-wave feminists understood patriarchy to denote male power and dominance (Randall 1987). Radical feminism accepted gender difference and criticised the earlier generation of egalitarian feminists for demanding women's equality with men by devaluing the feminism identity as something imposed by patriarchy, and not something that patriarchy justifies.

4. Post-modern feminism rejected the modernism of the Enlightenment Philosophy, namely the rational pursuit of truth, certainty and objectivity, and drew attention to the 'maleness' of its central concepts.
5. Zakaria (2003) believed it was just 2 per cent of the population.
6. Historically, the track record of communists in comparison to Social Democrats on the question of women's emancipation and empowerment has been both theoretically and practically inadequate. Communist tokenism was limited to granting equal political rights to women without considering additional measures that would create socio-economic equality. They retained the traditional male-headed family with the woman in a subordinate position, and therefore did not attempt to revamp the sexual division of labour. Theoretically, they attacked private families as economically wasteful and morally degrading, replacing it with communal households; however, they never conceived of men's share in domestic responsibilities. The erstwhile patriarchal totalitarian Soviet state made no effort to encourage independent women's movement. It strongly promoted and supported the view of women as mothers and workers. In spite of formal rights and privileges, high levels of education and access to their independent earnings, Soviet women were seen as resources for production and reproduction. In the former USSR, women's representation was 15.7 per cent. Its constitution guaranteed women equal rights. In the former Czechoslovakia, it was 25.9 per cent and in Cuba, 33.9 per cent. Traditionally, in contrast to the communists, the Social Democrats' approach to the women's question was pragmatic and non-doctrinaire. Its tone was set by August Bebel's *Woman and Socialism* (1879), republished as *Woman in the Past, Present and Future* (1884). Since the 1880s, the social democratic movement in Europe tried to include workers' wives, women workers, as well as middle-class women. Without forsaking the goal of socialism, Bebel emphasised the need for occupational, juridical and political equality for women to confront their dual oppression as wives and workers. The goal of class and gender equality, according to Bebel, was realisable through parliamentarism rather than revolution.
7. Since Eisenhower's presidency (1951–55), 15 women and 194 women have served in the cabinets of nine presidents. Eisenhower's cabinet had one woman, in charge of health, education and welfare, as compared to 20 men. The cabinets of the next presidents—Kennedy, Johnson and Nixon, from 1955 to 1975—were exclusively male. Ford, who succeeded Nixon, appointed a woman as secretary of housing and urban development. Carter (1977–80) had three women in his 21-member cabinet. Of the three, Patricia Harris held two different positions.
8. He has strengthened the social security system, since women are more dependent on it than men. One reason for this is that women live longer than men. An office for women's initiative and outreach at the White House, a cell to focus on violence against women in the Law Ministry, and an inter-agency council on women's business enterprises has been established. Clinton was the first president to sign an act concerning family and medical leave, granting 12 weeks leave without pay if a worker has an ailing relative to nurse or on the arrival of a newborn baby. He raised the minimum wages, benefitting 60 lakh women. He enacted the pay-cheque fairness act to eliminate the differences in pay between men and women. He provided tax benefits for children and initiated child health insurance, allocated a large portion of government grants for child welfare, and achieved a new standardisation in food for children. He provided substantive benefits to elders and breast cancer research, increased the grant for education, reduced the size of classrooms and provided for trained teachers. He opened a national hotline in order to handle cases of domestic violence, shelters for women in distress, severe punishment for sexual offences and pre-meditated torture against children and women, and stricter action against the trafficking of women and children across the globe, in cooperation with other countries.
9. Prior to the 1980s, it was an established fact that women in Western democracies were more conservative and right-wing than men (Almond and Verba 1963: 252). However, this scenario changed with the 1980s, which saw a weakening in women's traditional conservatism in advanced industrial societies or in the developing world. This was due to structural changes in the paid labour force, in educational opportunities for women and in the nature of modern families. Culturally, the rise of post-materialist values among younger generations has led to a gradual but continued decrease in gender inequality.

10. These two amendments oblige all states to reserve one-third of seats in the three-tiered system of local government (village, block and district levels), known as panchayati raj, for women. Elected directly by and from the villagers, the panchayats can take decisions concerning a wide range of fields, from agriculture to health, employment and primary education.
11. The bill was first introduced in the 11th Lok Sabha during the United Front Government in 1996, but lapsed with the premature dissolution of the house. It was introduced again in 1998 in the 12th Lok Sabha, but could not be taken up due to major disruptions in the House. It was introduced for the third time in 1999 in the 13th Lok Sabha as the 85th constitutional amendment, but has remained pending since then. It came up in 2003 and 2005, only to be deferred on both occasions following the failure to evolve an all-party consensus.

BIBLIOGRAPHY

Almond, G. A., 'The Return of the State', *American Political Science Review* 82 (3), 1988, pp. 855–74.

———, *A Discipline Divided: Schools and Sects in Political Science*, Newbury Park, CA: Sage Publications, 1990.

Almond, G. A. and G. Bingham Powell, *Comparative Politics: System, Process and Policy*, Boston: Little Brown, 1978, 2e.

———, *Comparative Politics: A Theoretical Approach*, New York: HarperCollins, 1996.

Almond, G. A., S. Kaare and R. J. Dalton, *Comparative Politics Today: A World View*, New York: Addison Wesley Longman, 2000, 7e.

Almond, G. A. and S. Verba (eds), *The Civic Culture Revisited*, Princeton, NJ: Princeton University Press, 1980.

Andrain, C. F., *Comparative Political Systems*, Armonk, NY: ME Sharpe, 1994.

Apter, D. E., *Rethinking Development: Modernization, Dependency and Postmodern Politics*, Newsbury, CA: Sage Publications, 1987.

Bellamy, R. (ed.), *Theories and Concepts of Politics*, Manchester: Manchester University Press, 1993.

Bara, J. and M. Pennington (eds), *Comparative Politics*, New Delhi: Sage Publications, 2009.

Berelson, Bernard, 'Behavioral Sciences', in *Encyclopedia of the Social Sciences*, Vol. 2, New York: The Free Press, 1968.

Bill, J. and R. L. Hardgrave Jr., *Comparative Politics: The Quest for Theory*, Columbus, OH: Charles Merrill Co., 1973.

Blondel, J., *Comparative Government*, London: Macmillan, 1969a.

———, *An Introduction to Comparative Government*, London: Weidenfeld and Nicolson, 1969b.

———, *Comparing Political Systems*, London: Weidenfeld and Nicolson, 1973.

———, *Comparing Legislatures*, London: Sage Publications, 1985.

Boix, C. and S. C. Stokes (eds), *The Oxford Handbook of Comparative Politics*, Oxford: Oxford University Press, 2007.

Burges, M. and A. G. Gagnon (eds), *Comparative Federalism and Federation*, Hemel Hempstead: Harvester Wheatsheaf, 1993.

Burrell, B. C., *Women and Political Participation: A Reference Handbook*, Santa Barbara, CA: ABC Clio, 2004.

Calvert, P., *A Study of Revolution*, Oxford: The Clarendon Press, 1970.

———, *Politics, Power and Revolution: An Introduction to Comparative Politics*, Brighton: Harvester, 1983.

———, *Comparative Politics*, Boston: Pearson, 2002.

Carsten, F. L., *The Rise of Fascism*, London: Methuen, 1967.

Chatterji, R., *Introduction to Comparative Political Analysis*, Kolkata: Sarat Book House, 2006.

Charlesworth, James S. (ed.), *The Limits of Behavioralism in Political Science*, Philadelphia: The American Academy of Political and Social Science, 1962.

Clapham, C., *Third World Politics: An Introduction*, Beckenham, Kent: Croom Helm, 1985.

Crick, B., *Basic Forms of Government: A Sketch and a Model*, London: Macmillan, 1973.

———, *In Defense of Politics*, Harmondsworth: Penguin, 2000, 5e.

Curtis, M. (ed.), *Introduction to Comparative Government*, New York: Harper and Row, 1993, 3e.

Dahl, R., *On Democracy*, New Haven: Yale University Press, 1998.

Dalton, R. J., *Citizen Politics, Public Opinion and Political Parties in Advanced Industrial Democracies*, Chatham: Chatham House, 2002.

Davis, M. R. and V. A. Lewis, *Modern Political Systems*, London: Pall Mall, 1971.

Diamond, L., *The Spirit of Democracy: The Struggle to Build Free Societies throughout the World*, New York: Holt, 2008.

Diamond, L, J. J. Linz and S. Martin (eds), *Politics in Developing Countries: Comparing Experiences with Democracy*, Colorado: Lynne Rienner Publishers, 1988–90.

Dobson, A., *Green Political Thought*, London: Unwin Hyman, 1990.

Dogan, M. and D. Pelassy, *How to Compare Nations: Strategies in Comparative Politics*, Chatham, NJ: Chatham House, 1990, 2e.

Dogan, M. and A. Kazancigil, *Comparing Nations, Concepts, Strategies, Substance*, Oxford: Blackwell, 1994.

Duverger, M., *Political Parties*, London: Methuen, 1954.

Eulau, H., *The Behavioural Persuasion in Politics*, New York: Random House, 1963.

Finifter, A. (ed.), *Political Science: The State of the Discipline*, Washington, DC: The American Political Science Association, 1993.

Fukuyama, F., *State Building, Governance and World Order in the Twenty-First Century*, London: Profile Books, 2004.

Grupp, J., *Corporatism: The Secret Government and the New World Order*, San Diego, CA: Progressive Press, 2008.

Gunther, R., J. R. Montero and J. J. Linz (eds), *Political Parties: Old Concepts and New Challenges*, Oxford: Oxford University Press, 2002.

Heywood, A., *Political Ideologies: An Introduction*, Basingstoke: Macmillan, 1992.

———, *Politics*, Basingstoke: Macmillan, 1997.

Horowitz, D., *Ethnic Groups in Conflict*, Berkeley: University of California Press, 2000.

Johari, J. C., *Comparative Politics*, New Delhi: Sterling Publishers, 1982.

———, *Comparative Political Theory: New Dimensions, Basic Concepts and Major Trends*, New Delhi: Sterling, 1987, 2e.

Kamrava, M., *Understanding Comparative Politics: A Framework for Analysis*, New York: Routledge, 2002.

Katz. R. S. and W. J. Crotty (eds), *Handbook of Party Politics*, London: Sage Publications, 2006.

Katznelson, I. and H. Milner (eds), *Political Science: The State of the Discipline*, New York: Norton, 2002.

King, R. and G. Kendall, *The State, Democracy and Globalization*, Basingstoke: Palgrave, 2003.

Kriegar, J. (ed.), *The Oxford Companion of Comparative Politics*, 2 vols., Oxford: Oxford University Press, 2013.

Landman, T., *Issues and Methods in Comparative Politics*, London: Routledge, 2000.

Leftwich, A. (ed.), *Democracy and Development*, Cambridge: Polity Press, 1996.

Lijphart, A., 'Comparative Politics and the Comparative Method', *American Political Science Review* 65 (3), 1971, pp. 682–93.

——— (ed.), *Parliamentary versus Presidential Government*, Oxford: Oxford University Press, 1992.

———, *Electoral Systems and Party Systems: A Study of Twenty-Seven Democracies 1945–90*, Oxford: Oxford University Press, 1995.

Lindblom, Charles E., 'Political Science in the 1940s and 1950s', *Daedalus* 126 (1), 1997, pp. 225–52.

Linz, J. and A. Valenzuela (eds), *The Failure of Presidential Democracy*, Baltimore MD: Johns Hopkins University Press, 1994.

Lowi, Theodore J., 'The State in Political Science: How We Become What We Study', *The American Political Science Review* 86 (1), 1992, pp. 1–17.

McNally, D., *Political Economy and the Rise of Capitalism: A Reinterpretation*, Berkeley: University of California Press, 1988.

Macridis, R. and B. E. Brown, *Comparative Politics: Notes and Readings*, Belmont, CA: Brooks/Cole, 1990.

Magstadt, T., *Nations and Governments: Comparative Politics in Regional Perspective*, New York: St. Martin's Press, 1991.

Marsh, D. and G. Stoker (eds), *Theories and Methods of Political Science*, London: Macmillan 1995.

Mayer, L. C., *Redefining Comparative Politics: Promise versus Performance*, California: Sage Publications, 1989.

Merkl, P. H., *Modern Comparative Politics*, New York: Holt, Rinehart & Winston, 1970.

Merritt, R. L., *Systematic Approaches to Comparative Politics*, Chicago: Rand McNally, 1970.

Nagle, J. D., *Introduction to Comparative Politics: Political Systems Performance in Third World*, Chicago: Nelson-Hall Publishers, 1992, 3e.

Needler, M. C., *The Concepts of Comparative Politics*, London and New York: Praegar, 1991.

Newton, K. and J. W. Van Deth, *Foundations of Comparative Politics*, New York: Cambridge University Press, 2009.

Norris, P., *Driving Democracy: Do Power-Sharing Institutions Work?* Cambridge: Cambridge University Press, 2008.

O'Donnell, G. and P. C. Schmitter, *Transitions from Authoritarian Rule: Tentative Conclusions about Uncertain Democracies*, Baltimore and London: Johns Hopkins University Press, 1986.

Paxton, Pamela and Melanie M. Hughes, *Women, Politics, and Power*, Los Angeles: Pine Force Press, 2007.

Pennings, P., H. Kennan and J. Kleinnijenjuis, *Doing Research in Political Science: An Introduction to Comparative Methods and Statistics*, London: Sage Publications, 1999.

Peters, G., *Comparative Politics: Theory and Methods*, New York: New York University Press, 1998.

Ray, A. and M. Bhattacharya, *Political Theory: Ideas and Institutions*, Kolkata: The World Press Pvt. Ltd., 2013 [1988].

Rotberg, R. I., *When States Fail: Causes and Consequences*, Princeton, NJ: Princeton University Press, 2003.

Rustow, D. A. and K. P. Erickson (eds), *Comparative Political Dynamics: Global Research Perspectives*, New York: HarperCollins Publishers, 1991.

Sartori, G., 'Concept Misinformation in Comparative Politics', *American Political Science Review* 64 (4), 1970, pp. 1033–53.

Schapiro, L., *Totalitarianism*, London: Pall Mall and Macmillan, 1972.

Skocpol, T., *Social Revolutions in the Modern World*, Cambridge: Cambridge University Press, 1994.

Smelser, N., *Comparative Methods in the Social Sciences*, Englewood Cliffs NJ: Prentice Hall, 1976.

Spanakos, A. P. and F. Panizza (eds), *Conceptualizing Comparative Politics*, New York: Routledge, 2015.

Stiglitz, J. E., *Globalization and Its Discontents*, New York: Allen Lane, 2002.

Tadros, M., *Women in Politics: Gender, Power and Development*, London: Zed Books, 2014.

von Beyme, K., *Political Parties in Western Democracies*, Aldershot: Gower, 1985.

Waldo, Dwight, *Political Science in the United States of America*, Paris: UNESCO, 1956.

———, 'Political Science: Tradition, Discipline, Profession, Science, Enterprise', in Fred I. Greenstein and Nelson W. Polsby (eds), *Handbook of Political Science*, Vol. 1. Reading, Mass.: Addison-Wesley, 1975.

Ware, A., *The Logic of Party Democracy*, London: Macmillan, 1979.

———, *Citizens, Parties and the State: A Reappraisal*, Cambridge: Polity Press, 1987a.

———, *Political Parties: Electoral Change and Structural Response*, Oxford: Blackwell, 1987b.

Webb, P., D. Farrell and I. Holliday, *Political Parties in Advanced Industrial Democracies*, Oxford: Oxford University Press, 2002.

Webb, P. and S. White (eds), *Party Politics in New Democracies*, Oxford: Oxford University Press, 2007.

Weiner, M. and S. P. Huntington (eds), *Understanding Political Development: An Analytic Study*, Boston, MA: Little Brown, 1987.

Wiarda, H. J. (ed.), *New Directions in Comparative Politics*, Boulder, CO: Westview Press, 1985.

———, *Corporatism and Comparative Politics: The Other Great Ism*, New York and London: M. E. Sharpe, 1997.

——— (ed.), *Comparative Politics: Critical Concepts in Political Science*, London and New York: Routledge, 2005.

———, *Comparative Politics: Approaches and Issues*, UK: Rowman and Littlefield Publishers, 2007.

Williamson, P. J., *Varieties of Corporatism: A Conceptual Discussion*, Cambridge: Cambridge University Press, 1985.

Wilson, G. K., *Interest Groups*, Oxford: Blackwell, 1990.

REFERENCES

Adamson, W. L., 'Gramsci's Interpretation of Fascism', *Journal of the History of Ideas* XLI, 1980, pp. 615–34.

Alavi, H., 'The State in Post-Colonial Societies: Pakistan and Bangladesh', *New Left Review* I/72 (July–August), 1972, pp. 59–81.

Almond, G. A., 'Comparative Political System', *Journal of Politics* 18 (3), 1956, pp. 391–406.

———, *Political Development*, Boston, MA: Little Brown, 1970.

———, *A Discipline Divided*, London: Sage Publications, 1990.

———, 'Political Science: The History of the Discipline', in R. E. Goodin and H. D. Klingemann (eds), *A New Handbook of Political Science*, Oxford: Oxford University Press, 1996.

Almond, G. A. and J. S. Coleman, *The Politics of Developing Areas*, Princeton, NJ: Princeton University Press, 1960.

Almond, G. A. and S. Verba, *The Civic Culture: Political Attitudes and Democracy in Five Nations*, London: Sage Publications, 1963.

Almond G. A. and G. Bingham-Powell Jr., *Comparative Politics: A Developmental Approach*, Boston, MA: Little, Brown, and Co., 1966.

Althusser, L., *For Marx*, London: Allen Lane, 1969.

Amin, S., *Accumulation on a World Scale: A Critique of the Theory of Underdevelopment*, New York: Monthly Review Press, 1970.

Apter, D. E., *The Politics of Modernization*, Chicago and London: The University of Chicago Press, 1965.

Arat, Z. F., *Democracy and Human Rights in Developing Countries*, United States: Lynne Rienner Publishers Inc., 1992.

Arblaster, A., *Democracy*, New Delhi: World View, 1997.

Arter, D., *Scandinavian Politics Today*, Manchester: Manchester University Press, 1999.

Arendt, H., *The Origins of Totalitarianism*, New York: Meridian, 1951.

———, *On Revolution*, New York: Viking Press, 1969.

Aristotle, *The Politics*, E. Barker (trans.), Oxford: Oxford University Press, 1979.

Ash, T. G. 'Eastern Europe: The Year of Truth', *New York Review of Books*, 10 (February), 1990, pp. 17–22.

Austin, G., *Indian Constitution: Cornerstone of a Nation*, New Delhi: Oxford University Press, 1966.

———, *Working for a Democratic Constitution: A History of the Indian Experience*, New Delhi: Oxford University Press, 1999.

Avineri, S., *Karl Marx on Colonialism and Modernization: His Despatches and Other Writings on China, India, Mexico, the Middle East and North Africa*, New York: Cambridge University Press, 1969.

———, *Karl Marx: Social and Political Thought*, New Delhi: S. Chand, 1976.

Axford, B., G. K. Browning, R. Huggins, B. Rosamond, and J. Turner, *Politics: An Introduction*, London and New York: Routledge, 1997.

Baccaro, L., 'What is Dead and What is Alive in the Theory of Corporatism', *British Journal of Industrial Relations* 41, 2003, pp. 683–706.

Bachrach, P. and M. S. Baratz, 'The Two Faces of Power', *American Political Science Review* 56 (4), 1962, pp. 942–52.

Bagehot, W., *The English Constitution*, United Kingdom: Chapman and Hall, 1867.

Ball, T., 'American Political Science in Its Postwar Political Context', in James Farr and Raymond Seidelman (eds), *Discipline and History. Political Science in the United States*, Ann Arbor: University of Michigan Press, 1993.

Ballington, J., Stockholm, Sweden: International Institute for Democracy and Electoral Assistance, 2004.

Barker, E. (trans.), *Aristotle's The Politics*, Oxford: Oxford University Press, 1979.

Barry, B., 'Political Accommodation and Consociational Democracy', *British Journal of Political Science* 5 (4), 1975, pp. 477–505.

———, *Democracy: Power and Justice: Essays in Political Theory*, Vol. I, Oxford: The Clarendon Press, 1991.

———, *Culture and Equality: An Egalitarian Critique of Multiculturalism*, Cambridge: Polity Press, 2001.

Batliwala, S., *Changing their World: Concepts and Practices of Women's Movements*, Toronto, Mexico City, Cape Town: Association for Women's Rights in Development, 2012, 2e.

Batora, J., 'Does the European Union Transform the Institution of Diplomacy', *Journal of European Public Policy* 12 (1), 2005, pp. 1–23.

Bay, C., 'Politics and Pseudo Politics: A Critical Evaluation of Some Behavioral Literature', *The American Political Science Review* I, 1965, pp. 39–51.

Bellah, R., R. Madsen and S. Tipton, *The Good Society*, New York: Knopf, 1991.

Bell, D., 'The Power Elite Reconsidered', in *C. Wright Mills and the Power Elite*, compiled by G. William Domhoff and Hoyt B. Ballard, Boston: Beacon Press, 1968.

———, 'American Exceptionalism Revisited: The Role of Civil Society', *The American Review*, 1990, pp. 9–14.

Benhabib, S. and D. Cornell, *Feminism as Critique*, Cambridge: Polity Press, 1986.

Bentham, J., *Constitution Code*, 2 vols, F. Rosen and J. H. Burns (eds), Oxford: The Clarendon Press, 1983.

Bentley, A. F., 'The Units of Investigation in the Social Sciences', in *Annals of American Academy of Political and Social Science*, Boston: Arena Publishing Company, 1895.

———, *The Process of Government: The Study of Social Pressures*, Chicago: University of Chicago Press, 1908.

Berlin, Sir I., *Karl Marx*, New York: Time Books, 1939.

———, 'Does Political Theory Still Exist?' in P. Laslett and W. G. Runciman (eds), *Philosophy, Politics and Society*, Second Series, Oxford: Basil Blackwell, 1962, pp. 1–33.

———, *Concepts and Categories*, London: Hogarth Press, 1980.

Bertalanffy, L. von, 'An Outline of General System Theory', *British Journal for the Philosophy of Science* 1, 1950, pp. 114–29.

———, 'General system theory—A new approach to unity of science' (Symposium), *Human Biology*, 23 December 1951, pp. 303–61.

———, *Modern Theories of Development*, New York: Harper, 1962.

———, *General System Theory*, New York: George Braziller, 1969.

Beyme, K. von, 'Political Institutions—Old and New', in R. A. W. Rhodes, S. A. Binder and B. A. Rockman (eds), *The Oxford Handbook of Political Institutions*, Oxford: Oxford University Press, 2006.

Bingham Powell Jr., G., *Contemporary Democracies: Participation, Stability and Violence*, Cambridge, MA: Harvard University Press, 1982a.

———, *Contemporary Democracies: Participation, Stability and Violence*, Cambridge, MA: Harvard University Press, 1982b.

Blackburn, R. (ed.), *After the Fall: The Failure of Communism and Future of Socialism*, London: Verso, 1991.

Black, A., *Guilds and Civil Society in European Political Thought: From the Twelfth Century to the Present*, New York: Cornell University Press, 1984.

Blondel, J., *Voters, Parties and Leaders*, London: Penguin, 1963.

———, 'Then and Now: Comparative Politics', *Political Studies*, XLVIII, 1999, pp. 152–60.

———, 'About Institutions, Mainly, but not Exclusively Political', in R. A. W. Rhodes, S. A. Binder and B. A. Rockman (eds), *The Oxford Handbook of Political Institutions*, Oxford: Oxford University Press, 2006.

———, *Comparative Government Introduction*, Oxford: Routledge and Kegan Paul, 2014.

Bodenheimer, S., 'Dependency and Imperialism: The Roots of Latin American Underdevelopment', in S. I. Fann and F. Hodge (eds), *Readings in US Imperialism*, Boston, MA: Cambridge University Press, 1974.

Bonder, G. and M. Nari, 'The 30 percent Quota Law: A turning point for women's political participation in Argentina', in A. Brill (ed.), *The Rising Public Voice: Women in Politics Worldwide*, New York: The Feminist Press at the City University of New York Press, 1995.

Bormann, N. C., 'Patterns of Democracy and its Critics', *Living Reviews in Democracy*, 2010, pp. 1–19. Available at democracy.livingreviews.org.

Bottomore, T. B., *Political Sociology*, London: Hutchinson, 1979.

———, *A Dictionary of Marxist Thought*, Oxford: Blackwell, 1983.

Bove, A., 'The Limits of Political Culture: An Introduction to G.W.F. Hegel's Notion of *Bildung*', *IWM Junior Visiting Fellows Conferences* XII (6), 2002, pp. 1–18.

Bowler, S., 'Electoral Systems', in R. A. W. Rhodes, S. A. Binder and B. A. Rockman (eds), *The Oxford Handbook of Political Institutions*, Oxford: Oxford University Press, 2006.

Brinton, C., *The Anatomy of Revolution*, New York: Vintage Books, 1938.

Bronowski, J. and B. Mazlish, *Western Intellectual Tradition*, Harmondsworth: Penguin, 1960.

Brown, G. T., *Korean Pricing Policies and Economic Development in 1960s*, Baltimore: Johns Hopkins University Press, 1973.

Brunsson, N. and J. P. Olsen, 'Organization theory: Thirty years of dismantling and then…?' in N. Brunsson and J. P. Olsen (eds), *Organizing Organizations*, Bergen: Fagbokforlaget, 1998.

Bryce, J., *Modern Democracies*, New York: Macmillan, 1921.

———, *American Commonwealth*, Indianapolis: Liberty Fund, 1995 [1888].

Burnham, J., *The Managerial Revolution: What is Happening in the World*, New York: John Day, 1941.

Burgess, M. and A. G. Gagnon (eds), *Comparative Federalism and Federation: Competing Traditions and Future Directions*, London: Harvester Wheatsheaf, 1993.

Canel, E., 'Democratization and the Decline of Urban Social Movements in Uruguay: A Political-Institutional Account', in A. Escobar and S. E. Alvarez (eds), *New Social Movements in Latin America: Identity, Strategy, and Democracy*, Boulder, Colorado: Westview Press, 1992.

Caporaso, J. A. and Z. Behrour, 'An Interpretation and Evaluation of Dependency Theory', in *Dependency to Development: Strategies to Overcome Underdevelopment and Inequality*, New York and Boulder: Monthly Review Press, 1981.

Caramani, D. (ed.), *Introduction to Comparative Politics*, New York: Oxford University Press, 2011.

Carr, E. H., *The Russian Revolution: Lenin to Stalin*, Harmondsworth: Penguin, 1979.

Cassese, A., *International Law in a Divided World*, Oxford: The Clarendon Press, 1986.

Castles, F. G., *The Social Democratic Image of Society*, London: Routledge and Kegan Paul, 1978.

Chilcote, R. H., *Theories of Comparative Politics: The Search for a Paradigm Reconsidered*, Boulder: Westview Press, 1994.

Clapham, C. and G. Philip (eds), *The Political Dilemmas of Military Regimes*, London and Sydney: Croom Helm, 1985.

Cohen, J. and J. Rogers, 'Secondary Associations and Democratic Governance', *Politics and Society* 20, 1992, pp. 393–412.

Cole, G. D. H., *Self Government in Industry*, London: G. Bell and Sons, 1917.

———, *Guild Socialism Revisited*, London: Leonard Parsons, 1920.

Coleman, J. S., *Foundations of Social Theory*, Cambridge, MA: Harvard University Press, 1990.

Colletti, L., *From Rousseau to Lenin*, New Delhi: Oxford University Press, 1969.

Cooke, A., *America*, New York: Alfred A. Knopf, 1974.

Crevald, M. V., *The Rise and the Decline of the State*, Cambridge: Cambridge University Press, 1999.

Crick, B. R., *The American Science of Politics: Its Origins and Conditions*, Berkeley: University of California Press, 1959.

Crosland, A., *The Future of Socialism*, London: Cape, 1956.

Cunningham, F., *Theories of Democracy: A Critical Introduction*, London: Routledge, 2000.

Curtis, M., *The Great Political Theories*, 2 vols, New York: Avon, 1961.

Czada, R., 'Corporativism (Corporatism)', in Bertrand Badie, Dirk, Berg-Schlosser and Leonardo Morlino (eds), *International Encyclopedia of Political Science*, London: Sage Publications, 2011.

Dahl, R. A., *A Preface to Democratic Theory*, Chicago: University of Chicago Press, 1956.

———, 'The Behavioral Approach in Political Science: Epitaph for a Monument to a Successful Protest', *American Political Science Review*, 55 (4), 1961a, pp 763–72.

———, *Who Governs? Democracy and Power in an American City*, New Haven, London: Yale University Press, 1961b.

———, *Modern Political Analysis*, Englewood Cliffs, N.J.: Prentice-Hall, 1966.

———, *Pluralist Democracy in the United States*, Chicago: Rand McNally, 1967.

———, 'A Critique of the Ruling Elite Model', in G. W. Domoff and H. B. Ballard (eds), *C. Wright Mills and the Power Elite*, Boston: Beacon Press, 1968.

———, *Polyarchy*, New Haven CT: Yale University Press, 1971.

———, *A Preface to Economic Theory*, Berkeley: University of California Press, 1985.

———, *Democracy, Liberty and Equality*, Oslo: Norwegian University Press, 1986.

———, *Democracy and its Critics*, New Haven, Connecticut: Yale University Press, 1989.

———, 'The Ills of the System: Do we need Basic Constitutional Changes', *Dissent* Fall, 1993.

———, *How Democratic is the American Constitution?* New Haven CT: Yale University Press, 2001.

Dahlerup, D. (ed.), *Women, Quotas and Politics*, London and New York: Routledge and Kegan Paul, 2009.

Daly, H. E., *Steady State Economics*, San Francisco: W. H. Freeman, 1977.

Davis, J. C., 'Towards a Theory of Revolution', *American Sociological Review* 43 (1), 1962, pp. 5–19.

Dicey, A. V., *Introduction to the Study of the Law of the Constitution*, Oxford: All Souls College, 1885, 1908.

Dickinson, H. T., *Liberty and Property: Political Ideology in the Eighteenth Century*, New Delhi: Holmes and Meier, 1977.

Djilas, M., *The New Class*, London: Thames and Hudson, 1957.

Dolgoff, S., *Bakunin on Anarchy*, edited, translated and introduced, New York: Vintage, 1973.

Dos Santos, T., 'The Structure of Dependency', *American Economic Review*, 60 (May), 1971, pp. 231–36.

Downs, A., *An Economic Theory of Democracy*, New York: Harper and Row, 1957.

Draper, H., *Karl Marx's Theory of Revolution: State and Bureaucracy*, New York: Monthly Review Press, 1977.

Duchacek, I., *Power Maps: Comparative Politics of Constitutions*, Santa Barbara, California: Abc Clio, 1973.

Duncan, G. and S. Lukes, 'The New Democracy', in S. Lukes (ed.), *Essays in Social Theory*, London: Macmillan, 1963.

Dunn, J., *Modern Revolution*, London: The Clarendon Press, 1989.

Duodo, C., 'Why Strong States are the Bane of Africa', *Guardian Weekly*, 8 May 1994.

Durkheim, E., *The Division of Labour in Society*, New York: Free Press, 1964 [1893].

Duverger, M., *Political Parties: Their Organization and Activity in the Modern State*, New York: Wiley, 1951.

Easton, D., *The Political System: An Inquiry into the State of Political Science*, New York: Wiley, 1953.

———, 'Introduction: The Current Meaning of "Behavioralism" in Political Science', in James S. Charlesworth (ed.), *The Limits of Behavioralism in Political Science*, Philadelphia: The American Academy of Political and Social Science, 1962.

———, *A Framework of Political Analysis*, Englewood Cliffs, NJ: Prentice-Hall, 1965.

———, 'The New Revolution in Political Science', *American Political Science Review* 63 (December), 1969, pp. 1051–61.

———, 'The future of the post-behavioural phase in political science', in K. R. Monroe (ed.), *Contemporary Empirical Political Theory*, Berkeley: University of California Press, 1997.

Echlin, E. P., 'Theology and Sustainable Development after Rio', *The Newman* 30, 1993, pp. 2–7.

Eckstein, H., 'A perspective on comparative politics, past and present', in H. Eckstein and D. E. Apter (eds), *Comparative Politics: A Reader*, London: Free Press of Glencoe, 1963.

Eckstein, H. and D. Apter (eds), *Comparative Politics: A Reader*, London: Free Press of Glencoe, 1963.

Elazar, D. J., *Exploring Federalism*, Tuscaloosa: University of Alabama Press, 1987.

Eisenstadt, S. N., 'Modernization and conditions of sustained growth', *World Politics* 16, 1973, pp. 576–94.

Elliot, C., 'Problems of Marxist Revisionism', *Journal of the History of Ideas* 28, 1967, pp. 71–89.

Elliott, L., 'The Rolling Economic Disaster', *The Guardian*, 20 August, 1991.

Emmanuel, A., *Unequal Exchange: A Study of the Imperialism of Trade*, London: New Left Books, 1969.

Engels, F., *Selected Writings*, 3 vols, Moscow: Progress Publishers, 1977.

Epstein, L. D., *Political Parties in Western Democracies*, New Jersey: Transaction Publishers, 1980.

Evans, P. B., D. Rueschemeyer and T. Skocpol (eds), *Bringing the State Back In*, Cambridge: Cambridge University Press, 1985.

Evans, R., *The Feminists*, London: Croom Helm, 1977.

Ferguson, A., *Principles of Moral and Political Science*, UK: Edinburgh, 1792.

Finer, H., *The Theory and Practice of Modern Government*, London: Methuen, 1962, 4e.

———, *The Major Governments of Europe*, London: Methuen, 1966.

Finer, S. E., *The Man on the Horseback: The Role of the Military in Politics*, London: Pall Mall Press, 1962.

———, *Vilfredo Pareto: Sociological Writings*, London: Pall Mall Press, 1966.

———, 'Almond's concept of the political system', *Government and Opposition* 5, 1970, pp. 3–21.

———, *Comparative Government: An Introduction to the Study of Politics*, New York: Basic Books, 1971 [1970].

Fong, E., P. Lim and Y. C. Linda, 'High Tech and Labour in the Asian NICs', *Labour and Society* 14, 1989, pp. 15–27.

Forsyth, M. G., *Union of States: The Theory and Practice of Confederation*, Leicester: Leicester University Press, 1981.

———, 'State' in D. Miller (ed.), *The Blackwell Encyclopaedia of Modern Political Thought*, Oxford: Basil Blackwell, 1987.

Forbes, G., *Women in Modern India*, Cambridge: Cambridge University Press, 1996.

Frank A. G., 'The Development of Underdevelopment and Sociology of Development and Underdevelopment of Sociology', in F. Cockcroft and J. Johnson (eds), *Dependence and Underdevelopment- Latin America's Political Economy*, New York: Monthly Review Press, 1972.

———, *Dependent Accumulation and Underdevelopment*, London: Fontana, 1978.

———, *Crisis in the Third World*, New York: Holmes and Meier, 1980.

Friedman, T., *The World is Flat* 3.0: *A Brief History of the Twenty-first Century*, New York: Farrar, Straus and Giroux, 2005.

Friedrich, C. J., *Constitutional Government and Democracy*, Calcutta: Oxford and IBH Publishing Co., 1968.

Friedrich, C. J. and Z. Brzezinski, *Totalitarian Dictatorship and Autocracy*, Cambridge, MA: Harvard University Press, 1965.

Fukuyama, F., *The End of History and the Last Man*, Harmondsworth: Penguin, 1992.

Galston, W., 'Two Concepts of Liberalism', *Ethics* 105 (3), 1995, pp. 516–34.

Gamble, A., 'Critical Political Economy', in R. J. B. Jones (ed.), *Perspectives on Political Economy*, New York: St Martin Press, 1983.

Gandhi, M. K., *Modern India Review*, October 1935.

Gasset, O. Y., *The Revolt of the Masses*, London: Unwin Books, 1961.

Gereffi, G. and P. Evans, 'Transnational Corporations, Dependent Development and State Policy in the Semi-periphery', *Latin American Research Review* 16 (3), 1981, pp. 30–45.

Giddens, A., *Durkheim*, London: Fontana Modern Masters, 1978.

———, *A Contemporary Critique of Historical Materialism*, Vol. 2, 'The Nation State and Violence', Cambridge: Polity, 1985.

———, *Modernity and Self Identity: Self and Society in the Late Modern Age*, Cambridge: Polity Press, 1991.

———, *Beyond Left and Right—the Future of Radical Politics*, Cambridge: Polity, 1994.

Glazer, N., *Affirmative Discrimination: Ethnic Inequality and Public Policy*, New York: Basic Books, 1975.

Goldsmith, E., *The Way*, London: Faber, 1992.

Goldstone, J. A. G., 'Theories of Revolution', in D. Miller (ed.), *The Blackwell Encyclopedia of Modern Political Thought*, Oxford: Basil Blackwell, 1987.

Goodin, R. E. and H. D. Klingemann, 'Political Science: The Discipline', in R. E. Goodin and H. D. Klingemann (eds), *A New Handbook of Political Science*, Oxford: Oxford University Press, 1996.

Goodwin, B., *Using Political Ideas*, Chicester: John Wiley, 1992.

Government of India, *Towards Equality: Report of the Committee on the Status of Women in India*, New Delhi: Ministry of Education and Social Welfare, Department of Social Welfare, 1974.

Gray, T., 'Electoral Gender Quotas: Lessons from Argentina and Chile', *Bulletin of Latin American Research* 22 (January), 2003, pp. 52–78.

Greenleaf, W. I., *British Political Tradition*, 2 vols, London: Methuen, 1973.

Grenville, J. A. S., *A World History of the 20th Century*, Vol. 1, London: Fontana Press, 1987.

Gurr, T. R., *Why Men Rebel*, Princeton, NJ: Princeton University Press, 1976.

Habermas, J., *The Theory of Communicative Action*, 2 vols, Boston, MA: Beacon Press, 1981 & 1987.

Hague, R., M. Harrop and W. Breslin, *Comparative Government and Politics*, Basingstoke: Macmillan, 1992 & 2001.

Hall, P. A. and R. Taylor, 'Political Science and the Three New "Institutionalisms"', *Political Studies* XLIV, 1996, pp. 936–57.

Hall, J. A., *Liberalism: Politics, Ideology and the Market*, Chapel Hill: University of North Carolina Press, 1988.

Hardin, G., *Tragedy of the Commons*, San Francisco: Freeman, 1968.

Harris, N., *The End of the Third World—Newly Industrialized Countries and the Decline of Ideology*, Harmondsworth: Penguin, 1986.

Harrison, S., *India: The Dangerous Decades*, Princeton NJ: Princeton University Press, 1960.

Havel, V., *The Power of the Powerless: Citizens against the State in Central-eastern Europe*, John Keane (ed.), Armonk, NY: M. E. Sharpe, 1985.

Heclo, H., 'Thinking Institutionally', in R. A. W. Rhodes, S. A. Binder and B. A. Rockman (eds), *The Oxford Handbook of Political Institutions*, Oxford: Oxford University Press, 2006.

Hegel, G. W. F., 'Philosophy of Law', in Jacob Loewenberg (ed.), *Hegel: Selections*, New York: C. Scribner's Sons, 1929.

———, *Philosophy of Right*, T. M. Knox (trans.), Oxford: Oxford University Press, 1969.

Held, D., *Models of Democracy*, Cambridge: Polity Press, 1987.

———, *Political Theory and the Modern State*, Cambridge: Polity Press, 1989.

Hempel, C. G., *Philosophy of Natural Sciences, Englewood Cliffs*, New Jersey: Prentice-Hall, 1966.

Heywood, A., *Political Theory: An Introduction*, London: Macmillan, 1997.

Hewlett, S. A., *The Cruel Dilemmas of Development: Twentieth Century Brazil*, New York: Basic Books, 1980.

Hill, C. (ed.), *The English Revolution of 1640: Three Essays*, London: Lawrence and Wishart, 1940.

———, *The World Turned Upside Down*, Harmondsworth: Penguins, 1972.

Hobsbawm, E., *Industry and Empire*, Harmondsworth: Pelican Books, 1968.

———, 'Goodbye to All That', *Marxism Today*, October 1990, pp. 19–23.

Horowitz, D. L., 'The Cracked Foundations of the Right to Secede', *Journal of Democracy* 14 (2), 2004, pp. 5–17.

Hunt, R. N., *The Political Ideas of Marx and Engels*, New Haven, CT: Yale University Press, 1975.

Huntington, S. P., *The Soldier and the State: The Theory and Practice of Civil-Military Relations*, United States: Belknap Press, 1957.

———, 'Political Modernization: America vs Europe', *World Politics* 18, 1966, pp. 378–414.

———, *Political Order in Changing Societies*, New Haven, CT: Yale University Press, 1968.

———, 'Will more countries become democratic', *Political Science Quarterly* 99 (Summer), 1984a, pp. 193–218.

Huntington, S. P., *The Third Wave: Democratization in the late Twentieth Century*, Norman, Oklahoma: University of Oklahoma Press, 1984b.

———, 'Democracy's Third Wave', *Journal of Democracy* Spring, 1991, pp. 12–34.

———, *The Clash of Civilizations and the Breaking of World Order*, New York: Simon and Schuster, 1996.

Inglehart, R., *The Silent Revolution: Changing Values and Political Styles Among Western Publics*, Princeton, NJ: Princeton University Press, 1977.

———, *Culture Shift in Advanced Industrial Society*, Princeton, NJ: Princeton University Press, 1990.

Jacobson, N., 'Political Science and Political Education', *American Political Science Review* 57, 1963, pp. 561–67.

Jackson, J. H., 'Tom Paine and the Rights of Man', in D. Thompson (ed.), *Political Ideas*, Oxford: Clarendon Press, 1969.

Jaegar, W., *Aristotle: Fundamentals of the History of His Development*, Oxford: Clarendon Press, 1923.

Joll, J., *Europe Since 1870: An International History*, Harmondsworth: Penguin, 1981.

Johnson, C., *MITI and the Japanese Miracle*, Stanford, CA: Stanford University Press, 1982.

Johnson, H. C., *Revolutionary Change*, Boston, MA: Beacon Press, 1966.

Jones, C., *The Presidency in Separated System*, Washington, D.C.: Brookings International, 1994.

Jones, M. P., 'Increasing Women's Representation via Gender Quotas: The Argentine Ley de Cupos', *Women and Politics* 16 (4), 1996, pp. 75–98.

Kamp, S., 'Introduction', in *Graham Wallas' Human Nature in Politics*, Boston, MA: Beacon Press, 1981.

Karsten, P., 'Military Interventions and Democracy, security policy and defence in Finland', Papers presented at the 1988 Munich Interim Conference of the Research Committee 01/ISA: Armed Forces and Conflict Resolution, München, 1989.

Kaufman, R., H. Cheronosky and D. Geller, 'A Preliminary Test of the Theory of Dependency', *Comparative Politics* April 1979, pp. 26–42.

Kavanagh, D., *Political Culture*, London: Macmillan, 1972.

———, *Political Science and Political Behaviour*, London: Allen and Unwin, 1983.

Kent, Frank R., *Political Behaviour: The Heretofore Unwritten Laws, Customs, and Principles of Politics as Practised in the United States*, New York: William Morrow and Company, 1928.

King, P., *Federalism and Federation*, Baltimore: Johns Hopkins and London, Croom Helm, 1982.

Kissinger, Henry, *World Order: Reflections on the Character of Nations and the course of History*, London: Allen Lane, 2014.

Knutsen, O., 'The Materialist/Post Materialist Value Dimension as a party cleavage in the Nordic Countries', *West European Politics* 13, 1990a, pp. 254–78.

———, 'The Materialist/Post Materialist Values and Social Structure in the Nordic Countries: A Comparative Study', *Comparative Politics* 23, 1990b, pp. 85–104.

Koelble, T., 'The New Institutionalism in Political Science and Sociology', *Comparative Politics* 27, 1995, pp. 231–43.

Kohli, A., *Democracy and Discontent: India's Growing Crisis of Governability*, Cambridge: Cambridge University Press, 1990.

Kolakowski, L., *Main Currents of Marxism*, 3 vols, Oxford: Oxford University Press, 1981.

Kothari, R., *Politics in India*, New Delhi: Orient Longman, 1970.

Kornhauser, W., *The Politics of Mass Society*, Glencoe Ill: The Free Press, 1959.

Krouse, R. W., 'Classical Images of Democracy in America: Madison and Tocqueville', in G. Duncan (ed.), *Democratic Theory and Practice*, Cambridge: Cambridge University Press, 1983.

Kukathas, C., 'Liberalism and Multiculturalism: The Politics of Indifference', *Political Theory* 26 (5), 1998, pp. 686–99.

Kuhn, T., *The Structure of Scientific Revolutions*, Chicago: University of Chicago Press, 1962.

Kymlicka, W., *Liberalism, Community and Culture*, Oxford: Oxford University Press, 1989.

———, *Multicultural Citizenship: A Liberal Theory of Minority Rights*, New York: Oxford University Press, 1995a.

——— (ed.), *The Rise of Minority Cultures*, Oxford: Oxford University Press, 1995b.

Laski, H. J., *Rise of European Liberalism*, London: Unwin Books, 1936.

Lasswell, H. D., *Politics: Who Gets What, When, How*, New York, London: Whittlesey house, McGraw-Hill, 1936.

Lehmbruch, G., 'Liberal Corporatism and Party Government', in P. Schmitter and G. Lehmbruch (eds), *Trends towards Corporatist Intermediation*, London: Sage Publications, 1979.

Lele, S. M., 'Sustainable Development: A Critical Review', *World Development* 19 (6), 1991, pp. 607–21.

Lenin, V. I., *The State and Revolution and Proletarian Revolution and Renegade Kautsky*, Moscow: Progress Publishers, 1977.

Leys, C., 'Underdevelopment and Dependency: Critical Notes', *Journal of Contemporary Asia* 7 (1), 1977, pp. 92–107.

Lichtheim, G., *A Short History of Socialism*, Glasgow: Fontana, 1975.

Lijphart, A., *The Politics of Accommodation: Pluralism and Democracy in the Netherlands*, Berkeley: University of California Press, 1968.

———, 'Religious vs. Linguistic vs. Class Voting: The "Crucial Experiment" of Belgium, Canada, South Africa and Switzerland', *American Political Science Review* 73 (2), 1979, pp. 442–58.

———, *Democracies*, New Haven, CT: Yale University Press, 1984.

———, *Democracy in Plural Society: A Comparative Exploration*, Bombay: Popular Prakashan, 1989.

Lim, H. C., *Dependent development in the world-system: The case of South Korea, 1963–1979*, Cambridge, MA: Harvard University Press, 1982.

Linz, J. J., 'A Case for Parliamentary Democracy', *Span*, July 1991, pp. 12–15.

———, *Totalitarian and Authoritarian Regimes*, Boulder, Colorado: Lynne Rienner Publishers, 2000.

Lipset, S. M., 'Some Social Requisites for Democracy: Economic Development and Political Legitimacy', *American Political Science Review* 53 (1), 1959, pp. 69–105.

———, 'The Changing Class Structure and Contemporary European Politics', *Daedalus* 93, 1964, pp. 271–303.

———, *Political Man: The Social Bases of Politics*, New York: Doubleday, 1960.

———, *The Third Country: America as a Post Industrial Society*, Stanford: Hoover Institute Press, 1979.

Lipset, S. M. and S. Rokkan, 'Cleavage structures, party systems and voter alignments: An introduction', in S. M. Lipset and S. Rokkan (eds), *Party Systems and Voter Alignments: Cross National Perspectives*, New York: Free Press, 1967.

List, Friedrich, *National System of Political Economy*, Sampson S. Lloyd (trans.), London: Longman, Green, and Co., 1909 [1841].

Lively, J., *Democracy*, Oxford: Basil Blackwell, 1975.

Locke, J., *Two Treatises on Civil Government*, P. Laslett (ed.), Cambridge: Cambridge University Press, 1960.

Mack, M. P., 'The Fabians and the Utilitarians', *Journal of the History of Ideas* 16, 1955, pp. 76–88.

Macpherson, C. B., *The Real World of Democracy*, Oxford: Oxford University Press, 1966.

———, *The Political Theory of Possessive Individualism: Hobbes to Locke*, Oxford: Clarendon Press, 1973.

———, *Democratic Theory: Essays in Retrieval*, Oxford: Clarendon Press, 1977.

Macridis, R. C., *The Study of Comparative Government*, New York: Random House, 1955.

———, 'A Survey of the field of Comparative Government', in H. Eckstein and D. E. Apter (eds), *Comparative Politics: A Reader*, New York: Free Press of Glencoe, 1963.

Mackenzie, R. T., *British Political Parties: The Distribution of Power within the Conservative and Labour Parties*, US: Heinmann, 1955.

Mair, P., 'Comparative Politics: An Overview', in *A New Handbook of Political Science*, WordPress.com, 1998.

Malik, K., 'Europe's Dangerous Multiculturalism: Why the Continent Fails Minority Groups', *Foreign Affairs* 8 December 2015, pp. 145–56.

Mamay, S., *Theories of Social Movements and their current development in Soviet Society*, Kent: The Centre for Social Anthropology and Computing publication, The University of Canterbury, 2007.

March, J. G. and J. P. Olsen, 'The New Institutionalism: Organizational Factors in Political Life', *American Political Science Review* 78 (3), 1984, pp. 734–49.

———, 'Elaborating the "New Institutionalism"', in R. A. W. Rhodes, S. A. Binder and B. A. Rockman (eds), *The Oxford Handbook of Political Institutions*, Oxford: Oxford University Press, 2004.

Marx, Karl, *The Eighteenth Brumaire of Louis Bonaparte*, Moscow: Progress Publishers, 1869 [1962].

———, *Critique of Hegel's Philosophy of Right*. Cambridge Studies in the History and Theory of Politics, Cambridge: Cambridge University Press, 1970 [1844].

Marx, K. H. and F. Engels, *The Communist Manifesto*, Moscow: Progress Publishers, 1975.

———, *Selected Works*, 3 vols, Moscow: Progress Publishers, 1977.

Marion-Young, I., 'Impartiality and the Civic Public: Some Implications of Feminist Critiques of Moral and Political Theory', in S. Benhabib and D. Cornell (eds), *Feminism as Critique*, Minneapolis: University of Minnesota Press, 1987.

———, 'Polity and Group Difference: A Critique of the Ideal of Universal Citizenship', *Ethics* 99 (2), 1989, pp. 250–74.

———, *Justice and the Politics of Difference*, Princeton, NJ: Princeton University Press, 1990.

———, 'Social Groups in Associative Democracy', *Politics and Society* 20, 1992, pp. 529–34.

———, *Inclusion and Democracy*, Oxford: Oxford University Press, 2000.

McCarthy, J. D. and M. N. Zald, 'Resource Mobilization and Social Movements: A Partial Theory', *The American Journal of Sociology* 82 (6), 1977, pp. 1212–41.

McCoy, C. A. and J. Playford (eds), *Apolitical Politics: A Critique of Behaviouralism*, New York: Thomas Y. Crowell, 1967.

McLellan, D., *Marxism after Marx*, London: Macmillan, 1979.

Meadows, D. H., D. Meadows, J. Randers, and W. W. Behrens, *The Limits to Growth*, New York: Universe Books, 1972.

Medvedev, R., *Let History Judge: The Origins and Consequences of Stalinism*, New York: Alfred A. Knopf, 1982.

Meisel, J. H., *The Myth of the Ruling Class: Gaetano Mosca and the Elite*, Ann Arbor: University of Michigan Press, 1958.

Meyerson, A., 'Adam Smith's Welfare State', *Policy Review* 50 (Fall), 1989, pp. 66–67.

Michels, R., *Political Parties*, New York: Free Press, 1962.

Miliband, R., 'C. Wright Mills', in *C. Wright Mills and The Power Elite*, compiled by G. William Domhoff and Hoyt B. Ballard, Boston: Beacon Press, 1968.

———, *The State in Capitalist Society*, London: Weidenfeld and Nicholson, 1969.

———, *Marxism and Politics*, Oxford: Oxford University Press, 1977.

Mill, John Stuart, *Considerations on Representative Government*, London: Parker, Son and Bourn, 1861.

Miller, D., *On Nationality*, Oxford: Oxford University Press, 1995.

———, 'Justice and Global Inequality', in A. Hurrell and N. Woods (eds), *Inequality, Globalization and World Politics*, Oxford: Oxford University Press, 1999.

———, *Citizenship and National Identities*, Cambridge: Polity Press, 2000.

———, 'Nationality in Divided Societies', in A. G. Gagnon and J. Tully (eds), *Multinational Democracies*, Cambridge: Cambridge University Press, 2001.

———, 'Nationalism', in J. S. Dryzek, B. Honig and A. Phillips (eds), *The Oxford Handbook of Political Theory*, Oxford: Oxford University Press, 2006.

Mills, C. W., *The Power Elite*, New York: Oxford University Press, 1956.

———, *The Sociological Imagination*, Oxford: Oxford University Press, 1959.

Mitchell, T., 'The Limits of the State: Beyond Statist Approaches and their Critics', *The American Political Science Review*, 85 (1), 1991, pp. 77–96.

Morall, J. B., *Political Thought in Medieval Times*, New York: Harper & Row, 1960.

Moore Jr., B., *Social Origins of Dictatorship and Democracy: Lord and Peasant in the Making of the Modern World*, Boston: Beacon Press, 1967.

Morris-Jones, W. H., *Government and Politics in India*, London: Hutchinson, 1971, 3e.

———, *Politics Mainly Indian*, New Delhi: Orient Longman, 1978.

Mosca, G., *The Ruling Class*, New York: McGraw Hill, 1939.

Mukherjee, S. and S. Ramaswamy, *Political Science Annual 1994–1995*, New Delhi: Deep and Deep Publications, 1995.

———, *A History of Socialist Thought: From the Predecessors to the Present*, New Delhi: Sage Publications, 2000.

———, *Democracy in Theory and Practice*, New Delhi: Macmillan, 2005.

———, *A History of Political Thought: Plato to Marx*, New Delhi: Prentice-Hall, 2011, 2e.

Myrdal, G., *Asian Drama: An Inquiry into the Poverty of Nations*, Harmondsworth: Penguin, 1968.

———, *Objectivity in Social Research*, New York: Pantheon, 1969.

Naess, A., *Ecology, Community and Lifestyle*, Cambridge: Cambridge University Press, 1989.

Nehru, B. K., 'A Fresh Look at the Constitution', in S. C. Kashyap (ed.), *Reforming the Constitution*, New Delhi: UBSPD, 1992.

Neustadt, R. E., *Presidential Powers and the Modern Presidentia: The Politics of Leadership from Roosevelt to Reagan*, New York: The Free Press, 1990.

Nisbet, R., *The Quest for Community*, New York: Oxford University Press, 1962.

———, *The Twilight of Authority*, New York: Basic Books, 1975.

North, D. C., *Understanding the Process of Economic Change*, Princeton, NJ: Princeton University Press, 2005.

Novack, G., *Uneven and Combined Development in History*, New York: Merit Publishers, 1966.

Nove, A., *The Economics of Feasible Socialism*, London: George Allen and Unwin, 1983.

Oakeshott, M., 'Political Education', in P. Laslett and W.G. Runciman (eds), *Philosophy, Politics and Society*, 1st Series, Oxford: Blackwell, 1956.

Offe, C., 'New Social Movements: Challenging the Boundaries of Institutional Politics', *Social Research* 52 (4), 1985, pp. 817–68.

Okin, S. M., 'Gender, the Public and the Private', in D. Held (ed.), *Political Theory Today*, Cambridge: Polity Press, 1991.

Olson, M., *Logic of Collective Action: Public Goods and the Theory Today*, Cambridge, MA: Harvard University Press, 1965.

O'Neil, P. H., *Essentials of Comparative Politics*, New York and London: W. W. Norton and Company, 2009.

O'Riordan, T., *Environmentalism*, London: Pion Press, 1981.

Organski, A. F. K., *The Stages of Political Development*, New York: Alfred A. Knopf, 1968.

Ostrogoski, M., *Democracy and the Organization of Political Parties*, London: Macmillan, 1902.

Ostrom, E., *Governing the Commons: The Evolution of Institutions*, Cambridge: Cambridge University Press, 1990.

Owens, E., *The Future of Freedom in the Developing World: Economic Development and Political Reform*, New York: Pergamon Press 1987.

Parekh, B., *Rethinking Multiculturalism: Cultural Diversity and Political Theory*, London: Macmillan Press, 2000.

Pareto, V., *The Mind and Society*, S. E. Finer (ed.), London: Pall Mall Press, 1966.

Parry, G., *Political Elites*, New York: Praeger, 1969.

Parsons, T., 'The Distribution of Power in American Society', Review of C. Wright Mills' *Power Elite, World Politics* 10 (1), 1957, pp. 123–43.

———, *The structure of social action: a study in social theory with special reference to a group of recent European writers*, Vol. 1, New York: Free Press, 1968.

Pateman, C., 'The civic culture: A philosophic critique', in G. Almond and S. Verba (eds), *The Civic Culture Revisited*, Newbury Park, CA: Sage Publications, 1989.

Pathak, B., 'Facets of the System: Presidential vs Parliamentary', in S. C. Kashyap (ed.), *Perspectives on the Constitution*, New Delhi: Allied Publishers, 1993.

Patrick, G., *The Concept of Political Culture*, International Studies Association Working Paper No 80, 1976.

Pearce, D. W., 'Sustainable futures: The economic issues: The Compatibility of industrial development and care of the environment', *Sustainable Development in an Industrial Economy*, Proceedings of a Conference held at Queen's College, Cambridge, UK, Centre for Economic and Environmental Development, 1985.

Perrin, R., 'Durkheim's Misrepresentation of Spencer: A Reply to Jones' "Durkheim's Response to Spencer"', *The Sociological Quarterly* 16, 1975, pp. 544–50.

———, 'Émile Durkheim's *Division of Labor* and the shadow of Herbert Spencer', *The Sociological Quarterly*, 36, 2005, pp. 791–808.

Peters, G., *Institutional Theory in Political Science: The New Institutionalism*, London: Continuum, 2005, 2e.

Phillips, A., *The Politics of Presence*, Oxford: The Clarendon Press, 1995.

Pierson, P. and T. Skocpol, 'Historical Institutionalism in Contemporary Political Science', in J. Katznelson and H. V. Miller (eds), *Political Science: State of the Discipline*, New York: Norton, 2002.

Pitkin, H., *The Concept of Representation*, Berkeley: University of California Press, 1967.

Plamentaz, J., *German Marxism and Russian Communism*, London: Longman, 1969.

Polsby, N. W., 'How to Study Community Power: The Pluralist Alternative', *The Journal of Politics* 22 (3), 1960, pp. 474–84.

———, 'The Institutionalization of the House of Representatives', *American Political Science Review* 62, 1962, pp. 144–68.

Poulantaz, N., *Political Power and Social Classes*, London: New Left Books, 1973.

Prebisch, R., *The Economic Development of Latin America and its Principal Problems*, New York: United Nations, 1971.

Putnam, R., *Making Democracy Work: Civic Traditions in Modern Italy*, Princeton, NJ: Princeton University Press, 1993.

Pye, L., *Asian Power and Politics: The Cultural Dimensions of Authority*, Harvard: Belknap Press, 1988.

———, 'Political Science and the Crisis of Authoritarianism', *American Political Science Review* 84 (1), 1990, pp. 3–17.

Pye, L. and Sidney Verba (eds), *Political Culture and Political Development*, Princeton, NJ: Princeton University Press, 1965.

Randall, V., *Women and Politics*, London: Macmillan, 1987.

Rapoport, A., *Prisoner's Dilemma*, Ann Arbor, MI: The University of Michigan Press, 1965.

———, *Two-Person Game Theory: The Essential Ideas*, Ann Arbor, MI: The University of Michigan Press, 1966.

———, *N-Person Game Theory. Concepts and Applications*, Ann Arbor, MI: The University of Michigan Press, 1970.

Raz, J., *The Morality of Freedom*, Oxford: The Clarendon Press, 1986.

———, 'Multiculturalism: a liberal perspective', in J. Raz (ed.), *Ethics in the Public Domain*, Oxford: The Clarendon Press, 1994.

Rey, P. P., *Colonialism, Neo Colonialism et Transition au Capitalisme*, Paris : Presses Universitaires de France, 1971.

———, *Alliances de Classes*, Paris : Presses Universitaires de France, 1973.

Rhodes, R. A. W., S. A. Binder and B. A. Rockman (eds), *The Oxford Handbook of Political Institutions*, Oxford: Oxford University Press, 2006.

Robinson, D. L., 'Why Americans Choose Parliamentary Government for Japan', in S. Mukherjee and S. Ramaswamy (eds), *Issues in Comparative Politics*, New Delhi: Deep and Deep Publications, 1996.

Rogowski, R., 'Comparative politics', in A. W. Finifter (ed.), *Political Science: The State of the Discipline II*, Washington, DC: American Political Science Association, 1993.

Rorty, R., 'Strangers and Liberals', *Political Theory*, 22, 1994, pp. 167–75.

Roos, L., 'Two Fundamental Mistakes that doomed the centrally planned economy', *The German Tribune*, 1408, 1990, p. 6.

Ross, M. H., 'Culture in Comparative Political Analysis', in M. I. Lichbech and A. Zuckerman (eds), *Rationality, Culture and Structure*, New York: Cambridge University Press, 2009, 2e.

Ross, W. D., *Aristotle*, London: Methuen, 1924.

Rostow, W. W., *The Stages of Economic Growth: A Non Communist Manifesto*, Cambridge: Cambridge University Press, 1960.

Rudolph, L. I. and S. H. Rudolph, *In Pursuit of Lakshmi*, New Delhi: Orient Longman, 1998.

Routh, G., *The Origins of Economic Ideas*, London: Macmillan, 1975.

Sabine, G. H., *A History of Political Theory*, revised by J. L. Thorson, New Delhi: Oxford and IBH, 1973, 4e.

Sachs, W. (ed.), *Global Ecology: New Area of Global Conflict*, London: Feuwood Books and Zed Books, 1993.

Samuelson, P. A., 'The illogic of Neo-Marxian doctrine of unequal exchange', in K. Belsey and P. A. Samuelson (eds), *Inflation, Trade and Taxes*, Ohio: Ohio University Press, 1976.

Sartori, G., *Parties and Party System: A Framework of Analysis*, Vol. 1, New York: Cambridge University Press, 1976.

———, *Parties and Party System: A Framework of Analysis*, UK: ECPR Press, 2005.

Saul, J. S., 'The State in Post-Colonial Societies: Tanzania', *The Socialist Register* 1974, pp. 349–70.

Schmitter, P., 'Still the Century of Corporatism', in P. Schmitter and G. Lehmbruch (eds), *Trends Towards Corporatism Intermediation*, London: Sage Publications, 1979.

Schumpeter, J., *Capitalism, Socialism and Democracy*, London: George Allen and Unwin, 1976 [1943].

———, *History of Economic Analysis*, Oxford: Oxford University Press, 1954.

Scruton, R., 'Multiculturalism: RIP', *The American Spectator* 7 December 2010, pp. 23–25.

Selznick, P., 'Theory of Organization', *American Sociological Review* 13 (1), 1948, pp. 25–35.

Sen, A., 'Socialism, Markets and Democracy', *The Hindu*, 9 January 1990.

———, 'Human Rights and Asian Values', Morgenthau Memorial lecture on ethics and foreign policy 16, Carnegie Council on Ethics and International Relations, 2003.

Shacher, A., *Multicultural Jurisdictions: Cultural Differences and Women's Rights*, Cambridge: Cambridge University Press, 2001.

Shane, P. M., 'Analyzing Constitutions', *Oxford Handbooks of Political Science: Political Institutions*, Ohio State Public Law Working Paper No. 220, 2006.

Skinner, Q., *The Foundations of Modern Political Thought*, 2, Cambridge: Cambridge University Press, 1978.

Skocpol, T., *States and Social Revolutions: A Comparative Analysis of France, Russia and China*, Cambridge: Cambridge University Press, 1979.

———, 'Bringing the State Back In: Strategies of Analysis in Current Research', in P. Evans, D. Rueschemeyer and T. Skocpol (eds), *Bringing the State Back*, Cambridge: Cambridge University Press, 1985.

Slater, D., 'Singapore's final Authoritarian election', *East Asia Forum*, 14 September 2015.

Smelsar, N., *Theory of Collective Behaviour*, New York: Free Press, 1962.

Smith, A., *An Inquiry into the Nature and Causes of the Wealth of Nations*, London: Everyman, 1776.

———, *Essays on Philosophical Subjects*, Indianapolis: Liberty Classics, 1980.

Smith, A. D., *Theories of Nationalism*, London: Duckworth, 1971.

———, *National Identity*, Harmondsworth: Penguin, 1991.

Smith, G., *Federalism: the Multiethnic Challenge*, New York: Routledge and Kegan Paul, 1995.

Smith, M., 'Pluralism', in D. Marsh and G. Stoker (eds), *Theory and Methods in Political Science*, Basingstoke: Macmillan, 1995.

Smith, S. B., *Hegel's Critique of Liberalism*, Chicago: University of Chicago Press, 1989.

Solzhenitsyn, A., *The Gulag Archipelago 1918–56*, USA: HarperCollins, 1973.

Stewart, D., 'The Hermeneutics of Suspicion', *Journal of Literature and Theology* 3, 1989, pp. 296–307.

Stokes, W., *Women in Contemporary Politics*, Cambridge: Polity Press, 2005.

Streeck, W. and K. Thelen, 'Introduction: Institutional change in advanced political economies', in W. Streeck and K. Thelen (eds), *Beyond Continuity: Institutional Change in Advanced Political Economies*, Oxford: Oxford University Press, 2005.

Susser, B., *Approaches to the Study of Politics*, London: Macmillan, 1992.

Sweezy, P., 'Power Elite or Ruling Class? Review of C. Wright Mills' *Power Elite*', *Monthly Review Press* 8 (5), 1956, pp. 3–28.

Tagore, R., *Letters from Russia*, Calcutta: Visva Bharathi, 1960.

Talmon, J. L., *The Origins of Totalitarian Democracy*, New York: Praegar, 1960.

Taylor, C., 'The Politics of Recognition', in A. Gutman (ed.), *Multiculturalism: Examining the Politics of Recognition*, Princeton, NJ: Princeton University Press, 1994.

Tawney, R. H., *Religion and the Rise of Capitalism*, New York: Harcourt, Brace and Company, 1926.

Tingsten, Herbert, *Political Behaviour: Studies in Election Statistics*, London: P. S. King and Son, 1937.

Tilly, C., *The Formation of National States in Western Europe*, Princeton, NJ: Princeton University Press, 1975.

———, 'Does Modernization Breed Revolution?', *International Social Science Journal* 134, 1991, pp. 22–43.

Tocqueville, A. de, *The Old Regime and the French Revolution*, New York: Doubleday, 1955 [1856].

Touraine, A., *The Post-Industrial Society. Tomorrow's Social History: Classes, Conflicts and Culture in the Programmed Society*, New York: Random House, 1971.

———, *The Voice and the Eye: An Analysis of Social Movements*, Cambridge: Cambridge University Press, 1981.

Tripp, A. M. and A. Kang, 'The Global Impact of Quotas: On the Fast Track to Increased Female Legislative Representation', *Comparative Political Studies* 41 (3), 2008, pp. 338–61.

Truman, D., *The Governmental Process*, New York: Alfred A. Knopf, 1951.

Tucker, R., *Political Culture in the Soviet Union*, New York: W. W. Norton and Co., 1987.

Tully, *Strange Multiplicity: Constitutionalism in an Age of Diversity*, Cambridge: Cambridge University Press, 1995.

———, 'Ethical Pluralism and Classical Liberalism', in R. Madsen and T. B. Strong (eds), *The Many and the One: Religious and Secular Perspectives on Ethical Pluralism in the Modern World*, Princeton, NJ: Princeton University Press, 2003.

Turner, R. K., *Sustainable Environmental Management: Principles and Practice*, London: Belhaven, 1988.

Verba, S., K. L. Schozman and H. E. Brady, *Voice and Equality: Civic Voluntarism in American Politics*, Cambridge, MA: Harvard University Press, 1995.

Vig, N. J., 'Political Science and Political Economy' in Norman J. Vig and Steven E. Schier (eds), *Political Economy in Western Democracies*, New York: Holmes and Meier, 1985.

Vincent, R. J., *Human Rights and International Relations*, Cambridge: Cambridge University Press, 1986.

von Hippel, K., *Democracy by Force: US Military Intervention in the Post-Cold War World*, Cambridge: Cambridge University Press, 2000.

Waldo, D., 'Political Science: Tradition, Discipline, Profession, Science, and Enterprise', in F. I. Greenstein and N. W. Polsby (eds), *Handbook of Political Science*, Vol. I: *Political Science: Scope and Theory*, Reading, Mass.: Addison-Wesley Pub. Co., 1975.

Waldron, J., *Liberal Rights*, Cambridge: Cambridge University Press, 1993.

———, 'Minority Cultures and the Cosmopolitan Alternative', in W. Kymlicka (ed.), *The Rights of Minority Cultures*, Oxford: Oxford University Press, 1995.

Wallas, Graham, *Human Nature in Politics*, London: A. Constable and Co., Ltd., 1908.

Wallerstein, I., *The Capitalist World Economy*, New York: Cambridge University Press, 1979.

———, *The Modern World System*, 3 Vols, 1974, 1980 and 1989, New York: Academic Press, 1974–89.

Walzer, M., *What it means to be an American*, New York: Marsilio, 1992.

Ware, A., *Political Parties and Party Systems*, New York: Oxford University Press, 1996.

Wasby, S., *Political Science: The Discipline and its Dimensions*, Calcutta: Scientific Book Agency, 1970.

Weale, A., *The New Politics of Pollution*, Manchester: Manchester University Press, 1992.

Webb, S., *History of Trade Unionism*, London: Longman, 1920.

Weber, M., 'Politics as a vocation', in H. H. Gerth and C. W. Mills (eds), *From Max Weber*, New York: Oxford University Press, 1958.

Weingast, B. R. and D. A. Wittman, *The Oxford Handbook of Political Economy*, Oxford: Oxford University Press, 2006.

Welch, S., *The Concept of Political Culture*, New York: St. Martin, 1993.

Wheare, K. C., *Federal Government*, London and New York: Oxford University Press, 1963 [1946].

———, *Modern Constitutions*, Oxford: Oxford University Press, 1966 [1951].

Wieviorka, M., 'After New Social Movements', *Social Movement Studies* 4 (1), 2005, pp. 1–19.

Williams, M. S., *Voice, Trust and Memory: Marginalized Groups and the Failings of Liberal Representation*, Princeton, NJ: Princeton University Press, 1998.

Williams, R., *Culture and Society*, Harmondsworth: Penguin, 1958.

Wilson, E., *To The Finland Station*, Glasgow, Harmondsworth: Penguin, 1941.

Wilson, G., *Special Interests and Policy Making*, Chilcester: John Wiley, 1977.

Wolfe, B., *Marxism: One Hundred Years in the Life of a Doctrine*, New York: Doubleday, 1969.

Wolin, Sheldon, *Politics and Vision: Continuity and Innovation in Western Political Thought*, Princeton: Princeton University Press, 1960.

———, 'Contract and Birthright', *Political Theory* 14, 1986, pp. 179–93.

———, 'Democracy and the Welfare State', *Political Theory* 15 (4), 1987, pp. 467–500.

Wood, G., *The Creation of the American Republic 1776–1787*, Chapel Hill: The University of North Carolina Press, 1969.

Woodcock, G., *The Anarchist Reader*, Glasgow: Fontana, 1944.

Zakaria, F., *The Future of Freedom: Illiberal Democracy at Home and Abroad*, New York: Viking, 2003.

Zald, M. N. and J. D. McCarthy, *Social Movements in an Organizational Society: Collected Essays*, New Jersey: Transaction Books, 1987.

Zuckert, C., 'On the Theory of Political Economy', in N. J. Vig and S. E. Schier (eds), *Political Economy in Western Democracies*, New York: Holmes and Meier, 1985.

Zweigenhaft, R. L. and W. Domoff, *Diversity in the Power Elite: Have Women and Minorities Reached the Top?* New Haven and London: Yale University Press, 1998.

INDEX